Region, Regional Identity and Regionalism in Southeastern Europe

Part I

Edited by

Klaus Roth and Ulf Brunnbauer

Ethnologia Balkanica

Journal for Southeast European Anthropology
Zeitschrift für die Anthropologie Südosteuropas
Journal d'anthropologie du sud-est européen

Volume 11/2007

LIT

ISSN 1111–0411

Printed in Germany

The journal is published by the International Association for Southeast European Anthropology (InASEA). It publishes articles by members of InASEA as well as by non-members. All articles are anonymously reviewed.
Languages of publication: English, French, German
Contributions must be supplied with a short abstract in English.

Cover: On the basis of a map by the European Commission (http://ec.europa.eu/regional_policy/images/map/cooperat2007/transnational/southeasteurope .pdf) the map shows both the new administrative regions designed by the EU (NUTS 1) and (in red) some of the historical regions in Southeast Europe, many of which cross national boundaries.

Subscription: Subscription price (one volume per year):
Students: 10 €, Individuals: 16 €, Institutions: 20 €
Individuals and institutions in Southeast Europe: 10 €.

Bibliographic information published by the Deutsche Nationalbibliothek
The Deutsche Nationalbibliothek lists this publication in the Deutsche Nationalbibliografie; detailed bibliographic data are available in the Internet at http://dnb.d-nb.de.

ISBN 978-3-8258-9903-5

A catalogue record for this book is available from the British Library

Chausseestr. 128 – 129
D-10115 Berlin

Auslieferung/Distribution:

LIT Verlag Fresnostr. 2, D-48159 Münster
Tel. +49 (0) 2 51/620 32 - 22, Fax +49 (0) 2 51/922 60 99, e-Mail: lit@lit-verlag.de

Distributed in the UK by: Global Book Marketing, 99B Wallis Rd, London, E9 5LN
Phone: +44 (0) 20 8533 5800 – Fax: +44 (0) 1600 775 663
http://www.centralbooks.co.uk/acatalog/search.html
Distributed in North America by:

Transaction Publishers
New Brunswick (U.S.A.) and London (U.K.)

Transaction Publishers
Rutgers University
35 Berrue Circle
Piscataway, NJ 08854

Phone: +1 (732) 445 - 2280
Fax: + 1 (732) 445 - 3138
for orders (U. S. only):
toll free (888) 999 - 6778
e-mail:
orders@transactionspub.com

Contents

Editorial

A hundred years ago, when immigrants to the US were asked by immigration officials on Ellis Island to say where they came from, many people from the Balkans would identify themselves as, for example, "Dalmatian" or "Herzegovinian". For the modern Balkan national state, such a form of identification was anathema because it belied the founding ideology of nationalism. Hence, all modern states that were established in Southeastern Europe since the first half of the 19th century were centralizing polities that put an end to long-lasting traditions of local autonomy, be it in the Ottoman or in the Habsburg empires. They essentially followed the Western European model of political organization, in particular the French one of rigid centralization. Regions would exist only as *pars pro toto* of the nation without any real political significance, and regional cultures were assumed to be variants of the dominant national one.

Centralizing policies in terms of both concentrating political power in the national capital and imagining the nation as a cultural unity were most pronounced in those states which were created by joining regions with very distinctive historical traditions. Interwar Yugoslavia, where in 1929 the administrative division of the country into historical regions was replaced by the deliberately a-historical division in *banovine*, or Romania after World War One, where the differences between the Old Kingdom and the newly acquired provinces of Transylvania, Bukovina and Bessarabia were ignored, are cases in point. The autistic ultra-nationalism of Enver Hoxha's Albania can also be seen as a reaction to the deeply felt regional divisions between northern and southern Albania, evident not only in language differences but also in patterns of social organization, political affiliation and economic activities. Generally, the socialist period marked the apex of centralization in Southeastern Europe, especially in Albania, Romania, and Bulgaria. Even in the former Yugoslavia, although the federation as such was extremely decentralized especially after the 1974 constitution, decentralization stopped at the republican level, as the individual republics had a distinctly centralized political organization. The non-socialist states of Turkey and Greece were no exception to the rule: here as well, nation-building in a multi-ethnic environment and the state's dominant role in the modernization process resulted in strongly centralized polities. The fact that many border regions of Southeastern European countries host large minority populations also increased the deep mistrust felt by national elites for any articulation of regional self-awareness. Regions were seen as a threat to the fetish of the unified nation, and sometimes they still are.

Over the last years, though, centralism has become increasingly challenged and the region has become an important issue in Southeastern Europe in a political, economic and socio-cultural sense. The reasons for the growing relevance of regional policy and regional planning and for the increase in regional self-awareness and identity are manifold. First of all, the resurgence of regional self-consciousness was part of the general democratisation process after 1989. Members of minorities but also the majority nationalities in certain regions reclaimed what they considered their history and looked back at times of – imagined or real – autonomy and self rule. These dynamics could even be translated into political parties, as the case of Istria shows. Such regionalist or even autonomist movements challenged not only the marginalization of their traditions in the national master narrative but also the often unfair division of capital and investment across the country and the neglect shown by the centre for the periphery.

Some regions also discovered that they had certain advantages over the centre, for example with regard to geographical location, and that they would be better off if matters were decided locally. The district of Timişoara in north-western Romania is a case in point: it has received more foreign investment and has grown more prosperous than any other part of Romania, save for Bucharest. In this process the elites of the Romanian Banat have rediscovered the Habsburg heritage as an argument for the Central European nature of their region in contrast to the "Balkanic" rest of the country and put an imagined region against the notion of a centralized state. Such developments also point to the decreased capacity of national centres to create and extract feelings of attachment in the time of economic crisis during the transformation period. The processes of decentralization are also facilitated by the technicalities of European integration: the administration of funds for regional development, from which the new member states benefit significantly, is dependent on the creation and subsequent functioning of regional administrative bodies which, in time, may become loci of political power and identification. The non-member states are urged to create such regional capacities as well, which also serve the goal of accommodating demands of ethnic minorities (take the Republic of Macedonia as an example).

The process of increasing political self-awareness has seen a concomitant rise in the cultural dimensions of regionalism. Regional histories have experienced a surge, as did various manifestations of regional culture, such as carnivals and arts festivals. Regional elites also began to promote the distinctiveness of their region in order to locate it on the international tourist market and sometimes also as a means to dissociate themselves from a nation state with image problems abroad (see, again, the Romanian Banat but also the Vojvodina in Serbia, where despite its now predominantly Serb population, the demand for autonomy is strong and backed up by the stress on the "European" character of the region). Although we still lack sociological evidence, occasional evidence suggests that the identification with the region is growing at the level of everyday life as well – not the least because some of the Southeast European states have been rather dysfunctional in the 1990s which reduced their capacity to bind feelings of attachment and loyalty. The opening of borders has also helped to strengthen regional identities, especially in places where historic regions had been divided by national borders. These sentiments also result in the creation of Euro-Regions and other forms of cross-border cooperation.

At the same time we see dramatic processes of increasing regional differentiation. Economic growth, unemployment, levels of investment, access to resources and prosperity are unevenly distributed between the different parts of the Southeast European countries. This is also a result of the legacy of centralism which had disadvantaged certain regions and failed to build mechanisms for balancing regional interests. While some regions do increasingly well, even attracting old-age pensioners from Western Europe in search of a place with better climate and lower prices, others are falling behind, some obviously fatally. The depopulation of the latter – in stark contrast with the fast-growing metropolises – is one of the more obvious consequences. The degree of attachment one feels for one's native region will obviously also be affected by the increase in socio-economic differences. Occurrences of nostalgia for by-gone times of prosperity are evident in regions which today suffer from impoverishment. On the other hand, even the most marginalized regions in Southeastern Europe are today more integrated into the world than they had ever been in the past. New media and migration processes change social and cultural patterns also in the most peripheral place; hence, the impoverishment of region can go along with their increased integration into the globalized world.

While it is obvious that the notion of region is of growing importance in Southeastern Europe, with the two parallel processes of increased regional cooperation over the whole peninsula and of political and cultural decentralization, the study of region, regionalism and regional identities in Southeastern Europe is still in its infancy. This was the reason why the International Association for Southeast European Anthropology (InASEA) in 2005 decided to devote its fourth conference to these issues. We firmly believed that ethnologists and scholars from neighbouring disciplines could make an important contribution to the exploration of "region" in Southeastern Europe, taking into account also recent trends in the humanities which have been labelled the "geographic turn". Territory, as physical and symbolic reality, as experience and image, has come back into the cultural and social sciences. As a consequence we invited our colleagues to look into these new dynamics, but also into historical processes, in Southeastern Europe with a focus on territories and spaces below – but also above – the level of the nation state.

The fourth conference of InASEA which took place in Timişoara, Romania, on 24–27 May, 2007, was therefore devoted to "Region, Regional Identity and Regionalism in Southeastern Europe". It attracted more than 150 participants from

Europe and North America. The present volume is the first outcome of this endeavour; the second will be volume 12 of this journal. Both volumes together present a selection of papers which analyse various dimensions of "region" in Southeastern Europe and provide evidence of the productivity of approaches focussing on social and cultural processes from the point of view of their spatial dimension. They show that the region, although not less imagined than the nation, is also a sphere of experiences and expectations that draws on collective memories and sentiments which set themselves apart from the national master narratives.

The conference - and the two volumes - would not have been possible without the enormous efforts of Mircea Alexiu and Atalia Ştefanescu from the West-University of Timişoara. They and their team of devoted colleagues and students made the conference the success it was - and we owe many thanks to them. We also want to thank the Wenner Gren Foundation for Anthropological Research, the German Science Foundation (Deutsche Forschungsgemeinschaft) and the West University of Timişoara for their generous financial support of the conference. And finally, our thanks go to all InASEA members who took it upon themselves to critically review the submitted papers.

Ulf Brunnbauer, President of InASEA Berlin, February 2008

Nach der Landung auf Ellis Island gab so mancher Emigrant aus dem westlichen Balkan auf die Frage der US-Immigrationsbeamten, woher er denn komme, zu Protokoll, „Dalmatiner" oder „Herzegowiner" zu sein. Für die modernen Staaten am Balkan waren solche Identifikationen ein Gräuel, untergruben sie doch die Gründungsideologie des Nationalismus. Alle modernen Staaten, die in Südosteuropa seit der ersten Hälfte des 19. Jahrhunderts etabliert wurden, waren zentralistisch organisiert und versuchten, alte Traditionen der lokalen Autonomie (sei es im osmanischen oder habsburgischen Kontext) zu überwinden. Sie folgten dabei im Wesentlichen dem westeuropäischen Modell, wobei es ihnen v. a. die zentralistische Verwaltungsstruktur Frankreichs angetan hatte. Regionen würden nur mehr als *pars pro toto* der Nation ohne echte politische Bedeutung existieren; regionale Kulturen wurden lediglich als Varianten der dominanten nationalen Kultur gedacht.

Die zentralistische Politik sowohl im Sinne der Konzentration der politischen Macht in der Hauptstadt als auch der Imaginierung der Nation als kulturelle Einheit war am stärksten in jenen Ländern, die Regionen mit sehr unterschiedlichen historischen Traditionen umfassten. Das Jugoslawien der Zwischenkriegszeit etwa, wo 1929 die Unterteilung in historische Provinzen durch eine bewusst unhistorische in *banovine* ersetzt wurde; oder Großrumänien nach dem Ersten Weltkrieg, wo die Unterschiede zwischen dem alten Königreich (Regat) und den ehemals habsburgischen Provinzen Siebenbürgen und Bukovina sowie dem einst russischen Bessarabien ignoriert wurden. Der autistische Ultranationalismus von Enver Hoxha kann auch verstanden werden als Reaktion auf die intensiv wahrgenommenen regionalen Differenzen zwischen Nord- und Südalbanien, die sich sowohl in sprachlichen, als auch sozialen und ökonomischen Unterschieden widerspiegelten. Insgesamt markierte die sozialistische Periode den Höhepunkt der Zentralisierung auch in Südosteuropa, nicht nur in Albanien, Bulgarien und Rumänien, sondern auch in einigen der jugoslawischen Republiken, wiewohl die jugoslawische Föderation als Ganze spätestens seit der Verfassungsreform von 1974 ein extrem dezentralisiertes Gebilde darstellte. Die nicht-sozialistischen südosteuropäischen Staaten Griechenland und Türkei bildeten hier keine Ausnahmen: In ihnen hatten die Nationsbildung in einem multiethnischen Kontext sowie die dominante Rolle des Staates bei der Modernisierung des Landes ebenfalls zu einer sehr zentralistischen Organisation geführt. Die Tatsache, dass viele Grenzregionen in Südosteuropa große Minderheitenpopulationen aufwiesen, verstärkte ebenfalls das Misstrauen der nationalen Eliten gegenüber jeglicher Artikulation von regionaler Besonderheit. Regionen wurden als Gefahr für die nationale Einheit gesehen - und werden es teilweise auch heute noch.

Seit dem Ende des Sozialismus wurde der Zentralismus in Südosteuropa aber immer stärker kritisiert; die „Region“ wurde wichtig in politischer, ökonomischer und sozio-kultureller Hinsicht. Die Gründe für die steigende Bedeutung von Regionalpolitik und Regionalplanung, aber auch für das wachsende regionale Selbstbewusstsein sind vielfältig. Zum einen ist der Regionalismus Teil des allgemeinen Demokratisierungsprozesses nach 1989. Angehörige von Minderheiten, aber auch der Mehrheitsbevölkerung versuchten in bestimmten Regionen, ihre als spezifisch erachtete Geschichte wiederzubeleben und blickten zurück auf Zeiten echter oder vermeintlicher Autonomie. Solche Prozesse konnten in der Gründung regionalistischer Parteien münden (wie z. B. in Istrien). Diese Regionalismen oder sogar Autonomiebestrebungen kritisierten nicht nur die Marginalisierung ihrer Traditionen in der nationalen Meistererzählung, sondern auch die oft unfaire Aufteilung von Kapital und Investitionen im Land sowie das Desinteresse, das das Zentrum gegenüber der Peripherie zeigte.

Einige Regionen entdeckten auch, dass sie bestimmte Vorteile gegenüber dem Zentrum haben, z. B. hinsichtlich ihrer geografischen Lage, und kamen zu der Ansicht, dass es ihnen besser gehen würde, wenn wichtige Fragen vor Ort und nicht in der fernen Hauptstadt entschieden würden. Der Bezirk Timişoara in Nordwestrumänien macht dies besonders gut deutlich: Er hat mehr Auslandsinvestitionen als jeder andere rumänische Regierungsbezirk (mit Ausnahme der Hauptstadt) angezogen und erfreut sich eines höheren Lebensstandards als der Rest des Landes. Die politischen Eliten des rumänischen Banats haben in diesem Prozess das habsburgische Erbe der Region wiederentdeckt, das als Nachweis des mitteleuropäischen Charakters der Region hervorgeholt wird. Gleichzeitig setzen sie sich vo dem als „balkanisch" gesehenen Rest des Landes ab und stellen dem Bild des Zentralstaates dasjenige einer traditionsreichen Region gegenüber. Der Prozess der Dezentralisierung wird dabei durch die Mechanismen der europäischen Integration gefördert, denn die Verwaltung der Mittel aus den Strukturfonds zur Regionalförderung, von denen die neuen Mitgliedsstaaten enorm profitieren, verlangt funktionierende regionale Körperschaften, die mit der Zeit auch zum Ausgangspunkt regionaler Identifikation und politischer Macht werden können. Die beitrittswilligen Staaten sind ebenfalls aufgefordert, solche Regionalverwaltungen zu schaffen – wobei die Dezentralisierung auch dazu dienen kann, die Forderungen ethnischer Minderheiten zu befriedigen (wofür die Republik Makedonien ein Beispiel wäre).

Die Stärkung des politischen Selbstbewusstseins von Regionen ging einher mit dem Aufstieg des kulturellen Regionalismus. Regionalgeschichte erlebte einen Boom, ebenso verschiedene Manifestationen von regionaler Kultur wie z. B. Karnevals und Festivals. Regionale Eliten begannen die Einmaligkeit ihrer Region zu bewerben, um sie auf der Landkarte des internationalen Tourismus fest zu verankern, aber z. T. auch, um sich von ihrem Nationalstaat mit Imageproblemen im Ausland abzusetzen (auch hierfür wäre der Banat in Rumänien ein Beispiel, oder aber die Vojvodina in Serbien, wo Forderungen nach Wiedereinsetzung der Autonomierechte auch von Seiten der serbischen Bevölkerung geäußert werden und man den „europäischen" Charakter der Nation betont). Noch gibt es nicht ausreichend soziologische Daten, aber so manche Beobachtung lässt darauf schließen, dass die Identifizierung mit der Region auch auf der Ebene des Alltagslebens an Bedeutung gewinnt. Die Öffnung von Grenzen hat ebenfalls dazu geführt, regionale Zugehörigkeitsgefühle zu stärken, insbesondere dort, wo historische Regionen durch nationale Grenzen geteilt wurden. Solche Vorstellungen resultierten u. a. in der Etablierung von Euro-Regionen und anderen Formen der zwischenstaatlichen grenzüberschreitenden Zusammenarbeit.

Gleichzeitig können wir dramatische Prozesse steigender regionaler Ungleichheit beobachten. Wirtschaftswachstum, Arbeitslosigkeit, Investitionen, Zugang zu Ressourcen und Wohlstand sind zwischen den verschiedenen Teilen der Länder Südosteuropas sehr unterschiedlich verteilt. Dies ist auch eine Folge des Zentralismus, durch den manche Regionen benachteiligt worden sind und der es nicht vermocht hat, für einen vernünftigen Interessenausgleich zwischen den Regionen zu sorgen. Während es einigen Regionen immer besser geht – und sie sogar Rentner aus Westeuropa auf der Suche nach einem Alterswohnsitz in einer klimatisch angenehmeren und billigeren Gegend anlocken –, gehören andere Regionen zu den ärmsten der EU. Die Entvölkerung der letzteren – im Gegensatz zum raschen Wachstum der urbanen Metropolen – ist eine der offensichtlichsten Folgen davon. Der Grad der individuellen Identifikation mit der Heimatregion wird durch diese sozioökonomischen Prozesse nicht unberührt bleiben. Zu beobachten ist in heute verarmten Regionen Nostalgie nach verloren gegangenen Zeiten von Wohlstand. Auf der anderen Seite muss auch betont werden, dass selbst die am stärksten marginalisierten Regionen Südosteuropas heute mehr in die Welt integriert sind als je in der Vergangenheit. Neue Medien und Migrationen führen zu sozialen und kulturellen Veränderungen auch noch am Rande der Peripherie. Das bedeutet, dass die Verarmung einer Region mit ihrer verstärkten Integration in die globalisierte Welt einher gehen kann.

Obwohl es also evident ist, dass „Region" in Südosteuropa von wachsender Bedeutung ist – und zwar im Sinne sowohl der regionalen Kooperation in der Region als auch der politischen und kulturellen Dezentralisierung –, steckt die wissenschaftliche Untersuchung von Region, Regionalismus und regionalen Identitäten in Südosteuropa noch in ihren Kinderschuhen. Dies war Grund genug für die Internationale Gesellschaft für die Anthropologie Südosteuropas (InASEA), ihre vierte Konferenz diesen Fragen zu widmen. Wir waren davon überzeugt, dass Ethnologen und Wissenschaftler aus Nachbardisziplinen einen wesentlichen Beitrag zur Regionalforschung in Südosteuropa leisten können. Damit sollte auch auf den in den Geisteswissenschaften zu beobachtenden *„geographical turn"* Bezug genommen werden, der den Raum – in seiner physischen wie auch symbolischen Qualität als Erfahrung und Vorstellung – wieder zu einem zentralen Gegenstand gemacht hat. Die Konferenz verstand sich als Forum, auf dem Wissenschaftler sowohl die aktuellen Dynamiken von Region und anderen Räumen unterhalb des Nationalstaats, aber auch deren historische Dimensionen diskutieren konnten.

Die Konferenz zum Thema „Region, regionale Identität und Regionalismus in Südosteuropa" fand vom 24. bis 27. Mai 2007 an der West-Universität in Timişoara statt. An ihr nahmen mehr als 150 Wissenschaftler aus Europa und Nordamerika teil. Der vorliegende Band enthält eine erste Auswahl an Texten, die bei der Konferenz präsentiert wurden; Band 12 der *Ethnologia Balkanica* wird dem gleichen Thema gewidmet sein. Die beiden Bände stehen beispielhaft für die Fruchtbarkeit von Ansätzen, die soziale und kulturelle Prozesse auf ihre räumlichen Dimensionen hin untersuchen. Sie zeigen, dass die Region – obwohl kaum weniger imaginiert als die Nation – einen wichtigen Erfahrungsraum und Erwartungshorizont darstellt und auf kollektiven Erinnerungen und Gefühlen beruht, die sich von den nationalen Meistererzählungen absetzen.

Die Konferenz und damit auch die beiden Bände unserer Zeitschrift wären nicht möglich gewesen ohne den enormen Einsatz von Mircea Alexiu und Atalia Ştefanescu von der West-Universität in Timişoara, die Gastgeber unserer Konferenz. Sie und ihr engagiertes Team von Kollegen und Studierenden machten die

Konferenz zu dem Erfolg, der sie war. Wir schulden ihnen dafür großen Dank. Ebenfalls danken möchten wir der Wenner Gren Foundation for Anthropological Research, der Deutschen Forschungsgemeinschaft und der West-Universität in Timişoara für ihre großzügige finanzielle Unterstützung der Konferenz. Und schließlich gilt unser Dank all jenen InASEA Mitgliedern, die es auf sich genommen haben, die für diesen Band eingereichten Texte kritisch zu kommentieren und Verbesserungsvorschläge zu formulieren.

Ulf Brunnbauer, Präsident der InASEA Berlin, Februar 2008

Il y a un siècle, lorsque, interrogés par les fonctionnaires de l'immigration sur l'île d'Ellis au sujet de leur origine, de nombreux ressortissants des Balkans s'identifiaient comme «Dalmatiens» ou «Herzégoviniens» par exemple. Pour les Etats modernes des Balkans ce type d'identification était évidemment un crime perpétré contre l'idéologie nationaliste qui leur servait de fondement. Ainsi, tous les Etats modernes du Sud-est de l'Europe établis depuis la première moitié du 19e siècle étaient centralisateurs et visaient à éliminer la longue tradition d'autonomie locale, que ce soit dans le contexte impérial ottoman ou habsbourgeois. Ils suivaient en cela le modèle de l'Europe occidentale et en particulier celui de la France, fortement centralisateur. Les régions désormais n'existeront que comme *pars pro toto* de la nation, sans jouir d'aucun pouvoir politique réel, tandis que les cultures régionales deviendront de simples variantes de la culture dominante nationale.

Les politiques centralisatrices consistant à concentrer à la fois le pouvoir politique dans la capitale nationale et à imaginer la nation comme une unité culturelle, furent d'autant plus prononcées que les régions les composant avaient des traditions historiques différentes. La Yougoslavie d'entre les deux guerres, où l'on remplaça en 1929 la division administrative du pays en régions historiques par une division volontairement a-historique, les *banovine,* ou la Grande Roumanie, après la première guerre mondiale, où les différences entre l'ancien Royaume (Regat) et les provinces nouvellement acquises de Transylvanie, Bucovine et Bessarabie furent ignorées, en sont de bons exemples. L'ultra-nationalisme autiste de l'Albanie d' Enver Hoxha peut également être interprété comme une réaction aux divisions régionales profondes entre le Nordet le Sud de l'Albanie qui ne se manifeste pas seulement dans la différence des langues mais aussi dans les modes d'organisation sociale, de gestion politique et les types d'activités économiques. De manière générale, on peut dire que la période socialiste été le point culminant de la centralisation en Europe du Sud-est, particulièrement en Albanie, en Roumanie et en Bulgarie. Même dans l'ex-Yougoslavie, bien que la Fédération en tant que telle ait été très décentralisée après la Constitution de 1974, la centralisation des républiques individuelles demeura très prononcée. La Turquie et la Grèce, bien que non socialistes, ne faisaient pas exception à cette règle : la construction de la nation dans un environnement multi-ethnique et le rôle dominant de l'Etat dans le processus de modernisation en firent des Etats fortement centralisés. Le fait que de nombreuses régions frontières abritaient d'importantes minorités renforça la méfiance des élites nationales face à toute tentative d'expression de singularité régionale. Les régions étaient considérées comme une menace pour l'unité nationale, ce qui est encore parfois le cas aujourd'hui.

Au cours des dernières années cependant, la centralisation a été de plus en plus remise en question. Les régions ont pris de l'importance dans les préoccupations politiques, économiques et socio-culturelles en Europe du Sud-est. Les raisons de l'importance croissante des politiques, de la planification et de la conscience régionales sont nombreuses. Premièrement le réveil de la conscience régionale est issu du processus de démocratisation après 1989. Les minorités, mais également les membres de la majorité de la population se réclamèrent dans certaines régions, de ce qu'elles considéraient être leur histoire et se mirent à évoquer leur passé autonome, réel ou imaginaire. Ces dynamiques purent même se concrétiser dans la création de partis politiques, comme par exemple en Istrie. Ces mouvements régionalistes et autonomistes remirent en question non seulement la marginalisation de leurs traditions dans le discours national dominant, mais également la répartition souvent injuste des capitaux et des investissements dans le pays et finalement le désintérêt du centre pour la périphérie.

Certaines régions se sont aperçues aussi qu'elles disposaient d' avantages par rapport au centre, eu égard par exemple à leur situation géographique et qu'elles seraient en meilleure posture si les choses étaient décidées localement. Le district de Timisoara, au nord-ouest de la Roumanie, en témoigne. C'est le district qui a connu le plus fort investissement étranger et qui est devenu le plus prospère de tout le pays excepté Bucarest. Du coup, les élites du Banat roumain ont redécouvert l'héritage des Habsbourgs et en ont fait un argument d'appartenance à l'Europe centrale, en contraste avec le reste du pays demeuré «balkanique». L'image de leur région riche de traditions historiques s'oppose ainsi à celle d'un Etat centralisé. Il faut dire aussi que le processus de décentralisation est facilité par les mécanismes de l'intégration européenne. En effet l'administration des fonds structurels pour la promotion des régions dont les nouveaux Etats membres profitent largement, suppose des administrations locales efficaces susceptibles de devenir avec le temps des lieux d'identification régionale et de pouvoir politique. Les Etats en liste d'attente sont encouragés à créer de telles ressources régionales; la décentralisation va aussi pouvoir servir aux minorités ethniques de moyen pour faire entendre leurs revendications (que l'on songe à la République de Macédoine par exemple).

Au cours de la prise de conscience politique croissante les dimensions culturelles du régionalisme ont pris de l'ampleur. Les histoires régionales se sont multipliées de même que les manifestations culturelles comme les carnavals et les festivals d'art. Les élites régionales ont aussi commencé à promouvoir la spécificité de leurs régions de manière à les positionner sur le marché touristique international et parfois également pour se distancer d'un Etat-nation dont l'image à l'étranger n'est pas bonne (voir à nouveau le Banat roumain mais aussi la Voïvodine serbe où, malgré la prédominance serbe, la demande d'autonomie est forte et soutenue par la mise en évidence du caractère «européen» de la région). Bien que nous manquions encore de données sociologiques, il semble que l'identification avec la région soit en augmentation, même au niveau de la vie quotidienne. L'ouverture des frontières a également contribué à un renforcement des appartenances régionales, surtout là où les régions historiques se sont vues divisées par des frontières nationales. Ces sentiments ont également pour résultat la création d'Euro-régions et d'autres formes de coopération transfrontalières.

Parallèlement on assiste à l'avènement d'écarts considérables entre les régions. La croissance économique, le chômage, les niveaux d'investissement, l'accès aux ressources et au bien-être, sont inégalement distribués dans les diverses parties des pays du Sud-est. C'est encore un héritage du centralisme qui a désavantagé certaines régions et n'a pas réussi à répondre de manière équitable aux intérêts des diverses régions. Alors que certaines régions s'en sortent vraiment très bien et réussissent même à attirer des retraités des pays de l'Europe de l'Ouest à la recherche de climats plus cléments et de prix plus raisonnables, d'autres végètent et certaines font partie des régions les plus pauvres de l'Union Européenne. Dans ces dernières on assiste à un dépeuplement massif en faveur des grandes villes. L'attachement à sa région va évidemment être affecté par l'augmentation des différences socio-économiques. Dans les régions qui s'appauvrissent on peut observer la manifestation d'une nostalgie évidente pour le bon vieux temps plus prospère. Cela dit, même les régions les plus marginalisées sont aujourd'hui plus intégrées que jamais au monde en général. Les nouveaux medias et les migrations transforment les modèles culturels et sociaux même dans les endroits les plus reculés. L'appauvrissement peut donc très bien s'accommoder d'une intégration dans le monde globalisé.

Il est évident que le concept de région revêt une importance croissante en Europe du Sud-est, aussi bien parce que la coopération régionale augmente dans cet espace et à cause du processus de décentralisation. Pourtant l'étude des régions, du régionalisme et des identités régionales dans le Sud-est européen ne fait que commencer. C'est la raison pour laquelle l'InASEA a décidé en 2005 de consacre sa quatrième conférence à ce thème. Nous étions convaincus que les anthropologues et les spécialistes des disciplines voisines pourraient contribuer de manière significative à l'étude de la «région» en Europe du Sud-est, en prenant en compte aussi le *«geographical turn»* qu'ont adopté récemment les sciences humaines, à savoir la considération du territoire physique et symbolique en tant qu'expérience et représentation. C'est pourquoi notre conférence voulait être un forum de discussion de ces dynamiques régionales et autres espaces sub-nationaux dans le Sud-est européen, mais également de leur dimension historique.

La quatrième Conférence de l'InASEA qui eut lieu à Timisoara du 24 au 27 mai 2007 avait ainsi pour titre: «Région, Identité régionale et Régionalisme en Europe du Sud-est». Plus de 150 participants d'Europe et d'Amérique du Nord y prirent part. Ce volume contient une première série de communications présentées à la Conférence; le numéro 12 *d'Ethnologia Balkanica* complètera celui-ci avec une deuxième séries d'articles dédiés au même thème. Ces deux volumes témoignent de la richesse des approches relatives à l'espace régional. Ils montrent que la région, si elle n'est pas moins «imaginée» que la nation, est également un lieu d'expériences et d'attentes, puisant dans la mémoire collective et dans des sentiments qui s'écartent des discours dominants de la nation.

La Conférence et les publications qui en sont issues n'auraient pas été possibles sans l'engagement indéfectible de Mircea Alexiu et de Atalia Stefanescu de l'Université Ouest de Timisoara qui fut notre hôte. Grâce à leur dévouement et à celui de leur équipe de collègues et d'étudiantes, la Conférence fut un succès, et nous tenons à leur exprimer ici notre gratitude. Nous remercions également la Fondation Wenner Gren pour la recherche en Anthropologie sociale, la *Deutsche Forschungsgemeinschaft* ainsi que l'Université Ouest de Timisoara pour leur généreux soutien financier. Nous remercions enfin tous les membres de l'InASEA qui ont pris sur eux de faire la critique des communications soumises pour publication.

Ulf Brunnbauer, Président de l'InASEA Berlin, Février 2008

What's in a Region?
Southeast European Regions Between Globalization, EU-Integration and Marginalization

Klaus Roth, Munich

The conference in Timişoara, capital of the historical region of Banat, dealt with a topic which, according to some scholars, does not really have great relevance in our modern world of almost boundless mobility and transnational migration, of worldwide communication and virtual spaces, and of globalization permeating into all spheres of politics, economy, society and everyday life. The question was if, in view of all these "deterritorializations" that seem to render physical space almost meaningless, it made sense to devote a whole conference to the topics of "region" and "regionalism" - particularly in view of the fact that the very term "region" is so hard to define and is used in so many different ways and contexts.

The answer of the organizing committee of the International Association for Southeast European Anthropology to this question was in the positive, and the overwhelming interest of so many scholars from Southeast and West European countries in this topic was evidence that the right decision was made. The interest was instigated, we must assume, not only by the renewed attention directed to *space*, i.e., the rediscovery of territorial space which has been labelled *"spatial turn"*, but also by the fact that this renewed focus on space, and on the local and the regional in particular, appears to have become an antidote to the increasing social, economic and political acceleration, to the exasperating dynamics of globalization. As Rolf Lindner observed in as early as 1994 (Lindner 1994), there is a return to the local and to the regional,[1] both of them becoming the complementary side of globalization. Two years earlier, in 1992, the British sociologist Roland Robertson had coined the term *"glocalization"* for this phenomenon. And indeed, although many political borders have been lifted, territories and borders have again become very important - the Schengen border or the EU-borders towards Africa as well as the boundaries drawn by Samuel Huntington (1993) being only the better-known cases in point. Yet there appears to be a third important reason for the interest that refers directly to Southeast Europe, namely that its regions as well as their political, economic and socio-cultural significance have become problematic - and that for a number of reasons. These problems have been raised

[1] Cf. also Fassmann 1997, Gerdes 1980, Harvie 1994, Popović 2002, Telo 2001, Wagstaff 1994.

to the public consciousness particularly in those countries that have become members of the European Union, but they are extant in all parts of Southeast Europe.

I.

Physical space or territory, it thus appears, has not at all become irrelevant, and the *region* in particular has – in spite of or because of globalization and EU integration – become the focus of attention not only in the economy and in politics, especially EU politics with its concept of a "Europe of the Regions", but also in several academic disciplines. However frequent and ubiquitous the use of "region" may be in everyday life, in politics or in academic discourse, it is nevertheless a very vague concept. The discussion of "region" includes, as Celia Applegate (1999: 1158) has pointed out, "little certainty and less consensus about such fundamental issues as to what we mean by the term region". Even in geography, the discipline that deals most prominently with space, the concept of "region" is disputed and difficult to delimit, and the same holds true for such disciplines as political sciences, economics, regional planning, sociology, ethnology or history – leaving aside its use even in such disciplines as medicine ("regions of the body"), astronomy ("regions of the universe"), philosophy and psychology ("regions of the mind"), or theology ("heavenly regions"). Nevertheless, in spite of its many different uses and meanings and in spite of its vagueness both in everyday and in academic discourses, the term "region" appears to be indispensable and useful. It is useful as a practical concept of understanding, as everybody seems to know what it denotes, although most people would be hard pressed if asked to define what it means.

A closer look at the term can elucidate its meanings in everyday usage and in academic disciplines. In both discourses, "region", which is derived from the Latin *"regio"*, i.e., direction or district, is commonly defined as a territorial unit of a certain *spatial extension*, that is, of a certain physical size. The problem is, however, that the extension of this spatial entity can be of almost any size, ranging from a few square kilometres to whole continents. For practical reasons, one can distinguish four levels of spatial dimensions that are commonly referred to by the term "region":

1. The *micro region*. The size of the smallest kind of region is between that of the community (i.e., city, town or village) and that of the district. This kind of "region" usually denotes units of the size of a relatively small area, often the area around a city or town; for the individual, it may be the area around one's home town. This space is important insofar as it is equivalent to the actual space of everyday interaction and experience of individuals. In this way, one speaks of the region of Belgrade or of Bucharest, of Thessalonika or of Timi-

şoara. In EU terminology, this kind of region is largely equivalent to the NUTS 3[2] level.

2. The *meso region*. The term "region" is most frequently applied to this medium-size territory. It denotes a larger area of a size between the city or district level and the level of the nation. It often has a proper name and a history, and it exists as a concept in people's minds. In Southeast Europe, such well-known *meso regions* are, for instance, Istria or Krajina, Sandjak, Kosovo or Vojvodina, Banat or Transylvania, Epiros or Peloponnese, Šopluk or Dobrudja, but also larger ones such as Northwest Bulgaria, Southern Albania or Central Serbia. In some cases, such as Montenegro, a meso region has become a nation of its own, while in other cases, such as Banat, Dobrudja, Thrace or Macedonia, a historical region stretches across present national boundaries. In EU terminology, this size of region is equivalent to either NUTS 1 or 2.
3. The *macro region*. The term "region" is also applied to much larger areas of a size that lies between the nation and the continent. "Southeastern Europe" or "the Balkans" are often referred to as a "European region", very much like the "Baltic region", "Scandinavia" or the Iberian Peninsula. In March 2007, in Zagreb, the foreign ministers of eleven Southeast European countries founded the *"Council of Regional Cooperation"* in order to improve cooperation between all Southeast European countries.[3] In his famous essay, the Hungarian historian Jenő Szücs (1985) outlined the "three *historical regions* of Europe", i.e., three areas each of which includes large parts of Europe, and Larry Wolff (1994) described the process by which the "West" defined (and distanced from itself) "Eastern Europe" as a European region of its own, while Maria Todorova (1997) outlined the same process for the "Balkan region".
4. Finally the *global level region*. It is certainly confusing that even very large parts of continents or areas that transcend them are called "regions". Particularly in political discourse it is common to speak of the "Black Sea Region", the "Mediterranean Region", the "Gulf Region" or even the "Atlantic" or "Pacific Region", and likewise the entire "Near East" is often referred to as a region. All of these regions range between parts of continents and the globe. It is worth noting that since the Second World War "area studies" have focussed largely on macro or global regions,[4] a fact that has been criticized as displaying

---

[2] The acronym stands for *Nomenclature des unités territoriales statistiques;* see below.

[3] http://www.stabilitypact.org/pages/Press/detail.asp?y=2007&p=534; Deutsche Welle, Fokus Ost-Südost, 16 May 2007. Cf. Südosteuropa Mitteilungen 47, 3 (2007) 90–93.

[4] This finds expression, as Robert Hayden has pointed out, in a variety of interdisciplinary scholarly associations such as the Association for Asian Studies, the African Studies Association, the Middle Eastern Studies Association, the Latin American Studies Association or the American Association for the Advancement of Slavic Studies.

a hegemonic attitude, but has also been considered a necessity in the globalizing world (cf. Appadurai 1996: 16).

From the above follow two important observations: (1) Unlike the clearly defined concepts of "community" or "nation", "region" is always a *relative* term, a term that refers to something intermediate. Whatever its size, a region is always an entity of the "in-between", and the concept of "region" itself is a concept "in-between". (2) Any given territory can belong to several levels of region at the same time, one of them overlaying the other.

II.

While the term "region" is applied to all four above-mentioned levels, in most academic disciplines it usually refers to *micro* regions or, most frequently, to *meso* regions; and in most countries, particularly in Southeast Europe, this kind of "region" is almost synonymous to "rural region".

As diverse as the spatial dimensions are, so too are the theoretical approaches to the phenomenon. In geography, the discipline for which "region" is at the very centre of attention, the "realistic" approach to the region prevailed from the nineteenth century until the 1980s. This approach was based on the idea that regions are "containers" in which all physical-geographic and human elements form a kind of "natural" whole (Wardenga/Miggelbrink 1998: 35). In the 1990s, this "essentialist" view of the region gave way to an approach that perceived the region predominantly or even exclusively as a *social construct*. The geographers Peter Weichhart and Hans Blotevogel considered the region even as a "double construct": on the one hand, it is a "mental construct of science", and on the other hand regions are "to a very large extent the result of human actions and insofar historical and social constructs", or "cognitive constructs of the everyday world" (Weichhart 1996: 36 f.). For the geographic study of the spatial organisation or of the distribution and interrelation of certain elements, the term was consequently used as a category of description and analysis, for which the authors developed the terms "structural region" *("Strukturregion")* and "integrative region" *("Verflechtungsregion")*. As for the level of everyday life and discourse, regions are, on the one hand, seen as "regions of activity of economic and political-administrative organisations" which are "constituted by the actions of people (individuals, groups) and by social organisations (enterprises, associations, administrative bodies)" (Blotevogel 1996: 59). On the other hand, regions are constituted and reproduced by communicative processes and are thus *mental constructs* of spatial entities, either as "perceived regions" *("Wahrnehmungsregionen")* or as "identity regions" *("Identitätsregionen")* as expressions of the ingroup feelings of social groups. It is the latter type of region that can, under certain conditions, also become a "frame of reference of *active regionalism*".

It was somewhat surprising for a discipline like geography that physical space was reduced to just one out of many factors and was almost lost sight of; it was the above-mentioned *"spatial turn"* that brought real space, its physical qualities and limitations back in and put an end to radical constructivist approaches. The present view of "region" is a combination of both approaches, taking the "real qualities" of a given territory, its social constructedness and the social concepts about it into consideration. In other words, the factors that constitute and define a region can be both natural and human, both real and mental.

III.

But what are, in practice, the factors or *criteria* that turn a stretch of land into a "region". As a matter of fact, *any one* criterion can in principle suffice to make a "region", so that Rudolf Hrbek and Sabine Weyand (1994: 15) and other authors define "region" as a territory characterized by homogeneity in at least one specific aspect that differentiates and delimits it from other territories. In other words, the very concept of "region" is based on (real or perceived) internal homogeneity and external heterogeneity. The number of possible differentiating criteria is very large, and it makes sense to divide them into two groups, namely the so-called "hard" or "objective" criteria, and the "soft" or "subjective" ones. In almost any case, however, one can note an interplay or a combination of various factors in the constitution of a region.

The *hard* or objective criteria concern the tangible features, functions and factors that can shape a "region" and set it apart from others. Thus, a region can be defined and delimited by its sheer natural *morphology*, by plains and mountain ranges, by rivers and seas, by marshes and deserts. It can furthermore be defined by its predominant *economy*, for example by pastoralism, certain trades or industries, by its *infrastructure* or by its predominant means of transportation (e.g. river transport). In very many cases, "regions" are *politically* defined, that is, they are units of government or administration. Furthermore, a common *history* or historical experience can form a region, and likewise so can *social* factors such as religion, language, dialect, ethnicity or folk culture be differentiating criteria that constitute a region. In the 1920s, it was the principal goal of the school of "Culture Area Research" that was founded in Germany to determine "objective" culture regions or culture areas on the basis of *folk culture,* which resulted in large atlas projects in Europe (cf. Wiegelmann 1968) and in the United States (cf. Rooney 1982).

The *soft* or subjective criteria, on the other hand, are intangible, but they are by no means less important than the "hard" ones. For the individual or the group, the "region" around them is their space of daily life and experience *(alltäglicher Erfahrungsraum)*, a space of intensive social interaction, of networks and bonding. Such subjectively defined or constructed regions are spatial expressions of social or mental facts, offering the individual or the group not only a degree of familiarity and security, as Ina-Maria Greverus (1972, 1979) has pointed out, but also a sense of belonging, both spatially (my "home region", *"Heimat"*) and socially ("my people"). These subjective definitions constitute the above-mentioned "identity regions",[5] giving expression to feelings of belonging and attachment, to people's "sense of region".

Closely related to this dichotomy of "hard" and "soft" criteria is yet another important distinction that concerns the constitution or *formation* of regions. Having in mind both the "realistic" and the "constructivist" approaches, one can discern three different ways in which regions are constituted: they can be either "given", "grown" or "intentionally formed" – or a mixture of the three.

1. A *"given"* region would be a territory that is clearly defined through natural boundaries. Islands (such as Crete), peninsulas (such as Istria) or valleys between mountain ranges (such as the Rose Valley in Bulgaria) are such "natural" regions. But one must be careful, because the importance of natural boundaries is often overrated: rivers, for instance, can divide territories, as is the case with the Danube between Romania and Bulgaria (cf. Roth 1997), but they can also unite them, as is the case in the Upper Rhine Valley between France, Germany and Switzerland.
2. A *"grown"* region denotes a territory that has, on the basis of hegemonic, administrative, economic, structural, social or ethnic factors, through a historical process grown into a region – and is perceived as such by the people living in and around it. In many cases there is an initial element of forceful construction such as wars and hegemony: the Ottoman conquest shaped new regions, and likewise the Westphalian Treaty of 1648 established the principle of *"cuius regio – eius religio"* and thereby created many new regions, but in both cases most of these constructs became, in the course of time, unquestioned realities and people developed a sense of belonging and identity.
   Most of the historical or traditional regions have no exact boundaries. They can be called *"informal"* regions which are characterized by intense communication, social relations and economic interactions. Experience shows that even after longer periods of separation by national borders or political systems, the local populations re-establish the traditional ties as soon as the borders are open again;

[5] Cf. Becker 2005, Cole 1999, Giordano 1999, 2000, Kappus 1999, Lindner 1994, Weichhart 1990.

the western and southern border regions of Bulgaria are good cases in point, as Galia Valchinova (2003) and Ivaylo Ditchev (2005) have demonstrated.

3. *"Intentionally formed"* or *"formal"* regions are of a different kind. Their size and borders are always clearly defined. It is true that throughout history, regions and borders have always been constructed and shifted for hegemonic or administrative purposes: the Ottoman Empire was divided into administrative *vilayets* and *sandjaks*, and the Habsburg Empire also had fixed administrative regions. But never before in history have there been more systematic and radical attempts at subjecting territories to rational control and mastery than in the last two centuries. This policy of rational regional planning reached the Balkan Peninsula in the nineteenth century as part of the nation building processes, and here it is important to note that the model that was adopted already by the Ottoman Empire in the mid-nineteenth century and later by all young Balkan nations was the *centralist French model* which grants very little power to the regions, and not the federal model which grants the traditional provinces and regions much more autonomy. As a consequence, all new Southeast European nations divided their territories into politically weak and fully dependent administrative units, similar to the French prefectures, and often disregarded grown historical regions.

The purposeful creation and re-creation of formal territorial units – and the disregard of traditional, informal regions – was even stronger in the socialist countries (with the exception of Yugoslavia), where it was a direct result of conscious, politically motivated efforts of the communist regimes to centralize power and to maintain full control on all levels.[6] It was only logical that these administrative regions never took hold in, and remained almost meaningless for, the majority of the population. Bulgaria may be an extreme case, but it is nevertheless indicative that after the first establishment of administrative regions in 1880 the entire regional structure of the country was radically changed in 1887, 1901, 1934, 1944, 1947, 1948, 1959 and 1971 (Enciklopedija Bălgarija 1978, vol. 1: 37–39). This clearly demonstrates that for the central government the division of the country into regions was determined almost exclusively by its political interests.

This approach to regional policy in some Balkan countries is certainly extreme, but it is not at all unique. In modern nations, intentionally constructed or formal regions are an indispensable basis for regional and infrastructure politics and planning, so that the geographer Hans Blotevogel (1991) can call the region a "goal-oriented spatial construct". In this tradition of regional planning, the European Union has established two systems of regional structures, namely (1) on the

---

[6] In the GDR, for instance, the powerful traditional provinces *(Länder)* were dissolved and 16 weak districts *(Bezirke)* were established; after German unification, the old provinces were immediately re-established.

national and sub-national level the NUTS, i.e., *Nomenclature des unités territoriales statistiques* or *Nomenclature of Territorial Units for Statistics,* that was introduced in the EU in 1980, and (2) on the supranational level of the EU and its neighbours a large number of *"Euro-Regions"*, i.e., cross-border regions stretching into two, three or more countries.[7]

While the first ones were established for purposes of statistics, administration and planning in order to make the EU countries comparable and to facilitate the allocation of regional funds, the latter ones aim at overcoming national boundaries and at creating a more federally structured "Europe of the Regions". So, while the first ones are meant to be a tool for politicians, administrators and planners and need no acceptance by the population, the latter, in order to fulfill their proclaimed political goal, have to be accepted by the population and should ideally become "informal regions". The experience of the "old" EU countries has shown, however, that many of these (highly subsidised) Euro-Regions never really came to full life, and that only those that coincide with traditional regions have had a chance to thrive.

In some cases formal and informal regions overlap, but they rarely coincide. While the formal regions are easy to grasp and have well-defined boundaries, the informal ones have fuzzy boundaries and their definition is often quite subjective and vague. And while the formal regions have, as Blotevogel put it, a specific goal or primary *function*, the functions of the informal regions are multiple and complex. Therefore the categorizations of regions based on function that are offered in the literature are not consistent. Nobert Hölcker (2004: 13), for instance, distinguishes between four different functional types of region, namely the administrative, the economic, the social and the cultural region. The first two of them largely coincide with formal regions, while the latter two relate more to informal regions. As all of them are relevant for Southeast Europe, I will briefly discuss them.

1. The *administrative, political* and planning regions are the most clearly delimited territorial units, as they have legally sanctioned political and administrative borders. While these regions are the concern of political sciences, government administration, law, regional planning or geography, they are rarely, if ever, studied by ethnologists. As mentioned above, these formal administrative units in Southeast Europe are formed on the model of the French prefectures, a fact that is particularly obvious in Romania. In all new EU member countries, the existing administrative units were integrated into the European NUTS-system which, for the sake of harmonization, defines four levels of regions, namely NUTS 0 = nation states, NUTS 1 = larger regions/parts of nations, NUTS 2 = mid-size regions/districts, and NUTS 3 = small regions/cities. Bulgaria, for

[7] On Euro-Regions see e.g. Bauer-Wolf 2005, Blask 2003, Hrbek/Weyand 1994, Ilies 2004, Knemeyer 1994, Ruge 2003, Sempft 1995.

example, is divided into two NUTS 1, six NUTS 2 regions *(rajoni)*, and 28 NUTS 3 regions *(oblasti)*. One must not forget, though, that in spite of (or maybe because of) the centralist policy of the Southeast European governments these administrative units are nevertheless spaces of political action, for example in elections, and sometimes spaces of opposition to the political centre or of active regionalism.

2. The *economic* regions are often closely related to administrative regions, but they do not have to, and they are less formal. Depending on regional policies, legal regulations, taxes, border and customs regimes, etc., they can transcend administrative regions. Their boundaries are more flexible and vague, as they are defined by economic factors and policies. Economic regions are in the focus of economics, economic geography and tourism research which focus, among other things, on regional economic networks and interrelations, on the development of tourism or regional products (cf. Ermann 2005), and on regional cooperation and networking as a means to survive the pressures of global competition. Ethnology has so far touched economic regions only in studies of traditional regional economies (such as agriculture, pastoralism, crafts) and their socio-cultural consequences, more recently also in studies of tourism (cf. Pöttler 1994, Rolshoven 2005) and in efforts to market regional products such as folk art or food. In the European Union, economic regions gain in relevance because of their attempts to gain the legal protection of their regional trademarks. Can real *feta* cheese be produced in Denmark and sold under this name? For Greece, this is a question that has both economic and identificational implications. Ethnology should definitely take an active interest in this interplay of regional economy and identity.
3. Only over the last decade has the *social* region become an object of study of such disciplines as demography, sociology, geography, history, political sciences and ethnology. Social regions usually have the size of micro regions (NUTS 3), and they can be both *informal* or *formal* regions, depending on the perspectives and goals of practitioners or scholars: demographic or social data are usually available for *formal* regions, so that researchers prefer to make these their field of study. But the *informal* nature of social regions is more relevant than their formal aspects: On the one hand, they are the living spaces of social groups (defined by language or dialect, ethnicity, religion, class or typical economy), and the space of their collective social and political experience, of their "typical" social interactions and relations, and – very importantly – of their marriage circles. On the other hand, they are the spaces of their collective identity, which is often based on their opposition to external forces such as the national capital. This opposition is particularly strong in those European regions that are (or feel to be) *peripheral* and cut off from resources. In these cases the *spatial periphery* is identical with *social periphery,* an inter-

dependence between space and social class that has only recently become a topic of sociological research in Europe.[8]

4. The *cultural* regions are of course the most elusive, as they seem to exist largely in the eyes of the beholder. "Culture Area Research" attempted to overcome this problem and to objectify culture areas or regions by systematically comparing and mapping tangible forms and styles of folk culture. The method was applied to Southeast Europe by the cultural geographer Otto Maull (1938) and by ethnologists such as Milovan Gavazzi (1958) and Christo Vakarelski (1969). The Croatian ethnologist Gavazzi determined twelve larger culture regions on the basis of their traditional material culture, their food ways, customs, dialects, verbal traditions, etc. (Map No. 1), most of which cross national borders. Although the method of "Culture Area Research" was applied in several European countries and even in the United States (see Rooney 1982) and produced impressive atlases, it has to be remarked critically that it focussed on the dominant ethnic groups, excluding the cultural diversity of ethnic, religious and social groups, and it did not account for culture change, particularly for the change caused by modernization and by the homogenizing cultural policies of the nation states. This approach to cultural regions has therefore largely given way to constructivist concepts which focus more on *subjective* definitions of cultural regions based on collective and individual feelings of belonging and identity. There is good reason to apply these concepts even in our time of increased mobility, particularly of rural-urban migration, because for most people their home region still remains their predominant or exclusive space of everyday action and experience, of identity and stability in a fast changing world. This focus on the "own" region, however, inevitably contributes to the delimitation of the "others", both in everyday life and in research. It has to be added that objective and subjective cultural regions are a topic not only of the ethnological sciences, but also of dialect studies, cultural geography and architecture.

IV.

The interest of ethnologists in Southeast European regions and their problems has so far been quite limited. Both foreign anthropology and native ethnography or folklore have largely been locally oriented. While the *village* community has received a lot of attention from both native and foreign researchers ever since the Romanian "monographical method" (cf. Mihăilescu 1998) or Irwin Sanders' study of a "Balkan Village" (Sanders 1949), and even the *city* has meanwhile become a

---

[8] In June 2007, a sociological conference in Rostock, Germany, was devoted to this problem.

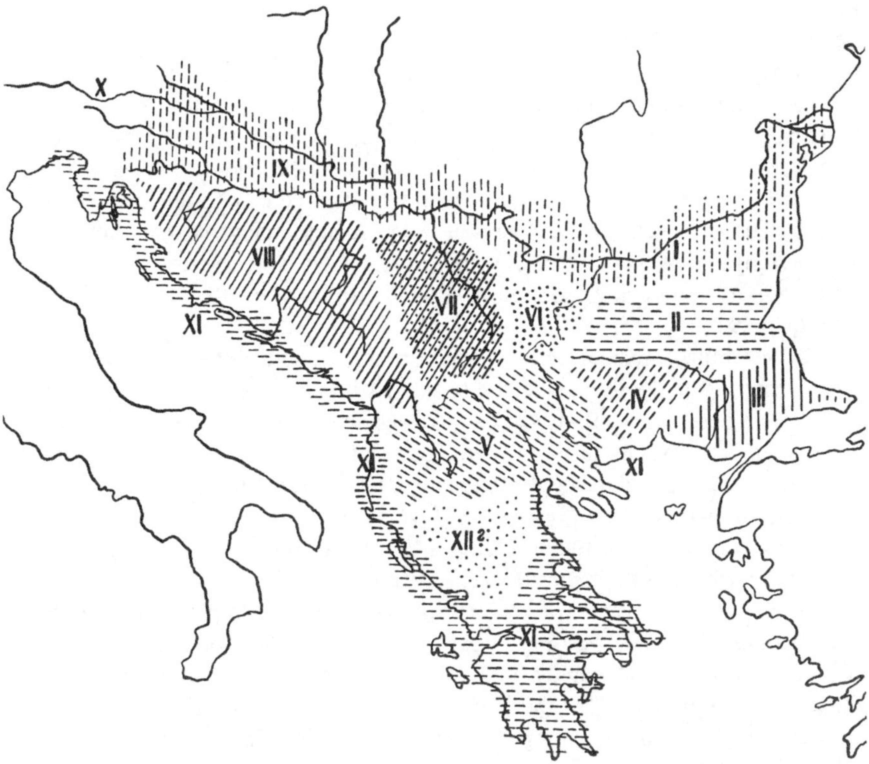

Map No. 1: The Culture Geographic Regions of Southeast Europe (from Gavazzi 1958: 12). I East-Danube Region, II Balkan Region, III Thracian Region, IV Rhodope Region, V Macedonian Region, VI Šop Region, VII Morava Region, VIII Dinaric Region, IX Pannonian Region, X East Alpine Region, XI Mediterranean Region (north, central and south Adriatic, Ionian-Agean), XII Intermediate Region (southern Albania, Epiros, Pindos)

focus of ethnological research[9], the *region* has only been used as an unquestioned locale of field studies either of folk culture in general[10] or of such aspects as

[9] Cf. vols. 9 and 10 of Ethnologia Balkanica which are exclusively devoted to urban life and culture in Southeast Europe.

[10] See e.g. the volumes by the Bulgarian Academy of Sciences on the folk culture of Bulgarian regions such as Pirinski kraj. Etnografski, folklorni i ezikovi proučvanija [Pirin region. Ethnographic, folkloristic and linguistic studies]. Sofia: BAN 1980; Plovdivski kraj. Etnografski i ezikovi proučvanija [Plovdiv region. Ethnographic and linguistic studies]. Sofia: BAN 1986; Sofijski kraj. Etnografski i ezikovi proučvanija [Sofia region. Ethnographic and linguistic studies]. Sofia: BAN 1993.

material culture, customs, epic traditions or narrating[11]. Apart from the above-mentioned works of Gavazzi (1958) and Vakarelski (1969), the "region" as such has not yet been problematised, nor have the specific political, economic, structural or socio-cultural problems of Southeast European regions been explicitly addressed from an ethnological perspective. In view of the processes of *glocalization* and increasing regional disparities, the ethnological sciences should therefore direct their attention to the actual developments in Southeast European regions. This means, that on the basis of sound ethnographic research, ethnologists should study the socio-cultural dimensions of all types of regions, including the formal administrative and economic ones and also the Euro-Regions. By studying them they can

- help determine informal regions, their culture, and the changes they undergo,
- help investigate the (objective and subjective) relations between the inhabitants and their region as well as between regions and the national centres of power,
- elucidate the extant normative and descriptive definitions and concepts of "region" in the Southeast European context before the background of EU definitions and concepts,
- but most of all address the problems of Southeast European regions and maybe even contribute to their solution (e.g. as consultants).

And problems there are in the regions of southeastern Europe. They are visible and palpable to anyone travelling through Southeast Europe with open eyes. Many of them are, or should be, the concern of politicians, administrators, regional planners or geographers, but there are just as many that concern the ethnological sciences. It goes without saying that several problems are the same as in other parts of Europe or the world, and here the ethnologist working in Southeast Europe should look at the wider European context and evaluate the international research literature.[12] Some problems, however, appear to have a specific nature or dimension on the Balkan Peninsula, mostly due to its historical legacy. Before the background of globalization, the expansion of the European Union and its goal of a *Europe of the Regions,* we must ask what the state of Southeast European regions is and what their most pressing problems are. Based on my personal experience, on literature and on sources such as the media, I want to discuss three aspects which I consider to be most relevant for ethnology.

[11] See e.g. the volume by D. Daskalova, D. Dobreva, J. Koceva, E. Minčeva: Narodna proza ot Blagoevgradski okrăg [Folk prose from Blagoevgrad region]. Sofia 1985 (= SbNU 58).

[12] See e.g. Giordano 1999, 2000, Göttsch 2000, Johler 2004, Köstlin 2005, Leimgruber 2005, Maase 1998, Pöttler 1994, Rolshoven 2005, Schilling/Ploch 1995.

Map No. 2: Core and Periphery in Europe (from Cole 1985: 9)

1. The increase in regional disparities

Ever since Ottoman times and the establishment of nation states, the Southeast European countries have been plagued by a number of sharp disparities or dichotomies. The fundamental one lies in the fact that since the development of the "world system" in the sixteenth to eighteenth centuries (cf. Wallerstein 1974, 1980) and the gradual decline of the Ottoman Empire from the early eighteenth century onward, the entire Balkan Peninsula became a region that was peripheral to the European centres, a disparity that has been studied from an anthropological perspective by John Cole (1985) (see Map No. 2). This historical dichotomy between European centres and the southeastern periphery continued throughout the twentieth century and was even exacerbated by the policy of the socialist regimes to integrate their countries into the "Eastern bloc" and to isolate them from the West. Today, this marginalization has its consequences not only in the fact that the GNP of the Southeast European EU members is the lowest in the EU, but also in the fact that virtually all regions with the weakest economies in the EU are located on the Balkan Peninsula; while in 1998, eight out of the ten weakest regions in the EU were in Greece (Vorauer 1998: 101), in 2007 twelve of the fifteen weakest regions were located in Bulgaria and Romania (see Table below).

Regions with the highest/lowest GDP per inhabitant in 2007[13]
(in PPS[14], EU-27 average of 2004 = 100%, EU = 268 NUTS 2 regions)

Regions with the highest GDP per inhabitant	GDP per inhabitant in percent of the EU-27 average	*Regions with the lowest GDP per inhabitant*	GDP per inhabitant in percent of the EU-27 average
Inner London (UK)	302.9	Vest (RO)	39.0
Luxemburg (LU)	251.0	Podlaskie (PL)	37.9
Region of Brussels (BE)	248.3	Centru (RO)	35.5
Hamburg (DE)	195.2	Podkarpackie (PL)	35.4
Vienna (AT)	179.7	Lubelskie (PL)	35.2
Île de France (FR)	174.5	Nord-Vest (RO)	33.0
Berkshire, Buckinghamshire, Oxfordshire (UK)	173.8	Sud-Est (RO)	30.7
Upper Bavaria (DE)	169.3	Jugoiztočen (BG)	29.9
Stockholm (SE)	165.7	Severoiztočen (BG)	29.3
Utrecht (NL)	157.7	Sud-Vest Oltenia (RO)	28.8
Darmstadt (DE)	157.3	Sud-Muntenia (RO)	28.4
Prague (CZ)	157.1	Severen centralen (BG)	26.4
Southern and Eastern (IE)	156.5	Južen centralen (BG)	25.6
Bremen (DE)	155.8	Severozapaden (BG)	25.6
NE Scotland (UK)	153.9	Nord-Est (RO)	23.6

Within the peripheral Southeast European macro region, there is yet another, a *second periphery*. The strong political focus on modernization and urban development ever since the late nineteenth century created a sharp dichotomy between developing *urban* regions and lagging behind *rural* regions. The neglect of the rural regions grew in the early twentieth century and it further increased in the socialist period, when the focus was on heavy industries, collectivization of agriculture and rapid urbanization.[15] In the 1990s, the impact of capitalism and globalization, combined with inadequate national policies (Creed 1995), increased the disparities between the urban centres and the rural peripheries even further:

[13] http://epp.eurostat.ec.europa.eu/cache/ity_offpub/KS-SF-07-104/EN/KS-SF-07-104-en.pdf.

[14] PPS = purchasing power standards.

[15] The rapid influx of village dwellers into the cities resulted in the "rurbanization" of southeast European cities, i.e., urbanization with strong rural elements (cf. Roth 1985, Prošić-Dvornić 1992).

Almost all Southeast European countries are today characterized by a sharp disparity between relatively strong and flourishing metropolitan regions and economically weak and backward rural regions which lack any adequate infrastructure,[16] many of which are depopulated or even devastated. They form both spatial and social peripheries which are "peripheries of the periphery" or "double peripheries" (cf. Axt 1997, Hofer 1987).

There are, of course, similar developments in many European countries (cf. Blotevogel 1997, Giordano 1994) and in North America, but the size of the problem on the Balkan Peninsula appears to be much larger. The growing discrepancy between developing and devastated regions in Southeast Europe has eminent social and cultural consequences (see Maier 2007). The almost empty peripheral regions with primitive agriculture and devastated villages are becoming more and more the refuge of ethnic minorities,[17] usually of Roma, or of the economically deprived, for example old-age pensioners surviving on subsistence agriculture and with "archaic cultural models" (Benovska-Săbkova 1995). In recent years, and increasingly with the EU accession, one can notice yet another development: more and more old-age pensioners from Western Europe buy houses – and sometimes whole villages – and repopulate regions that have been largely deserted by their original populations.

In the EU, the most important counter measures were and still are the funding of the improvement of the regional infrastructure and economy. In the 1980s and 1990s, Greece profited largely from this policy (cf. Lauth-Bacas 2004), but today there is less EU money available, and in the new member countries there seems to be less know-how and experience to acquire these funds[18] and more high-level corruption, as the progress reports of the EU Commission indicate. Other measures taken by the EU, by national governments, regional administrations, local authorities, and NGOs are the establishment and support of nature parks[19] and of tourism, especially "soft" village tourism, but it is very likely that the regional disparities will continue to grow in the foreseeable future.

---

[16] Cf. the keynote address by Robert M. Hayden on "Highways, Roadblocks and Empires" for the conference on "Building the Balkans Anew: From Metaphor to Market," University of Illinois at Urbana, Champaign, Sept. 21, 2007.

[17] In Bulgaria, for example, only 26,5% of the ethnic Bulgarians, but 63,1% of the ethnic Turks and 46,2% Roma live in villages (Genov 2007: 90); cf. also Aschauer 2007.

[18] In the summer of 2007, for example, radio reports indicated that Bulgarian wine-growing farmers were largely unable to file applications for EU funds for lack of know-how; the largest part of the funds earmarked for Bulgarian farmers remained unused.

[19] Most of these parks and reserves were established in the framework of the EU's "Natura 2000" programme, a European network of areas protected on the basis of the Flora-Fauna-Habitat Directive of 1992.

In view of these rather dramatic developments, ethnologists should direct their attention to the abandoned regions, but this time not in search of relics and survivals of "ancient" or "authentic" folk traditions, but rather to the socio-cultural consequences of the economic and demographic processes. These consequences include the shrinking of settlements and populations (cf. Becker 2005), regressive processes in everyday culture, the dying out of ethnic cultures (cf. Barna/Lönnqvist 2000 on the Banat region) or their replacement by other ethnic cultures, the growing "culture of the elderly", or the adaptation of new populations, e. g. Western old-age pensioners, to their new places of residence and their interactions with the local population. Worthy of ethnographic attention are also the political and economic attempts to turn the tide, for example through the production and marketing of regional products (with the help of EU subsidies or protection of trademarks), or the "folklorization" of such regions for domestic or international tourists.

2. From powerlessness to empowerment?

As mentioned above, the administrative regions of the new nation states were – and still continue to be – powerless and dependent on the strong power centres in the national capitals. With the partial exception of Yugoslavia, regional autonomy or any kind of self-determination or self-governance were impossible, so that the regions as well as the local communities remained in a state of almost complete dependency and non-responsibility. This in turn created a strong opposition between "us" and "them", between the weak periphery and the overpowering centre which, in the eyes of the people in the "province", was corrupt, abused its power, and totally neglected the rural regions. In Bulgaria, this political tradition of disregard and even contempt of the "backward" villages and regions continued after 1990, leading to catastrophic results (Creed 1995), with little change even after EU accession. It is hardly surprising that one of the basic political principles of the EU, the principle of "subsidiarity", is very difficult to implement in Southeast Europe. The principle demands that each political-administrative unit (from the village community up to the national government) should take care of *all* the matters that it can manage except for those that fall in the responsibility of the next higher administrative level. It is obvious that this federalist principle[20] grants a lot of local and regional autonomy and self-determination, but runs counter to the centralist structure of Southeast European countries.

For the outside observer it is striking that people in the "province" complain a lot about the capital and at the same time put up with their situation. They would

[20] Cf. Rose 2001, Sidjanski 2000, Vitzthum 2000.

rather try to escape their rural region and migrate to the urban centres or straight to the West as soon as they have the opportunity. Of course there is some identification with the region and interest in regional history and culture, and there are regional studies by local historians or ethnographers,[21] but this regional interest or regionalism is considerably lower than in West and Central European countries. Accordingly, there are few movements for *political regionalism*, i.e., for greater self-determination. If regions are less important in Southeast Europe, at least in the formerly Ottoman territories, it is worth asking for the reasons. A likely explanation could be that as a consequence of the Ottoman way of rule, the focus of life and of all social activities were – and largely continue to be – the smaller social units of the family, the kinship group and the village community (and maybe a few neighbouring settlements). The larger territorial or political units were governed by foreign Ottoman officials, so that an identification with the region could hardly develop. In view of this, the choice of the centralist French model of regional administration and the relatively low level of political regionalism, federalism or separatism was probably a logical consequences. It is worth noting that most regions striving for more autonomy within the national state[22] belong to that part of Southeast Europe that once was part of the Habsburg Empire.

It is the prevalent focus on village and kinship ties, the political powerlessness of the regions, and the resulting low regional cohesion that have – in conjunction with macro political and economic factors – contributed to the bleeding out of rural regions and to the excessive growth of urban conglomerations such as Athens (where over one third of all Greeks live!), Bucharest, Belgrade, Sofia or Istanbul. The opposition of the periphery against the centre is strong, but it is a silent and resigned one. The attitude towards the capital is characterized by a general *"culture of public mistrust"*, as Christian Giordano (2007) phrased it. The central government and all its institutions are viewed as the centres of corruption and mismanagement, and all mishap is blamed on them. Today, this criticism includes the way in which EU regional funds are allocated: officials in the capital are alleged to take ten or even twenty per cent in bribes or channel the funds to their relatives or friends (cf. Petrova 2006).

Although political counter action in the form of *political* regionalism is quite unlikely, there appears to be a growing *symbolic* or *nostalgic* revaluation of the regional and the local. This emerging *symbolic regionalism* derives largely from the strong kinship ties of most new urbanites to the places of origin of their families and kin and their nostalgia for "wholesome" village life vis-à-vis the disturbing effects of modernization, urbanization and globalization. In the last years,

---

[21] In Bulgaria, for example, there is a lot of literature on local and regional history and culture *("kraevedstvo")*, most of it written by devoted laymen.

[22] Montenegro, Kosovo, and the Republica Srpska are striving for, or have achieved, nationhood.

more and more city dwellers renovate the old village houses of their family or build new ones and spend their summer holidays in the region; regional or village tourism has become increasingly popular, as more and more historical and ethnographic museums have been opened and regional folklore festivals have greatly increased in number and popularity. The villages and regions make ever greater efforts to attract visitors with all kinds of old and new festivals and the sale of regional products, so that one can speak of a "musealization" and "festivalization" of rural regions and communities. It seems that the peripheral regions are becoming – as a kind of secondary development – the focus of nostalgic identification of the new urbanites, who as migrants to the big cities (or abroad) organize themselves in associations based on village or town origin (e. g. in Greece or Bulgaria) or on regional origin (*hemşer*, in Turkey), a kind of *regionalism by proxy*. They will get regional food from their relatives back in the village or buy the increasing number of "genuine" regional products; the advertizing industry has in any case discovered this new market. This sentimental return to the village or the region is certainly a "strategy of the powerless", but it can also create sentiments directed against the national capital or against "Brussels" which can be tapped by populist politicians.

On the other hand, one can observe a growing tendency that this regionalism leads to civic action, e. g. engagement for the protection of the natural habitat of the rural regions. Local and regional opposition to large and damaging infrastructural projects of big business or the government is supported by concerned citizens and NGOs in the cities, a new development that may lead to some degree of regional empowerment. All these developments are, in any case, important research topics for ethnologists or folklorists.

3. Transcending regional and national borders

Any definition of a region, be it a popular, political or scientific one, by necessity defines boundaries, and with that territories and people that do *not* belong to it. The vagueness of the boundaries of informal regions inevitably provokes the question of where a given region ends and where the neighbouring region begins. Regions are, in other words, also about inclusion and exclusion, about "us" and the "others". The spatial boundaries are reifications of social boundaries. And like every villager has stereotypical images of the people living in the next villages, in the same way people in any given region have images of themselves and of their neighbouring regions (cf. Hönnighausen 2000) which are often expressed in popular narrative forms such as sayings, slurs or jokes. In some cases there are even "regional characters" such as those of the *Šopi* in Bulgaria, the *Herzegovinians* in former Yugoslavia, or the *Cretans* in Greece.

Because of the vagueness of informal regions there is always a space "in-between", an intermediate or hybrid space of neither–nor which incorporates elements of both regions. It is marginal to both, but at the same time it is an important space of exchange and contact. This is particularly evident in regions that are located on national borders or even cross them. Such regions have always functioned as spaces of economic, social and cultural exchange between countries, particularly when the same language is spoken on both sides of the border, and in many cases there are special agreements between governments to facilitate the free flow of people, goods and services between these border regions[23]. It is this tradition that the European Union wants to continue and to strengthen by establishing and supporting trans-border Euro-Regions that make the national borders more permeable. Based on local or regional initiatives, trans-border regions were established in eastern and southeastern Europe even before EU accession, and there are more Euro-Regions to come. Meanwhile there are seventeen Euro-Regions that include Southeast European countries (see table), and there are plans to establish others. In 2007 Bulgaria, Greece and Turkey agreed to establish the Euro-Region "Trakia", but Bulgarian newspapers complained[24] that the Greek side was the least enthusiastic partner.

Euro-Regions in Southeast Europe[25]

Name of Euro-Region	*participating countries*
Adriatic Euroregion	AL BiH HR SM SL I
Carpathian Euroregion (Carpath. Foundation)	HU PL RO SK UA
Danube 21 Euroregion	BG RO SM
Danube-Drava-Sava	HU HR BiH
Danube-Kris-Mures-Tisza (DKMT)	HU RO SM
Drina-Sava-Majevica	BiH SM
Euregio Steiermark – Slovenija	SL AT
Euroregio Danube 21	BG RO SM
Euroregio Belasica	BG RO SM
Ister-Granum Euroregion	HU SK
Lower Danube (Dunarea de Jos)	RO MO UA
Nestos-Mesta Euroregion	BG GR

23 For the exchange in the Serbian-Romanian border region, see Radu 2007. For the regions on the Serbian-Bulgarian border there were in socialist times special privileges for the local population to cross the otherwise strictly closed and guarded border.

24 See, for example, the daily *Sega* of April 26, 2007, p. 14.

25 On the Romanian Euro-Regions see Ilies 2004.

Name of Euro-Region	*participating countries*
Niš-Skopje-Sofia Euroregion (Eurobalkans)	BG MK SM
Prespa/Ohrid Euroregion (Cultural Triangle)	GR MK AL
Siret-Prut-Nistru	RO MO
Upper Prut (Prutul de Sus)	RO MO UA
West Pannonia Euroregion	AT HU
planned: Euroregion Trakia	BG GR TR

SM = Serbia and Montenegro

Many Euro-Regions all over the EU have only a formal existence, i.e., in the actions of politicians, administrators, regional planners or economists, and only relatively few of them have really been accepted by the local population, usually those that had already been informal regions before (cf. Böttger 2006). Given the strong centralist tradition of the Southeast European countries and the reluctance of their governments to share power, there is good reason to be sceptical about the future of the Southeast European Euro-Regions. But whatever the outcome, the processes of their acceptance or rejection as well as the possible changes in everyday behaviours and the management of identities should be closely observed by ethnologists. The studies of Elke-Nicole Kappus (1999) and Pamela Ballinger (2004) of the region of Istria, which is part of the Adriatic Euroregion, have already produced fine results.

The present paper could touch only on some of the questions that concern the regions of Southeast Europe. Many more will be addressed in the papers of this volume whose main objective is to direct the attention of ethnologists, anthropologists, folklorists, sociologists and historians to the regions of the Balkan Peninsula and to the problems which they face in our time of EU integration and globalization.

Literature

Appadurai, Arjun 1996: Modernity at Large: Cultural Dimensions of Modernity. London, Minneapolis: University of Minnesota Press.

Axt, Heinz-Jürgen (ed.) 1997: Strukturwandel in Europa. Südosteuropa, Ruhrgebiet und Reform der EU-Strukturpolitik. Munich: SOG (Südosteuropa aktuell, 26).

Applegate, Celia 1999: A Europe of Regions: Reflections on the Historiography of Sub-National Places in Modern Times. In: The American Historical Review 104, 4: 1157–1182.

Aschauer, Wolfgang 2007: Ethnizität und Globalisierung regionaler Lebenswelten. Überlegungen zur Bedeutung ethnischer Kategorien in den Transformationsländern Südosteuropas aus sozial- und kulturgeographischer Sicht. In: Wilfried Heller et al. (eds.), Ethnizität in der Globalisierung. Zum Bedeutungswandel ethnischer Kategorien in Transformationsländern Südosteuropas. Munich: Sagner, 71–85.

Ballinger, Pamela 2004: "Authentic Hybrids" in the Balkan Borderlands. In: Current Anthropology 45.1: 31–60.

Barna, Gábor, Bo Lönnqvist 2000: The Lost Future - die expatriierte Kultur. In: Schweizerisches Archiv für Volkskunde 96: 121–143.

Bauer-Wolf, Stefan (ed.) 2005: "Europaregionen". Herausforderungen, Ziele, Kooperationsformen. Wien: Österreichische Raumordnungskonferenz (ÖROK).

Becker, Franziska 2005: Ortsidentitäten im "Europa der Regionen". Das Beispiel einer schrumpfenden Stadt an der deutsch-polnischen Grenze. In: Beate Binder, Silke Göttsch et al. (eds.), Ort. Arbeit. Körper. Ethnographie Europäischer Modernen. Münster: Waxmann, 175–183.

Benovska-Subkova, Milena 1995: Archaic Cultural Models and Totalitarianism. In: Ethnologia Balkanica. Sofia, 162–178.

Blask, Falk (ed.) 2003: Europa an der Grenze. Ost Odra West Oder. Münster: LIT.

Blotevogel, Hans Heinrich (ed.) 1991: Europäische Regionen im Wandel. Strukturelle Erneuerung, Raumordnung und Regionalpolitik im Europa der Regionen. Dortmund.

Blotevogel, Hans Heinrich 1996: Auf dem Weg zu einer "Theorie der Regionalität": Die Region als Forschungsobjekt der Geographie. In: G. Brunn (ed.), Region und Regionsbildung in Europa. Konzeptionen der Forschung und empirische Befunde. Baden-Baden, 44–68.

Blotevogel, Hans Heinrich 1997: Räumliche Disparitäten und Bevölkerungswanderungen in Europa. Regionale Antworten auf Herausforderungen der europäischen Raumentwicklung. Hannover: Verlag der ARL.

Böttger, Katrin 2006: Grenzüberschreitende Zusammenarbeit in Europa. Erfolge und Misserfolge der Kooperation am Beispiel der EUREGIO (Rhein-Ems-Ijssel), der Euregio Maas-Rhein und der Euroregion Neisse-Nisa-Nysa. Tübingen: Europ. Zentrum für Föderalismus-Forschung, 32.

Cole, John W. 1985: Culture and Economy in Peripheral Europe. In: Ethnologia Europaea, Journal of European Ethnology 15: 3-26.

Cole, John W. 1999: The Reproduction of Identity in Contemporary South Tyrol. In: Ethnologia Europaea, Journal of European Ethnology 29: 109–115.

Creed, Gerald W. 1995: The Politics of Agriculture: Identity and Socialist Sentiment in Bulgaria. In: Slavic Review 54, 4: 843-868.

Ditchev, Ivaylo 2005: Cities on Borders: the Stronghold Complex. In: Ethnologia Balkanica 9: 201–212.

Ermann, Ulrich 2005: Regionalprodukte. Vernetzungen und Grenzziehungen bei der Regionalisierung von Nahrungsmitteln. Stuttgart: Steiner.

Fassmann, Heinz (ed.) 1997: Die Rückkehr der Regionen. Beiträge zur regionalen Transformation Ostmitteleuropas. Wien: Verlag der ÖAW.

Gavazzi, Milovan 1958: Die kulturgeographische Gliederung Südosteuropas (Ein Entwurf). In: Südostforschungen 15: 5–21.

Genov, Nikolai 2007: Globalisierung und Lebenslagen ethnischer Gruppen: Veränderungen in Bulgarien. In: Wilfried Heller et al. (eds.), Ethnizität in der Globalisierung. Zum Bedeutungswandel ethnischer Kategorien in Transformationsländern Südosteuropas. Munich: Sagner, 87–108.

Gerdes, Dirk (ed.) 1980: Aufstand der Provinz. Regionalismus in Westeuropa. Frankfurt am Main: Campus.

Giordano, Christian 1994: Historizität statt Modernisierung? Reflexionen über die Transformationsprozesse in Mittel- und Osteuropa. In: C. Brombach, A. Nebelung (ed.): Zwischenzeiten und Seitenwege - Lebensverhältnisse in peripheren Regionen. Münster, Hamburg, 217–232

Giordano, Christian 1999: Regionalizing Identities. Ethnicity in Italy between Crisis and Loyalty to Tradition. In: Ethnologia Europaea 29: 117–131.

Giordano, Christian 2000: Zur Regionalisierung der Identitäten und der Konflikte. Die Rückkehr des Nationalstaates und die Versuchung der „territorialen Ethnizität" in Mittel- und Osteuropa. In: Robert Hettlage, Ludgera Vogt (eds.), Identitäten in der modernen Welt. Wiesbaden: Westdeutscher Verlag, 383–408.

Giordano, Christian 2007: Privates Vertrauen und informelle Netzwerke. Zur Organisationskultur in Gesellschaften des öffentlichen Misstrauens. Südosteuropa im Blickpunkt. In: K. Roth (ed.), Social Networks and Social Trust in the Transformation Countries. Ethnological and Sociological Studies. Berlin: LIT, 21–49.

Göttsch, Silke 2000: Region und Regionales als Thema der Volkskunde. In: Uwe Meiners, Karl-Heinz Ziessow (ed.), Dinge und Menschen. Geschichte, Sachkultur, Museologie. Cloppenburg, 153–161.

Greverus, Ina-Maria 1972: Der territoriale Mensch. Frankfurt am Main.

Greverus, Ina-Maria 1979: Auf der Suche nach Heimat. Munich.

Hall, Derek R., Darrick R. Danta (Ed.) 1996: Reconstructing the Balkans: a Geography of the New Southeast Europe. Chichester, New York: Wiley.

Harvie, Christopher T. 1994: The Rise of Regional Europe. London: Routledge.

Hofer, Tamás 1987: Agro-Town Regions of Peripheral Europe. In: Ethnologia Europaea 17: 69–95.

Hölcker, Norbert 2004: Regionen in Europa. Gewinner oder Verlierer des europäischen Einigungsprozesses? Eine Betrachtung des Bedeutungswandels der Regionen in Europa am Beispiel der europäischen Regional- und Strukturpolitik von 1957 bis heute. Marburg: Tectum.

Hönnighausen, Lothar (ed.) 2000: Regional Images and Regional Realities. Tübingen: Stauffenburg.

Hrbek, Rudolf, Sabine Weyand 1994: Betrifft: das Europa der Regionen. Fakten, Probleme, Perspektiven. Munich: Beck.

Huntington, Samuel 1993: Clash of Civilizations? In: Foreign Affairs 72, 3: 22–49.

Ilies, Alexandru 2004: România. Euroregiuni. Oradea: Ed. Univ.

Johler, Reinhard (ed.) 2004: Daheim in Europa. Formen von Europäisierung in der Region. Tübingen.

Kappus, Elke-Nicole 1999: Euroregionen - Identitätsmanagement über die Grenzen hinweg. In: Christian Giordano, Johanna Rolshoven (ed.), Europäische Ethnologie - Ethnologie Europas. Fribourg, 291–216.

Knemeyer, Franz-Ludwig 1994: Europa der Regionen - Europa der Kommunen. Wissenschaftliche und politische Bestandsaufnahme und Perspektive. Baden-Baden: Nomos.

Köstlin, Konrad 2005: Region in europäischen Modernen. In: Beate Binder, Silke Göttsch et al. (ed.), Ort. Arbeit. Körper. Ethnographie Europäischer Modernen. Münster: Waxmann, 119–126.

Lauth Bacas, Jutta 2004: Greek Attitudes towards EU Inclusion: Controversial Discourses of Belonging. In: Ethnologia Balkanica 8: 7–21.

Leimgruber, Walter 2005: Alpine Kultur: Welche Kultur für welchen Raum? In: Beate Binder, Silke Göttsch et al. (eds.), Ort. Arbeit. Körper. Ethnographie Europäischer Modernen. Münster: Waxmann, 147–155.

Lindner, Rolf (ed.) 1994: Die Wiederkehr des Regionalen. Über neue Formen kultureller Identität. Frankfurt am Main: Campus.

Maase, Kaspar 1998: Nahwelten zwischen "Heimat" und "Kulisse". Anmerkungen zur volkskundlich-kulturwissenschaftlichen Regionalitätsforschung. In: Zeitschrift für Volkskunde 94: 53–70.

Maier, Jörg 2007: Verlierer der Transformation - ein Hemmnis der Europäischen Integration? Empirische Studien in der Tschechischen Republik, Ungarn und Rumänien. Bayreuth (= Arbeitsmaterialien zur Raumordnung und Raumplanung, vol. 265).

Maull, Otto 1938: Einheit und Gliederung Südosteuropas. In: Leipziger Vierteljahrsschrift für Südosteuropa 1, 4: 3–20.

Mihăilescu, Vintilă 1998: The Monographical School of Dimitrie Gusti. How is a "Sociology of the Nation" Possible? In: Ethnologia Balkanica 2: 47–55.

Petrova, Ivanka, Klaus Roth 2006: "Europäisierung" und Vergabe von EU-Mitteln. Das Beispiel bulgarischer Unternehmen. In: Helga Schubert (ed.), "Europäisierung" - Begriff, Idee und Verwendung im interdisziplinären Diskurs. Forost Arbeitspapiere No. 38, Munich, 51–58.

Popović, Dragoljub 2002: European Regionalism. A Challenge to New Democracies. Basel, Munich: Helbing and Lichtenhahn.

Pöttler, Burkhard (ed.) 1994: Tourismus und Regionalkultur. Wien.

Prošić-Dvornić, Mirjana 1992: The Rurbanization of Belgrade After the Second World War. In: K. Roth (ed.), Southeast European Folk Culture in the Modern Era. Munich: SOG, 75–102.

Rafael, Vicente L. 1999: Regionalism, Area Studies, and the Accidents of Agency. In: The American Historical Review 104, 4: 1208–1220.

Rolshoven, Johanna 2005: Going South! Lokalität und Mobilität in einer touristischen Übergangsregion. In: Beate Binder, Silke Göttsch et al. (eds.), Ort. Arbeit. Körper. Ethnographie Europäischer Modernen. Münster: Waxmann, 135–146.

Rooney, John, Wilbur Zelinsky (eds.) 1982: This Remarkable Continent. An Atlas of United States and Canadian Society and Culture. Austin, Texas.

Rose, Jürgen (ed.) 2001: Federalism and Decentralization. Perspectives for the Transformation Process in Eastern and Central Europe. Münster, Berlin: LIT.

Roth, Klaus 1985: Großstädtische Kultur und dörfliche Lebensweise. Bulgarische Großstädte im 19. und 20. Jahrhundert. In: Th. Kohlmann, H. Bausinger (eds.), Großstadt. Aspekte empirischer Kulturforschung. Berlin, 363–376.

Roth, Klaus 1997: Rivers as Bridges - Rivers as Boundaries. Some Reflections on Intercultural Exchange on the Danube. In: Ethnologia Balkanica 1 (1997) 20–28.

Roth, Klaus, Ulf Brunnbauer 2006: Urban Life and Culture in Southeastern Europe. Anthropological and Historical Perspectives. Berlin: LIT (= Ethnologia Balkanica 10).

Ruge, Undine 2003: Die Erfindung des "Europa der Regionen". Kritische Ideengeschichte eines konservativen Konzepts. Frankfurt am Main: Campus.

Sanders, Irwin T. 1949: Balkan Village. Lexington; Westport, Conn. 1975.

Schilling, Heinz, Beatrice Ploch (ed.) 1995: Region. Heimaten der individualisierten Gesellschaft. Frankfurt am Main: Institut für Kulturanthropologie und Europ. Ethnologie.

Sempf, Harald L. 1995: Euroregion - Prüfstein auf dem Weg in die EU. Potsdam: Univ. Potsdam.

Sidjanski, Dusan 2000: The Federal Future of Europe. From the European Community to the European Union. Ann Arbor: Univ. of Michigan Press.

Szücs, Jenö 1985: Les trois Europes. Paris.

Telo, Mario (ed.) 2001: European Union and New Regionalism: Regional Actors and Global Governance in a Post-hegemonic Era. Aldershot; Burlington, VT: Ashgate.

Todorova, Maria 1997: Imagining the Balkans. Oxford.

Vakarelski, Christo 1969: Bulgarische Volkskunde. Berlin.

Valchinova, Galia 2003: Znepole. Western Bulgaria Between "Europe" and "America". In: Ethnologia Balkanica 7: 159–180.

Vitzthum, Wolfgang Graf (ed.) 2000: Europäischer Föderalismus. Supranationaler, subnationaler und multiethnischer Föderalismus in Europa. Berlin: Duncker & Humblot.

Vorauer, Karin 1998: Europäische Regionalpolitik - Regionale Disparitäten. Passau.

Wagstaff, Peter (ed.) 1994: Regionalism in Europe. Oxford: intellect.

Wallerstein, Immanuel 1974: Capitalist Agriculture and the Origins of the European World-economy in the 16. Century. New York.

Wallerstein, Immanuel 1980: Mercantilism and the Consolidation of the European World-economy, 1600–1750. New York.

Wardenga, Ute, Judith Miggelbrink 1998: Zwischen Realismus und Konstruktivismus: Regionsbegriffe in der Geographie und anderen Humanwissenschaften. In: Heinz-Werner Wollersheim, Sabine Tzschaschel, Matthias Middell (ed.), Region und Identifikation. Leipzig, 33–46.

Weichhart, Peter 1990: Raumbezogene Identität. Bausteine zu einer Theorie räumlich-sozialer Kognition und Identifikation. Stuttgart: Steiner.

Weichhart, Peter 1996: Die Region - Chimäre, Artefakt oder Strukturprinzip sozialer Systeme. In: G. Brunn (ed.), Region und Regionsbildung in Europa. Konzeptionen der Forschung und empirische Befunde. Baden-Baden, 25–43.

Wiegelmann, Günter 1968: The Atlas der deutschen Volkskunde and the Geographical Research Method. In: Journal of the Folklore Institute 5 (1968) 187–197.

Wolff, Larry 1994: Inventing Eastern Europe. The Map of Civilization on the Mind of Enlightenment. Stanford, CA: Stanford UP.

Ethnic versus Cosmopolitan Regionalism? For a Political Anthropology of Local Identity Constructions in a Globalized World-System

Christian Giordano, Fribourg

Introduction

The intent of this article is to analyse some of the phenomena induced by globalization that appear to radically alter the Old Continent's political map, especially after the end of the antagonism of the opposing blocs, i.e., the East-West tensions that lasted for more than forty years.

By means of a political anthropology approach, we shall examine various attempts to redefine the socio-political order established via the gradual achievement of that Europe of nations, which US President Thomas Woodrow Wilson in his days was so keen on. We must acknowledge that it is a Europe grounded in the institution of nation states, which, ever since their foundation, were nearly always administratively structured in line with the principle of bureaucratic centralism. We shall then illustrate how this set-up has been challenged by various regionalist movements that make use of the greater awareness of cultural diversity as well as plural identities fostered by globalization as a means to obtain specific political claims. As the article will highlight, these regionalisms in fact vary in accordance with two ideal types, i.e., ethnic regionalism and cosmopolitan regionalism.

At this point however, we need to address a further question: whether the actual cession of sovereignty by European national states over the last fifty years on the one hand, and the concurrent rise of various forms of regional entities on the other, have in fact entailed a significant change in political representations and consequently a mutation of their related practices and structures as well. An analysis of empirical evidence leads to the conclusion that in most cases the above-mentioned different forms of regionalism, despite their great variety, have seldom produced fundamental innovations. We can also note that neither the old political imagination nor the national states' models of organizational apparatus have been fully discarded.

Illusions and spectres of globalization

For a long time the first apostles of globalization would have us believe that the world is in the midst of an epoch-making socioeconomic, political and cultural mutation by which all societies are coming closer together and consequently becoming more similar. Whether neo-liberal or not, enthusiasts of this process view globalization as the chance to unify the world, thus making it more fair because less unequal (Fukuyama 1992); in which case, quite unlikely at any rate, globalization would ensure a totalizing process of democratization (perhaps even a totalitarian one) (cf. Giordano 2000: 383).

The most tangible example of an ideological use of this optimistic and illusory outlook on globalization has undoubtedly been the US administration's entire foreign policy project over the past eight years. Whether this project conceals a Machiavellian hidden agenda, as many fear, aimed at establishing or strengthening an imperial hegemony, or whether the purported political, social and economic conquests of Western civilization, specifically America's, could be naively and guilelessly presented to populations that have been barred from them till now, is not the point of this introduction. Accordingly, whether bestowing happiness on as many people as possible or a sinister scheme to dominate the world, at least a major portion of it, lay behind the idea of *spreading out* democracy is also not the concern of this paper. The significant aspect in this context is to point out how a possibilist discourse of the 1980s and 1890s about the future prospects of globalization gave rise to expectations – lofty or small-minded if not downright despicable is undetermined, but definitely quasi-messianic ones even amongst the most disenchanted and brazen political classes.

Radical critics of globalization, instead, fear that this process may lead to a dull, bleak future populated by obtuse and unidimensional societies like the ones already imagined by some exponents of the *Frankfurt School*, specifically Herbert Marcuse (1964). Yet, this quite pessimistic view of globalization can actually be traced back to the theory of increasing bureaucratization of Western societies developed by Max Weber (1956, vol. 2: 843 f.). According to the latter, bureaucratization is closely associated to socio-cultural standardization and uniformity and thus gives rise to *homologous* societies, quoting Italian writer Pier Paolo Pasolini (1999). In time, these societies confine their members within the well-known *iron cage*, which, according to Max Weber, is the harrowing point of arrival of an excessive rationalization brought on by an ominous hyperbureaucratization (Bendix 1960: 459; Baehr 2001: 153 f.). American sociologist George Ritzer linked rationalization and political-administrative bureaucratization, socio-cultural uniformity and globalization; the *McDonaldization of society*, an expression he coined, is an appropriate metaphor of the near-future world whose characteristics, according to this author, are already clearly perceivable (Ritzer 1996, 1998; Smart 1999). Globalization, therefore, is imposing a uniform social system organized in accordance with the totalizing and, gastronomically at least, totalitarian model of the notorious global chain of *standardized feeders* known as McDonald's.

Political expressions of this disquieting view of globalized society are those movements known as *altermondialistes, no global,* and even *ecologist*. They oppose the neo-liberal model of the Davos *World Economic Forum*, the *G8* projects or those of the *World Trade Organization*, by now the leading negative symbol and the chief enemy to challenge, as the frequent protest rallies in Geneva have highlighted.

Neither one of these nearly opposite projects of society is particularly enticing or suggestive of rosy visions. Their interesting aspect however is that despite antithetical visions they both stem from a shared premise, i.e., that differences, especially cultural ones, will gradually decrease and finally come to an end in the near future. Though opposites, both outlooks after all pursue the same hypothesis that can be traced back to a prophecy already found in some lesser-known writings by Friedrich Engels, to which the theoreticians of the *homo sovieticus* would subsequently refer to (Engels 1981, vol. 13: 267). Paradoxically, this prophecy practically matches the one of the *end of history* proposed by Francis Fukuyama, standard-bearer of neo-liberalism (Fukuyama 1992). Drawing analogies between neo-liberalism and socialism may appear contradictory and out of place, yet these similarities are not incidental, especially if we bear in mind that they are the outcome of two doctrines grounded in a universalistic fundamentalism.

It is common knowledge that the prophecy of the *end of history* as an outcome of globalization as formulated by Francis Fukuyama is countered by Samuel Huntington's theory of the *clash of civilizations*. In short, contrary to Fukuyama this author has upheld that globalization does not result in a socio-cultural levelling out and a flattening of otherness along the lines of the occidental model. Globalization, instead, heightens and exacerbates differences amongst cultures, thus creating highly conflictual political and social rifts between different types of civilizations, which, according to Huntington, in the end have always been incompatible (Huntington 1993, 1996). To express the different approaches to globalization with the aid of ironic metaphors, one could say that as far as socio-cultural dynamics are concerned Fukuyama's *end of history* proposes something resembling a strong tranquilizer if not a sleeping pill, while Huntington's highly dramatic *clash of civilizations* is more akin to a hefty snort of cocaine.

Nevertheless, all three of the above-mentioned models of globalization are highly debatable and ultimately rather untenable for those social scientists who work with empirical evidence, not abstract speculation. In fact, there certainly are experts of social sciences other than the ones indicated in this introduction who have proposed far more discerning and differentiated visions concerning globalization processes. We need only mention, for instance, the works of Saskia Sassen on "global cities" (Sassen 1994, 2001), those of Manuel Castells on the "network society" (Castells 1996), or the socio-historical analyses of Immanuel Wallerstein on the "world-system" (Wallerstein 1974), and the more recent historical-economic-political studies reflections of Niall Fergusson (2004). Yet, all these authors as well as for example Anthony Giddens (1990), Michael Hardt and Antonio Negri (2000) or Ulrich Beck (2007), have focussed on fundamental aspects of globalization that could be defined as *structural, institutional* and *technological* ones. If not utterly neglected, the cultural dimension of globalization has been somewhat overlooked to say the least.

It is always interesting instead to bear in mind that the three models presented in more detail are nevertheless the most popular ones in public debates, though they present a misleading view of the cultural dimension in globalization processes precisely because of their too universalistic call that tends to underestimate complexity, which can be grasped only with the help of some degree of relativism.

In conclusion, neither the *end of history* nor the *McDonaldization of society*, nor again the *clash of civilizations* are corroborated by empirical evidence; thus, none of the three scenarios seems likely to occur in the near future.

Undeniably, due to globalization processes many sections of society, especially in the economy – such as stock exchanges, banking and insurance systems, airlines, etc., – willingly or not have to conform to standardizing drives to survive in global markets. Likewise, the world of mass media is increasingly uniform; the same movies, TV series, commercials, quiz shows, music videos, etc. can now be seen in Italy, Russia, Malaysia and Venezuela. Several other examples come to mind such as some sports events or large hotel chains.

However, the socio-cultural reality of the globalized world is, and continues to be, far more diversified than many would have us believe. Featherstone is correct in pointing out that globalization leads to a greater awareness of differences, especially cultural or social ones. After all, even the great nerve centres of globalization, such as television networks like CNN or worldwide fast-food chains like McDonald's, have become producers and managers of difference. We need only view infomercials and tourism ads such as *"Sights and Sounds", "Malaysia, truly Asia", "India, incredible India"* broadcasted by the former, and the various ads devised by the latter for specific local contexts. By now, McDonald's hamburger is presented as something entirely different depending on whether we are in Kuala Lumpur, Berne or Fortaleza. This is definitely no coincidence, since McDonald's opted for a regional fare differentiation after a disastrous financial crisis at the end of the 1990s, which led to the collapse of the old model based on the worldwide standardization of culinary suggestions. Ironically, even McDonald's had to retrace its steps to avoid an impending bankruptcy, thus forgoing *McDonaldization*.

We also ought to mention Arjun Appadurai's diagnosis according to which we should be aware that globalization, except maybe in some extremely specialized economic sectors, coincides with a global landscape of cultures on the verge of increasing differentiation (Appadurai 1990, 1996). Joel Kahn (1995) has rightly added that globalization not only heightens the awareness of differences, as Featherstone stresses (Featherstone 1990: 1 f.), and not only goes hand in hand with the development of an increasingly diversified global landscape of cultures as Appadurai shows. Globalization is also concurrent with a veritable industry of distinctions, as defined by Pierre Bourdieu (1979), perceived as such by end-users and consequently purchased and used by the latter as if they were actual goods. Apparently, therefore, the notion of *glocalization* coined by Roland Robertson (1995: 25 f.) is legitimate, albeit rather contrived, and highlights that the standard response to globalization is local social strategies which always produce new cultural differences as well.

In this context, we can also mention the global tourism industry that has, given the higher demand for difference, amazingly increased its supply of *cultural tourism*. Nowadays, even the most popular destinations of *seaside tourism* like the Maldives or Mauritius cannot afford to offer beach, sky, sea and palm trees alone, but invite tourists to take part in cultural programs in customized venues based on the hosting country's purported or genuine ethno-cultural plurality. An evening show in Mauritius featuring a performance of *sega*, the Creole slaves' dance, will invariably include local gourmet foods, i.e., Indian and Chinese cuisine. To further increase the impression of local cultural variety, Thai or Vietnamese dishes will be added, though they are unrelated to the multiculturality of this small island in the Indian Ocean. The example illustrates that – as far as cultural pluralism is concerned – globalization is rather a *Disneyfication* than a *McDonaldization* (Wood 1998: 218).

If the previously mentioned trends are not utterly incongruous, then we should not be surprised if the globalization process seems a mammoth apparatus in which borders are undone and redone, inclusions and exclusions are deconstructed and reconstructed, and social equalities and inequalities between groups and individuals based on belonging and cultural affiliations are wiped out and redefined at an ever accelerating pace. For these reasons, the globalization process can be linked to the idea of a permanent *regionalization of identities*, accompanied by the inevitable conflicts and contrasts that these changes entail, but without these tensions necessarily escalating into a devastating and widespread *clash of civilizations* or into a single collective animosity.

Regionalization of identities and political regionalisms

There is a wide range of collective discourses and social strategies in the globalized landscape that thematize and put into practice the current manufacturing of cultural differences, which are devised in political and intellectual spheres as well as in everyday life.

Ethnicity, in terms of discourse, practice or process, is still an important opportunity, though certainly not the only one, to define boundaries by *inventing*, in this term's positive connotation, distinctions and thus *building* new belongings and affiliations. As such, *ethnic power* should not be regarded as a relic of the past, i. e., of the nineteenth and twentieth centuries, but should also be seen as a phenomenon linked to the several territorial redefinitions, regionalizations, and reconfigurations of identities in times of globalized late modernity. As we shall see, ethnicity is an extremely multiform phenomenon, which, according to circumstances, historical space of experience, and social needs, both symbolic and material, is conceived rather differently. While in many regions of sub-Saharan Africa and the Middle East the ethnicized regionalizations of identity and their associated conflicts are correlated to the colonial invention of tribal differences – as in the bloody war between the Hutu and Tutsi in Rwanda and Burundi or the violent struggles between segmentary communities in Somalia led by local warlords, or again the resurgence of rivalries between tribes along the Pakistani/Afghan border –, in Latin America we encounter other types of ethnicity-based regionalization of identities. In this part of the world actualization is brought into play, i. e., the revitalization and/or ethnicization of pre-Columbian era communities and affiliations when everything was – according to present-day managers of these regional identities – still authentic and not polluted by the influence of colonialism and Western capitalism. In these cases, the regionalization of identities, with somewhat populist overtones, rethinks the myths of the glorious past of *great empires* wiped out by Spanish colonial expansionism and the utopian vision of the *noble savage*, mindful of his fellows and nature: more specifically, the myth of the *land of no evil*, i. e., the primordial innocence of *indigenous peoples*. Paradigmatic in this sense are the regionalistic movements of the Maya populations of Guatemala and Mexico and particularly the *Zapatista Army* operating in Chiapas led by *subcommander Marcos*, the now legendary charismatic intellectual.

Europe: ethnic versus cosmopolitan regionalism?

Yet, even in old, jaded Europe, though probably more in its western than its eastern parts, we can observe multifaceted phenomena of regionalisation of identities, although in many cases less extreme, politically milder, and less socially conflictual ideological forms than on the continents mentioned above.

German anthropologist Rolf Lindner has rightly spoken of a *resurgence of regionalism*, a *Wiederkehr des Regionalen* that was perceivable already in the mid-1990s (Lindner 1994). He specifically mentions a resurgence of nationalism because, despite undeniable similarities, it differs substantially from Europe's regionalistic drives of the 1970s. Inspired by the disillusioned heirs of the 1968 protest movement, a wave of regionalism occurred in the 1970s, which some experts called *the provincial rebellion,* mainly because of its quite radical ideologies (Gerdes 1980, Lindner 1994: 7 f.). For the sake of argument we can say that, given the role played by some of the leaders of the student's movements frustrated by the political outcome of 1968, it was a shift from *class struggle* to a *struggle for subaltern identity recognition*. Saying that these movements patently stemmed from Gramscian-inspired ideological reflections (Gramsci 1975) adopted by the European radical left of the time would not be an overstatement. Ironically, for their own political ends they discovered the concepts of *identity* and *ethnicity*.

In contrast, current political regionalisms cannot, as Lindner credibly indicates, be likened to rebellions, in any case not to solely ideological ones, and thus not to mass uprisings, but rather to arrangements; hence, present-day regionalisms are not *counter*- but *co*-phenomena. As such, sociologist Lothar Baier points out that today all over Europe, unlike in the past, the term regionalism has lost its original dissenting, subversive, transgressive, and thus pejorative connotations, with public authorities exercising hegemonic functions (Baier 1991: 14, 1992: 3 f.). Today, established authorities have also come to accept it and thus it is now part of the common parlance of politicians and bureaucrats. We need only mention catchwords such as the *Europe of the Regions* or *devolution*. In the end, the latter political concept is simply regionalism from the opposite standpoint, i.e., of those who wield power and grant the demanded autonomies.

Current regionalisms in Europe can thus no longer be regarded as movements that fight back or openly challenge globalization, but rather as political orientations trying to reach arrangements or compromises through negotiations. From the point of view of political anthropology, we could venture a preliminary characterization of regionalism in the current European context. Agreeing with Lindner, the following necessary though still insufficient and thus partial definition of regionalism can be formulated:

Current regionalisms in Europe are foremost a political phenomenon based on the appeal to local identitary belongings in an attempt to adapt to radical socio-structural changes triggered and/or imposed by the globalization process. Furthermore, they are social strategies aiming to overcome difficulties and problems caused by globalization through the mobilization of local societies whose members think and/or believe they belong to the given group due to specific shared qualities. Thus, these local identities are the expression of what Max Weber called *Gemeinsamkeitsglauben*, i.e., a belief in commonality (Weber 1956, I: 234 f.) Finally, regionalism is a response in line with the national states' gradual cession of sovereignty to social, political, and economic institutions of *global governance*.

In fact, most of Europe's national states have more or less willingly handed over shares of political, economic, and social sovereignty to a supranational organization known as the European Union. At the same time, some global governance institutions, such as the WTO or NATO, have increasingly limited the sovereignty of the above national states, which, though certainly not at a crisis point, are definitely on the defensive.

Since these structural changes are crucial to the overall globalization process, on the one hand they certainly kindled neo-nationalistic ambitions (see the over-reactions of intellectuals and people alike in Poland, the Baltic nations, and Bulgaria), while on the other hand they just as certainly fostered regionalistic drives.

Admittedly, between the gradual cession of national states' sovereignty and regionalistic claims, there is now a dialectic relation which, through constant accommodations, generates new political settings, in some cases even based on a lasting, though often shaky, *power sharing*, both locally and nationally. Not to mention that today in Spain or Romania, Italy or Bulgaria, governing is a difficult or impossible task at all levels without the support of parties advocating regionalism. The recent victory of the Scottish National Party in the latest regional elections seems to confirm this trend even in Great Britain where the single majority voting system, precisely because of the electoral structure, leaves few chances to regionalistic political forces.

At this point, our analysis introduces differentiations by distinguishing between various types of regionalism. Accordingly, we have conceived two ideal types in a Weberian sense, placed at the opposite ends of a continuum (Weber 1968: 235 f.). Being ideal types, we are dealing with abstractions for heuristic purposes which, as Max Weber stressed, in their pure form are not corroborated by empirical reality but are extremely useful for comparative analysis. We shall thus distinguish between *ethnic regionalism* and *cosmopolitan regionalism*. By ethnic regionalism we mean a socio-political movement striving to build an imagined collectivity whose belief in commonality is based on ethnic criteria regarded as qualities unique to one's own group such as origin, ancestry, history, traditions, culture, religion, language, and – not least – territory.

To clarify these aspects we will use two examples out of the several available ones, namely, so-called Padania and Catalonia, which, though very different from each other, can be regarded as classic cases of ethnic regionalism in Europe.

The Lega Nord as the most endorsed representative of regionalism in northern Italy has constantly endeavoured to imagine and popularize the idea of an ethnically homogeneous community in the vast and culturally multifaceted territory of the Po Valley, which the Leghisti purposefully call Padania (Giordano 2001: 126 f.). Consequently, with quite some political success, following the Herderian notion of *Volk*, the term *popolo padano* (people of Padania), was created. Umberto Bossi, undisputed leader of the Leghisti movement, addresses his torrential speeches to a purported *popolo padano* or *popolo della Padania* (Giordano 2001: 129).

Apparently, matters were rather clear-cut, but the question turned thorny once the characteristics of the imagined regional community called Padania had to be established during the ethnicization process intentionally set in motion by the Lega Nord. It could not be language, given the huge variety of the region's dialects. Neither could religion be taken into account because laic constituents and politicians in the Leghista movement would not appreciate a *Catholic discourse* evoking ghosts of the defunct Democrazia Cristiana party, historic enemy of the Lega because of its unitary outlook. Likewise, territory was difficult to establish. In fact, neither the movement's leaders nor its backers have ever been able to establish boundaries nor have they been able to clarify where *Padania* begins or ends (Giordano 2001: 130).

To overcome these problems, managers of the Padania regional identity had to fall back on two other criteria, probably slightly less dubious than the others: shared history and origins, i.e., a shared ancestry. These two aspects are used quite often in several ethnicity-building projects. Accordingly, they claimed an *historical right* to a federalist, thus an autonomist political set-up, based on a regionalist tradition grounded in a distant and glorious past. To corroborate a historical right, choice past events, represented as exemplary, needed to be actualized. Consequently, Leghista regionalism revitalized and reinterpreted events dating from the Lombard Middle Ages in order to claim the *historical right* of the *people of Padania* to regional autonomy. The two crucial events of the past used by the Lega are the Pontida oath of allegiance and the Battle of Legnano against Frederick Barbarossa, the foreign alleged centralizer who wanted to put an end to municipal autonomies. Frederick Barbarossa thus becomes a metaphor of the centralizing aims of the Italian unified state. Bizarrely enough, a similar strategy employing the same events was produced during the Risorgimento with a unifying and anti-Austrian slant. Giuseppe Verdi, surely the most popular ideologist of Italy's unification, composed the opera *La Battaglia di Legnano* (Battle of Legnano), while a minor Risorgimento poet, Giovanni Berchet, wrote a poem called *Il giuramento di Pontida* (the Pontida Oath of Allegiance), which was learned by heart by generation after generation of Italian students. The original, unabridged version of this poem can be found on the website of the *Movimento dei Giovani Padani* (http://www.giovanipadani.leganord.org). Besides, the name Lega is inspired by the Lombard League against Frederick Barbarossa (Giordano 2005: 57).

In addition, resorting even to the ancient historian Polybius, shared origins have been imagined, according to which the present-day *people of Padania* are direct descendants of legendary *Celtic populations* who settled the Po Valley in pre-Roman times (http://www.legavarese.com). Based on this, traditions have been invented, e.g. a veritable cult with allegedly ancestral rituals and ceremonies performed along the banks of the Po River believed to be the sacred river of the people of Padania ever since Celtic times.

In contrast to this Italian regionalism, Catalan regionalism dates much further back and is far more acknowledged nationally and internationally (Nagel 1994). Jordi Pujol, the historic leader during the post-Franco period, is definitely regarded as the most charismatic, skilled, expert and acknowledged representative of European regionalism in the world. However, Catalan autonomy, which currently governs at the national level in Spain, is probably the best example of an ideal type of ethnoregionalism on the Old Continent. It is based on a concept of ethnicity that includes various characteristics, but language plays a major and nearly obsessive role. The region's linguistic Catalanization after the downfall of Francoism and the subsequent recognition of political autonomy have been applied radically, although the population is mainly bilingual and using Spanish and/or switching from one language to the other is very widespread in everyday life. Yet, all public acts (including official statements or affidavits for foreigners), road signs, place names, etc., are strictly in Catalan.

Although to a lesser extent, Catalan regionalism has also employed other hallmarks of regional identity, such as (1) shared history, i. e., the fact that Catalonia was a distinct political entity ever since the Middle Ages, (2) culture and traditions, ranging from architecture (Catalan gothic and the modernism of Antoni Gaudì) to gastronomy (the fabled Catalan cream), and (3) territory, expressed by the concept of *Paisos Catalans,* which includes not only present-day Catalan territory but also the Spanish *Levante* (reaching Elche) and the Balearic Islands, as well as territories outside Spain, i. e., in southern France (Perpignan) and the Catalan enclave of Alghero in Sardinia. We may also add that the term *Paisos Catalans* brings to mind the representation of a *Great Catalonia*, which in many ways resembles similar conceptions such as the Greek *Megali Idea*, Great Hungary, Great Serbia, Great Romania, Great Bulgaria, as well as *Großdeutschland*.

Given its long history, Catalan ethnoregionalism has gone through various phases (Payne 1991: 479 f., Llobera 2004). The current one, however, apparently confirms Rolf Lindner's thesis. In fact, we could call it a politically moderate regionalism which avoids head-to-head conflict and seeks answers to its requests through apt compromises and accommodations; even in recent times it was able to take over further areas of sovereignty that traditionally belonged to the national state. This lack of aggressiveness has been patent, despite recent frictions and strong tensions with Madrid in relation to Catalonia's request to achieve a new state of autonomy and recognition as *a nation without a state of its own* within Spain (McRoberts 2001). Due to the above-mentioned characteristics, Catalan ethno-regionalism is also frequently defined as a very specific form of nationalism.

If, based on these two examples, we wonder what ideological or structural novelty there might be in ethno-regionalism, then we have to admit that the old national state model still survives. In fact, nearly all ethno-regionalisms tend to rehash old *ethnic discourses* and reproduce territorially scaled-down institutions of the national state. Above all, no one can rule out that these movements, apparently amenable for the time being, will in the future catch the virus of nationalism and turn into regional ethno-nationalisms.

Cosmopolitan regionalism is based on a social imaginary which, at least in intent, endeavours to address the challenges of globalization and the national states' consequent gradual loss of sovereignty to aggregation projects that try to move beyond the limited range of current political boundaries and/or of purported ethno-cultural homogeneity. For these reasons, this regionalism is – as an ideal type – located at the extreme opposite side of ethnic regionalism.

At first glance at least, by its very nature, cosmopolitan regionalism should be (in line with David Hollinger's definition of this term) considered *post-ethnic* (Hollinger 1995), *transboundary* and *transnational*. In principle – and we strongly emphasize this expression – cosmopolitan regionalism, according to Hollinger's argumentation, should (1) make boundaries between groups involved in these types of regionalism more flexible, if not indeed variable, (2) allow the involved individuals to have plural belongings, and (3) accept hybrid identities for these same individuals.

What we need to find out is if, and to what extent, this model of regionalism is indeed feasible or put to practice; moreover, there are several projects of regionalism in Europe that could in theory be considered cosmopolitan or post-ethnic. Yet, how many of these projects have been achieved to date in line with their original intentions?

Firstly, we ought to mention the Euroregions which by juridical definition are transboundary and thus transnational (Anderson, O'Dowd, Wilson 2003). Because of that they could become the institutions in charge of carrying out cosmopolitan and post-ethnic projects locally. In most cases, however, despite the proliferation of these projects and some examples of zeal and initial enthusiasm that led to believe and hope in the formation of *bottom-up* participation movements, the *top-down* aspect was strikingly prevalent. This demoted Euroregions to a question of bureaucracy and technocracy that led local societies to back out of the projects.

In a famous article, Clifford Geertz wrote that a world atlas of modernity, aside from oceans and seas, is an absolute continuum of nations. Willingly or not, every person, every place, every tree, etc., belongs to a nation. Despite the manifold activities carried out, Euroregions were unable to create *authentic autonomous areas between nations* and thus interrupt the absolute continuum of the world atlas Geertz mentions. Cosmopolitan and post-ethnic *social imaginary* is still part of a noble utopian thought, which has rarely been achieved, however, in either Western or Eastern Europe.

Out of several possible examples, we would like to specifically introduce the one linked to the notion of *Black Sea Identity* recently observed in Georgia. This model of regionalism is outside the European Union's institutional framework, but its *transboundary, transnational* or *transcultural social imaginary* with purposefully *post-ethnic* connotations is strongly supported by the country's intellectuals and politicians, particularly after the dramatic political changes that occurred a few years ago. Based on the assumption of a shared identity due to a history of constant and deep cultural, social, and economic contacts, the Black Sea coastal countries plus Greece would create a region together (Vahl, Celac 2006: 169 f.). This model, certainly fascinating but probably too intellectual, evidently refers back to the idea of the Mediterranean as a historical dimension set forth in Fernand Braudel's renowned book *La Mediterranée à l'époque de Philippe II.* (Braudel 1982, Troebst 2006: 93 f.). We need to add a slightly unpleasant comment at this point. In the end, the *Black Sea Identity* project resembles a *Verlegenheitslösung* by which the Georgian elite in particular, cloaked by a smokescreen of regionalism, strives to renegotiate and redefine traditional geopolitical settings, in an endeavour to countervail supposed discriminatory or indeed humiliating labels such as *Caucasian, Balkans* or *Russian* in exchange for politically correct and thus well-respected attributes. The underlying reason is probably a relatively covert urge to revalorize national honour.

Nonetheless, it definitely is a very enticing project, which, on paper at least, strives to improve on the classic patterns of ethno-regionalism. The main problem remains its feasibility, since it has not been truly problematized yet, nor indeed set to work. In all likelihood, this vision is too intellectual and abstract, too far removed from the *social imaginary* of common people who are still too accustomed to the pattern of nation. All these projects of cosmopolitan regionalism are hardly feasible precisely because they try to override the nation's *social imaginary*, even though the latter has lost none of its appeal, although the national state has actually had to cede sovereignty during the globalization process. Finally, we ought to wonder whether the present consensus surrounding the *Black Sea Identity* project, beyond the enthusiastic endorsement of the Georgian intellectual elite, can conceal the diverse aims and diverging interests which are probably incompatible with each other. We can hypothesize, for example, that Turkey, contrary to Georgia, will use the *Black Sea Identity* vision for national hegemonic purposes. But if each country involves itself in this project of regionalism only for its own ends, the cosmopolitan character would go to waste and everything would become a sort of supermarket where everyone shops according to their own needs.

Finally, we should discuss the rather interesting case of current regionalism in the Romanian Banat. Local elites quite insistently present this region as being by definition intercultural. Actually, the notion of interculturality appears within a cosmopolitan and post-ethnic regionalistic discourse that refers to a glorious past but is employed to address present-day reality. Stressing the peaceful and cordial coexistence among different "ethnic groups" (Romanians, Hungarians, Germans, Serbs, Jews, Bulgarian Catholics, etc.), this discourse strives to highlight the existence of a cosmopolitan regional identity determined by "unity in diversity". Though this may have been true for social practices up to the beginning of the Second World War, conditions nowadays are quite different. In fact, cultural diversity gradually decreased significantly over the past seventy years. The Jewish community (consisting of both Ashkenazim and Sephardim) was notoriously all but physically annihilated during the holocaust, the Germans, i.e., the *Donauschwaben*, to a great extent emigrated to Germany (especially after 1989), while government-promoted internal migrations during socialism have significantly strengthened the Romanian presence in the Banat, thus making it by far the dominant community. The loudly extolled interculturality has sadly dwindled, though compared to the country's other multiethnic regions (for example, Transylvania and the city of Cluj in particular) a kind of *entente cordiale* prevails amongst the various ethnic groups (especially between Romanians and Hungarians). Considering regionalism in the Banat in terms of cosmopolitan regionalism is a striking overstatement, given especially the obvious divergence between the discourse brought forth by a small political and cultural elite on the one hand, and current ethno-demographic data as well as the reality of everyday social practices on the other.

Conclusion

As some regionalism experts have pointed out, national states today could be, and most probably are, too large to manage local issues and concurrently too small to run global affairs. Rosi Braidotti, the high priestess of postmodern *nomadic identities*, recently stated in a similar context that Europe *does not make us dream anymore* because its *social imaginary* continues to tap almost exclusively the reservoir of ideas – and we can add, institutions – deriving from the national state (Braidotti 2005: 760). In full agreement with her diagnosis, we believe that in a slightly modified form this could also be said about regionalisms as political phenomena. In fact, regionalisms frankly *do not make us dream.* For the most part, extant regionalisms are ethno-regionalisms based on the *social imaginary* deriving from the national state, moreover from its ethnic aspects. Cosmopolitan regionalisms, instead, at least in principle, have a *social imaginary* that certainly lies outside that of the national state, but, as far as their currently inadequate political realization is concerned, for the time being we can only be skeptical. The idea of a *postnational Europe* may appeal to the open spirits, but for the present it is a chimera and will remain so also in the near future. On this disenchanted note, we would like to end this contribution.

Literature

Anderson, James, Liam O'Dowd, Thomas M. Wilson (eds.) 2003: New Borders for a Changing Europe. London: Frank Cass.

Appadurai, Arjun 1990: Disjuncture and Difference in the Global Cultural Economy. In: Public Culture 2, 2: 1–24.

Appadurai, Arjun 1996: Modernity at Large: Cultural Dimensions of Globalization. Minneapolis: University of Minnesota Press.

Braidotti, Rosi 2005: L'Europa non ci fa sognare. Europa lässt uns nicht träumen. In: Kölnischer Kunstverein et al. (eds.), Projekt Migration. Köln, 760–769, 832–835.

Braudel, F. 1982: La Méditerranée et le monde méditerranéen a l'époque de Philippe II. Paris: Librairie Armand Colin (2 vols.).

Baehr, Peter 2001: The "Iron Cage" and the "Shell as Hard as Steel": Parsons, Weber, and the *Stahlhartes Gehäuse* Metaphor in the Protestant Ethic and the Spirit of Capitalism. In: History and Theory 40, 2: 153–169.

Baier, Lothar 1991: Abschied vom Regionalismus. In: Freibeuter 43: 14–20.

Baier, Lothar 1992: Neun Thesen zum real existierenden Regionalismus. In: Allmende 34–35: 3–7.

Beck, Ulrich 2007: Was ist Globalisierung? Irrtümer des Globalismus - Antworten auf Globalisierung. Frankfurt am Main: Suhrkamp.

Bendix, Reinhard 1960: Max Weber: An Intellectual Portrait. New York: Doubleday Anchor.

Bourdieu, Pierre 1979: La distinction. Critique sociale du jugement. Paris: Les Editions de Minuit.

Castells, Manuel 1996: The Rise of the Network Society. Cambridge, Mass.: Blackwells.

Engels, Friedrich 1981: Po und Rhein. In: Institut für Marxismus-Leninismus beim ZK der SED (ed.), Karl Marx und Friedrich Engels Werke. Berlin: Dietz, vol. 13: 225–268.

Featherstone, Mike 1990: Global Culture: An introduction. In: idem (ed.), Global Culture: Nationalism, Globalization and Modernity. London, Thousand Oaks: Sage, 1–14.

Fergusson, Niall 2004: Colossus. New York: Penguin.

Fukuyama, Francis 1992: The End of History and the Last Man. New York: Macmillan.

Gerdes, Dirk 1980: Aufstand der Provinz. Regionalismus in Westeuropa. Frankfurt am Main, New York: Campus.

Giddens, Anthony 1990: The Consequences of Modernity. Cambridge: Polity.

Giordano, Christian 2000: Zur Regionalisierung der Identitäten und der Konflikte. Die Rückkehr des Nationalstaates und die Versuchung der *territorialen*

Ethnizität in Mittel und Osteuropa. In: Robert Hettlage, Ludgera Vogt (eds.), Identitäten in der modernen Welt: Wiesbaden: Westdeutscher Verlag, 383–407.

Giordano, Christian 2001: Regionalizing Identities. Ethnicity in Italy between Crisis and Loyalty to Tradition. In: Peter Niedermüller, Bjarne Stocklund (eds.), Europe: Cultural Construction and Reality, Copenhagen: Museum Tusculanum, 117–131.

Giordano, Christian 2005: The Past in the Present. Actualized History in the Social Construction of Reality. In: Don Kalb, Herman Tak (eds.), Critical Junctions. Anthropology and History beyond the Cultural Turn. New York, Oxford: Berghahn, 53–71.

Gramsci, Antonio 1975: Quaderni dal carcere. Torino: Einaudi Editore.

Hardt, Michael, Antonio Negri 2000: Empire. Cambridge: Harvard UP.

Hollinger, David 1995: Postethnic America: Beyond Multiculturalism. New York: Basic Books.

Huntington, Samuel 1993: The Clash of Civilizations. In: Foreign Affairs 72, 3: 22–49.

Huntington, Samuel 1996: The Clash of Civilizations. New York: Simon & Shuster.

Kahn, Joel 1995: Culture, Multiculture, Postculture. London, Thousand Oaks: Sage.

Lindner, Rolf (ed.) 1994: Die Wiederkehr des Regionalen. Frankfurt am Main, New York: Campus.

Llobera, Josep R. 2004: Foundations of National Identity: from Catalonia to Europe. New York, Oxford: Berghahn.

Marcuse, Herbert 1964: One-Dimensional Man: Studies in the Ideology of Advanced Industrial Society. Boston: Beacon Press.

McRoberts, Kenneth 2001: Catalonia: Nation Building without a State. New York, Oxford: Berghahn.

Nagel, Klaus, 1994, Katalanistische Bewegung und Gesellschaft 1898–1939. In: Zeitschrift für Katalanistik 7: 9–36.

Pasolini, Pier Paolo 1999: Saggi sulla politica e sulla società. Milano: Mondadori: Meridiani.

Payne, Stanley G. 1991: Nationalism, Regionalism and Micronationalism in Spain. In: Journal of Contemporary History 26, 3/4: 479–491.

Ritzer, George 1996: The McDonaldization of Society. An Investigation into the Changing Character of Contemporary Social Life. Thousand Oaks, London: Pine Forge (revised edition).

Ritzer, George 1998: The McDonaldization Thesis: Explorations and Extensions. Thousand Oaks, London: Pine Forge.

Robertson, Roland 1995: Glocalization: Time-Space and Homogeneity-Heterogeneity. In: Mike Featherstone (ed.), Global Modernities. London, Thousand Oaks: Sage, 25–44.

Sassen, Saskia 1994: Cities in a World Economy. Thousand Oaks, London: Pine Forge.

Sassen, Saskia 2001: The Golbal Citiy. New York, Princeton: Princeton UP.

Smart, Barry (ed.) 1999: Resisting McDonaldization. Thousand Oaks, London: Sage.

Stalder, Felix 2006: Manuel Castells: The Theory of the Network Society. Cambridge: Polity.

Troebst, Stefan 2006: Geschichtsregion Schwarzmeerwelt. In: Südosteuropa-Mitteilungen 46, 5–6: 93–102.

Vahl, Marius, Sergiu Celac 2006: Ready for a Breakthrough: Elements for a European Strategy towards the Black Sea Region. In: Southeast European and Black Sea Studies 6, 2: 169–191.

Wallerstein, I. 1974: The Modern World-System. Capitalist Agriculture and the Origins of the European World-Economy in the Sixteenth Century. New York, San Francisco: Academic Press.

Weber, Max 1956: Wirtschaft und Gesellschaft (2 vols.). Tübingen: Mohr.

Weber, Max 1968: Die *Objektivität* sozialwissenschaftlicher Erkenntnisse. In: idem, Soziologie, Weltgeschichtliche Analysen, Politik. Stuttgart: Kröner.

Wood, Robert E. 1998: Touristic Ethnicity: A Brief Itinerary. In: Ethnic and Racial Studies 21, 2: 218–241.

Beyond the "New" Regional Question? Regions, Territoriality, and the Space of Anthropology in Southeastern Europe

Pamela Ballinger, Brunswick, Maine

The theme of this special issue and the conference dedicated to "Regions, Regionalism, and Regional Identity" out of which it developed points to the growing importance and strength of regional processes in Southeastern Europe, as well as Europe more generally. Writing in 1998, Jouni Hakli wondered whether "the emerging regional question [is] merely a logical continuation in the long disintegration process of the great European polyethnic empires, or an altogether new development reflecting the late modern networked form of organization in the areas of communication, [and] technology?" (cited in Zhurzhenko 2004: 512). Yet Hakli's question could have been asked, albeit with slightly different phrasing, in the 1970s or 1930s or even the late 19th century, reminding us that notions of the region and regionalism - and queries about their relationship to industrialization, modernization, and thus both technological and political change - are not new. Indeed, the regional question in Europe and beyond appears to have been emerging for a long time. Or perhaps, more accurately, we can say that the regionalism question as both a topic of scholarly attention and object of political action has periodically re-emerged in key moments marked by the realignment of states, nations, and the international system. In contemporary debates about regionalism, anthropologists have brought their long-standing expertise at analyzing local worlds to bear upon questions about how the region reflects articulations of the "local" with larger frameworks and, in turn, how those interactions produce understandings of locality and place.

My own interest in regionalism and regional identity developed as the result of fieldwork I carried out in the 1990s in Istria, a peninsula at the borders of Croatia, Slovenia, and Italy. The dramatic reconfigurations of state borders brought about by the end of the Cold War, Yugoslavia's dissolution, and the integration process that established the European Union gave rise to a regionalist movement - the Istrian Democratic Assembly (Istarski Demokratski Sabor) - that rejected the logics of nationalism then dominating public life in newly independent Croatia. Newfound "Istrians" accepted neither the rigid demarcation of new state borders across once shared territory nor the exclusivist ethno-national identifications of Croat or Slovene or Italian. A distinctive regional Istrian identity thus became a means of embracing multiple identities and recognition of the territory's historical intermixture.

Throughout post-Cold War Southeastern Europe, there exist many analogues to the Istrian case, in places like Transylvania and Bukovina (and many others discussed in this volume), zones that had been the meeting points for what Hakli calls "the great European polyethnic empires". This most recent period has witnessed the growth of regional political structures that range in size from the supranational to the sub-national. The post-1989 transformations in Europe have also given some broad regional or culture area classifications, such as the Balkans or Southeastern Europe, new salience. What do we mean, then, when we talk about the region and regionalism? And what analytical purchase does the region concept offer, particularly for anthropologists studying Southeastern Europe?

In attempting to answer these questions, in this article I first historicize scholarly interest in regions and regionalism. However brief and incomplete, this exercise directs attention to the essentially contested nature of the region concept, given the wide range of definitions ascribed to the region.[1] Furthermore, the rhetoric of a "new regionalism" as either alternative or complement to the nation has, in fact, a deep-rooted genealogy. I then return to the Istrian case to reflect upon the possibilities and limitations opened up for anthropology by the recent interest in regions, regionalism, and regional identity. In this growing literature, what is the space and role of anthropology?

The "New" "New Regionalism"?

In her influential work on a "Europe of the regions," historian Celia Applegate notes that "far from being a product of the post-Communist, post-Maastricht Treaty era in European affairs, this attention to a resurgent or a renewed or a reinvented or a rediscovered regionality in fact stretches back through several decades of Euro-punditry" (1999: 1157). Despite this, she maintains, "surprisingly little sustained historical analysis of 'regional Europe' nourishes the contemporary debate" (1999: 1158). In her attempt to fill this gap, Applegate offers a

---

[1] For a useful overview of various definitions of the region, regionalism, and regionalization in Europe, consult Loughlin (1996). Loughlin argues that debates about these terms in Europe must be considered alongside the ideology and history of federalism. He highlights the "elastic and inflated use of the basic term 'region' as well as the ambiguities of the term federalism … [that] brings home the potential for conceptual confusion when analyzing the 'regional question' in Europe and the necessity of clarifying the way in which one is using the terms" (1996: 145–146). Thus, despite early cautions about distinguishing clearly "between regionalism as a political phenomenon and regionalism in the social sciences" (Heberle 1943: 280), conceptual ambiguity continues to mark studies of regionalism.

helpful tour through European historiography, tracing the ways in which regional histories long occupied a subordinate position and only began to be taken seriously by historians in the 1960s and 1970s. This occurred, for example, as economic historians like Sidney Pollard began to rethink the history of industrialization along regional rather than national tracks and as scholars employing world systems approaches began to focus on regions as underdeveloped peripheries.[2]

Applegate confines her gaze to that of historiography, however, neglecting the ways in which scholars in fields like sociology, anthropology, and geography have examined regions and regionalism (though she does urge greater engagement with political geography). In her analysis of contemporary European regionalism, she also takes the Western European experience as normative. In historicizing the so-called new regionalism of the 1990s, she focuses on the rise in the 1960s and 1970s of separatist regionalist movements like those in the Celtic fringe, the Alto Adige, and the Pyrenees. This narrow geographic and disciplinary focus likely leads Applegate to date interest in the region and regionalization processes too shallowly.

Applegate is not alone in either her attention to regions or her sometimes too limited historicization of the phenomenon. In the 1990s, scholars in a variety of fields produced a large body of work on regions and regionalism, seeing the Cold War as having put "regionalism back on the map" (Wigen 1999: 1183) or as giving rise to a "new regionalism". When contemporary scholars talk about regions or regionalism, however, they do not always mean the same things. At times, regions refer to supranational economic or political blocs, such as the European Union. At other moments, regions refer to entities – political, economic, and/or cultural – that crosscut state borders, as in the Euroregion concept. At other points, regions represent administrative units and/or areas recognized as having a distinctive culture within national borders. Likewise, scholars sometime use regionalism as a label for the processes by which such regional blocs or entities are formed (this is sometimes also called regionalization), as a name for the political ideology promoting regional structures and the recognition of regions, or as a tag for the scholarly studies of processes of regionalization and the region.

And, of course, not all of these meanings are mutually exclusive. Istrian regionalism, for example, coalesced in the early 1990s as a political movement seeking a territorial entity that would cut across the borders of the Italian, Slovene, and Croatian states. Accused by the Tudjman regime of being separatists and secessionists, the regionalists then pushed a model of political decentralization and

---

[2] This work dovetailed with that of scholars like Michael Hechter (1975) and, for the anthropology of Southern Europe, Peter Schneider, Jane Schneider, and Edward Hansen (1972, 1975) and Katherine Verdery (1979), who analyzed regional underdevelopment and regional political movements through the framework of "internal colonialism".

devolution based on the administrative divisions of counties and regions within Croatia. Recently, the efforts of the Istrian Democratic Assembly have paid off with the establishment of an Adriatic Euroregion of which Istria constitutes one small part. In the Istrian case, then, different understandings of region and regionalism have been privileged at different moments in a process of political contestation. In their vision of regionalism, the Istrian Democratic Assembly and its supporters have promoted a regional identity as an alternative to the straitjacket of exclusive ethnic and national identities, even as the political climate of the Tudjman years forced the regionalists to stress that regionalism did not fundamentally challenge the nation-state's sovereignty but rather could complement or modify it in ways that did not directly weaken the state. In this case, both subnational and supranational visions of regionalism operate – rhetorically, at least – as complements to the nation-state, even as at points they provide political actors with resources by which to challenge the nation-state.

Much of the scholarly work since the 1990s on regional questions and processes in places like Istria has focused on regionalism as part and parcel of a globalizing world in which meanings of space and place do not disappear but become reconfigured and reterritorialized. In seeking to identify what is actually new about the *new regionalism* – in contrast to *old regionalisms* of the 1970s or even earlier – observers have pointed to a variety of factors, including the centrality of the regional framework to the EU architecture; the rise of new social movements, including those of regionalist movements that posit the modern vitality of the periphery against the corruption and decrepitude of the center (thereby reversing an older view of the region as repository of the traditional) (Woods 1995: 187–189); the restructuring of capitalism and the new competitive advantages held by regions with "institutional thickness" favoring democracy and economic prosperity (see Giordano 2001: 26–29); the new contexts created by an expanded multilateral framework for trade; the fact that the leading global power, the United States, has taken an active role in the promotion of preferential trade associations like those embodied by the North American Free Trade Agreement (NAFTA) and the Asia-Pacific Economic Cooperation (APEC) Forum; and the potential role of regions as sites for "the democratization of globalizing processes" (Larner, Walters 2002: 423). Other observers point to the explicit politicization of regional geography (i.e., the notion that scholarly work on regionalism from the field of geography should have political applications and can serve as an instrument for change) (Holmén 1995: 58) as a distinctively new feature of the latest wave of regionalism. Yet many of the questions that scholars today ask – How do we understand the region in relation to the nation? How do we understand regionalism in relation to increased connectivity and communications (what today we call globalization)? – recapitulate earlier debates. This brings us back to the nagging question of how new the new regionalism (understood as both processes of regionalization and the body of scholarly work dedicated to these topics) actually is.[3]

In thinking about this question, consider the fact that one prominent school of regionalist thought developed in the interwar period, another era in which states and the international system had undergone dramatic realignment and in which the world appeared increasingly connected as the result of technological transformations. Writing in 1939, for example, sociologist J. O. Hertzler situated regionalism in the context of processes of standardization. Though his vocabulary differs slightly from that employed by contemporary social observers, Hertzler's characterization of the interwar period nonetheless could stand in for a description of regionalism in today's globalizing world.

> "... uniformity-producing forces and processes [that] reached a new high. The means of communication ... vastly increased their [nation-wide] range. Technological advances ... increased migration and mobility ... Standardizing influences, such as advertising, motion pictures, newspapers and periodicals, styles and fashions, become more universal in their scope ... In spite of these factors producing [nation-wide] uniformities of behavior and consciousness, the regions have become more important in an economic, demographic, sociological, psychological, artistic, and political sense" (Hertzler 1939: 17–18).

In contemporary debates, globalization and its sub variants, like European Unionization, stand in as the new centralizing processes.

Current debates about supranational regional blocs also find relevant precursors and points of comparison in the interwar period. The 1920s and 1930s witnessed the growth of both economic and political regional arrangements in Europe, most of them supranational blocs made up of sovereign states. Scholars today typically compare the interwar regionalism unfavorably to that which preceded it in the 19th century, as well as to the post-World War II reorganization of commerce and trade (and, today, politics) on a regional basis. Scholars observe that the interwar regionalism, for example, was "often associated with the pursuit of beggar-thy-neighbor [economic] policies and substantial trade diversion, as well as heightened political conflict" (Mansfield, Milner 1999: 597).

In the same period, however, regionalism also appeared as a sub-national phenomenon or issue articulated in the context of regional planning in places like Great Britain (O'Brien 1999: 1205) and the United States. In the United States,

---

[3] Of course, even the question of the newness of the "new regionalism" is not an original one. For a summary of critical questioning of the newness of the "new regional geography", the reader is directed to Holmén (1995). Ultimately, Holmén himself calls for a new (or revitalized) regional geography rooted in "grounded theory" (1995: 60).

regional planning carried out by groups such as the National Resources Committee intersected with the work of geographers and sociologists in articulating specific concepts of the region – for instance, the single factor region (defined by a key aspect, such as cotton), composite region, and the administrative region – in considering how to best carry out planning and development of "backwards" regions, like the Tennessee Valley (Odum 1945: 253–255; also Hewes 1950: 250–251).[4] This type of regionalist study paralleled a more literary exploration of regionalism focused on the "folk" and, quite frequently, on the American South.[5] Though sociologists like Howard Odum stressed that the sentimental and romantic regionalism of the literary crowd had nothing to do with the rigorous "scientific regionalism" of the social scientists (Odum 1931: 6), both schools of thought positioned the region as archaic or traditional in contrast to the emerging modern "mass society". For the literary scholars, the persistence of local identities provided a welcome antidote to the ruthless processes of industrialization, centralization and homogenization, whereas for the planners, regionalism was often equated with "sectionalism", defined by historian Frederick Jackson Turner (most famous for his frontier thesis) as the means "by which a given area resists national uniformity" (cited in Hewes 1950: 244).[6]

The applied uses to which "scientific" regionalism was put in the 1930s compel us to question the newness of current attempts in a field such as geography to make regionally informed geography politically relevant. These past applications for regional planning also reveal the deep-rooted tradition of viewing the region as bound up with projects of national development and modernization/industrialization. This issue of how to understand the region vis à vis the nation informs much of the work, past and present, on region and regionalism. As Applegate puts it,

---

[4] On regional planning during World War II, consult Riemer (1943: 275–276). For the rise of "regional policy" in the context of the European community during the 1970s, the reader is directed to Loughlin (1996: 144).

[5] One strand of this regionalist study in the U.S. developed out of an older tradition focused on "community studies of race and folk culture" (Odum 1945: 245). In the first decade of the twentieth century, these studies centered on "Negro folk culture" in Georgia and Mississippi. Another body of work dedicated to regional research developed out of initiatives launched by the Institute for Research in Social Science at the University of North Carolina, particularly its program of Regional Research and Study (Odum 1945: 245–248). For a more detailed discussion of different schools of American regionalist thought in the first half of the twentieth century, see Odum (1945) and Hertzler (1939: 19). Fraser Hart traces later efforts within the discipline of geography to establish a "science of regions" and to render the region a "technical tool" (1982: 8–9). On the aspects of romanticism attached to area studies (as successor to earlier regional studies in the U.S. social sciences), the reader is referred to Rafael (1999).

[6] Other scholars at the time also equated regionalism with sectionalism or, at the very least, the potential for "localism, provincialism, and sectionalism" (Botkin 1936: 181).

> "Whether regional identity has entailed resistance or accommodation to the nation-state, the nation itself, at least from a constructivist perspective, appears to have been the controlling value system, the hegemonic concept. Resistant regional identities have for the most part taken shape around a claim to nationhood, while accommodating ones have emphasized a distinctiveness that can reinforce national markers of difference – in effect, performing variations on a common national theme" (1999: 1179).

Whereas in the 19th and early 20th century, the region appeared to scholars as undeveloped relative to the national center, by the 1960s and 1970s some regions now appeared to be the product of underdevelopment precisely as a result of the core/periphery relationship. Though the understanding of the nature of the relationship of region/nation had changed, the broader terms (questions of development) had not, for the most part. The resurgence of regionalist movements in Western Europe post-1968 and scholarly interest in regional identity also reinforced this enduring image of the region in opposition to the nation (whether as problem or panacea). The work of French intellectuals such as Emmanuel Le Roy Ladurie, Daniel Fabre, and even Pierre Bourdieu tended to locate the authentic in the regional and the regional in rural village life (Mark 1987). The brief historicization offered here thus suggests strong continuities in scholarly accounts of the old regionalism [that of the interwar] and the old new regionalism that emerged on the European intellectual and political scene in the 1960s and 1970s, continuities that we can follow down to accounts of the "new" "new regionalism" (that is, regionalism today).

Apart from these questions, however, the discussion here of region and regionalism in the American tradition may at first glance seem far from and, indeed, irrelevant to the European experience of regionalism, particularly in the contemporary moment. Yet I would argue that these scholarly genealogies cannot be so easily disentangled. Regionalist scholars in the U.S. in the first part of the 20th century, for instance, drew heavily on the work of German geographers like Friedrich Ratzel, Friedrich List, Carl Ritter, and Alexander von Humboldt, whose work proves critical for the intellectual genealogies of all the "regionalisms" mentioned here.[7] Some of the pioneering work of geographers like Ratzel and List was, in turn, informed by experiences in the United States early in their scholarly careers. Back in 1944, Werner Cahnman pointed out, "It seems obvious that Ratzel's conception of the frontier as a zone of transition and a peripheral organ rather than as a rigidly defined and legally drawn boundary-line, was derived, not only from his early interest in plant and animal ecology, but also from his obser-

[7] For an account of French political geography and its adoption as an "alternative geopolitics" by some American scholars during and after World War II, see Parker (2000).

vation of the expanding capacity of the American frontier in his time" (1944: 456). Furthermore, scholars in the U.S. have shared the definitional dilemmas that plagued scholars of the region in Europe, fretting endlessly over how to define the region. Some took their cues from Louis Wirth, arguing for a "high degree of conformity between the geographic, economic and cultural contour lines" (Hertzler 1939: 21), others followed Odum and Moore's phrasing of the region in terms of gestalt ["organic unity not only in its natural landscape, but in [that] cultural evolution"] (cited in Hertzler 1939: 23), and others articulated ideal types and operational definitions (Riemer 1944: 278). The end result of what John Fraser Hart has called the "sterile 'regionalizing ritual'" of trying to delimit regions was that some geographers and other scholars in both the U.S. and Europe lost sight of the fact that the goal of regional study was "to understand areas, not merely to draw lines around them" (Hart 1982: 8).

Scholarship in the 1960s and 1970s suffered less from these problems, as scholars began to focus more on what regions and regionalism did than what they consisted in, though almost every account of regions and regionalism to the present day (including this article) feels compelled to at least mention the continued lack of consensus over how to conceptualize the region. Certainly, the political dimensions of regions have received more emphasis in work on regionalism from the 1960s on, as scholars shifted away from a focus on defining environmental-geographical features and towards the political economy and ecology of regions (Mansfield, Milner 1999: 591; also Mansfield, Milner 1997). Scholars increasingly examined regional elites, organized political expressions of regionalism, and contests over the imagining of regions.[8] These studies implicitly recognized the etymology of the term region, which derives from Latin *regere*, to rule, and which in English carries associations of a place capable of being governed (O'Brien 1999: 1204).

In the most recent phase of regionalism, there appears to be much less overlap or dialogue between the studies of American and European regionalism. British historian Michael O'Brien has raised the intriguing possibility, however, that as he puts it, "the new availability of the language of regionalism in Europe and Asia may be partly due to the cultural influence of the United States, whose political language is now so broadly available and serves to reinforce the regionalist concept at the same moment that it has validated the efficiency of supermarkets" (1999: 1206–1207). He adds that scholars of the European and Asian scenes "are certainly discerning an indigenous movement in foreign cultures, but they may also be listening to an echo of American ideology" (1999: 1207). Though I am not at all sure that I agree with O'Brien's reading (indeed, it seems

[8] In 1944, Cahnman lamented the dearth of work on regional ecology, here understood as ecological relationships within and between regions (Cahnman 1944: 21–22).

counterintuitive for a Southeastern Europe dominated by particular versions of supranational, subnational, and crossnational regionalism promoted by the European Union), I include it here – as I did my brief discussion of the sociological body of work on American regionalism – because it unsettles some of our ideas about various genealogies of European regionalism as both political process and scholarly tradition.[9]

Conventional historicizations of regions and regionalisms in Europe may risk being "regionalized" themselves by failing to consider the influences on European regionalism from outside the European frame. Here I have highlighted the dialogue between European and North American ideas about regionalism. I might just as easily have considered the experimentation with regional political forms and ideologies in the colonial possessions of various European powers and the interplay between domestic and overseas ideas about regionalism and regional identities.

In considering various genealogies for regional processes in contemporary Europe and our understandings of them, we see that questions about the region today remain bound up with the issue of the nation. Anthropological research on the most recent expressions of regionalism and regional identity building projects in Europe follows out of the constructivist turn in studies of the nation and nationalism, using similar methods and theoretical tools with which to interrogate the "invention" and "imagining" or re-imagining of regions, regionalism, and regional identities in the wider context of the state making. Whereas scholars in the 19th century, the interwar, and even some in the 1970s typically saw the region as pre-national, anthropologists today recognize the "modernity" of the region and its frequently post-national character. Once viewed as archaic, backwards, and provincial [literally and figuratively (see Rafael 1999: 1208)],[10] the region and regional identity now often figure as the space of multicultural, even "cosmopolitan", imaginings.[11] Anthropologist Jonas Frykman voices a common view in his assessment of regions "as a kind of cultural interstices or imaginaries, in-between spaces of experimentation which make room for something different ... [in which] tolerance of diversity appears to be greater than in national centres" (2002: 47–48). With the resurgence of ethnic and national violence in post-Cold War Europe, particularly Southeastern Europe, political actors and scholars alike have

---

9 Likewise, the vision of a "regional Europe" reflects a historic dialogue between European and North American notions of federalism (for debates about "integral federalism" versus "Hamiltonian federalism", see Loughlin 1996: 141–143).

10 In the 1930s, literary critic Botkin deemed regional writers "provincial" writers, associated with the rural and agrarian, in contrast to metropolitan ones who bore urban values (1936: 184–185).

11 On this, see Christian Giordano, this volume. Giordano also discusses exceptions to this "benign" regionalism, as with the case of the Italian Northern Leagues. On the Northern Leagues, go to Agnew (1995), Woods (1995), Stacul (2005), and Giordano (2001).

turned to the region and regionalism as a promising alternative to the nation, i. e., as going beyond the nation.

Celia Applegate contends, "Murderous separatist movements aside, it is the rare observer of the European scene who regards contemporary manifestations of regional sentiment as anything but a healthy antidote to bellicose and exclusionary national ones. Hence investigations into the practices and idioms of regional identification have often lacked the sense of urgency that informs many studies of nationalism" (1999: 1176). I would argue that in parts of Southeastern Europe like the former Yugoslavia, however, there does exist a sense of political and scholarly urgency around the issue of regions. As crossnational and subnational regions are rediscovered, reinvented, and reconfigured by political actors (including intellectuals), the roots of *post-national* regional identities are often located in an idealized *pre-national* past that views the multiethnic, multilingual, and multiconfessional empires as zones of tolerance and pluralist coexistence. Although anthropologists have taken to heart the lesson that identity – whether national, regional, gendered, classed, or otherwise – is constructed, does intellectual sympathy for regional identity as a counterweight to national identity risk buying into the regionalists' visions and thereby inadvertently *naturalizing* the region? Does the perceived inclusivity of those regional identifications that explicitly privilege multiculturalism and multiethnic living together make those regional identifications appear as a more logical or natural outcome than the "artificial" homogenizations of ethnic and national identity? Do examinations of the "transcultural past" and present in the effort to rethink what Dirk Hoeder has called the "monocultural nation-state paradigm" (2003) problematize the nation-state paradigm while taking the transcultural experience at face value?

In exploring these questions, I could cite many examples from Southeastern Europe and beyond but I will focus briefly on the case that I know best, that of Istrian regionalism. In examining the Istrian case, I want to emphasize the ways in which regions and regional identities, like nations, remain trapped in the logics of territoriality and historic projects of state-making, even if the exclusivisms of the region are not exactly the same as those of the nation. This dilemma underscores the challenge for anthropologists to carve out an analytical space that is not bounded by the place-making projects of regions and regionalists.

Istrian Regionalism and the Dilemmas of Territoriality

Istria has received scholarly attention for its experiment in multiculturalist regionalism since the early 1990s, when there arose a political regionalist movement that claims to offer a model for coping with, and even celebrating, cultural diversity. The Istrian Democratic Assembly or IDS has held power in Croatian Istria since independence. Through 1999, the IDS stood in opposition to the national government headed by Franjo Tudjman and his Croatian Democratic Union (HDZ) party. Although a sense of victimization underwrote a new account of Istrian regional history, unlike in other parts of Yugoslavia the identities of victimizers and victims were not cast predominantly in ethno-national or religious terms but rather in terms of state centers dominating and exploiting peripheries. This move portrayed all Istrians – whether ethnically identified as Italian, Slovene, Croat, Rumeni, Montenegrin, Albanian, or Serb – as denizens of a region whose cultural and linguistic intermixture had survived in spite of the heavy-handed policies of distant centres of power. Political leaders and supporters of the regionalist movement have cited awareness of the non-congruence of political and socio-cultural borders as an explanation for why Istria did not experience inter-ethnic violence in the 1990s.

Discourses of Istria's multiethnic and multilingual character have a deep history in the region. Previous versions of political multiculturalism (i.e., self-conscious expressions of multiculturalism in service to politics) in Istria have often worked, albeit unintentionally (as in the Habsburg Monarchy or socialist Yugoslavia), to reinforce the understandings of separate ethno-national groups. In some aspects, then, the contemporary project of Istrianity reveals the same conceptual limits as its predecessors. The emphasis on being from a particular *place* (Istria) builds upon an intellectual tradition in the region that sees peoples as "belonging" to particular places and kinds of environments (think Jovan Cvijić and the "Dinaric Man"). By the same logic, then, migrations may move groups to environments in which they are deemed territorially incompatible. Such notions run through the ways in which "Istrians" often describe their new neighbors (e.g. the Bosnian or Kosovar who has no experience of the coast and its lifeways). Equally deep-rooted ideas about Istria as historically part of a Western or European civilizational realm in contrast to an "Eastern," Oriental (Ottoman) sphere further demarcate the symbolic boundary between civilised and "tolerant" Istrians and the "Balkan others" in their midst. Yet the forms such exclusions have taken in contemporary Istria, as opposed to other parts of the former Yugoslavia, differ dramatically. Violence and intolerance have not characterised life in Croatian Istria. Rather, a strong distinction between authentic Istrians and "non-Istrians" now living in Istria (particularly Muslims from Bosnia and Kosovar Albanians) marks everyday life in the peninsula, where difference becomes visible in things such as residential patterns, cuisine, practices of home care, gender relations, and the *perceptions* of such things on the part of different groups.

Language, in particular the capacity to speak various Istrian dialects, serves as a pronounced marker of difference. Croats from Slavonia or Muslims from Sarajevo living in Istria possess a common tongue with which to communicate with their Istrian neighbors but often find themselves excluded when Istrians code shift between various forms of čakavski Croatian, distinct town or village dialects, and Istro-Veneto (an Italian variation). Likewise, Istrians may feel excluded when newcomers "speak amongst themselves", reinforcing ideas about the "clannishness" of these recent arrivals.[12]

At the political level, the protection of Italian-Croatian bilingualism has provided a key element in the regionalist project, reflecting the refusal to accept one exclusive national or ethnic identity. In the language politics of everyday life, however, bilingualism often constitutes a border between authentic Istrians and others – that is, bilingualism and use of dialect become the markers of a regional identity from which many living in the region are effectively shut out. In practical terms, as well, the focus on bilingualism – so admirable when compared to the monolinguistic homogenizing policies of the Tudjman regime – may be fostering a sort of reductive multiculturalism that envisions Istrianity as a common house for Croats and Slovenes and Italians, to the neglect of other "minorities" such as the Montenegrins of Peroj, the Istro-Rumeni, Serbs, Albanians, and others.

Throughout the 1990s, the dangers of this reductivism were less apparent, as the Istrian regional concept operated effectively as a form of opposition to Tudjman's party and its centralizing efforts. When Tudjman died in 1999 and a center-left democratic coalition came into power in 2000, the IDS suddenly became part of the governing coalition. It did not take long, however, for differences among the governing parties to surface and for the IDS to withdraw from the coalition. Although its leaders have created a working relationship with the subsequent center-right (reformed HDZ) government, the IDS continues to nurture an oppositional role, a role that suits the sense of Istrian difference and superiority to other areas of Croatia. To some degree, then, the regionalist project remains positioned *against* the state, even if the stance of the central government towards the EU has transformed completely since the days of Tudjman and as the IDS continues to insist that it represents the ("European") model for the rest of Croatia.

Istrian regionalism remains not just positioned "against the state" (to some extent), however, but paradoxically contained "within the (Croatian) state".[13] Notwithstanding the IDS' claims (and hopes) to overcome the divisions created in 1991 by the drawing of a new political border between Slovenian and Croatian Istria, that border has dramatically altered the social fabric of life in Istria. Anthropologist Borut Brumen's work in the Slovene village of Sv. Peter, three kilometers from the Dragogna River, suggests that along this part of the border social distance between inhabitants has increased since 1991. When Brumen asked his informants how they viewed their neighbors just across the border, they

[12] For more details on such exclusions in everyday life, refer to Ballinger (2003, 2004). See also Ashbrook (2006) on the politicization of Istrian identity by the regionalists.

[13] For a more detailed discussion of various genealogies of political multiculturalism in Istria and the ways in which regionalism is positioned "against the state", see Ballinger (2006).

responded, "They were Istrians, just like us. We spoke the same language, the only difference being that they used more of the Croatian and we more of the Slovene words. It is only now that we call them Croatian Istrians. Before we were all just Istrians" (Brumen 1996: 146). After the establishment of the new border, economic relationships and patterns of marriage between inhabitants on opposite sides of the Dragogna became increasingly rare. As a consequence, the villagers of Sv. Peter "have now invented 'Others' who are not Istrian anymore but Croats from the other side of the border" (Brumen 1996: 151).

The harnessing of a once diffuse Istrian cultural identity to a more narrow political regionalist project centered in Croatia – together with the changes wrought by the imposition of a new territorial border – has made the Istrian label less salient for some residents of the peninsula, even as it has politicized the Istrian identity for others. When viewed from Slovene Istria, then, the "Istrian" identity's capacity to embrace all the peninsula's inhabitants appears to have shrunk since 1991.

In her work in two villages on the Croatian side of the border, anthropologist Lidija Nikočević likewise found that the border had severely disrupted previous patterns of reciprocity, labor, and kinship. The villagers in Pasjak and Gradinj viewed themselves as Istrians and resisted a strict ethnic definition as "Croats". Nikočević discerned greater "hesitancy" to identify with the putative ethno-national group on the Croat, as compared to the Slovene, side of the border. She explains this hesitancy not in terms of a greater (Croatian) Istrian tolerance or rejection of nationalism but as a result of "the deep dissatisfaction with the inferior economic status of the individuals and villages as a whole, which constantly compare themselves with examples across the border, and the general frustration with the border in all its aspects" (2003: 102). Here, then, Istrianness serves as a symbolic resource with which villagers on the Croatian side of the border seek to maintain the sense of shared culture that once linked them with their now divided "Slovene" counterparts, who no longer profess a sense of common Istrian identity.

The EU integration process (another form of regionalism, of course) has sharpened, rather than diminished, these feelings of difference.[14] Istrianity thus represents a sense of identity that increasingly differentiates Croatian Istria from Slovene Istria. This difference does not remain restricted to the level of discourse or sentiments. Rather, it represents a deep transformation in the forms of what Brumen calls "inter-cultural communication" (1996: 152) or Klaus Roth characterizes as "inter-cultural competence ... developed over a long period of time and integrated into the systems of interethnic coexistence" (2001: 41). Certain practices of regional inter-cultural communication are thus in sharp decline in Istria,

[14] This has become particularly evident to me in recent work I have carried out on the Istrian border zone near Piran and Savudrija and in interviews with fishermen on both sides of the border there; see Ballinger (2006b).

even as regionalist discourse intensifies. The territorial dimensions of contemporary Istrian regionalism, heir to its Habsburg and Yugoslav predecessors, significantly constrain the structure and scope of this project. The territorialised understanding of identity – of belonging to a *place,* as well as to a community of speakers of various linguistic variants – means that this regionalism does not entirely escape the logics of territorialised states, even when it positions itself against the state (and beyond the state, below the state, and so on).

The Space of Anthropology?

The conclusions that I have drawn here about the limits of Istrian regionalism are conclusions made using the tools of anthropological fieldwork and theory, combined with those of historical analysis. These tools better position anthropologists than some other scholars to interrogate critically the realities of the latest wave of regionalism and its expressions in Southeastern Europe. I still worry, however, about the seductive appeal of the region and regional identity as an "alternative" in an area that has become stereotypically known for nationalism. The proponents and ideologues of recent regional movements in Southeastern Europe, such as that of Istria, include sociologists and anthropologists. If as scholars we shift our attention to regional processes in order to provide a counterweight to nationalist histories and views of the world, we may risk reifying a larger "regional" distinction, that of Southeastern Europe, just as scholars of European regionalism risk reifying Europe (as noted in my discussion of the "new" "new regionalism"). Could regionalism become a new gatekeeping concept (Appadurai 1986) to replace the old one of nationalism and ethnic conflict? These potential dangers can be avoided if we remember that both regional and national constructions of identity do not occur only in the regionally and nationally bounded spaces under study. In this, we need to listen carefully to the "Song of the Non-aligned world" that Gupta (1992) "broadcast" over a decade ago.

Reflecting on the "reinscription of space in late capitalism" and after the end of the Cold War, Gupta used the 1987 anthem, "Song of the Non-Aligned World" to recuperate the history of the Non-aligned movement and highlight its usefulness as "a good example of such a transnational imagined community" (1992: 64). Gupta took nonalignment as a starting point for his critical discussion of the ways in which the making of the nation can only be understood by going beyond the national frameworks that too often delimit the boundaries of scholarly inquiry. He concluded,

> "On the one hand, we need to study structures of feeling that bind space, time, and memory in the production of location. By this I mean processes by which certain spaces become enshrined as 'homelands', by which ideas

> of 'us' and 'them' come to be deeply felt and mapped onto places such as nations. On the other hand, we need to pay attention to those processes that redivide, reterritorialize, and reinscribe space in the global political economy. Only then can we understand why the naturalized divisions and spaces that we have always taken for granted become problematic in certain circumstances, and only then can the 'problem' of nationalism be posed adequately" (1992: 76).

Replacing the terms "nationalism" and "nation" in Gupta's formulation with those of "regionalism" and "region" underscores the obvious but often overlooked point that merely using the territorialized region to interrogate the idea of nation proves insufficient. Region, like nation, must be examined at the intersection of processes of both deterritorialization and reterritorialization. Whereas Gupta took up the example of nonalignment to focus on the postcolonial world order, anthropologists of Southeastern Europe would do well to remember that the record album and song that frames Gupta's account was released in Belgrade in 1987 and features on its cover a photograph of state leaders at the first Nonaligned Summit, convened in Belgrade twenty six years earlier. Southeastern Europe is ripe for the kind of transnational and transregional analysis suggested by Gupta.

Anthropological work like that carried out by Loring Danforth (1995) on the Macedonian Question, Daphne Winland (2002, 2007) on the Croats of Toronto, and Maja Povrzanović Frykman on the Croatian diaspora (2001, 2004), to offer just a few well-chosen examples, illustrates the value of a transnational perspective (broadly conceived) for reframing scholarly understanding of national and other identities, including regional identity. Danforth analyzed transformations in Macedonian identity in the late 1980s and early 1990s not only through a transnational frame that traversed the borders of the Greek and newly independent Macedonian state but also encompasses the Greek and Macedonian diasporas in Australia. These "transnational national communities", together with transnational organizations like those of human rights activists, played a key role in the rearticulations of Macedonian and Greek identities (including a regional Greek Macedonian identity). Likewise, Daphne Winland's work with the Croats of Toronto complicates understanding of the processes of building Croatian identity in the newly independent state, demonstrating the signal role played by members of the diaspora but also the frequently divergent understandings of nation held by diasporic and homeland Croats. In those dialogues between homeland and diaspora, regional identities often come to the fore.

Maja Povrzanović Frykman (2001, 2004) has written extensively on the Croatian diaspora and the methodological implications of studying what she calls "meetings in the diaspora," particularly for a "native anthropologist" who is simultaneously insider and outsider in such contexts. Drawing on the work of

Steven Vertovec, Povrzanović Frykman understands diaspora in deterritorialized terms: as "social form", as a "type of consciousness", and as "a mode of cultural production" (2004: 85). She thus sees the object of her study as that of "diasporic conditions" and attends to what she deems "the hidden maps of 'transnationalism from below'" (ibid: 94). These maps do not match those of the cartographer tracing territory and political borders but rather refer to spaces of the imagination crisscrossed by emotions, language, and kinship. These maps also become embodied by material objects such as cooking pots and passports.[15] Here, too, we might think about Gupta's vinyl record and its hymn to nonalignment.

The kind of transnational, diaspora-focused work presented here as models decenters both regionalist and nationalist narratives about territorial integrity. Though transnational approaches have begun to transform European historiography[16], they have perhaps not made as many inroads into the history of Southeastern Europe. Anthropologists of this area, however, have paid more (if not enough) attention to these processes.[17] In putting into question some of the territorial assumptions of region and nation by using methods that refuse to be narrowly territorialized, anthropology can occupy an important *space*. This space is a very particular one, though, in which understandings of place are reterritorialized in unusual ways.

Literature

Agnew, John 1995: The Rhetoric of Regionalism: The Northern League in Italian Politics, 1983–94. In: Transactions of the Institute of British Geographers NS 20, 2: 156–172.

Appadurai, Arjun 1986: Theory in Anthropology: Center and Periphery. In: Comparative Studies in Society and History 28, 2: 357–361.

[15] See here Frykman's (2002) phenomenological emphasis on the life of things and the role of material culture in understandings of the region. Gerber offers an intriguing analysis of immigrants' letters that "recast[s] very familiar aspects of the history of those migrants into transnational terms that have yet to be employed to understand them" (2001: 67).

[16] The significant role played by the Italian diaspora in the making of Italian identity, for example, has begun to transform understandings of the Italian nation-state. For exemplars of this transnational, diasporic work in Italian studies, consult Cavazza (1997), Gabaccia (2000), and Gabaccia, Ottanelli (2005).

[17] I include my own work on Istria in this critique. Although I conducted research in a broad regional framework that crosscut state borders, my perspective did not venture beyond that of the geographically contiguous (albeit transnational) region. Having spent more time with the Istrian diaspora in North America since I did my initial work, I have come to realize the important role played in regional constructions by these more far-flung Istrians.

Applegate, Celia 1999: A Europe of Regions: Reflections on the Historiography of Sub-national Places in Modern Times. In: The American Historical Review 104, 4: 1157–1182.

Ashbrook, John E. 2006: Locking Horns in the Istrian Political Arena: Politicized Identity, the Istrian Democratic Assembly, and the Croatian Democratic Alliance. In: East European Politics and Societies 20, 4: 622–658.

Ballinger, Pamela 2003: History in Exile: Memory and Identity at the Borders of the Balkans. Princeton: Princeton UP.

Ballinger, Pamela 2004: "Authentic Hybrids" in the Balkan Borderlands. In: Current Anthropology 45, 1: 31–60.

Ballinger, Pamela 2006a: Multiculturalism Against the State: Lessons from Istria. Paper presented at the conference "Multiculturalism: The Central European Experience and its impact on identity-formation in a globalized world". Bellagio: Rockefeller Conference and Study Center.

Ballinger, Pamela 2006b: Watery Spaces, Globalizing Places: Ownership and Access in Postsocialist Croatia. In: Janet Laible, Henri Barkey (eds.), European Responses to Globalization. Amsterdam: Elsevier, 153–177.

Botkin, Benjamin A. 1936: Regionalism: Cult of Culture? In: The English Journal 25, 3: 181–185.

Cahnman, Werner J. 1944: The Concept of *Raum* and the Theory of Regionalism. In: American Sociological Review 9, 5: 455–462.

Brumen, Borut 1996: The State Wants It so, and the Folk Cannot Do Anything Against the State Anyway. In: Narodna umjetnost 33, 2: 139–155.

Cavazza, Stefano. 1997: Piccole Patrie: Feste popolari tra regione e nazione durante il fascismo. Bologna: Il Mulino.

Danforth, Loring. 1995: The Macedonian Conflict: Ethnic Nationalism in a Transnational World. Princeton: Princeton UP.

Frykman, Jonas 2002: Place for Something Else: Analysing a Cultural Imaginary. In: Ethnologia Europaea 32, 2: 47–68.

Gabaccia, Donna 2000: Italy's Many Diasporas. Seattle: University of Washington Press.

Gabaccia, Donna, Fraser M. Ottanelli (eds.) 2005: Italian Workers of the World: Labor Migration and the Formation of Multiethnic States. Urbana: University of Illinois Press.

Gerber, David A. 2001: Forming a Transnational Narrative: New Perspectives on European Migrations to the United States. In: The History Teacher 35, 1: 61–78.

Giordano, Benito 2001: "Institutional Thickness", Political Sub-culture and the Resurgence of (the "New") Regionalism in Italy: A Case Study of the Northern League in the Province of Varese. In: Transactions of the Institute of British Geographers NS 26, 1: 25–41.

Gupta, Akhil 1992: The Song of the Nonaligned World: Transnational Identities and the Reinscription of Space in Late Capitalism. In: Cultural Anthropology 7, 1: 63–79.

Hansen, Edward, Jane Schneider, Peter Hansen 1975: From Autonomous Development to Dependent Modernization: The Catalan Case Revisited: A reply to Pi-Sunyer. In: Comparative Studies in Society and History 17, 2: 238–241.

Hart, John Fraser 1982: Presidential Address: The Highest Form of the Geographer's Art. In: Annals of the Association of American Geographers 72, 1: 1–29.

Heberle, Rudolf 1943: Regionalism: Some Critical Observations. In: Social Forces 21, 3: 280–286.

Hechter, Michael 1975: Internal Colonialism: The Celtic Fringe in British National Development, 1536–1966. Berkeley: University of California Press.

Hertzler, J. O. 1939: Some Sociological Aspects of American Regionalism. In: Social Forces 18, 1: 17–29.

Hewes, Amy 1950: A Plea for Regional Studies. In: The Journal of Higher Education 21, 5: 243–252.

Hoeder, Dirk 2003: Revising the Monocultural Nation-state Paradigm: An Introduction to Transcultural Perspectives. In: Dirk Hoeder, Christiane Harzig, Adrian Shubert (eds.), The Historical Practice of Diversity: Transcultural Interactions from the Early Modern Mediterranean to the Postcolonial World. New York: Berghahn, 1–11.

Holmén, Hans 1995: What's New and What's Regional in the "New Regional Geography"? In: Geografiska Annaler. Series B, Human Geography 77, 1: 47–63.

Larner, Wendy, William Walters 2002: The Political Rationality of "New Regionalism": Toward a Genealogy of the Region. In: Theory and Society 31, 3: 391–432.

Loughlin, John 1996: "Europe of the Regions" and the Federalization of Europe. In: Publius 26, 4: 141–162.

Mansfield, Edward D., Helen V. Milner 1997: The Political Economy of Regionalism: An Overview. In: Edward D. Mansfield, V. Milner (eds.), The Political Economy of Regionalism. New York: Columbia UP, 1–19.

Mansfield, Edward D., Helen V. Milner 1999: The New Wave of Regionalism. In: International Organization 53, 3: 589–627.

Mark, Vera 1987: In Search of the Occitan Village: Regionalist Ideologies and the Ethnography of Southern France. In: Anthropological Quarterly 60, 2: 64–70.

Nikočević, Lidija 2003: Negotiating Borders: Myth, Rhetoric, and Political Relations. In: Focaal 41: 95–105.

O'Brien, Michael 1999: On Observing the Quicksand. In: The American Historical Review 104, 4: 1202–1228.

Odum, Howard W. 1931: Notes on the Study of Regional and Folk Society. In: Social Forces 10, 2: 164–175.

Odum, Howard W. 1945: From Community Studies to Regionalism. In: Social Forces 23, 2: 245–258.

Parker, Geoffrey 2000: Ratzel, the French School and the Birth of Alternative Geopolitics. In: Political Geography 19, 8: 957–969.

Povrzanović Frykman, Maja 2004: "Experimental" Ethnicity: Meetings in the Diaspora. In: Narodna umjetnost 41, 1: 83–102.

Povrzanović Frykman, Maja 2001: Constructions of Identities in Diaspora and Exile: Croats in Sweden in the 1990s. In: Maja Povrzanović Frykman (ed.), Beyond Integration: Challenges of Belonging in Diaspora and Exile. Lund: Nordic Academic Press, 166–194.

Rafael, Vicente L. 1999: Regionalism, Area Studies, and the Accidents of Agency. In: The American Historical Review 104, 4: 1208–1220.

Riemer, Svend 1943: Theoretical Aspects of Regionalism. In: Social Forces 21, 3: 275–280.

Roth, Klaus 2001: Toward "Politics of Interethnic Coexistence": Can Europe Learn from the Multiethnic Empires? In: Peter Niedermüller, Bjarne Stoklund (eds.), Europe: Cultural Construction and Reality. Copenhagen: Museum Tusculanum Press, 37–51.

Schneider, Peter, Jane Schneider, Edward Hansen 1972: Modernization and Development: The Role of Regional Elites and Noncorporate Groups in the European Mediterranean. In: Comparative Studies in Society and History 14, 3: 328–350.

Stacul, Jaro 2005: Natural Time, Political Time: Contested Histories in Northern Italy. In: Journal of the Royal Anthropological Institute 11, 4: 819–836.

Verdery, Katherine 1979: Internal Colonialism in Austria-Hungary. In: Ethnic and Racial Studies 2, 3: 378–399.

Wigen, Kären 1999: Culture, Power, and Place: The New Landscapes of East Asian Regionalism. In: The American Historical Review 104, 4: 1183–1201.

Winland, Daphne 2002: The Politics of Desire and Disdain: Croatian Identity Between "home" and "homeland". In: American Ethnologist 29, 3: 693–718.

Winland, Daphne 2007: We Are Now a Nation: Croats between "Home" and "Homeland". Toronto: University of Toronto Press.

Woods, Dwayne 1995: The Crisis of Center-Periphery Integration in Italy and the Rise of Regional Populism: The Lombard League. In: Comparative Politics 27, 2: 187–203.

Zhurzhenko, Tatiana 2004: Cross-Border Cooperation and Transformation of Regional Identities in the Ukrainian-Russian Borderlands: Towards a Euroregion "Slobozhanshchyna"? Part 2. In: Nationalities Papers 32, 3: 497–514.

Abstract

This article draws on ethnographic research on the Istrian region to explore the use of the concepts "region" and "regional identity" by anthropologists and other social actors in Southeastern Europe. The first part of the article excavates multiple genealogies and definitions of the region, examining key moments (such as the 1930s and 1990s) in which both the region and regionalism assumed particular importance as either complements or alternatives to the "nation". The article then explores the continued emphasis on the logics of territoriality of contemporary understandings of regions, regional identity, and regionalism. Recent anthropological work on regions has tended to undervalue de/re-territorializing processes, such as diaspora. As anthropologists have examined the constructed nature of nation-ness and national identity, they have paradoxically risked naturalizing the region and regional identity. In addressing these issues, the article reflects on the "space of anthropology" between region and nation in the study of Southeastern Europe.

Nationalism and the Re-Invention of Early-Modern Identities in the Ottoman-Habsburg Borderlands

Claire Norton, London

Introduction

> For history is the raw material for nationalist or ethnic or fundamentalist ideologies [...] The Past is an essential element, perhaps *the* essential element, in these ideologies. If there is no suitable past, it can always be invented. Indeed in the nature of things there is usually no entirely suitable past, because the phenomena these ideologies claim to justify is not ancient or eternal but historically novel (Hobsbawm 1998: 6).

> [F]orgetting, I would even go so far as to say historical error, is a crucial factor in the creation of a nation (Renan 1990: 11 quoted in Özkırımlı 2000: 36).

At a time when the nation state and nationalism are the predominant means of delineating geo-political space and articulating identity, histories of South-east Europe often unconsciously, and without it being explicitly acknowledged, articulate and reproduce primordialist or essentialist explanations of nationalism, and employ models that conceive of identity as inherent and unitary. That is to say, historians assume that national communities have always existed *sui generis* and that national identity is co-extensive with a distinct ethnic identity or community "essence", and thus is immutable and enduring. While such an "essence" may be dormant during periods of external oppression, the enduring ethno-national id of the community will always struggle for political and territorial autonomy and self realisation.

The modernist or constructivist understanding of nationalism, that national identity is contingent, invented, flexible, and constantly being negotiated and re-defined in response to environmental factors and contexts, is not widely accepted.[1] This, in conjunction with the predilection of historical writing for teleology, results in evidence being narrowly interpreted as establishing enduring, constant identities and thus the uncritical and anachronistic retrospective projection of

[1] Özkırımlı (2000) offers a summary and critique of the three main approaches to nationalism; primordialism, modernism and ethno-symbolism. In the last chapter he recommends a binary classification into essentialist and constructivist approaches which may be more useful.

current national identities onto early modern communities.[2] Such a practice is further exacerbated at times of fervent nation building when historians and their histories are drafted to help establish a national identity, and legitimise claims for nation-state status through the establishment, or "invention" of a glorious past that exemplifies the longevity and enduring nature of the nation. Earlier identities not congruent with the new vision are forgotten or re-interpreted, and history becomes a tool to serve new, contemporary agendas. At best one could argue that to uncritically project back nation-state influenced conceptions of identity onto earlier communities is not particularly heuristically beneficial or scholarly, at worst it can lead to history being used to justify or legitimise extremist political or separatist aims that can, and have, led to "ethnic cleansing" and violence.

New work on nationalism, identity and frontiers has, however, challenged the implicit presumption in many histories that proto-ethno-national communities congruent with contemporary nation-states have existed for hundreds, if not thousands, of years. In this article I intend to apply some of these approaches and findings to the question of the construction and representation of identities on the Ottoman-Habsburg frontier in the early modern and modern periods. I will explore how the employment of different interpretative frames or discourses has affected both remembrances of a particular event, and the construction of identities. Thus, I will challenge the view that the early modern Habsburg-Ottoman frontier was characterised by distinct and antagonistic communities defined along ethno-confessional or linguistic fault-lines. I will argue that the reification of identity as natural, constant and immutable arises from the pervasive influence of the essentialist understanding of nationalism and the dominance of the nation-state interpretative frame as a means of apprehending and constructing the past, and is therefore to be found in nineteenth- and twentieth-century narratives of the early modern border, but is not readily apparent in earlier sources. Instead many early modern sources offer alternative articulations of identity and ontologies of community centred around the fulcrums of class, occupation, local loyalties to commanders or elites and specific regional circumstances and customs.

The first section of the article will discuss in more detail theories of nationalism, frontiers, and identity construction that challenge the position implicit in many histories of South-east Europe. I will then present evidence from a variety of sources that suggest that the identities of individuals and communities inhabiting

---

[2] I use Fine's conception of ethnicity: defined as someone who "feels that he belongs to a community with others of his kind, and believes that he and these others are truly members of a community (even when they do not know each other), bound by common ingredients, usually common language, territory, history and a feeling that those who share this history, language, and other valued ingredients are somehow related and members of a larger common family" (Fine 2006: 2).

the early modern Ottoman-Habsburg frontier do not unproblematically map onto the proto-ethno-national identities assumed in some modern historians' accounts. By way of further illustration I will focus on an analysis of identity in early-modern Ottoman narratives describing the sieges of Nagykanizsa castle in 1600 and 1601 to exemplify how, despite sources sometimes superficially reinforcing the notion that communities fashioned identity in ethno-confessional or linguistic terms, these narratives, to be read coherently, require the audiences to construct or imagine identities of self and other in far more complex terms and thus articulate a counter discourse that contests that of empire or the nation.[3] Lastly, I will demonstrate how and why these narratives changed, and earlier identities were forgotten as they were re-inscribed within a nation state interpretative framework by nineteenth-century Ottoman, and twentieth-century Turkish scholars.

I have chosen to use narratives of the sieges of Nagykanizsa, a castle that was located just south of Lake Balaton in what is today Hungary, for three reasons. Firstly, narratives of antagonism and confrontations with oppositional "others" have a very effective ontological role in the imagination of communities: conflict requires a clear understanding on the part of the implied audience of who "we", the heroes, are, and who "they", the enemy are (Shapiro 1997: 42). Moreover, when we "work to construct the identity of someone else, we are constructing something that involves who *we* are at least as much, and often much more, than who *they* are" (Joseph 2004: 3). Secondly, the sieges took place in the Habsburg-Ottoman border region which I argue operated as a "middle ground", a place where diverse communities interacted and imagined more complex, plural and inclusive identities, and it thus offers an interesting example to counter the notion that this border only had a divisive role.[4] Lastly, the narrative has been repeatedly re-interpreted and re-written over the past four centuries and thus the various differences in later versions can be analysed as evidence for the affect on the text of the shift in interpretative frames and geo-political contexts: most noticeably the spread of nationalism as both a concept and way of delineating space.

Nationalism, history and identity

Nationalism as an ideology and practice has had a very close relationship with historians, history writing and the construction of the past over the past two hundred years. Renan argued that a common heroic past was more important as a

[3] Nagykanizsa castle was a key fortress in the Habsburg border defence line against the Ottomans. In 1600 the Ottoman army captured the castle from the Habsburgs after a long siege. The following year the Habsburgs attempted to retake the castle from the Ottomans, but were defeated by the Ottoman garrison commanded by Tiryaki Hasan Pasha.

[4] The term "middle ground" is from White 1991.

constituent ingredient for a nation than race, language or religion; that a nation "presupposes a past" (Renan 1990: 19 cited in Özkırımlı 2000: 35). It is of no surprise therefore that historians have always been willing to "invent" or discover suitable pasts for nations (Hobsbawm, Ranger 1983, Hobsbawm 1998: 6, Gellner 1964: 169 cited in Anderson 1991: 6)[5]. However, it is not only nationalist historians who are affected by the discourse of nationalism: the nation state and its concomitant explanatory discourse is now so pervasive that it constitutes the dominant interpretative-frame by which we all apprehend and make sense of the world. National entities and identities have become reified to the extent that to scholars not directly concerned with theorising about nationalism and identity, it can seem natural to assume that nations and national communities have always existed: the projection back of current identities onto early modern communities therefore seems reasonable, and thus identity is conceived of as predetermined, unitary and enduring.

The retrospective projection of identity also, as the quote by Renan at the beginning of the article suggests, requires historians to forget, as well as remember, the past in the writing of history. Both the national community and historians writing in an intellectual context which is dominated by the discourse of nationalism, tend to elide the differences that exist between the diverse communities that constitute a nation and focus instead upon their shared characteristics. More importantly, they also forget that the inhabitants of a particular region did not always identify as an "ethnic" community; that previously identity was constructed according to different criteria (Joseph 2004: 114 f.). Many histories of South-east Europe have, as a result of implicitly adopting particular essentialist models of identity, and theories of nationalism, in effect, elided the existence of more diverse communal identities and forgotten the existence of widespread co-operation and synthesis between ostensibly different groups. This forgetfulness is reinforced through the selection of sources, and reliance upon official narratives which often have a rhetorical or propaganda function that oversimplifies the relationship between us and them and can gloss over the ambiguities, tensions and complexities of border communities (Power, Standen 1999: 24 f.).

Within the context of Ottoman history historians often contend that medieval and early modern Balkan states were constituted by proto-ethno-national communities which retained their integrity and essence despite a period of quiescence under the yoke of Ottoman oppression. This, it is argued, was successfully achieved because there was very little association and interaction between the Ottomans and these communities: there was no, or limited, political cooperation, no economic or

---

5 I agree with Anderson (1991: 6) that the term invention should not be assimilated to the terms "falsity" and "fabrication", instead its corollaries should be "imagined", "created" or "culturally constructed".

cultural integration, and no voluntary religious conversion. For example, some scholars of Croatian history have interpreted early modern references to the term "Croatian" exclusively as evidence of an ethnic consciousness which has led them to speculate that Croatian ethno-genesis occurred in the early medieval period and thus the past thousand years can be characterised as a struggle for a self-governing Croatian state (Fine 2006: 12–15). Likewise, Hungarian historians have also, on occasion, depicted Hungarians as constituting a singular, unchanging ethno-nation which preserved a pre-Ottoman fifteenth-century ethnic, linguistic, cultural and religious identity throughout the period of Ottoman "subjugation" until its eventual emancipation and self-actualisation as the nation state of Hungary.[6]

There are, however, a number of theoretical and evidential problems with uncritically projecting current identities back onto earlier communities and interpreting evidence of identity exclusively in ethnic terms. Recent research has argued against models that conceive of identity as essential, static and enduring. Instead it is argued that identity is socially constructed and maintained through a variety of social processes and practices: it is performed, and requires the active, ongoing participation of individuals and communities. Identities are therefore constantly renegotiated, reinvented, and redefined according to the circumstances and dominant ideological explanatory frameworks in force (Ivanič 1998: 10, Bourdieu 1991: 223, Eller, Coughlan 1993: 188 cited in Özkırımlı 2000: 75). However, individuals are not free to adopt any identity that they choose: identity is a product of, and thus determined by, existent discourses, social "fields" and the social practices that individuals engage in (Joseph 2004: 10). Thus as contexts and discourses have altered over the centuries, so too have identities. Moreover, individuals do not possess just one identity, instead they adopt and perform a whole range of group identities that reflect their multiple roles in society (Ivanič 1998: 10).

The theoretical models of identity as socially constructed, plural and fluid are confirmed by the evidence when considering South-east Europe. The notion of an unchanging community essence and cultural homogeneity enduring through the centuries is firstly problematic in practical terms because of the impact of migration, conquest, intermarriage, and conversion throughout the region: how can a community essence be maintained during periods of mass migration or conversion? And what impact does inter-marriage have on identity? Secondly, the ruling elite frequently articulated different identities to that of the subject population: they often spoke a different language, had a different culture, and a different religion to

[6] Dávid, Fodor 2000: xviii, xix–xx, Fekete 1944: 308 quoted in Dávid and Fodor 2002: 318 f., Dávid 1995: 83 and 85–87, Hegyi 1995 quoted in Dávid and Fodor 2002: 320. For a detailed discussion of Hungarian historiography on this topic see Norton 2007. Hickok (1997: xi, 114 f.) and Minkov (2004: 65) also discuss nationalist historiography and the projection back of twentieth century identities in both a Slavic or Bosnian, and Bulgarian context.

their subjects. Thus extrapolating from elite conceptions of identity to that of the wider community is frequently misleading. The allegiances of individuals in times of peace and conflict also do not reflect the existence of homogeneous ethnic communities: members of the same religious, linguistic or cultural group could frequently be found on different sides of a conflict and in the service of different lords. Moreover, identities can be transitory or multiple: as discourses and geo-political contexts change so too the identities of communities are redefined. Fine has noted that those described as Croat in the early modern period were also often simultaneously described with the broader, more inclusive identity labels of Slav or Illyrian (Fine 2006: 560). Similarly, the Catholic Janjevci from the Kosovo region today have a Croat identity, but in nineteenth century Austro-Hungarian consular reports they were described as Catholic Serbs (Frantz 2007).

A critical argument against ascribing ethno-national identities to early modern communities however, is that although identities based upon a common language, religion or culture existed in the medieval and early modern world they were not of crucial importance to communities in constituting a group identity at that time. While individuals before the eighteenth century often felt patriotic and thus some kind of collective empathy or identity with their city, locality, ruler or empire, they did not, on any large scale or with any regularity, evince a sense of a collective ethno-national id (Hayes 1955: 6, Özkırımlı 2000: 37). Fine argues that there is very little, if any, evidence for the existence of such ethnic-type identities existing among the medieval Balkan peoples largely because state ideology was centred on loyalty to the ruler rather than on the idea of a collective or civic entity: subjects served the individual not the state (Fine 2006: 8). He concludes that any expression of a specifically Croat identity before the nineteenth century was predominantly an expression of political or geographic, not ethnic, identity: when individuals were described as Croats this generally denoted that they either lived in the territory called Croatia or that they served a Croatian king, ban or other ruler, not that they imagined themselves as part of a larger Croatian cultural community to which they felt inextricably bound (Fine 2006: 2 and 9).

Discussions of identity in this border region in Southeast Europe are also frequently problematic because historians' models of life along the frontier position it as a space that divides, and thus over-emphasise conflict, separation, mutual hostility and antagonism: they exaggerate cartographies of difference. While Dávid and Fodor acknowledge that borders are generally places of mediation, linkage and transfer, they argue that the Ottoman-Habsburg borders are an exception and deny that any long lasting interaction between communities in the area occurred (Dávid, Fodor 2000: xii, xviii, xix–xx). Recent scholarship, however, has suggested that early modern borders and frontiers were not always barriers dividing communities, but perhaps as a result of their nature as contested spaces, they were places which permitted, and facilitated, interaction between communities, and thus opportunities for integration and synthesis (White 1991, Power, Standen 1999). Although White's model for border interaction is situated in the evidential base of North America and Indian-white relations, it may have some heuristic benefit if applied to South-east Europe. In particular his stress on individuals' and communities' efforts at creating or imagining "a common, mutually comprehensive world" or a "middle ground" may have particular resonance and relevance (White 1991: ix). White argues that such a "middle ground" was a place "between cultures, peoples, and in between empires and the non-state world of villages," a place where, although different peoples may have "remained identifiable" they also "shaded into each other" (Ibid., x–xi). Borders were therefore places where a diverse range of beliefs, ideologies, institutions, practices and customs clashed, co-existed and compromised. In other words, while local religious and linguistic, as well as cultural distinctions endured, they were also transformed: new identities were created and enacted that reflected a new common, shared reality centred around local concerns and practices. Relationships and ties based upon village, religion, family, occupation, loyalty to a local lord, economic interest, and other shared concerns meant that for many people ethno-religious or linguistic criteria were not the most important factors in distinguishing "us" from "them", "self" from "other". Such a model of border societies reflects a constructivist understanding of nationalism in that it recognises the contingency and intersubjective nature of identity formation, and the role changing environmental or contextual conditions have. It also coheres with evidence from the early modern Habsburg-Ottoman frontier, and it is to this that I will now turn.

The Habsburg-Ottoman frontier re-visited

Generally, identity in the Ottoman Empire was not articulated simply in terms of ethno-confessional or linguistic criteria: the ruling elite participated in and reproduced a distinct Ottoman identity, yet came from a variety of different religious, linguistic and cultural backgrounds. Evidence suggests that while regional, linguistic and religious identities were important, Ottoman subjects did not form proto-ethno-national groups and exclusively, or predominantly, identify with their co-religionists, fellow language users, or those with a common cultural background while remaining separate from, and resistant to, the Ottoman state and culture as broadly conceived.[7] This was particularly the case in the Ottoman border regions, including the Habsburg/Polish-Ottoman frontier. For much of the sixteenth and

---

[7] Kunt (1974) discusses the importance of regional origins and shared languages in creating ties of loyalty and patronage among the Ottoman elite. Such regional and linguistic connections, though, can not really be interpreted as evidence of proto-national ethnic identities.

seventeenth centuries this border zone stretched from the Dalmatian coast eastwards until it reached the Black Sea in the Crimea. Although this frontier fluctuated over time, the section of the border which I am concerned with here was generally stable; broadly running through the present-day states of Croatia and Hungary and then, after the Ottoman defeat at the second siege of Vienna, moving slightly south and following the borders of Bosnia east along the river Sava into Wallachia before turning north.

This border between the Habsburgs and the Ottomans has frequently been characterized not only as a line dividing two empires, but as demarcating two competing civilizations: the Christian West and the Islamic East. However, recent scholarship has challenged this notion of the frontier space as a divisive line, a "locus of separation" and has instead re-interpreted it as a "transitional zone of interaction" (Stein 2007: 6).[8] Tales, muster records, and personal and official correspondence all attest to the existence of integrated and diverse border communities where interaction, synthesis and co-operation existed not only among Ottoman subjects of different religious, linguistic and cultural groups, but also between inhabitants from different states in the Habsburg-Ottoman border region. Here identity was far more complex and transient, with individuals often simultaneously identifying with a multiplicity of quite diverse communities and also changing communities, allegiances, and identities when convenient or pragmatic to do so.

Stein has argued that this border did not work to divide peoples, but helped to create a space for integration and co-operation. It was "a socially and economically dynamic zone of transition, where different people and states met and interacted", "a joint community of sorts" (Stein 2007: 156). Christian communities were found on both sides of the border, as were speakers of Hungarian and Slavic languages. Moreover, the specific conditions brought about by the existence of the frontier between the Habsburgs and the Ottomans necessitated particular state responses and this helped to create both a shared environment and a shared set of cultural, economic and military practices which, because communities of practice tend to engender shared beliefs, norms, ideologies and identities, led to the evolvement of a degree of commonality and the imagination of common identities (Joseph 2004: 65). Communities on both sides of the border lived similar agrarian or military lives. Moreover, despite their putative separation by the border, informal commercial and personal connections were maintained.

Although the largely hypothetical linear border demarcated the theoretical limits of the two empires' juridico-political power, central power was much more diffuse in the liminal space of the frontier region and power was effectively in the

[8] To this extent it resembles an earlier Ottoman frontier region, that of the Byzantine-Ottoman frontier in Anatolia in the thirteenth and fourteenth centuries which Heywood described as a "zone of passage and interaction *and* a political barrier" (1999: 233).

hands of marcher lords from both sides who through the constant exchange of letters, presents and envoys, negotiated and implemented a code, or system of practices, beneficial to themselves and their clients.[9] For example, despite Habsburg and Ottoman imperial treaties forbidding cross-border raiding in times of peace, such raids were essential to the local economy of the border region. Therefore commanders and notables from both sides attempted to regulate the practice to ensure its continuation. In 1649 the chief janissary ağa of Nagykanizsa complains in a letter to Count Adam Battyány at Körmend that eighty Ottoman soldiers have been captured by the Habsburgs. He suggests an exchange of prisoners and threatens to contact the count's superiors in Vienna if he does not agree, but at no time does he argue that such raids, which in fact violated the peace treaties between the two empires, should stop.[10] Another practice vital to the local economy, involving cross border co-operation and often against imperial orders, was the collection of taxes from communities across the border: elites from both sides attempted to collect taxes from peasants in lands that they had previously held, but had now been captured by the other side. For example, local Ottoman authorities tolerated the collection of taxes by Habsburg agents from peasants in Ottoman territories because in return they received one percent of the total collected sum (Bayerle 1973: 22). This practice of double taxation not only facilitated "some sort of commonality" between the Habsburg and Ottoman commanders and troops involved in the collection, but it also bound the peasants on both sides of the border together in a "single frontier community" (Stein 2007: 25 f.). More orthodox economic practices such as the cross border trade in cattle, salt, wine and other goods also created a common ground between communities in the region and integrated the military into civilian networks through their participation in trade. Forts along the border region flourished as market centres for a variety of products and also drew customers from across the Habsburg border (Stein 2007: 26 f. and 137 f.). Thus, they acted as nexus in wider economic networks which facilitated the interaction and integration of a variety of different communities.

The environment of the frontier did not only create a middle ground between fortress commanders and local lords, it also united the garrison soldiers and peasants who inhabited and farmed the land. The consistency and longevity of "tours of duty" of the garrison soldiers helped to integrate them into local economic and socio-cultural networks. For example, although janissary units were usually assigned to a garrison for five years, occasionally it was for much longer. Similarly the same commanders of the *azeb* units in Nagykanzisa castle served

---

[9] See Fekete (1932: 21) for a very friendly letter between the Ottoman governor of Buda and Johann Molard in 1618 which refers to the exchange of present and ambassadors.

[10] Sugar (1971: 82) cites a letter located in the Hungarian National Archives, Budapest (Batthyany Family Archives, Collection No. P1313, Fascicle 249, Document 226a).

there throughout the 1650s (Stein 2007: chapter 3, especially 74 and 77). In addition, the border offered a variety of economic opportunities to settlers and migrants from both sides: adventurous young men from diverse communities were attracted to the border because of the opportunities available: the availability of arable land, the need for skilled workers, and the chance to volunteer as a *sekban* or *gönüllü* soldier in a border garrison with the prospect of eventually being awarded a more permanent, salaried military position (Stein 2007: 93–97).

Merchants, prisoners, peasants and tax collectors were not the only people to traverse the border zone: soldiers frequently did not perceive political, religious, and linguistic boundaries as insurmountable and put their own financial gain above loyalty to a specific ethno-national community or state. Evidence from Ottoman campaign treasury account books shows that Christians from Poland, Transylvania and Austria were paid for service to the Ottoman state in the Long War (1593–1606) between the Habsburgs and Ottomans (Finkel 1992: 452). Other soldiers deserted to the Ottomans if they felt it was in their interest, such as the French and Walloon mercenaries stationed in the Habsburg-held garrison of Pâpa who deserted to the Ottomans in 1600. Records show that these soldiers not only fought alongside Ottoman soldiers in the subsequent Ottoman capture and defence of Nagykanizsa castle, but also elected to remain in Ottoman service for many more years. Interestingly, although one of the French captains converted to Islam, his fellow soldiers remained Christian (Finkel 1992: 465–468).

The garrisons themselves were also places of interaction between communities. Despite the official imperial rhetoric of the Ottoman centre that non-Muslims were not permitted to fight in the Ottoman military, there is considerable evidence that Christian soldiers and auxiliaries were a significant presence in Ottoman border fortresses. Stein, through an analysis of primary sources including military pay registers and muster rolls, has demonstrated that Christian soldiers, organised into *martoloso*, *sekban* and *müsellem* units, were active in border garrisons where they not only fought alongside their Muslim compatriots for the Ottoman state, but also engaged in raids and trade for personal gain (Stein 2007: 89–96). Pakalın also notes the presence of Christian *sekban* soldiers among the Ottoman forces at the siege of Vienna in 1683 (Pakalın 1966: 326). While much of this evidence concerns the Ottoman-Habsburg border before the loss of Hungary at the end of the seventeenth century the new frontier zone continued as a space of interaction and opportunity into the nineteenth century. For example as late as the nineteenth century the Catholic Fandi of the Kosovo region were exempted from the *ciziye* tax in exchange for military service in times of war and policing duties in peace times. Moreover, their loyalties were very much directed towards the Muslim Ottoman state and sultan rather than another Catholic or Christian power (Frantz 2007).

The Nagykanizsa narratives

I now want to explore Ottoman and modern Turkish narratives of the sieges of Nagykanizsa for evidence of how different audiences conceived of, or imagined, identities of self and other in this border region. In particular, I want to ascertain whether there is evidence in early modern Ottoman narratives of the siege, of interaction, cooperation or synthesis between individuals of different linguistic, and ethno-confessional communities as suggested by the sources and authors cited above. I will initially examine a corpus of twenty five early modern Ottoman *gazavatname* [campaign narrative] accounts of the sieges: collectively known as the *Gazavat-i Tiryaki Hasan Paşa* variously dating from 1616 to 1815.[11] In particular I will use ms. A.E.Tar.187 and ms. o.R.12961. The former has been selected because it can be seen as representative of the majority of the manuscripts, whereas the latter is unusual in that it represents identities of self and other that are more complex, fluid and inclusive than the other manuscripts in the corpus.[12] In the following section I will both foreground the way in which characters in the narratives negotiate and perform identities of self and other, and demonstrate that for the implied early modern audiences, identities based upon criteria other than ethnicity, religion and language took precedence. Evidence from these *gazavatnames* suggests not only that there was considerable interaction between different religious and linguistic communities, but also that there was significant incorporation or synthesis. In other words, self and other, friend and enemy, did not easily map onto Muslim, Turkish-speaking Ottoman and Christian, Hungarian or Slavic speaking, non-Ottoman.[13]

Early-Modern Ottoman Narratives

It is important to note that I am not claiming or arguing that the constructions of identity implicit in these *gazavatname* narratives equate easily with the identity-label Ottoman. Rather I am arguing that imaginations of identity and community

---

[11] The manuscripts are best described as constituting an interrelated corpus rather than copies of a single original because some of them have been significantly re-inscribed by their scribes and thus present very different potential readings. I have described and analysed the various interrelations and differences between the manuscripts in more detail (Norton 2005). A shorter description of the manuscript corpus together with a more in depth exploration of the construction of identities of self and other in these manuscripts can be found in Norton 2005b.

[12] All of the manuscripts implicitly present a conception of Ottoman self which includes non-Muslims and non-Turkish speakers, it is just more exaggerated in ms. o.R.12961.

[13] It should be noted that these *gazavatnames* contain fictional or imaginative sections which do not easily cohere with other available sources. However, in generic terms many of the examples of interaction between ostensibly distinct communities narrated in the manuscripts are confirmed by similar cases in other sources.

were created that contested a division based solely or exclusively on ethno-confessional or linguistic criteria. I also wish to challenge the notion that all Turkish-speaking Muslims would automatically and unproblematically have conceived of themselves as Ottoman, whereas non-Muslim, Slavic or Hungarian speakers would not have, and would have conceived of Ottoman as a label of the other. The term Ottoman was often, but not exclusively, understood to refer to the military and administrative elite of the empire. However, there is evidence that non-elite employees of the state did, to some extent, identify with the label Ottoman, in so much as they evinced a loyalty to the Ottoman state.

Pace Hegy and Dávid who have argued that the Ottoman presence in Hungary amounted to little more than a military occupation with the castles "bristling with Ottoman soldiers" and "almost no civilian Muslim population", the Nagykanzisa *gazavatname* narratives illustrate that many audiences did not conceive of such an actual and ontological divide between a Muslim, military presence in garrisons and non-Muslim, non-Ottoman civilians (Hegyi 1975 quoted in Dávid, Fodor 2002: 319, quotes from Dávid 1995: 87 f.). For example, the Ottoman *gazavatname* manuscripts describe in some detail a counter-intelligence ploy by the Ottoman commander, Tiryaki Hasan Pasha. He commands his deputy Kara Ömer Ağa to pass some enemy prisoners through "the middle of the hundred and fifty bandur, and the five hundred Hungarian cavalry" present in the castle and ensure that the prisoners hear the soldiers speaking Hungarian.[14] The "escape" of the prisoners is then facilitated and they subsequently erroneously inform the Habsburg camp that the Ottomans have effected a secret alliance with the Hungarian and Croatian forces employed in the Habsburg army (ms. A.E.Tar.187, fol. 18r).[15] What is of relevance here is that the narrative suggests there were soldiers in the garrison, fighting for the Ottomans, who spoke Hungarian (and also maybe Croatian) and who may have previously been employed by the ban of Croatia. Such a possibility is obviously very convenient from a narrative perspective as it facilitates the stratagem of the Ottoman commander, but we do have other documentary evidence that various non-Muslim soldiers, some of whom presumably spoke Hungarian, were present in Nagykanizsa castle under Ottoman control either during or after the Habsburg siege of 1601: the soldiers who defected from the Pâpa garrison as well as those non-Muslims listed in the *martolos* units in the 1621–1622 register (Finkel 1992: 465–468, Stein 2007: 92).

[14] The word *bandur* or *pandur* has many referents, but it is generally understood to refer to troops in the service of the *ban* of Croatia, Dalmatia and Slavonia.

[15] The quote is from ms. A.E.Tar. 187, but the other manuscripts in the corpus contain very similar versions of this event. The various manuscripts describe the forces allied with the Habsburgs as Hungarian and Croatian. Presumably this is being used here not as an ethnic identity, but more as a geographical or political identity and describes troops fighting for commanders who rule over estates in Croatia or Hungary.

This stratagem is further elaborated upon in ms. o.R.12961. Here the captured Habsburg soldiers are again made to walk among groups of different Hungarian speakers, but this time the Hungarians are described as soldiers, commanders and notables suggesting that Hungarian-speakers were integrated into the Ottoman military-administrative structure at all levels: "The Hungarian soldiers who previously brought the provisions and munitions from the castles of Bubofça, Berzince and Sigetwar were commanders and *ayan* [notables]. The Pasha had not given them permission to go and they were dwelling in the castle" (ms. o.R.12961, fol. 56v). Presumably, but not necessarily, these commanders and officers would have been Muslim, that is to say, Hungarian-speaking converts to Islam. The same manuscript makes a further reference to Hungarian-speaking converts to Islam: "... put the peasants who brought the provisions which came to us from Bubofça in soldiers' uniforms and also put some of the people of Islam in Hungarian clothing and let them speak Hungarian together" (ms. o.R.12961, fol. 46v). This quote also presents civilian, non-Muslim, Hungarian peasants as associating with the Ottomans: the fact that the peasants are not described as "the people of Islam" suggests they retained their Christian faith. For the audience of this manuscript inscribed at the end of the eighteenth century, the notion of there being civilian Hungarian speaking Christians, and converts to Islam who associated and identified with the Ottomans was not out of the ordinary.

This manuscript also presents further evidence of links between the garrison occupants and the rural population. The *gönüllü ağası* or commander of the locally recruited troops is depicted as a local inhabitant as he acts as a guide in the border area for Tiryaki Hasan Pasha. He also mentions that his brother has a farm in the border region (ms. o.R.12961 fols 14r-v).

The depiction of Hungarian or other Balkan-language speakers as self is continued in the narration of the activities of Tiryaki Hasan Pasha's deputies: Kara Ömer Ağa, Osman Ağa, and Arab Oğlu were all men local to the area who spoke Hungarian or a Slavic language.[16] Kara Ömer Ağa feeds misinformation about the situation in the castle to captured Habsburg prisoners before releasing them. He speaks to the prisoners in "their" language and asserts that he was kidnapped when young by the Ottomans, so really he is "one of them" and thus wants to help them (ms. A.E.Tar.187 fol. 18v). Osman Ağa is described as a spy who is fluent in "Frenk, and Austrian and Hungarian and Croatian" and when dressed in Frenkish garments looks so "real" that he convinces Tiryaki Hasan Pasha that he is in fact one of "them" (ms. A.E.Tar.187 fol. 31v). Arab Oğlu is similarly able to pass as one of the enemy other: he infiltrates the parliament or *torvin* held by the enemy Habsburg commanders, insinuates himself into the Habsburg army and also

[16] While Kara Ömer Ağa and Osman are found in all the manuscripts, Arab Oğlu only appears in ms. o.R.12961.

persuades an enemy notable that he is a local Balkan guide (ms. o.R.12961 fol. 9v–10v, 11v, 13r, 21r and 22v). Paradoxically, for these men in service to the Ottoman state and loyal to the Ottoman commander Tiryaki Hasan Pasha, to be able to convince the Habsburgs that they were "one of them", in one way they really must have been "one of them": they must have been locals of the region and native speakers of Hungarian or a Slavic language who were familiar enough with the local Christian culture, and customs to convince others. Again, although there is no proof that these men actually existed, and their ability to pass as the enemy is required for narrative purposes, there is plenty of evidence of local Hungarian and Slavic speakers participating in, and identifying with, the Ottoman military-administrative structure. Most importantly, the existence of non-Muslim, non-Turkish speakers participating in a conception of "Ottoman" self made sense to the implied seventeenth and eighteenth-century audiences of these manuscripts.

The above examples also indicate that a single language was not exclusively associated with a sense of self. This is important with regard to conceptions of identity because common speech can be "a peculiarly potent symbol of the social solidarity of those who speak the language" (Sapir 1949: 15–18 cited in Joseph 2004: 54). As will be seen in later inscriptions, if Turkish is depicted exclusively as the language of self, then it in effect excludes all speakers of non-Turkish languages from participating in, or performing, an "Ottoman" identity. Similarly, the imagination of the enemy other also permits a more inclusive imagination of self: the language of the enemy is never directly specified because to do so would make it harder to incorporate other speakers of this language into a conception of self (see ms. o.R.12961 fol. 46v).

Lastly, in ms. o.R.12961 self and other are demarcated not in ethno-confessional terms, but along the lines of status or occupation. There is a marked sympathy for the enemy soldiers, yet a hostility is displayed towards not only the enemy commanders, but also the Ottoman commanders. The character of Tiryaki Hasan Pasha, the heroic, brave commander in other inscriptions, here exhibits tension: he is the hero, but he is also one of the elite; thus while his achievements are recognised, he is also mocked as a drooling, incapacitated opium addict (Norton 2007b). Such an implicit articulation of self and other together with other linguistic evidence suggests that the implied audience of ms. o.R.12961 may have largely consisted of military men on the frontier for whom the shared circumstances or conditions of the marches generated a camaraderie that in some way united them regardless of which side of the border they served. Such a shared sense of identity is reinforced by the evidence from other sources of frequent cross border raiding and ransoming practices, trade networks and desertions.

For seventeenth and eighteenth century audiences of these *gazavatnames*, especially of ms. o.R.12961, the imagination of the Habsburg-Ottoman border zone as a culturally, religiously and linguistically mixed space where non-Muslims, recent converts and speakers of Hungarian, and Slavic languages could identify to some extent with the Ottoman state either via employment in the Ottoman military-administrative structure or through loyalty to a local border commander such as Tiryaki Hasan Pasha made sense: it reflected their reality. The border zone was perceived by these audiences, and also attested to by other early modern sources, as a "middle ground" where people of different religions and ethno-linguistic backgrounds could, and did, interact. This perception of the frontier and the people living there was something that changed in subsequent centuries as both the circumstances and the dominant discourse for apprehending and constructing geo-political space altered.

Late Ottoman narratives

By the end of the nineteenth century when Namık Kemal wrote his account of the sieges of Nagykanizsa, both the reality of the Ottoman-Habsburg border and the dominant frameworks available for the conception of space and identity had changed, resulting in a significantly different narrative re-construction of the Nagykanizsa sieges and concomitant imagination of identity. The Ottomans had lost their Hungarian territories at the end of the eighteenth century, and the nineteenth century witnessed numerous wars and uprisings in the Balkans as various groups attempted to secede from the Ottoman Empire and establish new states. Ideologically, discourses centred upon notions of constitutionalism and nationalism within a framework of Ottomanism were becoming more dominant among Ottoman intellectuals and were providing a scaffold for the re-invention of an Ottoman identity in response to the challenge from Europe and the gradual fragmentation of the empire. One of these intellectuals and reformers Namık Kemal, attempted to construct a new common Ottoman identity and sense of self for the changed times though his writing.

Namık Kemal re-wrote the tale of the siege of Nagykanizsa castle at the end of the nineteenth century for a new audience. This new version was extremely popular and was published in a number of different editions. It constitutes not only the most famous nineteenth century version of the sieges, but together with Namık Kemal's other works on Islamic heroes attempted to provide new models of identity and interpretations of the past for a nineteenth century proto-nationalist Ottoman middle class and elite.[17] Another, much shorter, description of the sieges of Nagykanizsa was also published by Ahmed Refik as part of his larger 1900–1 work entitled *Famous Ottoman Commanders*. Ahmed Refik, like Namık Kemal, is concerned to re-invent an Ottoman past through a series of stirring historical

[17] See bibliography for the various editions. Namık Kemal also wrote stirring histories of Saladin and Mehmed II.

vignettes or heroic portraits to provide a new sense of self identity for an audience living through turbulent and transformative geo-political times.

Namık Kemal's re-inscription of the early modern Ottoman *gazavatname* version of the sieges of Nagykanzisa specifically responds to changes in Ottoman geography, and the employment of an alternative ideological framework to map and interpret this space (Norton 2004: 137–143). In contrast to the cartographies of geo-political power inherent in the early-modern *gazavatname* manuscripts which conceive of state influence as radiating out from various centres and gradually diffusing through porous and ontologically liminal border zones, the nation-state discourse presumes the existence of fixed, coterminous nation-states demarcated by linear borders and occupied by distinct national communities with their own ethno-national identities. Thus, although the early-modern *gazavatnames* described the enemy besieging Ottoman Nagykanizsa according to geographical or political identity labels as Austrians, Hungarians, Bohemians, Poles, Frenks, Croatians, Slovenes, Herzogovinians and Zirinoğlu and his men, in Namık Kemal's nineteenth century *Kanije* the enemy are named in nation-state terms as, Germany, France, Italy and Russia (A.E.Tar.187, fol. 6v, Namık Kemal 1311 [1893]: 47 f., 65 and 98). Likewise, the re-interpretation of the term *Frenk*, which essentially signified to early modern Ottoman audiences Christendom in general, as France within Namık Kemal's nation-state dominated framework has the unintentional and erroneous consequence of implying that France was part of the Habsburg coalition besieging Nagykanizsa when in fact France was allied with the Ottomans at this time. A similar assumption is made by Ahmed Refik (Ahmed Refik 1318 [1900–1]: 322). Lastly, Namık Kemal's inclusion of Russia in the enemy coalition reflects a changed geo-political context and articulation of the identity of the other: writing just after the Crimean war and a century of frequent Russo-Ottoman conflict Namık Kemal has the Russians firmly located in his cartography of antagonism and thus inaccurately names them as the enemy.

The loss of Ottoman power in Hungary also has an impact upon Namık Kemal's and Ahmed Refik's conceptions of identities of self and other. No longer is it appropriate or coherent to conceive of, or imply, a sense of self that includes Hungarian-speakers. Therefore the Hungarian soldiers, peasants and notables present in the castle in the early modern *gazavatname* accounts are here transformed into prisoners, despite a loss of narrative coherency (Namık Kemal 1311 [1893]: 79, Ahmed Refik 1318 [1900–1]: 340). Similarly, the locals of the border area, here implicitly imagined as non-Muslim, non-Turkish speakers, are transformed from individuals with whom various earlier audiences did, or could, empathise and identify with, into the enemy other. Namık Kemal has Tiryaki Hasan Pasha declare: "My sons! We are on the border. In our midst there are so many infidels, both prisoners and locals and, hey, you can't stuff up their ears. Won't they hear the discussion I have with you? If they hear, won't they give news to the enemy?" (Namık Kemal 1311 [1893]: 52). Namık Kemal also re-describes in his account the two young men who, in the *gazavatname* accounts, motivated by fear flee the castle and escape to the besieging Habsburg army. He presents them as Hungarians and now ascribes their motivation for flight to a desire to apostatise and abandon Islam. The border therefore is no longer a middle ground, a place of interaction, communication and synthesis; a space in which the forging of different, shared identities based upon local concerns occurs. Instead it is a place of hostility, fear and separation, a place inscribing the differences between communities. Moreover, this latter example, together with Namık Kemal's stated aim in writing the history "to humbly serve and increase the patriotism and zealous public spirit of the Muslims by remembering and reminding the soldiers of the imperial army of some of the glorious deeds of the Ottoman army", suggests that for a nineteenth century bureaucrat and intellectual a sense of self had a pronounced Islamic, if not yet Turkish, character (Namık Kemal 1311 [1893]: 3–4).

Republican Turkish narratives

In the twentieth century, with the demise of the Ottoman Empire and the establishment of the Republic of Turkey, the tale of the siege of Nagykanizsa castle was again co-opted, and this time re-interpreted, as a tool with which to forge a Turkish national identity and to inculcate audiences with a sense of self and Turkishness. Three different accounts of the siege were published by state-related publishing houses in the twentieth century: Savaşkurt 1945, Baysun 1950, Ersever 1986.[18] All three accounts are didactic in nature: Savaşkurt states in his introduction that his aim in writing the history of the siege of Nagykanizsa is to demonstrate that Turkish (not Ottoman) soldiers developed particular military strategies before their European counterparts and therefore were at least the equal of Europeans (Savaşkurt 1945: 3). All three accounts re-interpret the sieges within a Turkish nation-state framework and thus map ontological and geo-political space accordingly. Turkish nationalist history generally re-imagines the Ottoman Empire as the penultimate of a long series of Turkish states stretching back for more than a millennium (Ersanlı 2002: 115 f., 130). Therefore the self articulated in these accounts is an ethnically Turkish self and the Ottoman Empire is appropriated as a Turkish Empire. The most popular of these accounts, and the most widely available, is that by Baysun, and it is this account that I will focus on. In Baysun's re-inscription of the narrative, the siege of Nagykanizsa is positioned as part of a

[18] Baysun was published by the Ministry of Education, Ersever by the General Staff Military History and Strategic Studies Ministry Publications and Savaşkurt by the Istanbul Military Press.

larger Turkish-Austrian war fought by the Turkish army with Turkish soldiers (Baysun 1950: 5 f., 9, 11). Baysun further appropriates the poly-lingual, multi-faith Ottomans as Turks through his use of the first person plural; it is always *our* soldiers who defend *our* land (Baysun 1950: 3). Thus the two multi-faith, poly-lingual early modern empires in which loyalty was centred upon a dynasty have been re-imagined in nation-state terms as homogenous, monolithic, ethno-national entities. This shift in the way geo-political space is imagined, from a dynastic to a nation-state cartography, is reflected in the exaltations that Hasan Pasha shouts before battle: in the early modern Ottoman *gazavatnames* he shouts "long live the padishah" while in Baysun's twentieth-century account it is "long live the nation" (A.E.Tar. 187 fols 20r, 20v and 41r, Baysun 1950: 10, 16, 23, 27).

The influence of the nation state discourse and its emphasis on ethnicities also re-maps cartographies of antagonism: self now equates solely with Turk, and all non-Turks within the empire are viewed with mistrust and become symbols of alterity. Kara Ömer Ağa who was depicted in the *gazavatname* narratives as a local of Hungary and a native speaker of a non-specified Balkan language is in Baysun's account transformed into an ethnic Turk, and his ability to speak Balkan languages is forgotten. As with Namık Kemal's narrative, Hungarians are also exclusively depicted as the enemy other. The Hungarians in the castle, who in the *gazavatname* accounts were soldiers, peasants and notables, are now simply prisoners (Baysun 1950: 31).

This shift from religion to ethnicity as the determinant of "otherness" in the context of Turkish nationalism is also evident in Baysun's depiction of the enemy character Kozma. Kozma is a character who before his appearance in Baysun, only appears in Cafer Iyani's seventeenth-century Ottoman account of the sieges of Nagykanizsa, *Cihadname-i Tiryaki Hasan Paşa* [The Jihad narrative of Tiryaki Hasan Pasha] (Ms. A.E.Tar. 190), which is separate and distinct from the *gazavatname* narratives.[19] In Cafer Iyani's original Kozma had simply been ascribed the identity label of infidel, but in Baysun he is re-described as a Hungarian thus further presenting Hungarians as the archetypal other (Baysun 1950: 6, A.E.Tar. 190 fol. 6v). This re-ascription of identity is also evident in Çabuk's twentieth century transcription and Turkification of Cafer Iyani's seventeenth century account. In the index he describes Kozma not as an infidel, but as "a rebellious Hungarian Bey" despite there being no evidence in the original manuscript that he was Hungarian (Çabuk 1978: 196). Lastly, the affect of the nation-state interpretative frame can also be seen in Çabuk's re-interpretation and re-writing of Cafer Iyani's term *Beç Kralı* [King of Vienna] as *Avusturya Kralı* [King of Austria] in his transcription (Çabuk 1978: 27).

---

[19] The manuscript is undated, but was presumably written sometime between 1601 and the early part of the seventeenth century when the author died.

Conclusion

The various re-inscriptions of the sieges of Nagykanizsa castle discussed in this paper illustrate how different discourses, interpretative frameworks, contextual circumstances and community goals have affected the imagination of self-other identities in the context of the Ottoman frontier in South-east Europe. Despite the arguments of some historians stressing the distinctiveness and separation of communities along ethno-linguistic and confessional lines in the early modern Habsburg-Ottoman border zone there is considerable evidence from the early modern period that this frontier region was in fact a complex, integrated and heterogeneous society where identity was far more complicated than often assumed, and transcended simple religious, linguistic and ethnic divisions. This is not to argue that religion, nor the cultural and linguistic traditions associated with particular groups in the Ottoman Empire, did not matter. Degrees of solidarity and identification are apparent among Ottomans from the same region, those who are native-speakers of the same language, or who share a similar religious background, but these are identities that co-exist alongside more inclusive, broadly defined and fluid Ottoman identities. Individuals and communities imagined and performed plural, overlapping identities that were contingent on their own pragmatic concerns, and the wider frontier context, and which focussed upon shared common experiences, local loyalties, and occupation. Moreover, such identities did not automatically include or exclude one from having loyalty to, and identifying with, the Ottoman state and creating a common identity with others of different ethno-confessional and linguistic groups: being Christian, or non-Turkish speaking, did not exclude one from identifying as an Ottoman.

However, histories written, and identities imagined, from within a nation-state discourse have tended to elide these other competing identities. Therefore it is imperative that as historians and scholars we consciously articulate, and then critically engage with, the interpretative frames and models we employ in our works: an unreflective employment of essentialist explanations of nationalism or identity can lead to the forgetting of earlier identities and the reification of current identities as eternal, immutable and unchanging. It should be remembered that identities in this region of South-east Europe have been, and are constantly, in the process of being re-invented: today's identities are just that – today's.

References

Manuscripts

Istanbul, Millet Kütüphanesi [National Library], A.E.Tar. 190: Cafer 'Iyani Cihadname-i Tiryaki Hasan Paşa [The Jihad narrative of Tiryaki Hasan Pasha].

Istanbul, Millet Kütüphanesi [National Library], A.E.Tar. 187: Tarih-i Tiryaki Hasan Paşa [The History of Tiryaki Hasan Pasha] fols 1v–61r.

London, British Library, O.R.12961, 1203 H./1789 C.E.: Hikaye-i Tiryaki Gazi Hasan Paşa [The Story of Tiryaki Gazi Hasan Pasha] inscribed by Salih Ağa Divitdar on 21 March 1789 fols 1v-95r.

Bibliography

Ahmed Refik 1318 H. [1900–1 C.E.]: Meşhur Osmanlı Komandanlar [Famous Ottoman commanders]. Istanbul: Kitaphane-i Islam ve Askeri Ibrahim Hilmi.

Anderson, Benedict 1991: Imagined Communities: Reflections on the Origins and Spread of Nationalism. London: Verso [first edition 1983].

Bayerle, Gustav 1973: Ottoman Tributes in Hungary: According to Sixteenth Century Tapu Registers of Novigrad. The Hague, Paris: Mouton (= Near and Middle East Monographs 8).

Baysun, Cavid 1950: Tiryaki Hasan Paşa ve Kanije Savaşı [Tiryaki Hasan Pasha and the Kanije War]. Istanbul: Milli Eğitim Basımevi (= Milli Eğitim Bakanlığı Köy Kitaplığı no.15).

Bourdieu, Pierre 1991: Language and Symbolic Power: the Economy of Linguistic Exchanges. Ed. John B. Thompson. Cambridge: Polity, Basil Blackwell.

Çabuk, Vahit 1978: Tiryaki Hasan Paşa'nın Gazaları ve Kanije Savunması [The campaigns of Tiryaki Hasan Pasha and the defence of Kanije]. Istanbul: Tercuman 1001 Temel Eser.

Dávid, Geza 1995: Administration in Ottoman Europe. In: Metin Kunt, Christine Woodhead (eds.), Süleyman the Magnificent and his Age. The Ottoman Empire in the Early Modern World. London, New York: Longman, 71–90.

Dávid, Geza, Pal Fodor 2000: Introduction. In: Geza Dávid, Pal Fodor (eds.), Ottomans, Hungarians, and Habsburgs in Central Europe: The Military Confines in the Era of Ottoman Conquest. Leiden: Brill, xi–xxvii.

Dávid, Geza, Pal Fodor 2002: Hungarian Studies in Ottoman History. In: Fikret Adanir, Suraiya Faroqhi (eds.), The Ottomans and the Balkans: A Discussion of Historiography. Leiden: Brill, 305–350.

Eller, J. D., R. M. Coughlan 1993: The Poverty of Primordialism: The Demystification of Ethnic Attachments. In: Ethnic and Racial Studies 16, 2: 183–201.

Ersanlı, Büsra 2002: The Ottoman Empire in the Historiography of the Kemalist Era: A Theory of Fatal Decline. In: Fikret Adanir, Suraiya Faroqhi (eds.), The Ottomans and the Balkans: A Discussion of Historiography. Leiden: Brill, 115–54.

Ersever, H. Ziya 1986: Kanije Savunması ve Tiryaki Hasan Paşa [The defence of Kanije and Tiryaki Hasan Pasha]. Ankara: Basımevi (= Türk Asker Büyükleri ve Türk Zaferleri Seri no. 12, Genelkurmay Askeri Tarih ve Stratejik Etüt Baskanlığı Yayınları Gnkur).

Fekete, Lajos 1932: Türkische Schriften aus dem Archive des Palatins Niklaus Esterhazy 1606–1645. Budapest: Esterházy Miklós nadór iratai [2].

Fekete, Lajos 1944: Budapest a törökkorban [Budapest under Turkish rule]. Budapest.

Fine, John V. A. 2006: When Ethnicity Did not Matter in the Balkans. A Study of Identity in Pre-Nationalist Croatia, Dalmatia, and Slavonia in the Medieval and Early-Modern Periods. Ann Arbor: The University of Michigan Press.

Finkel, Caroline 1992: French Mercenaries in the Habsburg-Ottoman War of 1583–1606. The Desertion of the Papa Garrison to the Ottomans in 1600. In: Bulletin of the School of Oriental and Africa Studies 55, 3: 451–471.

Frantz, Eva Anne 2007: Regional Identities in Late Ottoman Kosovo (1870–1913). Paper given at the 4th InASEA Conference: Region, Regional Identity and Regionalism in Southeastern Europe. Timişoara, Romania, 24–27 May 2007.

Gellner, Ernest, 1964: Thought and Change. London: Weidenfeld and Nicholson.

Hayes, C. 1955: The Historical Evolution of Modern Nationalism. New York: Macmillan [first edition 1931].

Hegyi, Klara 1975: Egy világbirodalom végvidékén [On the borders of a world-empire]. Budapest.

Hegyi, Klara 1995: Török berendezkedés Magyarországon [Ottoman administration in Hungary]. Budapest (= Historiá Könyvtár, Monográfiák 7).

Heywood, Colin 1999: The Frontier in Ottoman History. In: Daniel Power, Naomi Standen (eds.), Frontiers in Question: Eurasia Borderlands 700–1700. Basingstoke: Macmillan, 228–250.

Hickok, M.R. 1997: Ottoman Military Administration in Eighteenth Century Bosnia. Leiden: Brill.

Hobsbawm, Eric 1998: On History. London: Abacus [first ed. 1997].

Hobsbawm, Eric, Terrance Ranger (eds.) 1983: The Invention of Tradition. Cambridge: Cambridge UP.

Ivanič, Roz 1998: Writing and Identity: the Discoursal Construction of Identity in Academic Writing. Amsterdam, Philadelphia: John Benjamins.

Joseph, John, E. 2004: Language and Identity: National, Ethnic, Religious. Basingstoke: Palgrave Macmillan.

Kedourie, Elie 1960: Nationalism. London: Hutchinson [4th ed. Oxford, Cambridge, Mass.: Blackwell, 1993].

Kunt, Metin Ibrahim 1974: Ethnic-Regional *(Cins)* Solidarity in the Seventeenth Century Ottoman Establishment. In: International Journal of Middle East Studies 5, 3: 233–239.

Minkov, Anton 2004: Conversion to Islam in the Balkans: Kisve Bahası Petitions and Ottoman Social Life, 1670–1730. Leiden: Brill.

Namık Kemal 1311 [1893]: Kanije. Istanbul: Ebuzziya Matbaası.[20]

Norton, Claire 2004: The Remembrance of the Sieges of Kanije in the Construction of Late Ottoman and Modern Turkish Identities. In: Parergon 21, 1: 133–53.

Norton, Claire 2005: Plural Pasts: The Role of Function and Audience in the Creation of Meaning in Ottoman and Modern Turkish Accounts of the Siege of Nagykanizsa. PhD thesis, University of Birmingham.

Norton, Claire 2005b: "The Lutheran is the Turks' luck": Imagining Religious Identity, Alliance and Conflict on the Habsburg-Ottoman Marches in an Account of the Sieges of Nagykanizsa 1600 and 1601. In: Marlene Kurz, Martin Scheutz, Karl Vocelka, Thomas Winkelbauer (eds.), Das Osmanische Reich und die Habsburgermonarchie in der Neuzeit. Vienna: Österreichische Akademie der Wissenschaften (= Mitteilungen des Instituts für Österreichische Geschichtsforschung, suppl. vol. 49), 67–81.

Norton, Claire 2007: Narrating the "Yoke of Oppression" Twentieth-Century Hungarian Scholarship of the Ottoman-Hungarian Borderlands. In: Claire Norton (ed.), Nationalism, Historiography and the (Re)Construction of the Past. Washington: New Academia Press, 187–200.

Norton, Claire 2007b: Smack-Head Hasan: Why Are All Turkic Superheroes Intemperate, Treacherous, or Stupid? In: Angela Ndalianis, Chris Mackie, Wendy Haslem (eds.), Super/heroes. Washington: New Academia Press, 263–274.

Özkırımlı, Umit 2000: Theories of Nationalism: A Critical Introduction. Basingstoke: Palgrave.

Pakalın, M.Z. 1966: Sekbân. In: İslam Ansiklopedisi 10: 325–327.

Power, Daniel, Naomi Standen 1999: Introduction. In: Daniel Power, Naomi Standen (eds.), Frontiers in Question: Eurasia Borderlands 700–1700. Basingstoke: Macmillan.

Renan, E. 1990 [1882]: What is a Nation? In: Homi Bhabha (ed.), Nation and Narration. London: Routledge, 8–22.

Sapir, Edward 1949: Selected Writings in Language, Culture, and Personality. Ed. Davod G. Mandelbaum. Berkeley, Los Angeles: University of California Press.

---

[20] Kanije was first published under the pseudonym of Ahmed Nafiz by the Hayal Matbaasi in 1290 [1873]. It was republished in 1303 [1886] and 1311 [1893] by Ebuzziya Matbaası and in 1335 [1917] by the Matbaa-i Amire. It has also been translated into Turkish: Namık Kemal 1941: Kanije. trans. Hakki Tarik. Istanbul: Vakit Basımevi.

Savaşkurt, Avni 1945: Kanije Mudafaası [The defence of Kanije]. Istanbul: Askeri Matbaası (= Askeri Mecmuanın Tarih Kısmıseri 138).

Shapiro, M. 1997: Violent Cartographies: Mapping Cultures of War. London, Minneapolis: University of Minnesota Press.

Stein, Mark 2007: Guarding the Frontier: Ottoman Border Forts and Garrisons in Europe. London: Tauris Academic Studies.

Sugar, Peter 1971: The Ottoman "Professional Prisoner" on the Western Borders of the Empire in the Sixteenth and Seventeenth Centuries. In: Études Balkaniques 7: 82–91.

White, Richard 1991: The Middle Ground: Indians, Empires, and Republics in the Great Lakes Region, 1650–1815. Cambridge: Cambridge UP.

Abstract

This article will explore how identity is reflected and contested in various inscriptions of the siege of Nagykanizsa castle in today's Hungary. It will challenge the view that the early modern Habsburg-Ottoman frontier was characterised by distinct and antagonistic communities defined along ethno-confessional or linguistic fault-lines. Instead it will argue that such a position arises from the pervasive influence of the essentialist understanding of nationalism and the dominance of the nation-state interpretative frame as a means of apprehending and constructing the past. It will present evidence that early modern communities inhabiting this border region articulated and performed a multiplicity of overlapping and often conflicting identities more often centred around the fulcrums of class, occupation, local loyalties to commanders or elites and specific regional circumstances and customs. Then it will look in more detail at Ottoman and modern Turkish inscriptions of the sieges of Nagykanizsa and consider how and why these narratives changed, and earlier identities were forgotten, as they were re-inscribed within a nation state interpretative framework by nineteenth-century Ottoman, and twentieth-century Turkish scholars.

Ethnizität und grenzüberschreitende ökonomische Beziehungen in der ungarisch-slowakischen Grenzregion

Wolfgang Aschauer, Chemnitz

Einführung

Staatsgrenzen beeinflussen Ausmaß und Gestaltung ökonomischer Aktivitäten tiefgreifend: Sie wirken sich sowohl auf die Grenzregion als auch auf die grenzüberschreitenden Wirtschaftsbeziehungen aus. Untersuchungen über Grenzen konzentrieren sich daher oft auf Differenzen in Preisen, Löhnen, Warenverfügbarkeiten, Steuern, Gesetzen und anderen Regulationsformen.

Aus diesem Blickwinkel ist es zunächst alles andere als selbstverständlich, dass auch Ethnizität als ein Element von Kultur von Relevanz für die Wirtschaft, im vorliegenden Fall für grenzüberschreitende Wirtschaftsbeziehungen, ist oder zumindest sein könnte. Daher soll im folgenden zunächst die Rolle von Kultur innerhalb der Ökonomie betrachtet werden. Dabei wird insbesondere auf die Entstehung von Netzwerken eingegangen und auf die Bedeutung von darauf basierenden grenzüberschreitenden Beziehungen für die Regionalentwicklung. In einem zweiten Schritt soll dann am empirischen Beispiel das Augenmerk auf Ethnizität als ein Element von Kultur und einen Faktor von Wirtschaftsbeziehungen im slowakisch-ungarischen Grenzraum gerichtet werden. Dabei soll untersucht werden, welche Formen grenzüberschreitender Interaktion existieren und welche Auswirkungen sie auf die Regionalentwicklung haben. Hierzu werden die zwei wichtigsten sog. ethnische Gruppen in dieser Grenzregion betrachtet: die Ungarn in der Slowakei und die Roma bzw. Zigeuner in der Slowakei und in Ungarn.

Zunächst jedoch gilt es zu untersuchen, warum es nötig ist, sich mit kulturellen Gruppen zu beschäftigen, wenn grenzüberschreitende Wirtschaftsbeziehungen betrachtet werden sollen, d. h. welche Verbindung zwischen Ökonomie und Kultur besteht. Dies soll an Hand des Begriffs „Vertrauen“ geschehen.

Formen der Organisation von Vertrauen

Keine Gesellschaft kann ohne ein Mindestmaß an Vertrauen zwischen ihren Mitgliedern funktionieren. Wie Piotr Sztompka (1999: 22) schreibt, „facing other people we often remain in the condition of uncertainty, bafflement, and surprise“. Diese doppelte Kontingenz führt zu einer Situation, in der keiner der Beteiligten zu handeln wagt. Der einzige Ausweg aus dieser Situation ist es, Vertrauen in die

Reaktion des jeweils anderen zu haben, so etwa in Form von vorhersehbaren Handlungsweisen unter gegebenen Umständen (Luhmann 2000). Dabei können verschiedene Formen von Vertrauen identifiziert werden. Rose-Ackerman (1999, 2001) unterscheidet zwischen einseitiger Verlässlichkeit oder Vertrauenswürdigkeit und zweiseitigem oder reziprokem Vertrauen.

Reziprokes Vertrauen ist Vertrauen zwischen zwei Personen, das innerhalb von Interaktionen besteht. Die Verbindung zwischen den Personen kann auf Überlegungen in bezug auf die Interessen des jeweils anderen basieren, auf Gefühlen von persönlicher Zuneigung und Verantwortung, wie es vor allem für Verwandtschaftsbeziehungen charakteristisch sein kann, oder auf gemeinsamen Werten. Reziprokes Vertrauen gründet auf persönlichen Bindungen, wird innerhalb von Interaktionen realisiert und konstituiert dadurch ein Netz von persönlichen Beziehungen (Abraham 2003).

Einseitiges Vertrauen kann ebenfalls in einer Beziehung zwischen zwei Personen vorkommen, z. B. in Form von Vertrauen gegenüber einer Person mit speziellen Fertigkeiten und Kenntnissen wie etwa gegenüber einem Arzt, einem Rechtsanwalt oder einem wissenschaftlichen Experten (Sztompka 1999: 46–48). Der Unterschied zum reziproken Vertrauen liegt hierbei nicht in der Interaktion als solcher, sondern in deren Qualität. Einseitiges Vertrauen bedeutet, dass es für die Person, der vertraut wird, irrelevant ist, ob die andere Person ebenfalls vertrauenswürdig ist oder nicht.

Der wichtigste Typ von einseitigem Vertrauen wird jedoch nicht in Interaktionen zwischen Einzelpersonen realisiert, sondern in Form von Vertrauen in das Funktionieren von Organisationen.

> „This is rule-based trustworthiness - that is, trust that an organisation's rules will be followed in a neutral and predictable way. One trusts the institution's rules irrespective of the particular people occupying positions of trust and authority“ (Rose-Ackerman 2001: 8).

Sowohl das einseitige als auch das reziproke Vertrauen sind unerlässliche Elemente von gesellschaftlichem Leben. Ihre jeweilige Bedeutung hat jedoch im Laufe der Geschichte Veränderungen erfahren.

> „In small and pre-modern societies individuals characteristically relate repeatedly with the same persons in practically all situations. The networks used to acquire things are primarily informal, face-to-face associations of people. Members of small societies tend to move within culturally prescribed roles, and these roles include the specification of mutual assistance. Everyone knows who is to be trusted and who is to be approached for help; confidence and trust is implicit in the social relation. As a society grows and becomes more complex the social, economic and occupational mobility

of its members increases and the total roles found in small societies become fragmented. In an ideal modern society where collective action is institutionalised, the individual is led increasingly to depend on formal institutions and informal interpersonal networks are relegated to certain areas such as affective aspects of social life (kinship, friendship)" (Adler Lomnitz, Sheinbaum 2001: 2).

Im Laufe der Entwicklung von der vormodernen zur modernen Gesellschaft hat eine Bedeutungsverschiebung zwischen den genannten Formen von Vertrauen stattgefunden. Dies steht nicht nur in Verbindung mit dem Bedeutungsverlust des reziproken Vertrauens zugunsten des einseitigen Vertrauens zumeist in formale Institutionen, sondern auch mit den permanenten Spannungen zwischen den beiden Typen von Vertrauen (Brie 2000). Zwischenmenschliches Vertrauen, das auf Empathie und auf Pflichtgefühl gegenüber Familienangehörigen und Freunden gründet, unterscheidet sich wesentlich vom Vertrauen in die Fairness und Neutralität von Institutionen und der dort Beschäftigten, wie es für komplexe moderne Gesellschaften charakteristisch ist. Die den modernen Gesellschaften inhärente Bestrebung, Organisationsformen zu schaffen, die neutral und ohne Rücksicht auf die Einzelperson funktionieren, konfligiert mit reziprokem, gefühlsbasiertem Vertrauen, das von engen persönlichen Beziehungen oder Verwandtschaft abhängt.

„One who relies on affect-based trust may believe that the trusted person will favour her whether or not she fulfils the formal qualifications and will aid her even if it imposes some costs on him in his institutional role" (Rose-Ackerman 2001: 8).

Diese allgemeinen Tendenzen moderner Vertrauensbildung sind jedoch nicht ubiquitär. Denn auch den modernen Gesellschaften sind zahlreiche Exklusionsprozesse inhärent. So sehen sich diejenigen, denen es unmöglich erscheint, Vertrauen in öffentliche Institutionen zu entwickeln – etwa weil ihnen staatliche Einrichtungen nicht dieselben Rechte einräumen wie anderen Bürgern (was als Diskriminierung bezeichnet wird) – mit einem grundsätzlichen Problem konfrontiert: Wenn Institutionen unvorhersehbare oder vorhersehbar negative Auswirkungen haben, ist regelbasiertes oder Institutionen-Vertrauen offensichtlich widersinnig. Statt dessen scheint die geeignete Lösung des Problems in der Reduzierung sozialer Beziehungen auf solche, die auf reziprokem Vertrauen basieren (Familienbande u. ä.) zu liegen.[1] Dies ist jedoch in einer funktional differenzierten modernen Gesellschaft, in der alle Aspekte gesellschaftlichen Lebens eigenständigen funktionalen Systemen zugeordnet sind, unmöglich. Wenn aber das Vertrauen

---

[1] Zum Problem der institutionellen und privaten Vertrauens in den Transformationsländern s. die Beiträge in Roth 2007.

in Freunde u.a. nicht ausreicht für eine gesicherte Inklusion in die moderne Gesellschaft und zugleich kein Vertrauen in (üblicherweise staatliche) Institutionen existiert, dann gibt es nur eine Alternative: die Schaffung von *imaginiertem* Vertrauen. Eine Person vertraut einer anderen, weil sie annimmt, dass diese deshalb, weil sie derselben (z.B. ethnischen) Gruppe angehört, dieses Vertrauen nicht enttäuschen wird. Dieser Glaube wird aufrecht erhalten, obwohl es keinerlei Möglichkeit gibt, Vertrauensbruch auf persönlicher oder institutioneller Ebene zu sanktionieren.

Eine solche Situation ist wie geschaffen für Missbrauch. Die Ausbeutung von Migranten in ihrer Community ist nur ein Beispiel für dieses Problem. Die Schaffung von imaginiertem Vertrauen und die darauf basierende ökonomische Handlungsfähigkeit kann aber auch erfolgreich sein. Ethnische Mobilisierung kann Vertrauensbildung auf informeller Ebene erzwingen, sie kann die „imagined community" (Anderson 1991) wirklich werden lassen. Eine solche ethnisch begründete Solidarität kann sogar institutionalisiert werden, etwa in Form von politischer Repräsentation oder als ökonomisches Subsystem der Gesellschaft. Wenn eine große Zahl von Individuen andernfalls gesellschaftlich ausgeschlossen wäre, kann eine ethnische Organisation eine Vielzahl von Funktionen annehmen und so die Inklusion dieser Personen sichern. Imaginiertes Vertrauen wird dadurch in eine Art institutionen-basiertes Vertrauen umgesetzt. Auf diesem Weg wird auch die imaginierte Gemeinschaft in ein real existierendes gesellschaftliches System umgewandelt, zumeist auf der Grundlage der Organisationsform des Netzwerkes (Granovetter 1992).

Vertrauen als Grundlage nicht nur von wirtschaftlichen Aktivitäten kann daher in verschiedenen Formen realisiert werden:

1. Vertrauen kann vorliegen als Vertrauen in staatliche Einrichtungen, in gesetzliche Regelungen oder in die Struktur des Staates insgesamt.
2. Vertrauen kann als zwischenmenschliches Vertrauen auftreten, basierend auf Verwandtschaft, gemeinsamen Werten oder anderen Faktoren.
3. Vertrauen kann auf Organisationsebene existieren. Damit ist weder öffentliches Vertrauen noch solches in die Staatsstrukturen angesprochen, sondern Vertrauen in gesellschaftliche Netzwerke. Ein derartiges Netzwerk ist abhängig von einer fortgeschrittenen Form des zwischenmenschlichen Vertrauens; es unterscheidet sich vom zwischenmenschlichen Vertrauen, wie es in einfachen Interaktionen auftritt, durch den Einbezug einer großen Anzahl von Mitgliedern. Vertrauen gegenüber einem Mitglied des Netzwerks hängt nicht von der Kenntnis der individuellen Vertrauenswürdigkeit des einzelnen ab, sondern davon, dass es Mitglied des Netzwerks ist. Die Existenz des Netzwerks selbst impliziert Vertrauen.

Von diesem Gesichtspunkt aus ist das Vertrauen in die Mitglieder eines Netzwerks ähnlich dem Vertrauen in staatliche Institutionen. Der grundlegende Unterschied liegt in der Exklusivität des Netzwerks. Ein Netzwerk ist im Gegensatz zu gesetzlichen Regelungen, die für alle Bürger gültig sind, hochselektiv. Netzwerke sind daher informell konzipiert, während Formen öffentlicher oder staatlicher Kooperation formal geregelt sind.

Die Rolle von Netzwerkbeziehungen für wirtschaftliche Aktivitäten

Die Bildung von Netzwerken ist die Reaktion auf imaginierte oder reale gesellschaftliche Exklusion, wie sie allen modernen Gesellschaften inhärent ist (Luhmann 1998: 630–634). Vertrauen auf diese Art aufzubauen und zu organisieren ist jedoch nicht nur ein grundsätzlicher Bestandteil gesellschaftlichen Lebens, sondern auch spezifischen, lokalen Faktoren unterworfen, so etwa den Inklusions- und Exklusionsmechanismen des jeweiligen Nationalstaates. Der vorliegende Artikel beschäftigt sich mit der slowakisch-ungarischen Grenzregion; hier ist der wichtigste Prozess, der die Vertrauensbildung beeinflusst, die Transformation der (ehemals) sozialistischen Länder.

Die Transformationsforschung diskutiert die Frage persönlicher Netzwerke und ihrer Relevanz für Vertrauensbildung auf zwei Arten. Zum einen wird die Bedeutung von Netzwerken als unerlässliche Elemente des Sozialismus hervorgehoben. Wie Ledeneva (1998) zeigt, war der Zugang zu einer möglichst großen Zahl von Netzwerken der einzig effektive und damit normale Weg, persönliche Bedürfnisse im Sozialismus zu befriedigen. Unter den Bedingungen der Planwirtschaft mit ihrem inhärenten System von Knappheiten konnten zahlreiche Güter nur durch die Mitgliedschaft in einem Netzwerk erhalten werden. Die unsichere Verfügbarkeit von Waren machte es unerlässlich, gute Verbindungen auf Gegenseitigkeit zu vielen Leuten zu haben. Die Grundelemente dieser Art von Netzwerk waren die folgenden:

- *Gegenseitigkeit:* die Bereitschaft, den anderen Mitgliedern des Netzwerks beizustehen, unabhängig von einer sofortigen Gegenleistung;
- *Dauerhaftigkeit:* auch wenn kein sofortiger Hilfsbedarf besteht, werden die Kontakte für einen zukünftigen Bedarf aufrechterhalten;
- *Übertragbarkeit:* der Anspruch auf Unterstützungsgewährung kann durch Vermittlung von Netzwerkmitgliedern auf andere Personen übertragen werden;
- *moralische Legitimation:* die Grundlage des Netzwerks – der gemeinsame Vorteil – wird hinter Begriffen wie Freundschaft oder Nachbarschaft versteckt.

Netzwerke sind jedoch nicht nur auf der zwischenmenschlichen Ebene von Bedeutung. Forschungsarbeiten haben darauf hingewiesen, dass auch Netzwerke zwischen Unternehmen, d.h. zwischenbetriebliche persönliche Netzwerke hochrelevant waren (Bohle 1996). Da sie die Pflicht hatten, die zentralen Pläne zu erfüllen, mussten die Manager Kontakte zu anderen Unternehmen aufbauen, um Produktionsmaterialien zu erhalten oder Kunden für eigene Waren zu finden. Die Unternehmen konnten keine Marktbeziehungen zur Erfüllung dieser Verträge nutzen, sie mussten vielmehr verschiedene Formen persönlicher Kontakte aufbauen, um die Vorhersehbarkeit, Stabilität und Dauerhaftigkeit ihrer Wirtschaftsbeziehungen zu sichern. Gute persönliche Kontakte zwischen Managern - die oft zu großen Netzwerken ausgebaut wurden - waren daher ein unerlässlicher Bestandteil der Funktionsweise der sozialistischen Ökonomie; „managerial socialism served as a training ground and a place for the original accumulation of informal network assets (‚network capital') for informal and managerial elite action" (Adler Lomnitz, Sheinbaum 2001: 14). Darüber hinaus waren immer wiederkehrende Phasen des Kapitalmangels Grundlage und Ausgangsbedingung der Substituierung formal definierter Produktionszusammenhänge, für die große Investitionen nötig gewesen wären, durch informelle Lösungen auf individueller oder Gruppen-Ebene (Adler Lomnitz, Sheinbaum 2001: 14; vgl. Delhey, Newton 2002)

Folgt man verschiedenen Transformationstheoretikern, behielten diese Netzwerke während der Transformation ihre Bedeutung als Hauptquelle von Vertrauensbildung bei. Einzelpersonen und Unternehmen lernten, dass Netzwerke ökonomisch wesentlich nützlicher und effektiver sind als sich auf formale Regeln zu beziehen, wie sie vom Staat vorgeschrieben und organisiert sind. Daher behielten sie ihr gewohntes Verhalten bei. Auch wenn die Marktwirtschaft viele Gründe für Netzwerkbildung obsolet hat werden lassen (so ist es nun z. B. effektiver, Güter in einem Laden zu kaufen als es über Interaktionen im Netzwerk zu erhalten), bleiben in komplexeren Situationen Netzwerke ein effektives Mittel zum Erreichen von Zielen. In Situationen, in denen Kontakte zwischen Individuen oder Unternehmen und Staatsorganen eine Rolle spielen, kann die Unsicherheit über die Qualität einer solchen Beziehung vermindert werden, indem Bezug hergestellt wird zu existierenden Netzwerken oder indem zumindest deren grundlegendstes Element angewandt wird – Gegenseitigkeit, die bei Beteiligung staatlicher Stellen Korruption genannt wird.

Ein zweiter Ansatz interpretiert die Bedeutung von Netzwerken in der Transformation nicht in erster Linie als Erbe des Sozialismus, sondern als ein Resultat des Transformationsprozesses selbst. In den 1990er Jahren diskutierten vor allem Stark et al. (Stark 1997, Grabher, Stark 1997) das Problem, das aus der Tatsache entstand, dass die Transformationsphase oft das Verschwinden der sozialistischen Institutionen mit der abrupten Implementierung neuer Institutionen verband, was zu einem Mangel an ökonomisch wirksamem Vertrauen führte. Das Resultat war sowohl die Reduktion ökonomischer Aktivitäten als auch die Umleitung von Vertrauen hin zu persönlichen Verbindungen. Netzwerke entstanden demnach, um die Funktionen noch nicht existierender formaler Institutionen zu erfüllen, d. h. als ein Mittel, um die Marktteilnehmer mit notwendigem Vertrauen in ihre Partner zu versorgen. Netzwerkbeziehungen tauchten in Situationen auf, in denen die alten formalen Institutionen aufgehört hatten zu existieren und neue noch nicht aufgebaut waren. Aus diesem Blickwinkel zeigt die Existenz von Netzwerken, dass der Transformationsprozess noch immer abläuft. Dieses Verständnis von Vertrauen impliziert darüber hinaus, dass die Rolle von Netzwerkbeziehungen sich mit der fortschreitenden Etablierung von demokratischen Staatsstrukturen und der Marktwirtschaft vermindern wird.

Der dritte Aspekt von Vertrauensbildung durch Netzwerke - neben der Erklärung als Erbe des Sozialismus und als Element des Transformationsprozesses - bezieht sich auf die besondere Situation in Grenzregionen. In einer Grenzregion, d.h. in einer Region mit grenzüberschreitenden ökonomischen Aktivitäten, ist Institutionenvertrauen üblicherweise deutlich schwächer als im Binnenland. Grenzüberschreitende Wirtschaftstätigkeit kann nicht als ebenso sicher angesehen werden wie innerhalb desselben Landes. Dies ergibt sich nicht nur aus unterschiedlichen rechtlichen und ökonomischen Systemen, sondern auch aus verschiedenen informellen Regeln und Verhaltensweisen. Denn zumindest zu Beginn von grenzüberschreitenden Beziehungen muss Vertrauen erworben, aufgebaut und vertieft werden.

Grenzüberschreitende Beziehungen haben in Überlegungen zur Regionalentwicklung aber nicht nur einen Wert an sich, d.h. für die daran beteiligten Wirtschaftssubjekte. Politische Analysen der Regionalpolitik innerhalb der EU stimmen im wesentlichen darin überein, dass ökonomische Integration und Kooperation für eine Grenzregion als Ganze von Vorteil ist (Niebuhr, Stiller 2002). Um dies zu überprüfen, ist zunächst zu untersuchen, was unter Kooperation überhaupt zu verstehen ist und welche Formen von Kooperation zwischen Unternehmen existieren. Verschiedene Untersuchungen in ostmitteleuropäischen Grenzregionen zeigen ein recht einheitliches Bild. So ist als primäres Motiv der grenzüberschreitenden Aktivitäten die Marktexpansion anzusehen, d.h. der Wunsch, wichtige Kunden zu erreichen oder in den Markt insgesamt einzutreten. Der Zugang zu öffentlichen Aufträgen hat eine geringere, auf beiden Seiten in etwa gleiche Bedeutung. Motive im Bereich der Produktionskosten (Effizienzkriterien) sind allgemein weniger relevant als marktbezogene Motive. Die Evaluierung der tatsächlichen grenzüberschreitenden Beziehungen zeigt aber oft ein sehr geringes Ausmaß der Zufriedenheit mit deren Effekten; v.a. die Instabilität der Beziehungen und das unsichere institutionelle Umfeld beeinträchtigen die Kontakte (vgl. Hunya, Telegdy 2003).

Zwar zeigen sich unabhängig von auftretenden Problemen bei der Realisierung grenzüberschreitender Beziehungen zahlreiche Unternehmen gewillt, mit Unternehmen auf der jeweils anderen Seite der Grenze zu kooperieren. Dennoch können solche rein bilateralen Kontakte nicht als identisch mit der wirtschaftlichen Integration der Grenzregion angesehen werden. Die Bildung einer Region impliziert multilaterale Kooperation, d.h. die Integration der Regionalökonomie als Ganzer.

Deshalb schließt sich hier die Frage an, wie eine Region wirtschaftlich integriert werden kann, d. h. zu einer tatsächlichen Interaktionsregion werden kann, nicht nur zu einer deklaratorischen Region, wie sie etwa auf politischen Plänen gezeichnet wird.

Regionsbildung, Wirtschaftsentwicklung und Vertrauen

Eines der wichtigsten Beispiel für Regionsbildung, das in der Literatur diskutiert wird, ist das sog. „Dritte Italien". Dabei handelt es sich zwar um keine Grenzregion, aber dennoch um ein Musterbeispiel für Regionsbildung. In den 1980er Jahren stellten Regionalwissenschaftler ein enormes wirtschaftliches Wachstum in der norditalienischen Poebene fest, und dies, obwohl dort keinerlei große Unternehmen oder Betriebseinheiten existierten, wie es etwa für nördlich angrenzende Regionen mit Standorten wie Turin oder Mailand charakteristisch ist. Stattdessen fanden sich hier ausschließlich kleine und mittlere Unternehmen, die einen erstaunlichen Erfolg auf dem Weltmarkt erzielen konnten. Die Antwort auf die Frage nach den Gründen für diesen Erfolg fand die Regionalforschung in einer bestimmten Art von Kooperation zwischen den regionalen Unternehmen, die als *milieu innovateur* oder innovatives Milieu bezeichnet wurde.

Das Konzept des innovativen Milieus wurde entwickelt, um Innovationsprozesse von Kleinunternehmen innerhalb von Industriedistrikten zu verstehen. Das theoretische Konzept der innovativen Milieus wurde im Laufe der Zeit auf größere Räume und umfangreichere Produktionsformen ausgeweitet (Camagni 1991). Das Konzept des innovativen Milieus versteht Raumentwicklung als

> „effect of innovative processes and synergies developing over limited territorial areas. It is defined as a set of relations which bring together and integrate a local production system, a group of actors and representations and an industrial culture, and which generates a localised dynamic process of collective learning. Basic constituent elements of the local milieu are: mobility of specialised labour within the local labour market, innovation, imitation, inter-firm co-operation and linkages, common codes and conventions, and a common sense of belonging together" (Camagni 2003: 16).

Grundlegendes Element eines Milieus ist die räumliche Nähe, die nicht nur zu einer Reduktion von Produktions- und Transaktionskosten führt, sondern auch mit soziokultureller Nähe verbunden ist:

> „We can define it as the presence of shared models of behaviour, mutual trust, common language and representations, and common moral and cognitive codes. Geographic proximity and socio-cultural proximity mean there is a high probability of interaction and synergy between economic

> agents, of informal repeated contracts, of absence of opportunistic behaviours, of high division of labour and co-operation within the milieu. What can be called local relational capital, composed of co-operative attitudes, trust, cohesion and a sense of belonging together“ (Camagni 2003: 16).

Das lokale oder regionale innovative Milieu hat drei Elemente (vgl. Abb. 1):

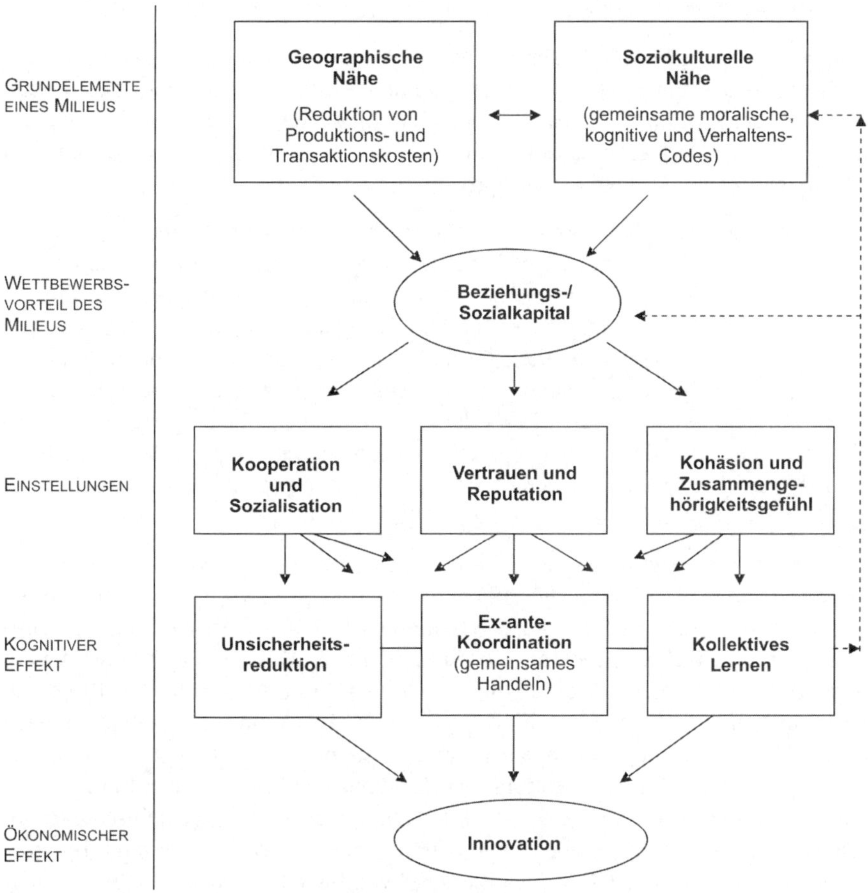

Abb.1: Grundlegende Elemente und Funktionen eines lokalen Milieus (Quelle: nach Camagni 2003:18)

Hier ist zum einen die Funktion der Unsicherheitsreduktion in Innovationsprozessen zu nennen:

> „Local relational space is seen as a means of reducing uncertainty, since - due to geographic and cultural proximity - collecting, evaluating and particularly transcoding information, selecting decisional routines, controlling and co-ordinating competitors are carried out collectively within the social context of the local and regional milieu“ (Camagni 2003: 17).

Zum anderen existiert die Funktion, lokale Akteure und kollektive Aktionsformen vor der eigentlichen Handlung auf der Grundlage von Konventionen, Verhaltensnormen, gemeinsamen Codes der sozialen Inklusion und Exklusion und von gegenseitigem Vertrauen zu koordinieren. Und zum dritten gibt es die Funktion der Unterstützung kollektiver Lernprozesse:

> „Learning processes require a host of tacit, immaterial, and informal exchanges, which happen usually mainly inside large firms. But an interesting parallel to this process exists, in the case of the local milieu: in this case the learning processes develop mainly outside the individual firm, but inside the local labour market, through the chains of professional upgrading, the mobility of skilled labour inside the area and the density of customer-supplier co-operation relations. The local milieu - which can be either an industrial district or a city - becomes the substratum in which long term ‚collective‘ learning processes are embedded to the advantage of the local economy“ (Camagni 2003: 18).

Die Abbildung zeigt, dass dem Milieu, das als Beziehungskapital bezeichnet werden kann und aus dem die (Interaktions-)Region erwächst, eine bestimmte Zusammensetzung von Verhaltensweisen entspricht. Die wirtschaftliche Zusammenarbeit gründet auf diesem Beziehungskapital. Dessen wichtigster Aspekt wiederum ist Vertrauen. Werden die oben aufgeführten Argumente zur Rolle von Vertrauen zusammengefasst, wird offensichtlich, dass kulturelle Elemente, die für die Sicherung von Vertrauen nötig sind, nicht nur Wirtschaften beeinflussen, welche die Transformation durchlaufen. Gemeinsame Werte, gemeinsame Denkweisen, gemeinsame Aspekte der Wirklichkeitswahrnehmung, gemeinsame Handlungsformen - kurz: die gemeinsame Kultur - beeinflussen tiefgreifend das wirtschaftliche Wachstum, die Innovationsgeschwindigkeit und den Wohlstand einer Region, da sie dazu beitragen, ein Vertrauensumfeld zu schaffen.

Dieses Verständnis der Rolle von Kultur innerhalb der Ökonomie im allgemeinen und in der Regionalentwicklung im Besonderen ist nun keine Eigenheit der Konzeption innovativer Milieus. Kulturelle Faktoren spielen in ähnlicher Weise auch in anderen Theorien zur Regionalökonomie, so etwa im Neoinstitutionalismus oder in der Theorie der lernenden Regionen eine wichtige Rolle.

Kultur als Element von Vertrauensbildung ist damit auch für grenzüberschreitende Regionsbildung von Bedeutung; eine Grenzregion kann als eine Sonderform einer vertrauenssuchenden und -bildenden Umgebung verstanden werden.

Hypothesen zur Empirie im ungarisch-slowakischen Grenzraum

Werden die skizzierten theoretischen Überlegungen als Ausgangspunkt empirischer Beobachtungen verwendet, lassen sich folgende Hypothesen über das Funktionieren grenzüberschreitender Kooperation und Regionalentwicklung im ungarisch-slowakischen Grenzgebiet ableiten:

1. Grenzüberschreitende Kooperation kann ökonomisch vorteilhaft für die Grenzregion sein.
2. Der beste Weg, eine Kooperationsregion zu schaffen, liegt in einer gemeinsamen vertrauensbildenden Umgebung, insbesondere in einem innovativen Milieu.
3. Großunternehmen benötigen ein solches Milieu nicht, aber im Fall von Klein- und Mittelunternehmen ist es notwendig, über ein Netzwerk an vertrauenswürdigen Beziehungen zu verfügen.
4. Netzwerkbeziehungen über Grenzen hinweg sind - zumindest solange keine starken formalen Beziehungen existieren - informell. Diese wiederum basieren auf gegenseitigem Vertrauen und einer gemeinsamen Kultur.

Wenn diese Hypothesen zutreffen, folgt aus ihnen, dass diejenigen Grenzregionen die besten Chancen für wirtschaftliches Wachstum haben, in denen auf beiden Seiten der Grenze dieselbe ethnische Gruppe lebt. Denn es sind gerade ethnische Bindungen, aus denen Vertrauen erwachsen kann, oder wie Horowitz es ausdrückt: „Ethnic affiliation provides a sense of security ... as well as a source of trust, certainty, reciprocal help, and protection“ (Horowitz 1993: 32).

Diese Argumentation ist deutlich substantieller als die sehr vagen Stellungnahmen in zahlreichen politischen Reden, wonach ethnische Gruppen eine Brücke zwischen zwei Ländern bilden können. Daher wurden im ersten Teil des Artikels konkrete Überlegungen vorgestellt, die eine erhöhte Wahrscheinlichkeit von grenzüberschreitenden Beziehungen postulieren, wenn diese über Kontakte innerhalb einer ethnischen Gruppe realisiert werden. Solch eine ethnische Gruppe kann die Möglichkeit zur Bildung eines informellen Netzwerks und eines innovativen Milieus bieten, was als Grundlage für wirtschaftliche Entwicklung dienen kann. Die slowakisch-ungarische Grenzregion bietet die Möglichkeit, diese Argumente zu überprüfen, indem sie auf die Sphäre von Ethnizität angewandt werden. Es gilt demnach die Frage zu untersuchen, in welcher Weise Ethnizität als Form einer angenommenen gemeinsamen Kultur sich förderlich auf grenzüberschreitende Wirtschaftsbeziehungen auswirkt.

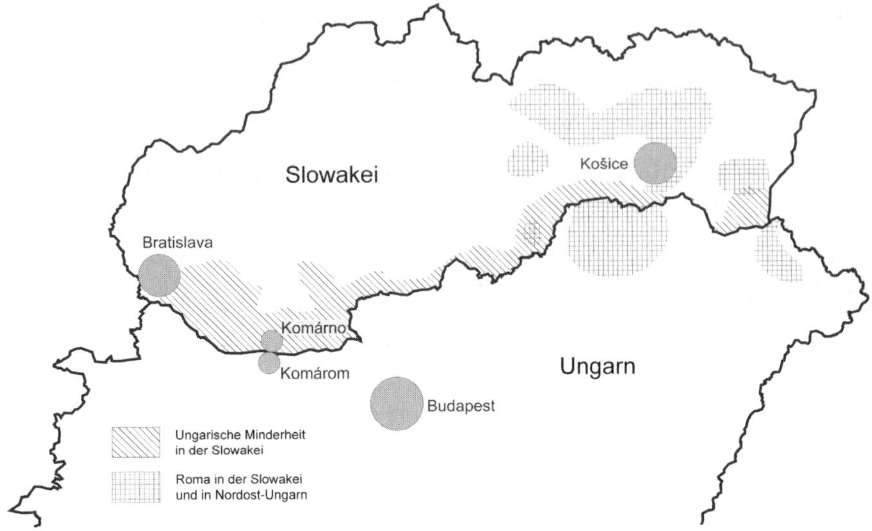

Abb. 2: Ethnische Gruppen in der ungarisch-slowakischen Grenzregion (Quelle: Eigener Entwurf)

Die beiden größten ethnischen Gruppen, die auf beiden Seiten der Grenze wohnen, sind die Ungarn und die Roma. Die Karte (Abb. 2) zeigt die Siedlungsgebiete der Ungarn in der Slowakei und der Roma in beiden Ländern. Die meisten ethnischen Ungarn - gemessen auf der Grundlage der Muttersprache, wie sie bei der Volkszählung angegeben wurde - sind entlang der gemeinsamen Grenze zu finden, konzentriert vor allem im Südwesten der Slowakei. Etwa 10% der slowakischen Bevölkerung von insges. 5,5 Mio. Einwohnern wird zu dieser ethnischen Gruppe gezählt. Während diese Zahl überwiegend als zutreffend verstanden wird, wird die Anzahl der Roma zumeist recht kontrovers diskutiert. So besteht eine sehr große Differenz zwischen der Zahl der Roma, die sich selbst als solche (oder auch als Zigeuner) bezeichnen - bei der Volkszählung 2001 waren es rund 45 000 - und verschiedenen staatlichen oder wissenschaftlichen Schätzungen, die von etwa einer halben Million Roma in der Slowakei ausgehen.

In Ungarn ist der Unterschied zwischen der Volkszählung und den Schätzungen deutlich geringer: den 175 000 Roma lt. Volkszählung steht eine geschätzte halbe Million gegenüber. Die Karte zeigt ausschließlich die „Volkszählungs-Roma“, deren größter Teil im Hinblick auf die Grenzregion in der Ostslowakei und in Nordost-Ungarn lebt.

Angesichts der Nähe der beiden ethnischen Gruppen zu ihrem jeweiligen Gegenüber auf der anderen Seite der Grenze können diese Gruppen empirisch dazu herangezogen werden, die Rolle von Kultur oder Ethnizität innerhalb ökonomischer Beziehungen zu untersuchen.

Die Ungarn im ungarisch-slowakischen Grenzgebiet

Im Fall der Ungarn im ungarisch-slowakischen Grenzgebiet sind zunächst einige allgemeine Bemerkungen zur raumwirtschaftlichen Lage voranzuschicken. Nordwest-Ungarn, insbesondere die Gebiete entlang der Straßenverbindung Wien-Budapest, ist der wohlhabendste und am schnellsten sich entwickelnde Teil des Landes nach der Hauptstadt Budapest. Dasselbe kann für Bratislava und seine Umgebung festgestellt werden. Beide Regionen sind nicht nur Standort multinationaler Unternehmen wie etwa Škoda/Volkswagen in Bratislava, Suzuki in Esztergom oder Audi in Győr, sondern ziehen auch viele kleine Firmen und Arbeitskräfte aus nahe gelegenen Städten und Dörfern an. Diese Regionen wachsen außerdem nicht nur sehr schnell und haben Pionierfunktion für das wirtschaftliche Wachstum, sondern sind auch treibendes Element der sozialen und kulturellen Modernisierung Ostmitteleuropas. Hier können sogenannte moderne, d. h. den Anforderungen der funktional differenzierten Gesellschaft entsprechende Verhaltensweisen wie etwa rationales Verhalten und moderne Werte wie das Leistungsprinzip weitaus öfter beobachtet werden als in anderen Teilen der Slowakei und Ungarns (vgl. dazu auch Aschauer 1995).

Die Ungarn v. a. in der West-Slowakei werden von beiden Prozessen beeinflusst. Obwohl die slowakische Seite der Grenzregion bis heute nicht sehr stark entwickelt ist, kann sie dennoch am Wachstum der Region Bratislava und Nordwest-Ungarns partizipieren, was durch einige Beispiele illustriert werden kann: Aufgrund von Arbeitskräftemangel im Suzuki-Betrieb im ungarischen Esztergom, der auch von der geringen Bereitschaft ungarischer Arbeitskräfte zu permanenter oder temporärer Migration hervorgerufen wurde, holt das Unternehmen slowakische Arbeiter mit Bussen von der anderen Seite der Grenze. Diese Arbeitskräfte sind zumeist Angehörige der ungarischen Minderheit. Ihre ungarische Muttersprache ist dabei ein wichtiges Argument, ihnen den Arbeitsplatz anzubieten, und dies nicht nur bei Suzuki, sondern auch in anderen nahe gelegenen Unternehmen.

Das zweite Beispiel ist die Doppelstadt Komárno und Komárom (Abb. 2). Komárno, der Kern der alten Stadt, die auf beiden Seiten der Donau lag, wurde im Friedensvertrag von Trianon der Slowakei zugeschlagen. Seit dieser Zeit entwickelte sich Komárom, das früher die Vorstadt auf der ungarischen Seite war, zu einer selbständigen Kleinstadt. Heute ist einer der wichtigsten Wirtschaftszweige in Komárno, dem slowakischen Teil der Stadt, der ungarische Einkaufstourismus, basierend auf dem relativ hohen Einkommen auf der ungarischen Seite. Komárom/

Komárno ist ein gutes Beispiel für alltägliche grenzüberschreitende Beziehungen und dies nicht nur aufgrund des Einkaufstourismus, sondern auch wegen der regelmäßigen Kontakte etwa zwischen den Stadtverwaltungen, wenn Verkehrsprobleme besprochen werden müssen, oder zwischen Schulen und Kulturgruppen auf beiden Seiten der Grenze.

In Komárno wurde zudem im Oktober 2004 eine ungarisch-sprachige Universität gegründet. Die Universität, die vom slowakischen Staat, vom ungarischen Staat und von der Europäischen Union finanziert wird, ist in erster Linie für Angehörige der ungarischen Minderheit bestimmt. Die guten Lernbedingungen machen es jedoch wahrscheinlich, dass sie auch Ungarn von der anderen Seite der Grenze anziehen wird, aber auch andere Studenten aus der Slowakei. Aufgegliederte Zahlen über die Studierenden liegen bisher jedoch noch nicht vor.

Bereits die wenigen Beispiele zeigen, dass es zahlreiche grenzüberschreitende Verbindungen und Aktivitäten gibt, all dies unter wirtschaftlich günstigen Gegebenheiten. Ethnische Ungarn nehmen an all diesen Aktivitäten teil. Sie pendeln aus der Slowakei nach Ungarn, sie sind Einkaufstouristen in Grenzstädten, sie sind Studenten in der ungarisch-sprachigen Universität, die dabei ist, nicht nur eine Bildungseinrichtung zu sein, sondern auch der Kern der regionalen intellektuellen und schließlich sogar der ökonomischen Entwicklung. Bei jeder Koinzidenz ist jedoch zu fragen, ob auch Kausalität vorliegt, hier also, ob tatsächlich die Mitgliedschaft in derselben ethnischen Gruppe diese Prozesse vorantreibt, noch genauer: ob es einen Bedarf an personengebundenem Vertrauen gibt, der Menschen dazu bringt, Kontakte zu Mitgliedern derselben Gruppe zu präferieren. Wahrscheinlich muss die Antwort im vorliegenden Fall „nein" lauten.

Für Suzuki spielt Ethnizität keine Rolle, der einzige Faktor von Bedeutung ist die Kenntnis der ungarischen Sprache. Für Einkaufstouristen sind Preise wichtig, nicht ethnische Beziehungen. Die sozioökonomischen Verhältnisse dieser Grenzregion bestimmen also die grenzüberschreitenden Kontakte. Der Prozess der Entwicklung von Institutionenvertrauen hat die Bindungen von Familie und Ethnizität geschwächt. Es besteht kein Bedarf an Vertrauen, das über einer reale oder imaginierte Gemeinschaft gewonnen wird, weil die formalen Institutionen als effektiv wirksam begriffen werden. Damit können die Effekte der Modernisierung sowohl die günstigen ökonomischen Bedingungen als auch das Ausmaß der grenzüberschreitenden Verbindungen und Aktivitäten in zufriedenstellendem Umfang erklären; Ethnizität hat demgegenüber nur geringe Erklärungskapazität.

Zwei wichtige Ausnahmen sollen hier jedoch nicht unterschlagen werden. Zum einen sind – wenig überraschend – alle Aktivitäten, die an kulturelle und Bildungs-Themen gebunden sind, mit der Mitgliedschaft in derselben ethnischen bzw. Sprach-Gruppe verbunden. Ungarischsprachige Kulturveranstaltungen in Komárom/Komárno gründen sich auf dem Medium der ungarischen Sprache und verstärken dadurch zugleich deren Bedeutung. Zum anderen hat die ungarische

Außenpolitik die Tendenz so zu handeln, als wäre Ungarn das Heimatland als Auslandsungarn.[2] Dies führt zu politischen Maßnahmen wie etwa der Gewährung einer Art doppelter Staatsbürgerschaft „light", wie sie sich im sog. Status-Gesetz findet – einem ungarischen Gesetz, das Auswirkungen auf die Bürger eines anderen Staates hat (hier: die ethnischen Ungarn in der Slowakei). Diese Art von Politik hat einen überwiegend negativen Einfluss auf die bilateralen Beziehungen und behindert die Verbesserung der grenzüberschreitenden Beziehungen. Auf der Mikroebene hinterlässt diese Politik aber nur geringe Spuren und ändert daher die geschilderte Situation nur in geringem Ausmaß.

Insgesamt kann festgestellt werden, dass Kooperationsnetzwerke zwischen Ungarn auf beiden Seiten der Grenze nicht nur regionaler Natur sind, sondern immer auch Teil internationaler Politik, und zwar

1. als Teil ungarischer politischer Bestrebungen, die ehemals ungarischen Gebiete mit dem Kernland auf kultureller oder persönlicher Ebene wiederzuvereinigen;
2. als Teil slowakischer politischer Anstrengungen, den Einfluss ungarischer staatlicher Aktivitäten auf das eigene Territorium zu reduzieren;
3. als Teil der Versuche seitens der EU, die Situation durch wachsame Beobachtung der Einflussnahme beider Seiten auf die grenzüberschreitenden Beziehungen zu kontrollieren.

Die Roma im ungarisch-slowakischen Grenzgebiet

Ganz anders sieht es bei den grenzüberschreitenden Beziehungen der anderen ethnischen Gruppe aus, die in der Grenzregion anzutreffen ist, bei den Roma, die vor allem im östlichen Teil des Grenzgebiets zu finden sind. Bereits aus ökonomischer Sicht unterscheidet sich der östliche Teil der slowakisch-ungarischen Grenze tiefgreifend vom westlichen Teil. Während des Sozialismus wurden beide Seiten dieser Grenzregion durch die Ansiedlung von Großunternehmen der Schwerindustrie, in denen die regionalen Arbeitskräfte Arbeitsplätze und Einkommen fanden, zu entwickeln versucht. Mit dem Ende des Sozialismus geriet die regionale Schwerindustrie in eine Krise, die zu einer Krise der gesamten Regionalökonomie wurde. Diese Krise führte zu einer selektiven Arbeitsplatzreduktion: Fast alle Roma der Region verloren ihre (zumeist un- oder angelernten) Arbeitsplätze, und dies auf beiden Seiten der Grenze.

Investitionen wie diejenige von U.S. Steel in Košice (Abb. 2), der zweitgrößten Stadt der Slowakei und in der Grenzregion gelegen, konnte die schwierige

---

[2] Dies illustriert die Bemerkung des ersten nachsozialistischen ungarischen Ministerpräsidenten József Antall, der sich nach seiner Wahl als Ministerpräsident von 15 Millionen Ungarn bezeichnete. Ungarn hat aber nur etwa 10 Millionen Einwohner.

Situation der Regionalökonomie nicht wesentlich beeinflussen. In dieser Situation setzen Regionalplaner ebenso wie europäische Pläne zur Regionalentwicklung ihre Hoffnungen in regionale Kooperationen, die regionales Wirtschaftswachstum entwickeln oder zumindest initiieren sollen.

In diesen Plänen könnten die Roma – entsprechend den oben diskutierten Theorien über die Bedeutung von gemeinsamer Kultur für die Regionalentwicklung – eine wichtige Rolle spielen aufgrund der grenzüberschreitenden Kooperation, von der angenommen wird, dass sie innerhalb ihrer ethnischen Gemeinschaft existiert. Es gilt daher zu untersuchen, inwieweit eine solche Annahme zutrifft, d. h. ob diese ethnische Gemeinschaft in der Lage ist, grenzüberschreitende ökonomische Beziehungen zu initiieren oder zumindest aufrechtzuerhalten.

Zunächst ist festzustellen, dass die Mehrheit der Roma eine sehr arme Bevölkerung ist. In ihrer profunden Studie über slowakische Roma fasst Zoon (2001) die Situation wie folgt zusammen:

> „Widespread joblessness is the main source of the poverty suffered by the bulk of Slovakia's Roma. Unemployment among the Roma has skyrocketed to about 80 percent in the last decade, a rate about four times higher than the national average; and most Romani young men take more than three years to find a job. Romani women are excluded from the work force almost entirely. Virtually all working-age Roma in some of the worst of Eastern Slovakia's segregated settlements are without gainful employment. Segregation and racial discrimination contribute to the low levels of education and training that prevent Roma from finding work. Roma account for 83 percent of the total number of unemployed persons who lack an elementary education and more than 41 percent of the total number of the job seekers with only elementary school certificates. Unemployment on such a scale translates directly into severe poverty. Approximately 25 percent of Slovakia's Roma have an income of less than U.S. $2 a day, compared with only 5 percent of the general population" (Zoon 2001: 2).

Über die Armut hinaus sehen sich die Roma mit zahlreichen und umfassenden, in Rassenvorurteilen gründenden Formen von Diskriminierung konfrontiert.

> „Local officials set the Romani citizens of Slovakia apart by denying them permanent residence status in the places where they live and by effectively prescribing the places where they are allowed to dwell. Laws and regulations, as well as decisions taken by government officials, limit Romani access to social protection benefits, health care services, and public housing and transportation. Discrimination and segregation in the education system are producing a sickly, ill-educated, unemployable generation of children. Some local and national political leaders in Slovakia argue openly that the

> only way to deal with the current situation is to further separate the Roma from the rest of Slovakia's population. Public opinion surveys indicate that many, if not most, people in Slovakia share these views" (Zoon 2001: 1–2).

Diese Situation hat nicht nur ökonomische und soziale Auswirkungen, sondern auch wichtige psychologische Komponenten. Menschen, die in segregierten Siedlungen leben, beschreiben Armut als verbunden mit Gefühlen von Hilflosigkeit und Ausschluss aus der größeren Gemeinschaft. Für viele ist Armut daneben auch mit Schamgefühlen verbunden. So ziehen diejenigen, die als extrem arm erscheinen, es vor, sich selbst als „fast", aber nicht völlig „arm" zu bezeichnen. Für die Allerärmsten bedeutet „fast arm" aber kaum mehr als nicht zu verhungern (The World Bank et al. 2002: 15). Dies ist auch ein Erbe des Sozialismus, der Armut innerhalb des Sozialismus als Konsequenz von persönlichem Versagen und Faulheit definierte und verstand - was sich kaum von der neoliberalen Erklärung von Armut innerhalb der Marktwirtschaft unterscheidet. Viele Roma fühlen, dass die existierenden Institutionen ihren Lebensbedingungen gegenüber feindlich oder zumindest indifferent sind. Sie haben deshalb kein oder nur sehr eingeschränktes Vertrauen in lokale Behörden und andere Institutionen wie etwa Sozialhilfeeinrichtungen und - in geringerem Ausmaß - Schulen und Gesundheitszentren.

Noch ein weiterer Punkt ist hier von Bedeutung: Um den Konsequenzen ihrer wirtschaftlichen Marginalisierung und sozialen Exklusion zu begegnen, bauen arme Menschen Netzwerke und andere Verbindungen auf, welche die formalen institutionellen Bindungen ersetzen. Diese Netzwerke kollidieren oft mit dem Gesetz und juristischen Einrichtungen wie den Strafverfolgungsbehörden und anderen Regulationsinstrumenten. Damit tendiert das, was auf der einen Seite ein wirtschaftlich wichtiges, manchmal sogar unerlässliches Netzwerk ist, auf der anderen Seite dazu, das Ausmaß an Exklusion zu vertiefen und zu gesellschaftlicher Teilung, Polarisierung und Konflikthaftigkeit beizutragen.

Zusätzliche Probleme ergeben sich aus den Strukturen und Verhaltensweisen, die in der sozialistischen Ära entstanden sind. Damals wie auch in der Transformationsphase verhielten sich die staatlichen Autoritäten auf eine nicht vorhersehbare Art und Weise; Regeln wurden gebrochen, und Angelegenheiten wurden über Bestechung oder persönliche Kontakte geregelt: „Hence informal networks were involved in protecting their members from the intrusion of state agencies, or exploiting these agencies, in substituting for the functions of formal organisations, or subverting them" (Castle-Kanerova, Jordan 2001: 10).

Für eine Lösung dieses Problems wären Bürgerorganisationen, die als Interessengruppen fungieren und die Verbindung zwischen zivilgesellschaftlichem Leben und den Strukturen politischer Herrschaft herstellen, geeignet gewesen. Doch dazu kam es nicht. Anstelle solcher Organisationen existierten und existieren informelle

Netzwerke, die es den Menschen ermöglichten, Dinge zu erreichen, ohne offen auf Korruption angewiesen zu sein.

> „Civil-society organisations were not training grounds for local or national politics; the norms of trust and co-operation generated by associations did not spill over into political culture; and there were few overt linkages between associational and political networks. This helps explain our finding that new NGOs in the field of social provision were isolated from each other, and that the local authorities sought to organise them, rather than draw on their social capital for their own purposes“ (Castle-Kanerova, Jordan 2001: 10).

Damit schwächt das institutionelle Erbe des Sozialismus zusammen mit der Armut nicht nur die Fähigkeit der Roma, grenzüberschreitende Beziehungen aufzubauen, sondern bereits ihre Fähigkeit, soziale Kontakte im eigenen Land herzustellen. Dieses Problem wird noch durch Beziehungsprobleme innerhalb der Gruppe der Roma verstärkt. Es wird immer wieder auf lokaler Ebene festgestellt, dass persönliche Konflikte, in die Roma verwickelt sind, gewöhnlich nicht zwischen Roma und Nicht-Roma existieren, sondern zwischen örtlichen Roma und solchen aus anderen Siedlungen.

All diese Beobachtungen beeinflussen die Antwort auf die diesem Beitrag zugrunde liegende Frage, inwieweit die Mitgliedschaft in einer ethnischen Gruppen die Basis für die Bildung von Vertrauen sein kann, indem sie sich vorteilhaft auf die Schaffung von Netzwerken auswirkt und damit ein wichtiger Faktor grenzüberschreitender Kontakte ist. Bevor aber diese Frage beantwortet werden kann, muss zunächst die ethnische Gruppe der Roma definiert werden. Hauptcharakteristika einer ethnischen Gemeinschaft sind üblicherweise folgende:

- Gemeinsame ethnische Merkmale wie Sprache, Gebräuche oder gemeinsame Geschichte sind unerlässliche Bestandteile für die Herausbildung einer ethnischen Gruppe. Dabei ist unerheblich, ob etwa die gemeinsame Geschichte real oder imaginiert ist, wie Benedict Anderson (Anderson 1991) hervorgehoben hat. Von Bedeutung ist ausschließlich, ob sich die Menschen darauf beziehen und sie in der gruppeninternen Kommunikation thematisieren.
- Solidarität und Sozialkapital sind sehr oft direkt an die Wahrnehmung gemeinsamer ethnischer Merkmale geknüpft, was folgendermaßen begründet wird: Da wir zur selben Gruppe gehören, praktizieren wir Solidarität, und diese auf Ethnizität gründenden Verbindungen sind eine Form sozialen Kapitals, das wir im Alltag nutzen können.
- Gemeinsame Ethnizität und die Bevorzugung persönlicher ethnischer Beziehungen sind wichtige Grundbedingungen für die Existenz einer ethnischen Gruppe, aber sie müssen erst öffentlich kommuniziert werden, damit die Idee und Praxis einer ethnischen Gemeinschaftsbildung organisiert werden kann. Die Akteure

dieser Kommunikation sind üblicherweise Intellektuelle. In einer ethnischen Bewegung übernehmen sie die Rolle der Führung.

- Programm und Ideologie bilden die Grundlage für die Verwirklichung der Organisation einer ethnischen Gruppe. Ideen und Ideologien bilden den Umriss und das Programm gibt die genaue Richtung dieses Prozesses. Programm und Ideologie sind der Hintergrund der Organisation einer ethnischen Gruppe und der Form ihrer Verbindungen mit der Gesellschaft als Ganze.
- Nicht zuletzt benötigen ethnische Gruppen auch finanzielle und politische Mittel, um als Gemeinschaft handeln zu können. Ohne Geld und ohne gesetzliche Zulassung der Organisation können ethnische Merkmale nicht in eine Gemeinschaft umgewandelt werden.

Werden die slowakischen und ungarischen Roma unter dem Aspekt dieser Merkmale analysiert, ergeben sich eindeutige Befunde. Es ist unzweifelhaft, dass den Roma unter den aktuellen Umständen von Armut und Diskriminierung alle finanziellen Mittel zur Gemeinschaftsbildung fehlen. Sie werden auch nur eingeschränkt politisch dazu motiviert, eine distinkte und politisch separate ethnische Gruppe zu bilden. Darüber hinaus sind auch wichtige ethnische Merkmale nicht als gemeinsame Merkmale anzusehen: Von den slowakischen und ungarischen Roma werden zumindest vier völlig unterschiedliche Sprachen gesprochen: Slowakisch in der Slowakei, Ungarisch sowie Romanes oder Lovári - Sprachvarianten, die vom Sanskrit abstammen - in beiden Ländern und ein altrumänischer Dialekt namens Beás in Ungarn. Aber nicht nur die Sprachen, sondern auch die Gebräuche, Werte und viele andere Charakteristika differieren in großem Ausmaß. Es besteht auch kaum ein Gemeinschaftsbewusstsein. Dies kann etwa durch die große Anzahl von Roma-Organisationen illustriert werden, die sich gegenseitig nach der Maßgabe, wer die „wahren" Roma vertritt, bekämpfen. Dies ist auch der Hauptgrund für den großen Unterschied zwischen den von den Volkszählungen registrierten Roma und den Schätzungen. Für diejenigen, die schätzen, ist jeder Roma ein Roma, und diese zusammen bilden ein Gruppe. Für die Mitglieder der so definierten (Merkmals-)Gruppe ist die Situation völlig anders. Nur wenige Personen gehören zur eigenen (Sozial-)Gruppe, und diese sind diejenigen, denen vertraut wird: Familienmitglieder, andere Verwandte und die Bevölkerung desjenigen Dorfes oder Stadtteils, in dem sie leben.

Das Ergebnis dieses kurzen Überblicks kann nun in Beziehung gesetzt werden zu Frage nach der Rolle persönlicher Kontakte innerhalb grenzüberschreitender Wirtschaftsbeziehungen. Die Roma haben sehr enge Beziehungen zueinander, aber die Definition des Anderen ist ebenfalls sehr eng. Daher reicht die Gemeinschaftsbildung auch nicht über die Grenze. Sogar die prinzipiell „grenzenlosen" Internetauftritte der slowakischen oder ungarischen Roma-Organisationen orientieren sich in ihrer Themenwahl strikt an den nationalstaatlichen Grenzen; auch Links etwa zu einer Organisation im Nachbarland finden sich gar nicht oder sehr versteckt.

Damit können folgende Schlussfolgerungen gezogen werden: Trotz des Umstandes, dass verschiedene Programme und Maßnahmen der jeweiligen Nationalstaaten, der Europäischen Union und von NGOs sich mit den Roma befassen, ist zu konstatieren, dass eine ethnische Gruppe der Roma nicht existiert - zumindest wenn der oben angeführten Definition von Ethnizität gefolgt wird, nach der Ethnizität für „a sense of security ... as well as a source of trust, certainty, reciprocal help, and protection“ (Horowitz 1993: 32) sorgt. All dies existiert fast ausschließlich auf der Ebene der Familie oder clanartiger Strukturen, nicht auf ethnischer Ebene. Es gibt kaum grenzüberschreitende oder sprachgruppenübergreifende Kommunikation, die Roma-Partner präferiert. Nur in sehr geringem Maße können bisher Prozesse einer wirklichen Gemeinschaftsbildung über die Sprach- und sonstigen Grenzen hinweg im Entstehen beobachtet werden.

Zusammenfassung

Zusammenfassend lässt sich die Situation in der slowakisch-ungarischen Grenzregion folgendermaßen charakterisieren: Von ethnischen Gruppen wird oft angenommen, dass sie Brücken über Grenzlinien hinweg bilden und so positive Auswirkungen auf die wirtschaftlich relevanten Beziehungen, ja sogar auf die Gesamtentwicklung der Grenzregion haben. Im slowakisch-ungarischen Grenzgebiet haben sich solche Hoffnungen (noch) nicht erfüllt. In der westlichen Grenzregion hat im Hinblick auf die Ungarn in der Slowakei die Einführung von Marktwirtschaft und Demokratie und damit die fortschreitende Realisierung einer funktional differenzierten Gesellschaft die wirtschaftliche Relevanz von persönlichen Beziehungen als Grundlage von Vertrauensbildung gemindert. Folglich ist die ökonomische Bedeutung von grenzüberschreitenden Aktivitäten auf ethnischer Grundlage marginal. In der östlichen Grenzregion könnten hingegen tatsächlich Beziehungen auf persönlicher Ebene einen Weg zum Aufbau oder zur Verbesserung grenzüberschreitender Wirtschaftsbeziehungen eröffnen. Doch bei der wichtigsten regionalen ethnischen Gruppe, den Roma, sind die persönlichen Beziehungen sehr eng begrenzt und reichen nicht über kleine Gruppen von Verwandten und Nachbarn hinaus. Daher sind grenzüberschreitende Beziehungen sehr selten und haben keine Auswirkungen auf wirtschaftliche Entwicklung. Bisher können nur geringe Wandlungen in Richtung auf einen größeren Umfang grenzüberschreitender Beziehungen festgestellt werden. Ob diese sich ausbreiten und die grenzüberschreitenden Wirtschaftsbeziehungen beeinflussen werden, kann kaum vorhergesehen werden. Aber es scheint ein interessantes Forschungsgebiet zu bleiben.

Literatur

Abraham, Martin 2003: With a Little Help from my Spouse: The Role of Trust in Family Business. Leipzig [http://www.uni-leipzig.de/~sozio/content/site/a_berichte/34.pdf].

Adler Lomnitz, Larissa, Diana Sheinbaum 2001: Trust, Social Networks and the Informal Economy: A Comparative Analysis. Prepared for the Workshop on Honesty and Trust in Post-Socialist Societies at Collegium. Budapest, May 25–26, 2001 [http://www.colbud.hu/honesty-trust/trust-informalecon.doc].

Anderson, Benedict 1991: Imagined Communities. Reflections on the Origin and Spread of Nationalism. London: Verso.

Aschauer, Wolfgang 1995: Auswirkungen der wirtschaftlichen und politischen Veränderungen in Osteuropa auf den ungarisch-österreichischen und den ungarisch-rumänischen Grenzraum. Potsdam (= Potsdamer Geographische Forschungen 10).

Bohle, Dorothee 1996: Governance im Spätsozialismus: die Herausbildung hybrider Koordinationsformen und informeller Vernetzungen in Ungarn und Polen in den achtziger Jahren. Berlin: Wissenschaftszentrum Berlin für Sozialforschung, Abteilung Organisation und Beschäftigung, Forschungsschwerpunkt Arbeitsmarkt und Beschäftigung (= Discussion papers FS I 96–102).

Brie, Michael 2000: Formal Institutions and Informal Institutional Arrangements. In: BISS public. Beiträge zur sozialwissenschaftlichen Diskussion 30, II: 101–119

Camagni, Roberto 1991: Local „Milieu", Uncertainty and Innovation Networks: Towards a New Dynamic Theory of Economic Space. In: Roberto Camagni (ed.), Innovation Networks: Spatial Perspectives. London, New York: Belhaven Press, 121–144.

Camagni, Roberto 2003: Regional Clusters, Regional Competencies and Regional Competition. Paper delivered at the International Conference on „Cluster management in structural policy - International experiences and consequences for Northrhine-Westfalia". Duisburg.

Castle-Kanerova, Mita, Bill Jordan 2001: Local Strategies for Civic Inclusion in a European Context: the Roma in the Czech Republic. Brighton (= ESRC „One Europe or Several?" Programme working papers 34/01) [http://netc.mcc.ac.uk/WoPEc/data/papers/erponeeurP0034.html].

Delhey, Jan, Kenneth Newton 2002: Who Trusts? The Origins of Social Trust in Seven Nations. Research Unit „Social Structure and Social Reporting" of the Social Science Research Center Berlin (WZB, FS III 02 - 402).

Grabher, Gernot, David Stark 1997: Organizing Diversity: Evolutionary Theory, Network Analysis, and Post-socialism. In: Gernot Grabher, David Stark (eds.), Restructuring Networks in Post-socialism. Legacies, Linkages, and Localities. Oxford: Oxford UP, 1–32.

Granovetter, Mark 1992: Problems of Explanation in Economic Sociology. In: Nitin Nohria, Robert G. Eccles (eds.), Networks and Organizations: Structure, Form, and Action. Boston: Harvard Business School Press, 25–56.

Horowitz, Donald L. 1993: Democracy in Divided Societies. In: Journal of Democracy 4: 18–38.

Hunya, Gábor, Álmos Telegdy 2003: Hungarian-Romanian Cross-Border Economic Co-operation. In: Revue Région et Développement 18: 13–30.

Ledeneva, Alena V. 1998: An Economy of Favors: Informal Exchanges and Networking in Russia. Cambridge UK: Cambridge UP.

Luhmann, Niklas 1998. Die Gesellschaft der Gesellschaft. Frankfurt am Main: Suhrkamp.

Luhmann, Niklas 2000: Vertrauen. Ein Mechanismus der Reduktion sozialer Komplexität. Stuttgart (orig. 1968).

Niebuhr, Annekatrin, Silvia Stiller 2002: Integration Effects in Border Regions – A Survey of Economic Theory and Empirical Studies. Hamburg (= HWWA Discussion Paper 179) [http://www.hwwa.de/Forschung/Publikationen/Discussion_Paper/2002/179.pdf].

Rose-Ackerman, Susan 1999: Corruption and Government: Causes, Consequences and Reform. Cambridge UK: Cambridge UP.

Rose-Ackerman, Susan 2001: Trust, Honesty, and Corruption: Theories and Survey Evidence from Post-Socialist Societies. Toward a Research Agenda for a Project of the Collegium Budapest. Prepared for the Workshop on Honesty and Trust in Post-Socialist Societies at Collegium. Budapest, May 25–26, 2001. Draft of April 24, 2001 [http://www.colbud.hu/honesty-trust/rose/pub01.PDF].

Roth, Klaus (Hg.) 2007: Soziale Netzwerke und soziales Vertrauen in den Transformationsländern. Ethnologische und soziologische Untersuchungen. Social Networks and Social Trust in the Transformation Countries. Ethnological and Sociological Studies. Zürich, Berlin: LIT.

Stark, David 1997: Recombinant Property in East European Capitalism. In: Gernot Grabher, David Stark (eds.), Restructuring Networks in Post-socialism. Legacies, Linkages, and Localities. Oxford: Oxford UP, 35–69.

Sztompka, Piotr 1999: Trust: A Sociological Theory. Cambridge UK: Cambridge UP.

The World Bank, Foundation S.P.A.C.E, INEKO, The Open Society Institute (eds.) 2002: Poverty and Welfare of Roma in the Slovak Republic. Bratislava [http://www.worldbank.org/eca/roma/data/povertyinslovak.pdf].

Zoon, Ina 2001: On the Margins. Slovakia. Roma and Public Services in Slovakia. A Call to Action to Improve Romani Access to Social Protection, Health Care, and Housing. New York: Open Society Institute.

Abstract

Belonging to the same ethnic group increases the trust towards another person of the same ethnicity and weakens the trust towards members of the out-group. In-group-relations, if defined ethnically, can therefore transcend borders. This understanding of an ethnic group leads to the hypothesis that cross-border economic relations are more frequent and stronger if the partners belong to the same ethnic group. Ethnic groups are therefore often thought to build bridges across border lines and thus provide support for economically relevant relations, or even spur the border region's common development. In the Slovak-Hungarian border regions these hopes do not (yet) seem to be fulfilled. In the western part, with regard to ethnic Hungarians in Slovakia, the modernisation process reduced the economic importance of personal relations. Consequently, the relevance of cross-border activities on ethnic grounds is marginal. In the eastern part, personally-based connections could offer a way to starting or improving economic cross-border relations. But in this region's primary ethnic group, the Romanies, personal ties are very close and do not reach outside their small groups of relatives and neighbours. Hence, cross-border relations are very rare and have no impact on economic development. Only slight changes towards a greater extent of cross-border ethnic connections can be observed.

Slavic Macedonian Nationalism: From "Regional" to "Ethnic"

Alexander Maxwell, Wellington

During the twentieth century, Slavo-Macedonian national feeling has shifted. At the beginning of the twentieth century, Slavic patriots in Macedonia felt a strong attachment to "Macedonia" as a multi-ethnic homeland. They imagined a Macedonian community uniting themselves with non-Slavic Macedonians: Greeks, Vlachs, Turks, Jews, etc. Most of these Macedonian Slavs also saw themselves as Bulgarians. By the middle of the century, however, Macedonian patriots began to see Macedonian and Bulgarian loyalties as mutually exclusive. "Regional" Macedonian nationalism had become "ethnic" Macedonian nationalism, not least because of a remarkably successful campaign to win recognition for a uniquely Macedonian "language". This transformation shows that the content of collective loyalties can shift: patriots can manipulate multi-cultural regional loyalties to generate new ethnic sentiments.

This argument raises political, terminological and methodological difficulties. The main political complication is vigorous Greek scholarly tradition that proclaims a Greek monopoly over things "Macedonian". This Greek scholarship rejects the very idea that a Slav can be a Macedonian, though some scholars have acknowledged the existence of Macedonian "Slavophones" (Vakalopoulos 1983, Kofos 1989a). Slavs in Macedonia have, however, long described themselves as *Makedonski*, with or without Greek approval, and since this article examines developments in Slavic thought, Greek sensibilities are essentially irrelevant to the analysis.

Terminological difficulties arise because this narrative touches on nationalism, a hotly contested term. Which collective loyalties count as "national" and which do not? At the turn of the century, Slavic patriots simultaneously described themselves as Macedonian and Bulgarian. Both regional Macedonianism and ethnic Bulgarianism, furthermore, can be credibly described as "nationalism". Some scholars might distinguish "regional" or perhaps "territorial" Macedonian loyalties from "ethnic" or "racial" Bulgarian loyalties. No terminology, however, can hope to be consistent with the usage of historical actors, who invoked diverse national concepts to promote various political goals.

Scholars often promote a political agenda by describing some historical phenomena as "nationalism" and discounting others as mere "regionalism". In an age when the "nation" is imagined as a legitimate political actor, whether by historical actors or scholars writing about the past, all definitions of the nation implicitly contain a statement of political legitimacy (Schnapper 1998: 15). Contrasting the "nation" to a mere "region" (or to a mere "ethnicity") inevitably confers legitimacy on some claims and delegitimates others. A non-partisan analysis cannot grant the status of a "nation" to some objects of collective loyalty, while denying it to others. In this analysis, therefore, coexisting "regional" and "ethnic" loyalties will both qualify as "nationalism".

Acknowledging all collective loyalties as "national", however, requires different sorts of "nationalism" to be classified and contrasted. Ignatieff's (1992: 3–5) distinction between "exclusive ethnic nationalism" with "multi-cultural civic nationalism", to use Anthony Smith's (2000: 16) formulation of this ubiquitous dichotomy, problematically implies a moral judgment against nasty ethnic nationalism in favor of tolerant civic nationalism (see Spencer, Wollman 2002: 96–106, Brubaker 2002). Replacing "civic" with "regional" to symbolize the conscious rejection of normative judgment, however, allows one to express this essay's hypothesis as follows: Macedonia's Slavs simultaneously espoused both "regional Macedonian nationalism" and "ethnic Bulgarian nationalism" in the early twentieth century, but by 1945 an "ethnic Macedonian nationalism" incompatible with Bulgarian loyalties had emerged. Some scholars may reject the very possibility of simultaneous Bulgarian and Macedonian national loyalties, but historical actors in other parts of the world have claimed multiple national loyalties (Maxwell 2005).

Gathering the historical evidence to support or disprove this hypothesis poses methodological and empirical problems. National sentiments are an elusive object of study. Macedonian Slavs at the turn of the century, furthermore, were mostly illiterate, and thus those literate Slavs preserved their national sentiments on paper, thus providing sources for subsequent historians to analyze, were by definition atypical: mostly partisan intellectuals writing polemical pamphlets. Obviously, these pamphlets are important primary sources, but must be viewed skeptically: political entrepreneurs using national concepts to promote their agendas cannot be trusted to provide a dispassionate description of popular national feeling.

Traveller accounts provide an alternative perspective. While some travel accounts were as frankly partisan as political manifestos, other travellers record credible conversations with ordinary Macedonians. British, German and American travellers in the Balkans, of course, bring their own biases to their texts, and Balkan scholars have recently spent considerable time applying Edward Said's analysis of "Orientalism" to Balkan studies (see Said 1978, Bakić-Hayden 1995, Todorova 1997, Wolff 1994, Fleming 1999). The insights of this literature, however, are secondary to this narrative. Foreign travellers may have seen the Balkans as backwards and exotic, and these perceptions may have shaped their descriptions, but this phenomenon on its own does not lead the foreigner to promote any given national concept for the Balkan peasantry. Foreign travellers, unlike polemical intellectuals, often acknowledged the diversity and complexity of Balkan national feelings.

Slavic Macedonian regionalism in the late Ottoman Empire

At the end of the nineteenth century, national sentiment existed mostly among a small social class of educated people, often described as the "intelligentsia." The Slavic rural peasantry did not participate in nationalist debates that had no meaning to their concerns. Henry Brailsford, a British journalist whose 1906 account is an indispensable source for this period of Macedonian history, even described a "wealthy peasant" in Bitola whose village changed national loyalties:

> We are all poor men, but we want to have our own school and a priest who will look after us properly. We used to have a Greek teacher. We paid him £5 a year and his bread, while the Greek consul paid him another £5; but we had no priest of our own. ... The Bulgarians heard of this and they came and made us an offer. They said they would give us a priest who would live in the village and a teacher to whom we need pay nothing. Well, sir, ours is a poor village, and so of course we became Bulgarians (Brailsford 1906: 102, see also the commentary in Danforth 1995: 198, Gounaris 1995).

While these villagers apparently lacked any strong feelings about their national loyalties, they adroitly manipulated outsider concerns to promote local goals. Perhaps the French consul in Salonica did not exaggerate too grossly when he joked that with a million francs he could turn the Macedonians into Frenchmen: "He would preach that the Macedonians are the descendants of the French crusaders who conquered Salonica in the twelfth century, and the francs would do the rest" (Brailsford 1906: 103).

At the end of the nineteenth century, Macedonia was famous for its heterogeneous population. Population figures were an important battlefront in the political struggle for Macedonia, and an extensive scholarly literature has examined the war of statistics.[1] Justin McCarthy described the magnitude of the problem while discussing the dishonest use of Ottoman census figures:

> Confident that few would ever see real Ottoman statistics, Greek and Bulgarian nationalist and governmental sources published "Ottoman statistics" to bolter their case that their group was dominant in the population.

---

[1] Duncan Perry (1988: 19) summarized that "studies using linguistic, cultural, historical and religious criteria usually yield different results, and various combinations of these modes of measurement add only new permutations, each ... inspired by the nationalist prejudices and preferences of the individuals making the assessments." For a detailed pro-Macedonian summary, see Anastasovski 2005: 128–73. See also Michailidis 1998, Gaber and Joveska 2004, Danforth 1995: 57. The standard work on Ottoman population statistics is Karpat 1985.

> Strangely the supposed Ottoman data were completely different depending on who published them (McCarthy 2001: 58).

Figure 1, taken from McCarthy, illustrates how much the various statistics varied.[2]

	Bulgarian Claims	Serbian Claims	Greek Claims	Ottoman Census Figures
Turks [Muslims]	499	231 000	634 000	1 112 000
Bulgarians	1 181 000	57 000	332 000	774 000
Greeks	229 000	201 000	653 000	514 000
Serbs	1 000	2 048 000	–	–

Figure 1: Claims to Macedonia's population using "Ottoman Statistics"

The extreme politicization of Macedonian population figures makes a cursory treatment inadvisable; limitations of space prevent an exhaustive analysis. For the purposes of this analysis, however, the true population figures are not important: note merely Macedonia's considerable ethnic diversity, the intense disagreement about the most fundamental facts of Macedonian demography, and the absence of "Macedonian" as an ethnic category.

While Macedonia's entire population was the subject of competing ethnic claims, the classification of Macedonia's Slavic population was doubly contested. Bulgarians argued that Macedonian Slavs were Bulgarians; Serbs that they were Serbs. A few brazen Greeks, equating Greek nationality with loyalty to the Orthodox Patriarch, even claimed they were "Slavophone Greeks"[3]. Foreign observers mostly favored the Bulgarian thesis.

Foreign observers discussing the struggle for Macedonia on the eve of the Balkan wars explicitly denied that "Macedonians" formed a distinct ethnic category: Macedonia was instead a region in which different ethnicities struggled for

---

[2] McCarthy (2001: 59) presented the Ottoman statistics as the "actual population", which strikes me as problematic not least because the Ottoman state classified its citizens on the basis of religion: Ottoman statistics dealt with "Muslims" not "Turks". The difficulty of calculating ethnic statistics from confessional data could explain some discrepancy between figures. Such quibbles do not, however, detract from McCarthy's main point about the Bulgarian, Serbian and Greek figures: "of course, they were all fakes".

[3] Arthur Evans discussed the "Bulgarophone Greeks", in a letter of 30 September 1903; see also the report of the Greek consul in Seres (Syar) of 31 January 1909, in Božinov and Panayotov 1978: 541. The "Slavophone Greek" discourse is also applied to the Slavic minority in northern Greece; see Nikoloudis 2002, Holevas 1991, Phillips 2004: 22. Special thanks to Svetlana Doncheva for her assistance with Greek historiography.

supremacy. For instance, John Fraser (1912: 174) wrote that "there is no distinct race that can be called Macedonian". In 1903, British Archaeologist Arthur Evans concurred in a letter to the *Times:*

> There are no *Macedonians*. There are Bulgars. There are Roumans ... There are Greeks, including more or less superficially Hellenized Roumans. There are "Turks", including Mohammedian Bulgarians ... There is an infusion of Skipetars or Albanians ... Finally there is the large Spanish Jew population in Soloun [Thessaloniki]. But there are no "Macedonians" (quoted in: Bozhinov 1978: 2: 540–1).

For Evans, a "Macedonian" might be Bulgarian, Romanian, Greek, Turkish, or Jewish: the term had no ethnic content.

Serbian propagandists, however, argued with some success that Macedonian Slavs were raw ethnographic material that might, with time and education, be formed into either Bulgarians or Serbs. Stojan Novaković, a philologist and Serbian diplomat, promoted Macedonianism as a counter-weight to Bulgarian feeling (see Banac 1984: 112, Džambazovski 1963: 141, Novaković 1884, 1906). Serbian geographer Jovan Cvijić also wrote influential works in a similar spirit (e.g. Cvijić 1906). Serbian patriots obviously had a nationalist incentive for adopting this constructivist approach to nationality: if Macedonian Slavs had not yet chosen their loyalties, as Henry Wilkinson observed (1951: 150), then "Serbia's claim to Macedonia would be on a par with that of Bulgaria". Bulgarians were quick to call Serbian motives into question (Šaldev 1993: 15). Note, however, that the theory of potential nationality also captures the attitude of peasants near Bitola as Brailsford described them. In any event, this Serbian argument had far-reaching consequences: the notion that Macedonian Slavs were not yet Serbs or Bulgarians was the germ of the idea that they formed a distinct ethnic category, neither Serbian nor Bulgarian.

As modern Macedonian scholarship has assiduously demonstrated, some Macedonian Slavs articulated Macedonian ethnic distinctiveness. Petko Slavejkov's essay on the "Macedonian Question" suggests that a certain tradition of anti-Bulgarian Slavic nationalism had become established by 1871: "we have heard many a time from the Macedonists that they are not Bulgarians but Macedonians – heirs of the ancient Macedonians and we have always sought some evidence of it but never found any" (Koneski 1960: 73). Giorgi Pulevski proclaimed in his 1875 *Rečnik od tri jezika* (Dictionary of three languages) that "a nation is a people who are of the same stock and who speak the same language ... the Macedonians are a nation, and this place of theirs is Macedonia" (Pulevski 1875, see also Lunt 1984: 103, Koneski 1960: 86–92).

Foreign travellers confirm the existence of Slavic intellectuals with Macedonian particularist sensibilities. Brailsford (1906: 19), for example, encountered "an ardent Macedonian nationalist, rather distrustful of Bulgaria and profoundly hostile to Russia".[4] Brailsford, however, saw him as exceptional, and characterized the Slavic movement in Macedonia simply as "the Bulgarian movement".

> Undoubtedly any Slav race which belonged to the Orthodox race might have won Macedonia, given the necessary tact and the necessary funds. Servia or Montenegro, or even Russia, might have done it. In point of fact it is Bulgaria which has succeeded. History and ethnology and comparative philology may take what side in the controversy they please. The Macedonians are Bulgars today because a free and progressive Bulgaria has known how to attract them (Brailsford 1906: 103).

Those linguists and journalists who articulated Macedonian particularist nationalism in the final years of Ottoman rule were eccentrics: most Macedonian Slavs at the turn of the century, if they felt any national sentiments at all, felt Bulgarian.

The "Bulgarian movement" in Macedonia, however, retained a sense of Macedonian regionalism by distinguishing the interests of the Bulgarian state from those of Bulgarians in Macedonia. The political context mattered: as Ivo Banac put it (1984: 327), Macedonian Slavs "were Bulgars in struggles against Serbian and Greek hegemonism, but within the Bulgar world, they were increasingly becoming exclusive Macedonians". In 1902, for example, the Sofia newspaper *Reformi* published an article called "Elements Necessary for Macedonia's Autonomy". This article started with the assumption that Macedonian Slavs were Bulgarians: "Macedonia has one element, which, in its numbers and culture, is in a position to maintain one government. This is undoubtedly the Bulgarian element. Of 2.25 million citizens, more than 1.25 million are Bulgarians." *Reformi*, however, also described Macedonia as a multi-ethnic region, arguing that "Bulgarians, Turks, Greeks, Wallachians have lived there from time immemorial". So it rejected union with Bulgaria, calling instead for an autonomous, multi-ethnic Macedonia:

> Macedonia ... bordering on all Balkan states, is serving as the arena for terrible struggles which conceal the political expansion of this or that state. ... These sentiments, when transferred to the local population, transform it into mutual irreconcilable enemies. And mind you, these enemies are the sons of one and the same land.

Reformi even claimed hopefully that "some non-Bulgarian and non-Slav elements already form part of the revolutionary organization. This is a reassuring fact for the present and a good omen for the future" (Božinov, Panayotov 1978, vol. 3: 465).

---

[4] This individual, a Bishop's secretary, is mentioned to illustrate that churchmen with treasonous opinions could hold office in late-Ottoman Macedonia thanks to the protection of the great powers.

The article in *Reformi* demonstrates that some Slavic Macedonian intellectuals felt loyalty to Macedonia as a region or territory without claiming any specifically Macedonian ethnicity. The primary aim of multi-ethnic Macedonian regionalism was an alliance of Greeks and Slavs (read: Bulgarians) against Ottoman rule. This sort of Macedonianism, notice, does not qualify as classic "civic" nationalism. The phrase "civic Macedonian nationalism" implies a multi-cultural tolerance. But Macedonian regionalism was strongly Christian, and usually excluded Macedonia's Muslims, though we shall see that some patriots accepted Muslim peasants as fellow Macedonians.

Secondly, theorists of "civic nationalism" usually equate the nation with the existing state, and proclaiming the equality of all citizens. Macedonian regionalism, by contrast, was directed against the Ottoman Empire. The Ottoman government had no administrative unit corresponding to Macedonia: the region in question was divided between the vilayets of Üsküb (Skopje), Salonica (Thessaloniki) and Monastir. Indeed, Macedonia existed in the symbolic geography of Europe mostly because of Alexander the Great and his glorious empire in antiquity[5]. Authors imagining Macedonia around 1900 delineated the territory in very different ways: Nick Anastasovski (2005: 128) took an unjustified liberty in proclaiming any geographic definition of Macedonia as "generally accepted". Indeed, a few contemporaries even refused to recognize "Macedonia" as a meaningful geographic entity: King Ferdinand of Bulgaria notoriously spoke simply of "the vilayets" (see Perry 1988: 46). In 1931, Wesley Gewehr (1931: 79) accurately summarized that "Macedonia has always been an area of indefinite boundaries", since, as Wilkenson (1951: 1) put it, "hardly two authorities can be found to agree on [Macedonia's] exact delineation". The only apparent points of consensus were that Salonica (Thessaloniki, Solun) was the capital city, and that Macedonia lay under Ottoman administration.

Figure 2 compares three definitions of Macedonia taken from the period 1899–1905; the three geographers agreed only that Macedonia did not extend northeast into Bulgaria, nor south into Greek Thessaly, nor east beyond the Mesta river. Macedonia's extent into the Ottoman lands in North and West was variously imagined.

---

5 The 1802 *English Encyclopedia* defined Macedonia as "a most celebrated kingdom of antiquity". The *Encyclopedia Britannica*'s 1810 and 1823 editions described the deeds of Alexander the Great and his successors, but even the 29 page entry in the 1823 edition described the medieval and modern history of Macedonia in one sentence "... the country was reduced to a Roman province in 148 B.C. To them in continued subject until the year 1357, when it was reduced by the Turkish sultan Bajazet, and it has remained in the hands of the Turks ever since". The *Bol'šaia entsiklopediia* (1896) also ended its description of Macedonia with the Roman conquest.

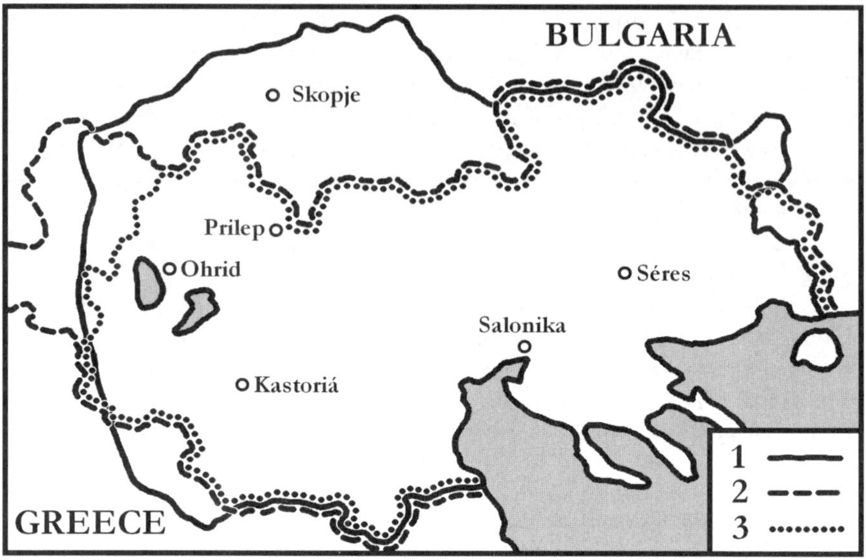

Figure 2: Three definitions of Macedonia, 1899–1905[6]

Macedonian regionalism and the 1903 Ilinden Rising

Both multi-ethnic Macedonian regionalism and ethnic Bulgarianism played important roles in a central event of late Ottoman Macedonia, the August 1903 Ilinden rising. Armed bands rose against Ottoman rule and attacked their mostly Muslim landlords. The revolutionaries hoped to provoke intervention from the great powers, but were disappointed. The Ottoman army quickly suppressed the uprising, though a revolutionary government in the town of Kruševo, known as the Kruševo republic, survived over a week.

Greek, Bulgarian and Macedonian historiographies describe the Ilinden rising quite differently. Greek historiography, as embodied in Douglas Dakin's *The Greek Struggle in Macedonia* (1966: 101), downplays the Ilinden rising as the work of extremists: "The story that the rising was a widespread popular movement is entirely a myth." Contemporary observer John Foster Frasier (1912: 179) concurred, writing that "the revolutionary movement, as it is in Macedonia today,

[6] The definitions shown are: (1) Greek, C. Nicolaides, 1899. (2) Anonymous, *Cartes ... de la Macédonie,* 1905 and (3) "a Greek definition given by D. M. Brancoff", 1905. Map by the author, based on a map in Wilkinson 1951: 2.

is the outcome of terror and murder", and that "the Bulgarian Macedonians help the 'bands', not because they regard them as brothers, but because they are afraid of assassination if they do not" (For a conversation with a peasant refugee, see also Booth 1905: 222 f.). These comments, of course, probably apply with equal force to all Balkan insurrections. Richard Clutterbuck, an expert on guerilla movements, suggests that at most 1% of the population will support a revolutionary cause, another 10% "follow the lead of activists on either side", while the remaining 89% "do their utmost to keep their families out of battle" (Clutterbuck 1977, see also Perry 1988: 153).

Slavic historians, both Bulgarian and Macedonian, glorify the Ilinden rising as a defining moment in the national struggle. Victor Roudometof (2002: 59) estimated that a fifth of all essays published in *The Macedonian Review* refer to it. Hristo Poljanski (1969: 167) described Ilinden as "one of the brightest scenes in the whole pageant of Macedonia's national liberation movement. In all the age long desire for freedom and a place in the sun for the Macedonian people found expression". Aleksandar Hristov's two-volume sourcebook on the rising, *Prilozi za Ilinden* (Contributions to Ilinden, 1972) contains almost two thousand pages. Ilinden's centrality to Macedonian nationalism provoked the Bulgarian Academy of Sciences to publish reference works highlighting the Bulgarian aspects of the rising. Six years after Hristo Poljanski's six-volume biography of Goce Delčev was published in Skopje (1972), for example, Hristo Hristov's *Goce Delčev. Spomeni, Dokumenti, Materiali* appeared in Sofia (1978).

Evidence of Bulgarian sentiments during the Ilinden rising is abundant; Bulgarian flags flew from housetops and the Bulgarian song *Makedonija, stara Bălgaria* (Macedonia, old Bulgaria) was sung (Adanir 1979: 184). Contemporary foreign observers treated the Bulgarian nature of the rising as self-evident. The organization responsible for the Ilinden rising, usually known to Anglophone scholars by the name Internal Macedonian Revolutionary Organization, or IMRO (alternatively as "VMRO" from its Slavic initials), enjoyed strong ties with the government in Sofia and received arms and financial support from the Bulgarian government (Perry 1988: 40). According to Duncan Perry, the correspondence of the aforementioned Goce Delčev "often states clearly and simply, 'We are Bulgarians'" (Perry 1988: 23). Giorge Petrov, another IMRO leader, wrote in 1896 that "The Macedonian population consists of Bulgarians, Turks, Albanians, Wallachians, Jews and Gypsies" (Božinov, Panayotov 1978, vol. 3: document 40). IMRO as an organization showed its Bulgarian sympathies by initially describing itself as "the Bulgaria-Macedonia-Edirne Revolutionary Organization" (see Perry 1988: 41).[7]

---

[7] A political party in contemporary Macedonia, attempting to claim the Ilinden heritage, calls itself IMRO-DPMNE, but this modern party must be distinguished from it predecessor.

The Bulgarian loyalties of IMRO's leadership, however, coexisted with the desire for multi-ethnic Macedonia to enjoy administrative autonomy. When Delčev was elected to IMRO's Central Committee in 1896, he opened membership in IMRO to all inhabitants of European Turkey, since his goal was to "assemble all the dissatisfied elements in Macedonia and the Adrianople region, *regardless of nationality or religion*, in order to win through revolution full autonomy for both regions" (emphasis added, see Pribichevich 1982: 121). He also declared his intention to "fight against chauvinist propaganda and nationalistic disputes". Delčev reiterated this multi-ethnic regionalism in 1902, proclaiming IMRO's goal "to unite in one whole all discontented elements in Macedonia and the Adrianople areas irrespective of nationality" (Perry 1988: 109–10).

The 2–3 August 1903 Manifesto of the Kruševo Republic, surprisingly, included a direct appeal to Macedonia's Muslim population: "We have not risen against the peaceful, diligent and honest Turkish people who, like ourselves, earn their living through sweat and blood – they are our brothers with whom we have always lived and would like to live again" (Radin 1993: 275). Nikola Karev, head of the ephemeral statelet, matched words with deeds, as Stoyan Pribichevich (1982: 128) summarized: "Karev called a council of sixty prominent citizens, in which each nationality was represented by twenty men. From those he selected six men as the Executive council, again two from each nationality." The leaders of the Kruševo Republic thus propounded a Macedonian regionalism that embraced non-Slavs, even while they rose against Ottoman rule.

IMRO's regionalism attracted some support from non-Slavic Macedonians. Salonica Jews donated money to the revolutionaries, and Pitu Gule, a noted martyr of the Kruševo Republic, was a Vlach (see Arslan 2003: 84). IMRO even managed to win the support of a few Turks who, Perry reports, "curiously ... were most often members of the gendarmerie" (Perry 1988: 175, see also Brailsford 1906: 187). Macedonian Greeks did not participate, however, and Greek historians downplay the significance of IMRO's multi-ethnicism. Dakin (1966: 93), for example, claimed that IMRO "forced Greeks, Serbians and Vlachs to follow them in their peripatetions ... to give a semblance of unity both to the local inhabitants and to foreign observers". Yet even Dakin admitted that the Slavs were able to reach a special understanding with Macedonian Vlachs: "Certain Rumanizing Vlachs, ... in return for a promise to favor the Rumanian liturgy, joined the revolutionary movement." Turkish historian Ali Arslan similarly found that "Vlach-Bulgarian convergence" took place in Ohrid (Arslan 2003).

One should not, however, over-estimate the multi-ethnic character of the Ilinden rising. IMRO was an overwhelmingly Slavic movement, and was prone to bouts of ethnic exclusiveness. In 1896, membership in IMRO was restricted to "any Bulgarian, regardless of sex, who has not comprised himself in the eyes of the community ... and who promises to be of service in some way to the revolutionary cause of liberation" (Perry 1988: 65). Additionally, the Ilinden rising should not be analyzed solely as a national uprising: IMRO won what popular support it enjoyed mostly by promising to abolish peasant debts and redistribute land (Dakin 1966: 93).

In 1903, in the wake of Ilinden's failure, a circle of Macedonian Slavs studying in Russia became so disillusioned with Bulgaria that they began to promote the idea of a distinct Macedonian ethnicity. In a letter of 17 February 1904, Dimiter Čupovski, founder of the Slav-Macedonian Literary Society in St. Petersburg, sought to promote "the notion that the Slavs of Macedonia are not the same as Serbs and Bulgars but a separate tribe representing something different from both", hoping that "the people and many representatives of its intelligentsia will come to recognize themselves as sons of a Slav Macedonian tribe which as closer links to the Russians than to the Serbs and Bulgars" (see Šaldev 1993: 17).

Similar ideas can be found in the seminal *On Macedonian Matters*, written in 1903 by Krsté Misirkov, who had studied history in both Odessa and Petersburg and been active in the Slav-Macedonian Society. Misirkov's greatest fear was that Macedonia would be carved up between Greece, Serbia and Bulgaria: "Could there be any greater misfortune for Macedonia than to be partitioned?"[8] But where Čupovski hoped that Russia would prevent this outcome, Misirkov sought to renew and revitalize the Ottoman state:

> We Macedonians are Turkish subjects and interested in maintaining the unity of Turkey ... the Macedonian intelligentsia, if they examine their own interests, should for their own sake and the sake of their people devote all their moral strength to the prime task of maintaining the unity of Turkey (Missirkov 1974: 63).

Misirkov, however, recognized that the Ottoman state could not survive without more support from its Christian population. He thus called on Macedonia's "intellectuals with Bulgarian, Serbian and Greek educational backgrounds" to work for a reformed Ottoman Macedonia (Missirkov 1974: 85). Misirkov's reformed Macedonia was, however, to enjoy autonomous administration, which in light of previous Serbian, Bulgarian and Romanian autonomy should be seen as a first step toward eventual independence.

Misirkov's support for the Ottoman state may surprise contemporary readers who inevitably see the Ilinden uprising as a step in the larger process of Ottoman collapse. Note, however, that several Macedonian Slavs supported a reformed Ottoman state while maintaining Bulgarian ethnic sentiments. In 1912, Pančo

---

[8] Note, however, that Misirkov did not feel threatened by any of these powers on its own: "From the Macedonian point of view, the unification of all Macedonia with Bulgaria, Serbia or Greece is not desirable, but neither is it particularly frightening." Missirkov 1974: 63 and 89.

Dorev, Bitola's MP in the Ottoman parliament, argued for the "emancipation of the Bulgarian nationality in Ottoman political life through individual civil, not the national communal, rights" (see Parvanova 2001: 66).

Misirkov saw both IMRO and the Ilinden rising as a catastrophe: its failure increased the danger of Macedonia's partition, threatening the integrity of Macedonia as a single region. He also saw IMRO as Bulgarian phenomena: "The only Macedonian Slavs who played a leading part in the uprising were those who called themselves Bulgarians." Misirkov lamented that "no local Macedonian patriotism"[9] existed and would have to be created. He anticipated that Macedonians would respond to his proposals with a series of baffled questions:

> What sort of new Macedonian nation can this be when we and our fathers and grandfathers and great-grandfathers have always been called Bulgarians? ... Macedonian as a nationality has never existed, they will say, and it does not exist now. There have always been two south Slav nationalities in Macedonia: Bulgarian and Serbian. So, any kind of Macedonian Slav revival is simply the empty concern of a number of fanatics who have no concept of South Slav history.

Misirkov answered these objections by observing that national loyalties change with time: "What has not existed in the past may still be brought into existence later, provided that the appropriate historical circumstances arise." He looked to the Ottoman state to help promote a specifically Macedonian ethnic loyalty by establishing "an Archbishopric in Ohrid which would be the Archbishopric of all Macedonia". Slavic Macedonian ethnicity would thus acquire a religious dimension:

> If it is officially acknowledged that there are not several Slav nationalities in Macedonia, but only one, which is neither Bulgarian nor Serbian, and if Macedonia secedes as an independent Bishopric, Turkey will be immediately freed from interference in Macedonian affairs by the three neighboring states.

Misirkov, in short, wanted the Ottoman state to promote Macedonian nation-building, calling for "official recognition ... for the Macedonian people; in all official documents and certificates the designation *Macedonian* must be introduced for all persons of Slav origin in Macedonia" (Missirkov 1974: 55, 174, 150–152, 62, 58).

---

[9] "Finally, many people will point out that our greatest misfortune is that we have no local Macedonian patriotism. If there were patriotism in Macedonia, we would think and work only for Macedonia. But now some of us still consider ourselves Bulgarian and link our interests with those of Bulgaria instead of studying our own country, Macedonia ..." (Missirkov 1974: 146).

Misirkov understandably saw Bulgarian feeling as the biggest threat to his national project. He even conceded, implicitly, that Macedonian Slavs might have become Bulgarians, though he felt that because of the failed Ilinden rising "Macedonia has become lost to the Bulgarian nation". Misirkov also acknowledged the impact of Serbian propaganda: "Over the last twenty-five years ... the Serbs have succeeded, if not in turning the Macedonians into Serbs, at least in convincing Europe that there are Serbs in Macedonia." Misirkov opposed the Serbian position, but nevertheless acknowledged its influence: "The Macedonian national revival ... is basically the result of the competition between Bulgaria and Serbia over the Macedonian question" (Missirkov 1974: 113, 140, 149). That said, it is worth noting that Misirkov himself returned to a Bulgarian nationalist position by 1907, and his 1913 diary articulates explicit Bulgarianism (see Nihtinen 1995, Hamm 1976).

Misirkov's arguments had little impact in their own time, since his ideas never reached a broad audience. IMRO activists seized and destroyed most copies of the book. Misirkov's work owes its present reputation to a 1946 reprint. Nevertheless, Misirkov's concept of Slavo-Macedonian ethnicity, caught between Bulgaria and Serbia, was a milestone, showing that political actors drew on Macedonian regional loyalty to imagine an "ethnic" Macedonian nation.

Macedonia's partition and interwar Macedonianism

Macedonian politics were transformed by the First and Second Balkan Wars, since the 1913 treaty of Bucharest partitioned Macedonia. The Treaty of Bucharest became a dead letter when the First World War broke out a year later, but the peace treaties signed after the First World War essentially confirmed the outcome of the Balkan wars. Greece gained the entire Macedonian coast and with it Thessaloniki, Macedonia's most important city. Bulgaria, despite its strong ethnic claim to the Slavic north of Macedonia, received the smallest slice, mostly because it fought alongside the defeated Central Powers. Serbia, which transformed into a part of the "Kingdom of Serbs, Croats and Slovenes", and then Yugoslavia, won the bulk of northern Macedonia, which was renamed "South Serbia". The Greek, Bulgarian and Yugoslav slices of Macedonia are also known as Aegean, Pirin and Vardar Macedonia, respectively.

The majority of Macedonia's rural population did not participate in either the Balkan wars or the First World War, but rather sought to escape the fighting. John Koliopoulos (1999: 26–7) wrote that

> Self-preservation in most cases was an infinitely stronger motive than attachment to abstract causes like nationalism. ... The fierceness of national animosities and claims and the consequent readiness of both sides to use

> force ... persuaded the peasants to describe themselves in whatever way seemed at the moment safest (Koliopoulos 1999: 26 f.).

The threat to their lives and property was real: this period witnessed traumatic upheavals in Macedonian demography. The most dramatic victims were Muslims in Greek Macedonia, expelled to Turkey under the so-called "transfer of populations". Nevertheless, the war affected people from every ethnic group (Hirschon 2003, Carnegie Foundation 1914: 148–185, Gewehr 1931: 105, Mihajlov 1965: 680, 692). Since Macedonian ethnic nationalism emerged primarily in Vardar Macedonia, however, the rest of this analysis will concentrate on the Slavic experience under Yugoslav rule.

The interwar Yugoslav state sought to Serbianize its bit of Macedonia. Bulgarian cultural institutions were closed; Bulgarian teachers and priests were expelled. The Carnegie foundation's *Report of the International Commission* (1914: 272) characterized the following incident, attributed to a "Bulgarian teacher", as "typical":

> One Sunday the Servian soldiers surrounded a Bulgarian church. When the worshippers came out at the close of the service, a table stood before the door upon which were a paper and a revolver. They were to choose between this; either they were to sign the paper, signifying that they thus became Servians, or were to suffer death. They all signed.

In official documents, family names ending with the Bulgarian suffix "-ov" were changed to end with Serbian "-ović" (Wendel 1922: 77, Ehrenburg 1947: 104, Bakeless 1935: 223, Mihajlov 1965: 680). These heavy-handed policies were ultimately unsuccessful, and may have even been counterproductive: in Herman Ullman's words (1943: 97), "Belgrade was unable to assimilate the Macedonians".

IMRO rejected the borders drawn at the Paris peace conference and continued military operations during the interwar period. Its leaders settled in Sofia and organized raids into Vardar Macedonia from both Bulgaria and Albania, though they devoted most of their energy to political infighting. IMRO had raised money through kidnapping before the Balkan wars (Carpenter 2003); but during the interwar period, it degenerated into an extortion racket, blackmailing the roughly 100000 Macedonian emigrants and the inhabitants of Bulgarian Macedonia into buying "protection" from terror and economic boycott through "voluntary" patriotic subscription and taxes. In the early 1930s it engaged in illegal drug traffic (Pribichevich 1982: 141).

IMRO also split into several camps, and many of its leading figures were murdered in factional infighting. Todor Aleksandrov, for example, was murdered in the mountains of Bulgarian Macedonia in 1924, and later that same year Peter

Čaulev was assassinated in Milan. Todor Panitsa was shot in the Vienna Opera in 1925, Aleksandar Protogerov on the street in Sofia in 1928.

The left faction of IMRO established ties with the Balkan Communist Federation, a Comintern-sponsored alliance between Bulgarian, Yugoslav and Greek Communist parties founded in Sofia in January, 1920. In March 1924, after negotiations with IMRO, the Federation praised IMRO as the "real organizer and leader of the Macedonian Slavs, regardless of nationality"; in May 1924, IMRO's "The New Orientation of the Macedonian Revolutionary Movement" called in turn for a "Balkan Federation", declaring that it could "*only count on the extreme progressive and revolutionary movements of Europe*, fighting against the imperialist policy of their governments". Elisabeth Barker concluded that "The New Orientation" so closely resembled the Balkan Communist Federation's March manifesto that it "might have been drafted by a Communist" (Barker 1950: 52, 57; for Todor Aleksandrov's account of the split, see Heathcote 1925: 148 f.).

Both the Balkan Communist Federation and IMRO's left wing proclaimed a multi-ethnic Macedonian regionalism. In 1924, the Balkan Communist Federation described its image of multi-ethnic Macedonia as follows:

> All the nationalities which dominate in the neighboring States are represented in Macedonia, but in such proportions that not one of them attains an absolute majority. Consequently the domination of any one of the Balkan states over Macedonia means national oppression of the majority of the Macedonian population and stirs up national struggles which are exploited by other interested states for their schemes of conquest ... A united Macedonia and autonomous Macedonia is now the slogan of Macedonians in all corners of their fatherland (Barker 1950: 52).

Ivo Banac (1984: 324) reports that the Federalists took ethnic tolerance so far that they supported neutral Esperanto as the official language of a "Federal Republic of Macedonia".

Multi-ethnic Macedonianism between the World Wars, much as in the late Ottoman period, differed from classic "civic" nationalism by opposing the existing state structure. In a Declaration of 29 April 1924, Todor Aleksandrov, P. Čaulev, and A. Protogerov resolved to fight the governments of Serbia, Greece and Bulgaria equally, hoping to attain "a Balkan Federation, which alone will be in a position to frustrate the attempts at annexation by the existing Balkan states, and to guarantee the cultural development of all ethnic minorities". That said, the same declaration promised that IMRO would struggle for "the liberation and unification of the dismembered parts of Macedonia into a completely independent political entity within its natural ethnic *[sic]* and geographical boundaries" (Božinov, Panayotov 1978, vol. 4: document 31). While this appeal to Macedonia's geographic boundaries suggests Macedonian regionalism, this reference to ethnic boundaries hints at Slavo-Macedonian ethnic distinctiveness, uneasily contradicting previous assertions of multi-cultural or multi-ethnic diversity.

Communist internationalists eventually followed Misirkov in explicitly proclaiming a distinctively Macedonian Slavic ethnic nation. In the *Federation Balcanique* of 1 April 1926, Dimitar Vlahov, a journalist who edited several patriotic newspapers, expressed the willingness of "United IMRO" to work with "persons of all social classes without distinction of nationality, citizenship, religion or sex" (Barker 1950: 68; on Vlahov's publishing career, see Najdoski 1987). Vlahov, like Čupovski and Misirkov, found his path to Macedonian particularism in Russia, when the executive committee of the Comintern met in Moscow to formulate its policy toward the Macedonian question. He described the events in his memoirs:

> One day I was informed that the consultation would be held. And so it was. Before the convening of the consultation, the inner leadership of the committee had already reached its stand, including the question of the Macedonian nation, and charged the Balkan secretariat with the drafting of [the] corresponding resolution ... In the resolution, which we published in *Makedonsko Delo* [The Macedonian Cause] in 1934, it was concluded that the Macedonian nation exists (Banac 1984: 328).

Vlahov's apparent willingness to accept the Comintern's decision blindly, without even offering any personal reaction, partly explains what Elizabeth Barker (1950: 69) called the "widespread belief, not eradicated by Vlahov's disclaimers, that he was in fact a Communist agent".

While Čupovski and Misirkov promoted a Macedonian ethnic nation to encourage Ottoman administrative reform, Vlahov and the Comintern promoted Macedonian ethnic distinctiveness to further socialist internationalism. None of these expatriate Macedonians could credibly claim to represent popular opinion in Macedonia itself; indeed, they could not even claim to represent the consensus of Macedonian diaspora opinion. In 1927, a Macedonian society in Indianapolis published a pamphlet on "The Macedonian Slavs; Their National Character and Struggles". The authors described themselves as "we Macedonians", claimed to speak for "the Macedonian people", and called for an "Independent and united Macedonia"; yet they also proclaimed that "the Macedonian Slavs are Bulgars", and that "the language of the Macedonian Slavs is Bulgarian" (Anon. 1927: 9 f.; for a pro-Bulgarian account of the Macedonian Slavic diaspora, see Mitev 1993: 2001). The *Macedonian Tribune*, published first in Indianapolis and later in Fort Wayne, began publishing regularly that same year, using Bulgarian orthography (Shea 1997: 209).

The squabbles of expatriate intellectuals held little interest for ordinary Macedonians: foreign observers continued to describe Macedonia's population as an anational peasantry. John Footman, a British diplomat in Skopje, estimated that 80% of Macedonia’s population “desire a firm, just and enlightened government, and regard nationality as of minor importance”. A British diplomatic report on “The Macedonian Question and Komitaji Activity” of 26 November 1925 concluded that while “amongst the Slav intellectuals there is violent partisanship, probably the majority of the Slavs ... do not care to what nationality they belong” (Rossos 1994: 377). German scholar Leonard Schultze-Jena (1927: 153) denied that “self-determination offered a way to decide between Serbian and Bulgarian loyalties” because for Macedonian Slavs “the desire to eat one’s bread in peace” trumped national sentiment.

Disillusionment with ethnic nationalism, whether Serbian, Bulgarian or Greek, sometimes strengthened the sense of Macedonian regionalism: one could reject ethnic politics by proclaiming loyalty to multi-ethnic Macedonia. A. C. Corfe, a League of Nations commissioner from New Zealand, found the Macedonian Slavs in 1923 weary of nationalist conflict: “To my question ‘what do you want? An autonomous Macedonia or a Macedonia under Bulgars?’ the answer was generally the same: ‘We want good administration. We are Macedonians, not Greeks or Bulgars ... We want to be left in peace’” (Rossos 1994: 380; on Corfe’s work in the Balkans see Michailidis 1996). German traveler and social-democratic member of the German Reichstag Hermann Wendel (1922: 77) reported that Muslims in traditional dress proclaimed themselves “Macedonians”, though when prompted, they also said “now we belong to the Serbian state, so we are now Serbs”. Wendel also encountered a vegetable shop owned by “Jordanović”; the shop sign clearly indicated that the last two letters had been freshly painted. Wendel speculated that the man had originally called himself Jordan, but “in 1912 he changed to Jordanov, changed to Serbian Jordanović in 1912, remained harmlessly in his stall as Bulgarian Jordanov until 1915, and two years later calmly continued life as Jordanović”. But when Wendel asked “What are you, a Serb or a Bulgarian?” the shopkeeper replied “Macedonian!”.

Some Macedonian Slavs rejected Bulgarian loyalties because wartime trauma had turned them against the kingdom of Bulgaria. On 19 April 1926, R. A. Gallop, a British diplomat visiting Skopje, wrote in a report on “Conditions in Macedonia” that “There seemed to be no love lost for the Bulgars in most places. Their brutality during the war had lost them the affection even of those who before the Balkan War had been their friends” (quoted in Rossos 1994: 380). A group of men in Skopska Cerna Gora expressed equally vigorous anti-Bulgarian sentiments to Rebecca West: “they are our *non-brothers*”. Yet West also encountered a Bulgarophile youth in Bitola who blamed the Yugoslav government for the lack of a proper road to the Adriatic: “What a shame it is that we do not belong to Bulgaria ... Did we but belong to Bulgaria, as we ought to, considering we are all Bulgarians, it would be done and well done.” West’s Bitola informant also claimed a certain Veles lawyer as a staunch Bulgarian patriot, though the lawyer himself rejected the description: "I am not a Bulgarian patriot. I am not even a Bulgarian. I can be quite sure about that, for when I was a child I saw my father, who was a Serbian schoolmaster in a village between here and Prilep, murdered by Bulgarians." The Veles lawyer further rejected nationalism as a virtue: "I believe it is time we stopped thinking of such little things as whether we are Serbs or Bulgarians. I believe we should rather realize with a new seriousness that we are all human beings" (West 1969: 676, 787, 797 f.).

Regionalism as the basis of Macedonian nationalism in communist Yugoslavia

Neither the Bulgarian government nor Macedonian revolutionary organizations in Sofia could reconcile themselves to a Serbian Macedonia. During the Second World War, when Bulgaria fought as a German ally, most of Vardar Macedonia fell under Bulgarian rule (Todorovski 1975). Bulgarian occupation initially enjoyed some support. On 15 July 1940, a series of pro-Bulgarian committees throughout Macedonia issued a joint declaration proclaiming that "Bulgarians from and in Macedonia" desired to "return to motherland Bulgaria" (see Hristov 1941).

The Bulgarian occupation of Macedonia, however, proved disastrously counterproductive for the Bulgarian cause. Serbian cultural institutions were Bulgarianized for the war's duration, but most key posts went to officials sent from Bulgaria. Many of these "Bulgarians" were originally Macedonians who had been uprooted during the Balkan Wars, but their imposition nevertheless displaced existing elites and created a sense of local grievance. The Bulgarian administration also coincided with the privations and violence of war, which hardly created positive associations. The war was a traumatic period of Macedonian history. Slavs in Aegean Macedonia became the target of Greek ethnic cleansing. Greek scholar Evangelos Kofos (1989b) estimates that some 15000–20000 Slavs were pushed into Yugoslavia at the end of the Second World War. Though he hopefully claims that "in Greek Macedonia persecution never reached genocide-like practices", Vardar Macedonia nevertheless had to cope with large numbers of displaced people. The summary in Barker (1950: 80) is probably accurate: "In so far as it is possible to generalize, it seems that the Bulgarian occupation ... was sufficiently unpleasant to disillusion most of the population of Yugoslav Macedonia about the advantages of belonging to Bulgaria."

The backlash against wartime national chauvinism, and the suffering it caused, created considerable popular support for Tito and the Communist Partisans. The Communists had promoted multi-ethnic Macedonia in the interwar period, and during the war tried to establish a common line with Communists in Greece and

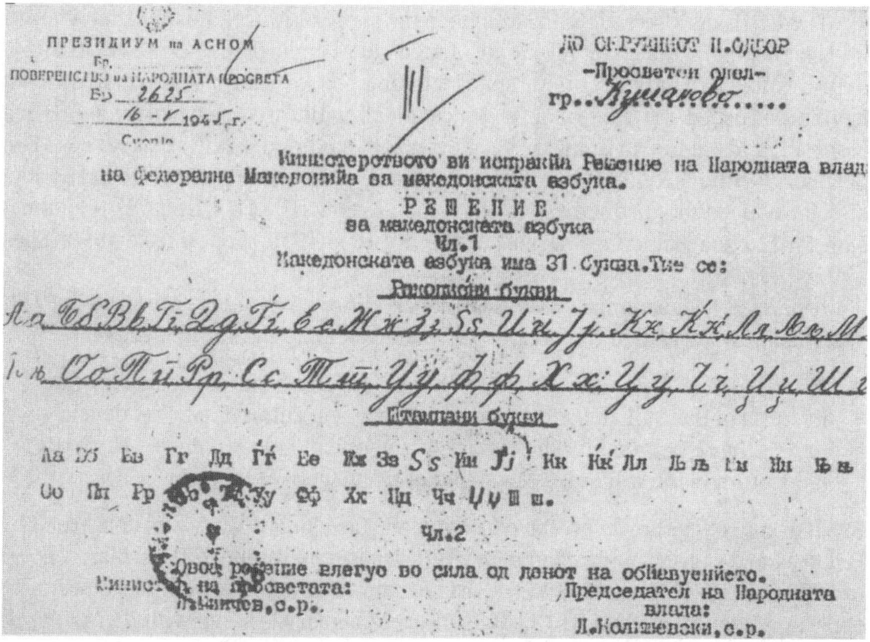

ПРЕЗИДИУМ на АСНОМ
ПОВЕРЕНСТВО на НАРОДНАТА ПРОСВЕТА
Бр. 2625
16-V 1945 г.
Скопје

ДО СЕРУЗИСОТ Н.ОДБОР
-Просветен оддел-
гр. Куманово

Министерството ви испраќа Решение на Народната влада на федерална Македонија за македонската азбука.

РЕШЕНИЕ
за македонската азбука
Чл.1
Македонската азбука има 31 букви. Тие се:
Ракописни букви

Штампани букви
Аа Бб Вв Гг Дд Ѓѓ Ее Жж Зз Ѕѕ Ии Јј Кк Ќќ Лл Љљ Мм Нн Њњ Оо Пп Рр Сс Тт Уу Фф Хх Цц Чч Џџ Шш.

Чл.2
Ова решение влегува во сила од денот на обнародувањето.

Министер на просветата:
[illegible]ичев, с.р.

Председател на Народната влада:
Л.Колишевски, с.р.

Figure 3: The Decree establishing the Macedonian alphabet, 1945 (Kempgen 2007)

Bulgaria. Milovan Djilas placed the Macedonian policy of Yugoslav communists in a wider Balkan context:

> A solution of the Macedonian question which not only is not prejudicial to either Serbs or Bulgars but in fact strengthens the brotherly ties between the two peoples and the Macedonians is one of the greatest historical events in the Balkans and one of the vital requisites for a general consolidation of the Balkan situation and for the ensuring of peace and independence for the Balkan peoples (quoted in Slijepcević 1958: 217).

Ever since the Comintern decision of 1934, Yugoslav Communists had recognized a distinctively Macedonian nation. For example Svetozar Vukmanović-Tempo, Tito's deputy in Macedonia, promoted a "Slavo Macedonian nation" as a counterweight to the propaganda of Axis Bulgaria (Sfetas 1995: 297). On 29 November 1943, at the Partisan congress in Jajce, Tito's partisans officially declared Macedonia a distinct national unit within re-founded, multi-national Yugoslavia: "Yugoslavia is being built up on a federal principle which will ensure full equality for the nations of Serbia, Croatia, Slovenia, Macedonia, Montenegro, Bosnia and Herzegovina" (Baker 1950: 94, Schoup 1968: 144–83).

The Partisans also sought to strengthen the sense of Macedonian distinctiveness by establishing a Macedonian literary language (Tomić 1992: 437–54). In 1944, they formed a linguistic commission including Venko Markovski, credited with having published the first book in Macedonian while living in Sofia, and Blaže Koneski, a Macedonian linguist. They eventually codified a new alphabet based on Serbian Cyrillic (see Figure 3). This used the "Serbian" letters {Љ} and {Њ}, but also introduced the distinctively Macedonian letters {Ѓ}, {Ќ}, and {Ѕ} (Commission for Language and Orthography 1945, Koneski 1950, Topolinjska 1998, Shea 1997: 207–210).[10]

A uniquely Macedonian script was not an entirely new idea: Missirkov (1974: 146) had also advocated the creation of a Macedonian literary language:

> As a devotee of the idea of complete separation of our interests from the interests of the Balkan nations and of independent cultural national development, I have written it in the central Macedonian dialect, which will be for me from now on a literary Macedonian language.

In Misirkov's day, however, the education of Macedonian Slavs was dominated by Bulgaria and Serbia, with around 781 Bulgarian schools and 260 Serbian schools in 1900 (Lange-Akhund 1998: 33). Risto Kantardzhiev (1974: 108), a Macedonian expert on literacy, counted 1 132 Bulgarian elementary schools with 63 763 pupils in 1911, as compared to 303 Serbian schools in 1906. Starting in 1944, with the war still raging, Partisans began distributing the Macedonian textbook *Bukvar na makedonsi jazik* in schools near Kostur and Lerin (Florina) (Shea 1997: 207). Postwar Yugoslavia introduced Koneski's orthography in all Macedonian schools, and starting on 3 May 1945, made it the official orthography for the Macedonian government.

Linguistic distinctiveness frequently acts as a marker of ethnic nationality in Eastern Europe and the Balkans, and the linguistic policy of the Tito government was a conscious attempt to transform Macedonian regionalism into ethnic nationalism. The postwar Yugoslav government also introduced "Macedonian" as an ethnicity in the census, and in 1948 counted 810000 Macedonians (Breznik 1974: 20). Promoting a Macedonian ethnic nation enabled the Communists to demonstrate their lack of Serbian chauvinism, underscoring their difference from the previous regime.

This project to promote a distinctive Macedonian ethnicity, complete with a distinctive language, proved popular and successful. American journalist Robert St. John emphasized the importance of language in his tour of Macedonia:

---

[10] Note that the Macedonian letter {Ѕ} is pronounced /dz/; Macedonian writes the sound /s/ with the Cyrillic letter {С}.

> The people are being allowed to speak their own languages, whatever that language was. To them this seemed more important than anything else. Even than how much food they had to eat. They said they didn't hate Belgrade any more. It was different now. Now Belgrade no longer meant Serbs who tried to force them to speak the language of the Master race (St. John 1947: 310).

St. John also wrote that Yugoslavia was "encouraging the use of the Macedonian language, which is quite different from the language of the Serbs. There are Macedonian schools, Macedonian newspapers and magazines, a Macedonian university" (1947: 99). John Morris (1948: 99) similarly wrote that Macedonians "unlike the other Yugoslav peoples, have attained their national identity only in the past three years ... the Macedonians are acutely conscious of their newly won status and are anxious to assert it". Morris laid great emphasis on the creation of a literary language as a symbol of this new status, declaring that the government had "done for Macedonians what Vuk Karadzic did for the Serbs and Croats a century ago, and given a literary form to a spoken language which was previously without literature".

While Serbs have reconciled themselves to their failure to Serbianize Macedonia, Bulgarians have not, perhaps because Bulgarophile Macedonian Slavs still exist. Indeed, some Macedonian Slavs still combine Bulgarian ethnic sentiment with the desire for an independent multi-ethnic Macedonia. In 1989, for example, Ivan Mihailov, a self-professed "Bulgarian from Macedonia", told Macedonian journalist Boris Višinsky (2001) that he sought "an independent Macedonia with recognized historical ethnic groups". Mihailov, however, represents a minority opinion in Macedonia itself.

The Macedonian National Movement and nationalism theory: a few conclusions

At the beginning of the twentieth century, then, the adjective "Macedonian" described a multi-ethnic region that inspired group loyalty and political action among its large Slavic population. Before the First World War, these Slavic activists mostly saw themselves as Bulgarians. A vigorous interwar campaign to Serbianize Macedonia's Slavs failed to convince Macedonian Slavs that they were Serbs, yet Macedonian Slavs increasingly became disillusioned with both Serbian assimilationism and Bulgarian irredentism. The trauma of the Second World War proved decisive: when the Communist Partisans promoted a Macedonian "ethnic" nation within the context of federal Yugoslavia, they won considerable popular support among the Macedonian public. This new ethnic project succeeded not least because it built upon powerful pre-existing loyalties to Macedonia as a multi-ethnic region.

This narrative, dating Slavic Macedonian particularism to the end of the Second World War, obviously rejects the primordialist explanation of modern nationalism. Some nationalism theorists, notably Anthony Smith (1998: 145–169), seem to regard the slaying of this particular dragon as redundant, but popular historiography, whether Greek, Bulgarian and Macedonian, routinely juxtaposes the "reality" of the preferred national concept with the "myths" of rival concepts (see Danforth 1995: 28–55). This modernist narrative, however, accounts for more evidence than traditional narratives: it accounts for both expressions "Bulgarian loyalty" and "Macedonian loyalty", and it reconciles the vitality of modern Macedonian nationalism with the national apathy recorded by foreign travelers at the beginning of the century.

Ironically, communist internationalism played a central role in promoting Macedonian ethnic particularism. Rogers Brubaker's powerful analysis of "nationalizing states" has suggested that socialist states frequently adopted policies that institutionalized national concepts. Brubaker (1996: 16, 79–106) has suggested that scholars ask what makes "the nation-evoking, nation-invoking efforts of political entrepreneurs more or less likely to succeed", and this narrative offers a historical explanation why the Yugoslav communist party enjoyed so much success with its Macedonian national concept. This analysis also explains why Tito and Koneski enjoyed greater success than Misirkov, whose ideas lend themselves to selective retroactive appropriation, but whose Ottoman political loyalties, belief in the Bulgarian character of IMRO, and rejection of primordialism put him at variance with contemporary Macedonian nationalism.

Multi-ethnic Macedonian regionalism calls into question the implicit moral assumption that multi-ethnic nationalism is democratic and tolerant: the movement for multi-ethnic Macedonia in the late Ottoman Empire was a nationalism of bombs, bloodshed, and the slogan "freedom or death". Meanwhile, Misirkov's call for Macedonian ethnic particularism respected existing frontiers and sought peaceful reform of government administration.

From the perspective of nationalism theory, however, the most striking aspect of this narrative is the "regional" Macedonian feeling of the early twentieth century. Most contemporary observers assume that Slavic Macedonian nationalism is "ethnic" nationalism: John Stremlau (1995: 408) assumes that American intervention is necessary for promoting civic nationalism in Macedonia, while Hugh Poulton (1995: 186) contrasts civic Albanian demands with Macedonian ethnic nationalism. Perhaps in the context of post-Communist Macedonian policy toward the Albanian minority, this terminology is understandable.

Macedonian regionalism, however, may also help scholars heed Michel Seymor's call (2000: 27) to "go beyond the ethnic/civic dichotomy". Several prominent nationalism theorists, including Hans Kohn (1969: 163–65) and Ernst Gellner (1983: 97), have described ethnic nationalism as "Eastern nationalism" or the "classical Habsburg (and points east) form of nationalism". National concepts in Slavic Macedonia problematize these assumptions: at the turn of the century, Slavic Macedonians sought, however unsuccessfully, to imagine a multi-ethnic "regional" nation distinct from both the "ethnic" nations in Macedonia and existing state structures. The Bulgarian-Vlach alliance, furthermore, suggests that this multi-ethnicism attracted significant political support, even if the implacable Greek opposition ultimately rendered multi-ethnic Macedonia an unrealistic political project.

Literature

Adanir, Fikret 1979: Die makedonische Frage. Ihre Entstehung und Entwicklung bis 1908. Wiesbaden: Franz Steiner.

Anastasovski, Nick 2005: Contestations over Macedonian Identity, 1870–1912. Melbourne: Victoria University Doctoral Thesis in Social Sciences.

Anon. 1927: The Macedonian Slavs, Their National Character and Struggles. Indianapolis: Central Committee of the Union of the Macedonian Political Organizations of the United States and Canada.

Arslan, Ali 2003: Greek-Vlach Conflict in Macedonia. In: Études Balkaniques 2: 78–102.

Bakeless, John 1935: The Macedonian Question. In: Annals of the American Academy of Political and Social Science 177: 223-231.

Bakić-Hayden, Milica 1995: Nesting Orientalisms: The Case of Former Yugoslavia. In: Slavic Review 54, 4: 917–931.

Banac, Ivo 1984: The National Question in Yugoslavia: Origins, History, Politics. Ithaca, London: Cornell University Press.

Barker, Elisabeth 1950: Macedonia: Its Place in Balkan Power Politics. London: Broadwater.

Bonsal, Stephen 1946: Suitors and Supplicants: The Little Nations at Versailles. Port Washington: Prentice Hall (http://www.hungarian-history.hu/lib/bonsal/bonsal13.htm).

Booth, John 1905: Trouble in the Balkans. London: Hurst and Blackett.

Božinov, Voin, Lyobomir Panayotov (eds.) 1978; Macedonia, Documents and Materials, 4 vols. Sofia: Bulgarian Academy of Sciences, Institute of History.

Brailsford, Henry 1906: Macedonia, Its Races and Their Future. London: Methuen.

Breznik, Dušan 1974: Nations and Nationalities of Yugoslavia. Belgrade: Medjunarodna Politika.

Brubaker, Rogers 1996: Nationalism Reframed. Cambridge: Cambridge University Press.

Brubaker, Rogers 2002: Ethnicity Without Groups. In: Archives européennes de sociologie 43, 2: 163–189.

Carnegie Foundation 1914: Report of the International Commission. Washington DC: Carnegie Endowment for International Peace.

Carpenter, Therese 2003: The Miss Stone Affair: America's First Modern Hostage Crisis. New York: Simon and Schuster.

Clutterbuck, Richard 1977: Guerillas and Terrorists. Athens, Ohio: Ohio University Press.

Commission for Language and Orthography, 1945: Makedonski pravopis [Macedonian Orthography]. Skopje: Državno izdavačko Pretprijatie.

Cvijić, Jovan 1906: Promatranja o etnografiji makedonskih Slovena [Observations on the Ethnography of the Macedonian Slavs]. Belgrade: Geca Kon.

Dakin, Douglas 1966: The Greek Struggle in Macedonia 1897–1913. Thessaloniki: Institute for Balkan Studies.

Danforth, Loring 1995: The Macedonian Conflict: Ethnic Nationalism in a Transnational World. Princeton: Princeton University Press.

Džambazovski, Kliment 1963: Stojan Novaković i makedonizam [Stojan Novaković and Macedonianism]. In: Istorijski časopis 14: 140–142.

Ehrenbug, Ilya 1947: European Crossroad: A Soviet Journalist in the Balkans, translated by Anya Markov. New York: Knopf.

Fleming, K. E. 1999: The Muslim Bonaparte. Princeton: Princeton University Press.

Frasier, John Foster 1912: Pictures from the Balkans. London: Cassel.

Gaber, Natasha Aneta Joveska 2004: Macedonian Census Results - Controversy or Reality? In: South-East Europe Review for Labour and Social Affairs 1: 99–110.

Gellner, Ernest 1983: Nations and Nationalism. Oxford: Blackwell.

Gewehr, Wesley Marsh 1931: The Rise of Nationalism in the Balkans. New York: Holt [reprinted by Archon 1967].

Gounaris, Basil 1995: Social Cleavages and national "awakening" in Ottoman Macedonia. In: East European Quarterly 29: 409–426.

Hamm, Josip 1976: Moj osvrt na K. P. Misirkova [My view of K. P. Misirkov]. In: Trajko Stamatoski (ed.), Krste P. Misirkov i nacionalno-kulturniot razvoj na makedonskiot narod do osloboduvanjeto [Krste Misirkov and the National-Cultural Movement for a Macedonian Nation to the Liberation]. Skopje: IMJ Krste Misirkov.

Heathcote, Dudley 1925: My Wanderings in the Balkans. London: Hutchinson.

Hirschon, Renée 2003: Crossing the Aegean: an Appraisal of the 1923 Compulsory Population Exchange Between Greece and Turkey. London: Berghahn.

Holevas, Ioannis 1991: Oi Ellines slavophonoi tis Makedonias [Slavophone Greeks in Macedonia]. Athens: Risos.

Hristov, Aleksandar 1978: Prilozi za Ilinden: Materijali od naučinot sobir na Ilindenskoto Vostanie i Kruševskata Republika [Papers on Ilinden: Materials from the Conference About the Ilinden Uprising and the Kruševo Republic]. Kruševo: Sovet Deset Dena Kruševska Republika.

Hristov, Hristo 1978: Gotse Delčev. Spomeni, dokumenti, materiali [Gotse Delčev, Memoirs, Documents, Materials]. Sofia: Nauka i izkustvo.

Hristov, K. 1941: The Declaration. In: Iljustracija Ilinden [Ilinden Illustration] 14: 5

Ignatieff, Michael 1992: Blood and Belonging. London: BBC Press.

Kantardzhiev, Risto, Lazo Lazaroski 1974: Schools and Education. In: The Socialist Republic of Macedonia. Skopje: Macedonian Review Editions.

Karpat, Kemal 1985: Ottoman Population, 1830–1914: Demographic and Social Characteristics. Madison: University of Wisconsin Press.

Kempgen, Sebastian 2007: Kultur und Kulturgeschichte Makedoniens (Slavo-Makedoniens) (http://kodeks.uni-bamberg.de/Macedonia/MakAlphabetDecree.htm).

Kofos, Evangelos 1989a: National Heritage and National Identity in Nineteenth and Twentieth Century Macedonia. In: European History Quarterly 19: 229–267.

Kofos, Evangelos 1989b: The Impact of the Macedonian Question on Civil Conflict in Greece (1943–49). In: Hellenic Foundation for Defence and Foreign Policy 3 (http://www.macedonian-heritage.gr/downloads/lirary/Kofos02.pdf).

Kohn, Hans 1969: Western and Eastern Nationalisms. In: John Hutchinson, Anthony Smith (eds.), Oxford Reader on Nationalism. Oxford: Oxford University Press, 1969, 163–165.

Koliopoulos, John 1999: Plundered Loyalties: Axis Occupation and Civil Strife in Greek West Macedonia, 1941–49. New York: New York University.

Koneski, Blaže 1960: Toward the Macedonian Renaissance: Macedonian Textbooks of the Nineteenth Century. Skopje: Nova Makedonija.

Lagne-Akhund, Nadine 1998: The Macedonian Question, 1893–1908: From Western Sources. New York: Colombia University Press.

Lunt, Horace 1984: Some Sociolinguistic Aspects of Macedonian and Bulgarian. Ann Arbor: University of Michigan.

Maxwell, Alexander 2005: Multiple Nationalism: National Concepts in 19th Century Hungary and Benedict Anderson's "Imagined Communities". In: Nationalism and Ethnic Politics 11, 3: 385–414.

McCarthy, Justin 2001: The Ottoman Peoples and the End of Empire. London: Arnold.

Michailidis, Iakovos 1996: Minority Rights and Educational Problems in Greek Interwar Macedonia: The Case of the Peimer "Abecedar". In: Journal of Modern Greek Studies 14, 2: 329–343.

Michailidis, Iakovos 1998: The War of Statistics: Traditional Recipes for the Preparation of the Macedonian Salad. In: East European Quarterly 32, 1: 9–21.

Mihajlov, Ivan 1965: Osvoboditelna borba 1919–24 g. [The Liberation War 1919–1924]. Brussels: Louvain.

Missirkov, Krsté 1974 [1903]: On Macedonian Matters, translated by Alan McConnell. Skopje: Macedonian Review.

Mitev, Trandafil 1993: Bălgarskata emigracija v Amerika i borbite za osvoboždenieto na Makedonija, 1919–1945 [The Bulgarian Emigration in America and the Struggle to Liberate Macedonia, 1919–1945]. Sofia: Sv. Georgie Pobedonosec.

Mitev, Trandafil 2001: A Short History of the Macedonian Patriotic Organization. Sofia: Macedonian Scientific Institute.

Morris, John 1948: Yugoslavia. London: St. Botolph.

Najdoski, Djordjia 1987: VMRO (Obedineta) i žurnalističkata dejnost na Dimitar Vlahov [IMRO-United and the Journalistic Activity of Dimitar Vlahov]. Skopje: NIO Studentski zbor.

Nihtinen, Atina 1995: Comments on Contradictions in the Life and Work of Kr. P. Misirkov. In: Studia Slavica Finlandensia 12: 96–103.

Nikoloudis, Georgios 2002: Oi ellenes Slavophonoi sti Makedonia e istoria kai to problima tis tautotitas tous [Slavophone Greeks in Macedonia, or History and the Problem of their Identity]. Thessaloniki: Irodotos.

Novaković, Stojan 1894: S Morave na Vardar – Putne veleške [From the Morava to the Vardar – Travel Notes]. Belgrade: Stamp.

Novaković, Stojan 1906: Balkanska pitanja i manje istorijsko-poličje beleške o Balkansom poluostrovu, 1886–1905 [The Balkan Question and Some Historical-Political Notes on the Balkan Peninsula, 1886–1905]. Belgrade: Kolarca.

Parvanova, Zorka 2001: Programme and Organizational Transformations of National Movements in Eastern Turkey (1910–1912). In: Études Balkaniques 66: 52–68.

Perry, Duncan 1988: The Politics of Terror: The Macedonian Liberation Movements 1893–1903. Durham: Duke University Press.

Phillips, John 2004: Macedonia: Warlords and Rebels in the Balkans. Yale: Yale University Press.

Poljanski, Hristo 1969: The Ilinden Rising. In: From the Past of the Macedonian People. Skopje: Nova Makedonija.

Poljanski, Hristo 1972: Delčev i negovoto vreme [Delčev and his Age]. Skopje: Misla.

Poulton, Hugh 1995: Who are the Macedonians? London: Hurst and Co.

Pribichevich, Stoyan 1982: Macedonia, Its People and History. University Park: Pennsylvania State University Press.

Pulevski, Gjorgji 1875: Rečnik od tri jezika [Dictionary of Three Languages]. Belgrade.

Radin, Michael 1993: IMRO and the Macedonian Question. Skopje: Kultura.

Rossos, Andrew 1994: The British Foreign Office and Macedonian Identity, 1918–1941. In: Slavic Review 53, 2: 367–394.

Roudometof, Victor 1996: Nationalism and Identity Politics in the Balkans: Greece and the Macedonian Question. In: Journal of Modern Greek Studies 14, 2: 253–301.

Roudometof, Victor 2002: Collective Memory, National Identity, and Ethnic Conflict: Greece, Bulgaria and the Macedonian Question. Westport, Conn.: Praeger.

Said, Edward 1978: Orientalism: Western Conceptions of the Orient. London: Pantheon.

Šaldev, Hristo 1993: Extracts from the Memoirs of Hristo Shaldev, Macedonian Revolutionary (1876–1962). Adeliade: Todor Alexandrov.

Schnapper, Domnique 1998 [1994]: Community of Citizens: On the Modern Idea of Nationality. New Brunswick: Transaction Publishers.

Schoup, Paul 1968: Communism and the Yugoslav National Question. New York: Colombia University Press.

Schultze-Jena, Leonard 1927: Makedonien: Landschafts- und Kulturbilder. Jena: Gustav Fischer.

Seymour, Michel 2000: On Redefining the Nation. In: Nenad Miščević (ed.), Nationalism and Ethnic Conflict: Philosophical Perspectives. Chicago: Open Court, 25–55.

Sfetas, Spyidon 1995: Autonomist Movements of the Slavophones in 1944: The Attitude of the Communist Party of Greece and the Protection of the Greek-Yugoslav Border. In: Balkan Studies 36, 2 (http://www.macedonian-heritage.gr/downloads/library/Sfetas01.pdf).

Shea, John 1997: Macedonia and Greece: The Struggle to Define a New Balkan Nation. Jefferston, NC: McFarland.

Slavejkov, Petko 1871: The Macedonian Question. In: Makedonija, 18 January 1871.

Slijepcević, Djoko 1958: The Macedonian Question Chicago: American Institute for Balkan Affairs.

Smith, Anthony 1998: Nationalism and Modernism. London: Routledge.

Smith, Anthony 2000: The Nation in History: Historiographical Debates about Ethnicity and Nationalism. Hanover, NH: University Press of New England.

Spencer, Philip, Howard Wollman 2002: Nationalism: A Critical Introduction. London: Sage.

St. John, Robert 1947: The Silent People Speak. New York: Doubleday.

Stremlau, John 1995: Antidote to Anarchy. In: Brad Roberts (ed.), Order and Disorder After the Cold War. Boston: MIT Press, 29–44.

Todorova, Maria 1997: Imagining the Balkans. New York: Oxford University Press.

Todorovski, Gligor 1975: Okupatsijata na Zapadna Makedonija [The Occupation of Western Macedonia]. Skopje: Misla [second edition: Skopje: NIO Studentski Zbor, 1982]).

Tomić, Olga Mišenka 1992: Macedonian as an Ausbau Language. In: Michael Clyne (ed.), Pluricentric Languages: Differing Norms in Different Nations. Berlin: Mouton de Gruyter, 437–454.

Topolinjska, Zuzanna (ed.) 1998: The Sociolinguistic Situation of the Macedonian Language. A themed issue of the International Journal of the Sociology of Language 131.

Ullman, Hermann 1943: Die Völker im Südosten. Jena: Eugen Diederichs.

Vakalopoulos, Konstantinos 1983: O Voreios Ellinismos kata tin proimi phasi tou Makedonikou Agona (1878–1894) [Northern Hellenism in the Early Stages of the Macedonian Struggle (1878–1894)]. Thessalonika.

Vidoeski, Bozidar 1998: Five Decades since the Codification of the Macedonian Language. In: Zuzanna Topolinjska (ed.), The Sociolinguistic Situation of the Macedonian Language. A themed issue of the International Journal of the Sociology of Language 131: 13–29.

Višinksy, Boris, written interview with Ivan Mihailov, 1 October 1989. Reprinted in Demokratsia, 8 January 2001: 10–11; English translation available online at http://www.macedoniainfo.com/Independent_Macedonia.htm, accessed 21 January 2007.

Wendel, Hermann 1922: Kreuz und quer durch den slawischen Süden. Frankfurt am Main: Societäts-Druckerei.

West, Rebecca 1969 [1940]: Black Lamb, Grey Falcon. New York: Viking Press.

Wilkinson, Henry 1951: Maps and Politics. A review of Ethnographic Cartography of Macedonia. Liverpool: Liverpool University Press.

Wolff, Larry 1994: Inventing Eastern Europe: The Map of Civilization on the Mind of the Enlightenment. Stanford: University Press.

Pratiques de la *coexistence* en milieu multiethnique transylvain et nouvelles mobilisations régionales

Bianca Botea, Lyon

Cet article relate quelques résultats d'une recherche menée principalement dans la ville de Cluj-Napoca, en Roumanie, recherche qui a porté sur la construction symbolique de la Transylvanie et les recompositions identitaires et régionales actuelles de cet espace. Cette recherche m'a amenée à observer que les discours sur la Transylvanie étaient fortement compétitifs et souvent conflictuels, polarisant des groupes et amenant à des phénomènes d'ethnicisation. Ces discours et les conceptions du territoire qui sont sous-jacentes traduisent plus largement un phénomène de «coexistence» des narrations et plus largement des groupes. Cet article présentera quelques facettes de ce phénomène de «coexistence» roumano-hongroise à Cluj-Napoca.

Mais les négociations à propos de la Transylvanie ne produisent pas seulement de la polarisation ethnique, mais aussi de la mise en commun entre individus ou collectifs différents. Ces négociations engagent parfois des actions communes à travers lesquelles certaines oppositions et lectures nationalistes de la Transylvanie sont en partie outrepassées. La deuxième partie de mon intervention s'arrêtera ainsi sur ces nouvelles mobilisations de type régional et régionaliste qui ont émergé récemment en Transylvanie sous l'influence de l'*Europe des Régions*, et qui interrogent des recompositions sociales et territoriales qui ont lieu dans cette partie d'Europe.

Cette recherche s'est appuyée sur différents lieux et objets de terrain à Cluj-Napoca: pratiques d'occupation de l'espace urbain et de patrimonialisation, usages conflictuels de la langue dans l'espace public, pratiques muséales, réseaux des associations magyarophones. J'ai privilégié le point de vue des acteurs engagés dans des structures institutionnelles et associatives, mettant l'accent davantage sur la production socio-politique de la Transylvanie que sur les pratiques des habitants de la ville dans leur vie quotidienne. C'est au niveau des discours et des actions des différents acteurs institutionnels et associatifs que cette catégorie est le plus évoquée et souvent de manière controversée.

Une remarque m'apparaît nécessaire d'entrée de jeu: mon propos s'inscrit dans une approche dynamique et constructiviste qui ne considère pas les groupes ethniques comme des groupes figés et existant en soi, mais plutôt comme des groupes en cours de constitution ou de réactualisation dans la pratique sociale, dans le processus de cohabitation et de partage du même territoire. Même si ces identifications ethniques ou culturelles sont parfois vécues comme une réalité par les individus, cela n'annule en rien leur caractère «performatif», dans le sens où ils font advenir une réalité qui n'existait pas auparavant. De la même manière, la Transylvanie est abordée comme une catégorie performative produite dans le processus de négociation entre acteurs multiples, et non comme une réalité pré-existante et univoque.

Contexte historique transylvain

Province historique de la Roumanie, la Transylvanie est restée jusqu'à nos jours une catégorie forte de l'imaginaire local, national et transnational, bien qu'elle n'ait jamais véritablement constitué un territoire administratif. La force symbolique de cet espace repose sur le caractère très mouvant de ses frontières historiques, sur les tensions politiques qui en ont découlé et les mémoires encore très vivantes liées à cette histoire. Principauté autonome entre 1541 et 1699, la Transylvanie fait ensuite partie de l'empire des Habsbourgs et du Royaume hongrois puis, après la première guerre mondiale, est rattachée à la Roumanie. Une partie de ce territoire redevient hongroise durant la seconde guerre mondiale, puis est de nouveau réintégrée à la Roumanie après 1945.

Cette situation historique, et finalement sociale et politique, a fait de ce territoire ce que Jöel Kötek (1996) appelle une «région-frontière»: un territoire controversé, «située à la charnière d'ensembles ethniques ou idéologiques». Ces controverses se sont cristallisées principalement autour de deux processus de construction nationale concurrentes, roumaine et hongroise, toutes les deux intégrant la Transylvanie dans leur récit national.

Aujourd'hui en Roumanie vit une forte «minorité» hongroise (environ 1415000 selon le recensement de 2002) qui habite majoritairement en Transylvanie[1]: 98,9% de la population hongroise de Roumanie vit dans cette région, ce qui représente 19,6% sur la population totale de la Transylvanie. Dans la ville de Cluj-Napoca, considérée comme la capitale historique de la région et la capitale culturelle des Hongrois de Roumanie, la population magyare représente 18,8% de la population totale de la ville.

Les changements territoriaux survenus dans l'histoire de la Transylvanie ont laissé de profondes traces dans la mémoire de ses habitants et la population hongroise est encore fortement liée – socialement, économiquement et symboliquement – à la partie restée de l'autre côté de la frontière étatique roumaine.

---

[1] La Transylvanie sera considérée ici comme le territoire désigné comme tel après 1918, et non le territoire «historique» transylvain de la Principauté ou d'avant 1918.

Citoyens roumains, les Hongrois de Transylvanie revendiquent une différenciation culturelle forte par rapport à la population roumaine (le premier marqueur identitaire étant la langue) et une appartenance à une «nation» culturelle (et non étatique) hongroise. Les pratiques économiques, sociales, culturelles et même politiques de cette population s'inscrivent fortement dans l'espace transnational de cette «patrie hongroise»[2].

Cette orientation culturelle, économique et professionnelle vers la Hongrie de la part des Magyars de Transylvanie, peut laisser l'impression d'un fonctionnement parallèle ou séparé (sur le critère de la langue) par rapport au paysage institutionnel et associatif de la ville. Cette logique de la «coexistence», si elle garantit la pérennité du groupe culturel hongrois, devient problématique quand elle se traduit par des phénomènes de repli sur soi allant jusqu'à des pratiques d'exclusion de l'*autre* (du côté roumain ou hongrois).

Territoires de la coexistence

Sans avoir l'ambition de présenter en termes exhaustifs le tableau de cette «coexistence» qui caractérise la cohabitation roumano-hongroise à Cluj-Napoca, et notamment ses raisons d'existence, je m'arrêterai uniquement à quelques dimensions. Rico Lie, analysant les différents «états des espaces de communication interculturelle», évoque la «coexistence», comme une situation dans laquelle les éléments culturels sont présents les uns à côté des autres, «sans qu'il existe une interaction orientée vers la négociation ou le changement» (Lie 2002: 19). Il est question d'une co-présence d'éléments culturels plutôt isolés et d'une forme passive de communication.

Ce modèle de la *coexistence* renvoie à un phénomène décrit par Robert Hayden (2002) dans ses recherches sur les Balkans et sur l'Asie du Sud: la «tolérance comme non-interférence» *(tolerance as noninterference)*. Cette dernière serait une forme de tolérance passive («tolérer» apparaît ici dans le sens de «permettre», de «ne pas interférer avec»). Elle caractériserait les situations à travers lesquelles, même si différentes populations partageaient par exemple un même espace physique, elles mèneraient une vie en communautés séparées. Néanmoins, cela n'entraînerait pas pour autant des hostilités et des affrontements entre les populations. La pratique de *komşiluk* (mot d'origine turque), rencontrée en Bosnie, est donnée comme exemple pour illustrer cette situation. Cette pratique comporte des obligations strictes quant à la réciprocité entre les individus des différents groupes ethniques vivant à proximité, alors qu'elle interdit les mariages entre les membres

---

[2] Pour une analyse de cette notion de «patrie hongroise», voir Losonczy (1999) et Zempléni (1996).

de groupes confessionnels différents. Elle règle donc les relations entre les individus en tant que représentants des groupes, mais également entre les groupes, lesquels, au contraire, ne se mélangent pas (cf. Roth 2006).

Ce fonctionnement de «coexistence», sans réel échange et rencontre, peut être aussi rencontré à Cluj, notamment dans l'univers des institutions et des associations rattachées au réseau étatique ou magyarophone de la ville. Cela ne suppose pas pour autant qu'il n'existe pas de lieux associatifs qui transgressent ces frontières ethniques. Mais la tendance générale, notamment au niveau des institutions culturelles, est celle d'un fonctionnement en parallèle, d'un manque de dialogue et de projets en commun entre ces structures.

Ce fonctionnement séparé des institutions culturelles n'est pas un phénomène récent. Cette tradition était déjà présente du temps de l'Empire austro-hongrois, vers la fin du XIXe siècle, avec des réseaux associatifs culturels et économiques liés à chaque communauté ethnique. Cette tradition est perpétuée à Cluj durant l'entre-deux-guerres alors que le réseau institutionnel hongrois fonctionne encore (sans doute avec certaines difficultés), mais également lors de la première période du communisme. Les années 60 marquent un renouveau, dans le sens d'une diminution et parfois d'une disparition des possibilités de fonctionnement d'un dispositif institutionnel autonome hongrois, la meilleure illustration étant l'unification des deux universités respectivement en langue roumaine et hongroise de Cluj en 1959. Après 1989, le réseau institutionnel hongrois est récréé, avec l'objectif de remettre en place les structures fonctionnant durant l'entre-deux-guerres et dans la première période communiste.

De nos jours, le paradigme national roumain (rencontré par exemple dans les musées transylvains), ainsi que les politiques de recrutement dans les institutions culturelles «roumaines» affaiblissant la présence des employés hongrois, n'encouragent pas la rencontre avec les acteurs et le public hongrois. Pour illustrer ceux-ci nous pouvons observer l'exposition permanente du Musée National d'Histoire de la Transylvanie. Reprenant les principes de rédaction des manuels scolaires d'histoire des Roumains, cette exposition met en avant une histoire qui, «depuis les origines à nos jours», relate l'unité du *peuple roumain*. La diversité culturelle de la région transylvaine se fond dans un tout monolitique national et l'histoire des autres communautés ethniques de la Transylvanie apparaît uniquement comme une dimension annexe, une dimension proportionnelle d'un tout unitaire, voire parfois une parenthèse dans l'histoire.

A propos de la question de la diminution des employés hongrois dans les structures culturelles et scientifiques (publiques) de la ville de Cluj, j'ai pu observer l'existence de ce phénomène dans les musées (à partir de l'analyse des organigrammes), mais il est présent aussi dans d'autres institutions de Cluj: *Bibliothèque Municipale*, *Archives Nationales*, *Institut de l'Histoire de l'Académie roumaine* ou autres. Ce phénomène n'est pas récent, nous pourrions nous rappeler par exemple que, pendant les deux dernières décennies du communisme, les Hongrois étaient parfois écartés des postes de direction. Après 1989, cette diminution de la présence hongroise dans les institutions culturelles a continué. Nous pouvons remarquer que ce phénomène a un impact direct sur les actions et la politique de ces dernières: il oriente les axes de travail et de a recherche de ces institutions, la politique des acquisitions et, implicitement, il oriente la documentation (l'information) fournie au public, ce qui a aussi un impact décisif sur la construction ou l'attirance d'un certain type de public. Cet aspect est très visible pour des institutions publiques de Cluj comme par exemple pour les musées, que de nombreux Hongrois refusent de visiter.

Si la politique de certaines institutions publiques n'appellent pas à un dialogue ou une rencontre avec le public et les organismes hongrois, en revanche, le fort réseau institutionnel magyarophone entretient lui aussi ce fonctionnement en parallèle. Le responsable d'une association magyarophone de tourisme et pour la connaissance de la «patrie», témoigne du rôle de la langue dans cette construction identitaire hongroise, usage de la langue qui amène, dans ce contexte de disparition du bilinguisme du côté roumain, à la séparation des activités et des publics:

> «Si on invite aussi des Roumains à nos activités, la langue parlée sera le roumain. Mais quand on parle le roumain c'est comme quand on marche dans une chaussure un peu étroite. Ça te gêne un peu. C'est sûr qu'on peut marcher comme ça, mais ça devient trop fatiguant de faire de la randonnée dans une chaussure qui te gène et au bout du compte nous perdons aussi l'envie (...). *Je me sens frustré. En tant que président de l'association, je me sens isolé. Je vois qu'il y a d'autres associations roumaines à Cluj, avec lesquelles je n'ai aucun lien. Nous avons les mêmes objectifs, sauf que je marche sur mes chemins dans ma langue ... Et, pour être un peu ironique, j'en vivrai et j'en mourrai. Nous nous isolons, mais au moins nous restons entre nous*».

Le paysage associatif témoigne pleinement de cette coexistence des activités. Les associations qui regroupent de manière systématique Roumains et Hongrois sont plutôt rares, hormis les domaines qui concernent le travail social (assistance sociale, associations de volontariat) et le champ artistique. De la même manière, comme le notait aussi Claude Karnoouh (1998) par rapport aux associations étudiantes, il n'existe pas, hormis les clubs sportifs, d'associations syndicales, culturelles ou civiques communes.

Dans le domaine culturel, le manque de collaboration entre les élites roumaines et hongroises doit être compris comme un désintérêt pour la culture de l'autre. Orientés davantage vers les cultures de l'Occident (ou, depuis récemment, des autres continents), les intérêts sont moins dirigés vers le développement des relations entre cultures cohabitant sur le même territoire. Il faut noter que la culture hongroise de Transylvanie est tournée vers les productions culturelles de Budapest: la reconnaissance d'un écrivain hongrois de Transylvanie est validée à Budapest et dans la grande majorité des cas il restera totalement méconnu dans le milieu culturel roumain de Transylvanie. Nous pouvons remarquer par ailleurs le nombre extrêmement réduit de traducteurs professionnels pour les deux langues, ce qui est encore un indicateur d'un espace vide d'interconnaissance entre les deux groupes, notamment au niveau des productions de la culture *savante*. Les domaines des arts plastiques, de la musique et du théâtre sont des exceptions qui connaissent, au contraire, d'échanges fréquents.

Ce manque de collaboration roumano-hongroise au niveau des institutions et associations de la ville de Cluj est entretenu par une politique de financement public orientée vers une mise en valeur de la «culture nationale» (comprise comme ethno-nationale) ou vers le soutien des «communautés minoritaires», par des financements du *Service des Minorités* de l'Etat roumain ou des financements en provenance de Hongrie. Les financements publics destinés à stimuler le travail en commun et les liens entre les différentes communautés ethniques sont inexistants. Dans ce contexte, des fondations internationales comme par exemple, le réseau ONG de la Fondation Soros, orientent leurs ressources vers de tels programmes de collaboration (pour des ateliers de dialogue interculturel, des publications bilingues, la coopération scientifique), mais une fois le réservoir fermé, la logique de développement ethno-nationale reprend le dessus.

A travers mes recherches à Cluj, j'ai pu observer qu'au sein de ces réseaux juxtaposés sont construites et diffusées des lectures différentes et souvent exclusives du territoire de la Transylvanie. Au centre de cette interprétation différente repose une lecture controversée de l'histoire de ce territoire. L'histoire de la région est décrite différemment avec les premiers manuels d'histoires que l'on enseigne dans les écoles primaires roumaines et hongroises. Aujourd'hui, les guides touristiques de la ville présentent des lectures différentes, selon qu'ils sont écrits en roumain ou hongrois. Beaucoup plus riche en informations que les guides roumains, des guides magyarophones que j'ai analysés présentent le patrimoine de la ville en faisant appel à l'ancienne toponymie hongroise. Les noms actuels des rues apparaissent entre parenthèses et, de manière similaire, les objectifs touristiques (bâtiments, statues, etc.) sont présentés sous leur nom et leur fonction antérieures à 1918, alors que l'usage actuel du lieu est rajouté brièvement à la fin de cette présentation. Les itinéraires touristiques cheminent des lieux de mémoire hongrois de la ville et inscrivent cette dernière dans une Transylvanie où la présence et la contribution roumaine apparaissent seulement comme une parenthèse ou un accident de l'histoire. Les guides en langue roumaine sont souvent une réplique et une construction en miroir reprenant cette même idée, valorisant cette fois un passé et un territoire «roumain».

Si deux interprétations différentes, voire parfois opposées, du territoire de la Transylvanie peuvent apparaître à travers leur mise en circulation par ces réseaux institutionnels, associatifs, commerciaux, etc., ces lectures ne sont cependant pas homogènes intérieurement, car nous rencontrons des rapports différents à ce territoire même au sein de chacun des deux groupes ethniques. Malgré cela, dans la pratique sociale - surtout dans ce contexte de ségrégation institutionnelle ou d'ethnicisation au niveau de la vie quotidienne - nombreuses sont les situations où les différenciations internes qui se manifestent au sein de chaque groupe arrivent plus facilement à un consensus, par rapport à la tendance très faible de rapprochement entre ces deux visions ethnicisées du territoire.

Sans avoir mené de travaux approfondis sur les pratiques urbaines et de cohabitation des habitants de la ville, mes observations, ainsi que certaines études existantes (Feischmidt 2003), montrent que les phénomènes de segmentation ethnique ne sont pas totalement étrangers à la pratique quotidienne des individus. Un de mes interlocuteurs me relate l'enterrement d'une de ces collègues de travail, muséographe, pour laquelle l'office religieux s'est déroulé en langue hongroise dans l'église romano-catholique de Cluj. Comme une partie des participants à cet évènement étaient des Roumains - collègues de travail ou voisins de la personne décédée - ceux-ci ont manifesté leur souhait que la cérémonie soit aussi officiée en langue roumaine. La demande fut refusée par le prêtre et les autres instances de l'église. Les exemples sont multiples. Dans un autre registre, la pratique de cohabitation des étudiants et, en particulier, une certaine disposition ethnique des étudiants dans les résidences universitaires, témoigne d'un phénomène similaire des réseaux de sociabilité ethnicisés. Comme l'observait aussi Claude Karnoouh (1998), ces lieux ne sont pas disposés ethniquement à l'avance, mais les étudiants cherchent souvent à se regrouper selon le critère ethnique, échangeant avec d'autres personnes afin de retrouver des collègues de chambre parlant la même langue.

Le même phénomène peut être observé dans d'autres domaines de la vie quotidienne des habitants de la ville. Margit Feischmidt a montré que l'organisation du marché du travail et des niches économiques suit souvent ces critères ethniques. Cet auteur met en évidence le fait que, de manière générale, les personnes hongroises d'un niveau d'éducation plus élevé résistent davantage à l'intégration et s'insèrent dans des réseaux de sociabilité magyarophone. Aussi, la socialisation au sein des jeunes hongrois du milieu ouvrier transgresse plus souvent les frontières ethniques. Les contacts entre voisins et collègues de travail provenant d'un milieu ethnique différent sont plutôt rares et superficiels parmi les classes sociales plus éduquées. En revanche, elles sont plutôt fréquentes au niveau des classes ouvrières, surtout celles provenant du milieu rural. Cette différence d'attitude est visible aussi par rapport au phénomène d'endogamie.

Cette ethnicisation des lectures du territoire et des réseaux de sociabilité, économiques, culturels ne domine pas complètement le paysage de la ville de Cluj.

Nous ne sommes pas devant un phénomène de fragmentation ethnique spatiale généralisée de l'espace urbain. Il n'existe pas de quartiers ethnicisés à Cluj. Aussi, nous pouvons évoquer la place centrale - haut lieu de mémoire hongroise - qui, malgré les nombreuses tentatives de destruction de la part de l'ancienne mairie nationaliste roumaine (entre 1992 et 2004), reste un lieu de rencontre pour des catégories de population extrêmement différentes. Des jeunes, des retraités, des touristes, des rockers, des personnes de passage dans la ville cohabitent tous dans cet espace, au-delà des appartenances ethniques. La proximité de l'université et des librairies dans cette ville universitaire qui compte environ 80000 étudiants ne peut pas annuler ou réduire la fréquentation de cette place centrale. En outre, l'attachement des habitants de la ville à la statue du roi Mathias, présente sur ce lieu, est indépendant des affiliations ethniques. Selon un sondage réalisé à Cluj (Lazar 2003b: 20), la statue la plus «représentative» parmi les monuments du centre-ville est, selon les habitants roumains, la statue du roi Mathias. Pour les Hongrois, cette statue exprime au mieux leur fierté.

Dans un autre registre, des rencontres transethniques ont lieu dans les «espaces de sous-sol» et dans la «ville souterraine», mentionnés par M. Lazar (2003a). Ainsi, des espaces tels que les bars ou les clubs se construisent au-delà des clivages existants parfois dans les «espaces de surface».

L'existence de ces pratiques de mise en lien et de rencontre entre les habitants de la ville, indépendamment de leur espace d'identification ethnique, nous amène à interroger autrement que de manière statique les phénomènes de «coexistence» ou de «tolérance comme non-interférence». A Cluj, nous pouvons observer une oscillation permanente entre des situations de non-interférence (d'exclusion de l'autre ou de tolérance passive) et de rapprochement entre individus s'identifiant à des groupes ethniques différents. L'*entre-soi* et la *coexistence* des groupes ne sont alors que des états temporaires de la même manière que le *communautaire* en tant que pratique de l'*entre-soi* n'est pas l'état habituel des sociétés mais une production sociale limitée dans le temps. Jean-Luc Nancy (1990) et Roberto Esposito (2000), entre autres, attiraient par ailleurs l'attention sur les mésinterprétations faites jusqu'à présent du terme «communauté» par la philosophie politique moderne. Selon ces auteurs, la conception fusionnelle de la communauté (abordée aussi par l'ethnologie classique) serait une fiction, la communauté étant une expérience du partage avec d'autres et d'exposition à l'autre.

Cette perspective dynamique d'analyse de la cohabitation multiethnique nous amène à nous interroger sur les situations où les groupes se croisent et se rencontrent. Face au constat d'une parole divisée sur la Transylvanie, ne pourrait-elle pas être aussi un lieu qui permette de construire des liens, de l'en commun, au-delà des séparations et crispations identitaires?

«Provincia»: le projet d'expérimentation d'une autre Transylvanie

Le défi était d'identifier des initiatives de mise en commun interethniques au niveau du fonctionnement associatif ou institutionnel. C'est à ce niveau que les clivages se ressentent davantage et, plus largement, dans des catégories plus éduquées de la population.

Un tel espace de rencontre entre Roumains et Hongrois et de construction d'un projet commun a pu voir le jour grâce à un groupe de réflexion, *Provincia*, et à une association, la *Ligue Pro Europa*, qui se sont proposés de rendre visible sur la scène publique un nouveau discours sur la *Transylvanie*, celui d'un territoire d'interférences culturelles et de complémentarités. Ce mouvement réunissait entre autres des écrivains, des journalistes, des politologues, des sociologues, des historiens, s'identifiant à des groupes ethniques différents (roumain, hongrois ou, en moindre partie, allemand).

La principale activité de *Provincia* a été la publication d'une revue bilingue mensuelle portant le même nom, dont l'initiateur fut un politologue né en Transylvanie, vivant entre Budapest et Oradea. Elle fut publiée à partir de 2000 avec le financement de la fondation internationale Soros (CRDE). Le projet est né entre Budapest, Bucarest et la Transylvanie, lieu où habitent ses membres, mais il est lancé sur la scène publique à Cluj. Le potentiel intellectuel et institutionnel de cette ville, ainsi que sa triple valeur symbolique en tant que capitale historique de la région, capitale culturelle des Hongrois de Roumanie et espace historique réputé pour des clivages roumano-hongrois, ont fait de Cluj une ville idéale où un tel projet pouvait acquérir une visibilité publique.

Provincia a pris la forme d'un groupe «virtuel», avec des membres permanents (environ 10–15 personnes) qui participaient généralement aux différentes actions du groupe (forums, séminaires, écoles d'été, quelques débats télévisés), et d'autres personnes, du pays ou de l'étranger (des diasporas ou non), qui avaient uniquement une activité de publication dans la revue. Celle-ci a eu un tirage de 5000 exemplaires pour chacune de ces deux versions (en roumaine et en hongrois). La revue a connu d'importantes difficultés de distribution, venant s'ajouter à d'autres types problèmes. En effet, dans un premier temps, par le caractère de la publication (essais journalistiques ou littéraires et analyses à profil sociologique, historique, de politologie, etc.), elle s'adressait un public restreint. Dans un second temps, la nouveauté de son message, centré sur la coopération roumano-hongroise, a été reçue avec réticence au sein des deux publics. Enfin, une mauvaise politique de distribution s'est rajoutée à tout cela.

La visibilité des actions et du discours de *Provincia* s'est avant tout exprimée dans les réactions fortement hostiles qu'elle a suscitées sur la scène publique, ses membres étant accusés de «sécessionnistes», «traîtres», voulant «vendre le pays», «manipulés de l'extérieur». Quelques réactions violentes ont existé aussi dans l'espace privé ou professionnel des membres actifs du groupe, allant de la méfiance jusqu'à certaines menaces de licenciement.

Malgré la disparition de la revue en septembre 2002 (par manque de financement et de mobilisation), laquelle a fortement ébranlé la cohésion du groupe, *Provincia* s'inscrit dans le fil des événements historiques qui ont joué un rôle important dans la construction de cette catégorie symbolique de la Transylvanie en lui donnant un cours particulier à un moment précis de l'histoire. En dépit d'une certaine marginalité du groupe, *Provincia* a fait «événement» (Bensa, Fassin 2002), car elle a marqué un moment de rupture dans un ordre existant, par rapport à la conception courante du territoire et du vivre ensemble. Dans le paysage des projets culturels ou politiques roumano-hongrois que la Transylvanie a connu à travers son histoire, l'initiative de *Provincia* est une première, aussi bien par son projet de créer une publication qui s'adresse à la fois à un public roumain et hongrois, que par son objectif de construire, sur d'autres bases, un espace de débat autour de la question transylvaine. L'introduction dans le débat public des idées sur la régionalisation de la Roumanie, idée tabou dans le pays dans les années 1990, marque également une contribution importante du groupe et de ses continuateurs.

Après la fin de la publication, les idées de *Provincia*, ainsi que les rencontres de ses membres ont été poursuivies à travers les actions de la *Ligue Pro Europa* (LPE). Celle-ci initie des ateliers et des forums dans plusieurs villes de Transylvanie et organise chaque année, entre autres, deux manifestations: l'*Académie Transsylvania* (un programme de formation destiné à des jeunes leaders d'opinion – étudiants, membres des partis politiques, des associations, etc.) et l'*Université Transsylvania* (qui s'organise sous la forme de journées de débats avec des hommes politiques, économistes, écrivains, des membres de *Provincia* et en présence d'étudiants et de membres de l'*Académie Transsylvania*). La question de la constitution d'un espace des complémentarités culturelles, de la spécificité régionale de la Transylvanie et de la régionalisation de la Roumanie ont été les thèmes principaux de ces rencontres.

L'Europe: moteur des recompositions régionales en Transylvanie

Si *Provincia* fut une première dans l'histoire de la Transylvanie, il convient de s'interroger sur les facteurs qui ont permis une telle entreprise. Au-delà de quelques transformations internes qui ont amélioré le climat des relations interethniques en Transylvanie, le nouvel acteur qui a impulsé cette initiative fut l'*Europe* (comme processus d'élargissement européen). C'est plus particulièrement sur les idées d'une *Europe des Régions* que *Provincia* a appuyé ses actions. Pour le rappeler, cette approche de l'Europe se développe à partir de 1993, plus ou moins en opposition à une *Europe des Nations*: «L'avenir sera marqué par le fait que les régions deviendront l'échelon de pouvoir après l'échelon communautaire, l'emportant ainsi sur les Etats nationaux, voués à une atrophie progressive, le principe de *subsidiarité* les rendant périmés. C'est la thèse de l'Europe des régions» (Palard 1998).

L'inscription du projet de *Provincia* dans une problématique européenne et d'intégration de la Roumanie dans l'UE a été un argument puissant contre les réactions nationalistes et hostiles de la part du pouvoir, des médias et d'une partie de la population. Ce phénomène de renaissance des régionalismes et de recompositions régionales (territoriales et identitaires) ayant l'Europe comme moteur, est visible dans de nombreux pays d'Europe centrale et orientale. Des études menées, par exemple en Bulgarie (Kabakchieva 2001) ou en Croatie (Ballinger 2004) témoignent de ces mutations culturelles et politiques en cours au sein de l'Europe.

Si les idées européennes en matière de construction régionale inspirent les nouveaux projets collectifs autour de la Transylvanie, un scénario du passé semble, dans une certaine mesure, se répéter. Rappelons qu'à la fin du XIXe siècle, l'influence des idées de construction des Etats-Nations, d'inspiration occidentale, se répandait en Europe centrale et orientale, et avec celles-ci l'institutionnalisation d'une conception particulière du territoire et de la nation. Aujourd'hui, l'arbitre européen a changé les règles du jeu, dans ce sens qu'en critiquant un modèle que lui-même a produit, le modèle de l'Etat-Nation, il tente de l'améliorer et même d'en imposer un autre: celui des régions. La construction des Etats-Nations a introduit une certaine conception de la relation entre territoire, culture et nation, avec des répercussions visibles partout en Europe. Il est alors important de comprendre quelle conception du territoire et de la culture est négociée dans ce nouveau cadre de pensée régionale ou régionaliste.

Toute la politique communautaire européenne est menée à partir des régions, mais la notion de «région» reste néanmoins assez vague dans les textes européens; les régions couvrent dans la pratique une diversité parfois très contrastée d'un pays européen à un autre. Il manque plus largement un consensus quant aux principes mêmes de construction d'une *Europe des régions*, projet considéré comme utopique par ceux qui défendent une *Europe des Etats nationaux*.

L'accueil et l'application de ces idées européennes en Transylvanie ont un grand intérêt pour le chercheur car le terrain transylvain traduit une tension entre plusieurs conceptions de construction régionale existantes au sein de l'Union Européenne. Dans toute la rhétorique de construction régionale, un accent est mis sur l'importance de la dimension historique et culturelle comme critère de découpage régional. Néanmoins, dans la pratique, le critère économique l'emporte souvent, comme nous pouvons l'observer pour le cas de la France, de l'Allemagne, de l'Italie et de l'Espagne (Dupoirier 1998: 188). En Roumanie, le même principe fut appliqué en 1998 pour la récente régionalisation du pays à partir de huit «régions de développement» économiques. Certains géographes (Rey

1998: 32, Groza et Muntele 2003) soulignent le caractère artificiel et le découpage «par la bande» de ces régions, qui ne tient pas compte des spécificités géographiques, historiques, politiques que certains territoires ont développées dans le temps.

Opposés à ces découpages artificiels et s'appuyant sur certains textes du Conseil de l'Europe,[3] différents mouvements intellectuels ou associatifs (*Provincia*, la *Ligue Pro Europa*, etc.) ont proposé un principe de découpage régional principalement en fonction du critère culturel. Les régions proposées dans ce cas rappellent, par leur contour, les anciennes provinces historiques et elles sont supposées avoir comme avantage une «cohérence culturelle et historique» déjà existante. La constitution des régions selon ce critère et certains droits d'autonomie à leur échelle apparaissent dans les textes du Conseil de l'Europe comme une solution possible pour les conflits politiques et pour l'amélioration du climat interethnique dans les pays d'Europe centrale et orientale.

La spécificité culturelle et historique de ces régions apparaît donc comme un facteur essentiel dans la construction des régions «naturelles» (en opposition aux régions «artificielles») et ce discours est loin d'être uniquement local. Pour les régions françaises, qui n'ont pas suivi les anciens maillages historiques, la dimension culturelle fait *a posteriori* partie des projets régionaux. Si la région française fut initialement pensée uniquement comme un acteur des politiques publiques, elle se veut de plus en plus une «région-territoire, lieu de mise en cohérence d'identités plurielles – historiques et culturelles – dont l'institution régionale veut être le gardien et/ou le promoteur» (Dupoirier 1998: 193). Les politiques culturelles régionales s'efforcent ainsi de faire de ce territoire «un lieu d'histoire et de culture» et de créer la conscience d'une «identité culturelle» régionale. Ce phénomène d'appropriation d'une image régionale a d'ailleurs des échos importants chez les habitants de ces territoires. Les études ont montré que l'existence de fondements historiques et culturels n'est pas une condition nécessaire à l'affirmation d'une identité régionale, même si elle est une ressource non-négligeable (Draï 1991, Dargent 2001). Cette identité régionale n'est pas «le résultat mécanique de la longueur de l'histoire autonome des différentes provinces» (Dargent 2001). Des régions jeunes sont fortement identitaires, comme Midi-Pyrénées, le Nord Pas de Calais, alors que c'est le contraire pour le cas de la Lorraine, même si cette dernière est la dernière province attachée à la France.

Indépendamment du fait que la dimension culturelle est mobilisée au moment de la légitimation des nouvelles constructions territoriales ou bien par la suite, ces

[3] Il est question de la *Résolution 1334 (2003): Expériences positives des régions autonomes comme source d'inspiration dans la résolution de conflits en Europe*, élaborée par l'Assemblée parlementaire du Conseil de l'Europe, et de la *Recommandation 158 (2004) sur les enjeux de la régionalisation en Europe du Sud-Est*, texte issu du Congrès des Autorités Locales et Régionales du Conseil de l'Europe.

projets mettent en jeu une conception qui essentialise les régions ainsi que les identités et les territoires afférents. Tôt ou tard, la rhétorique autour de ces espaces les qualifie comme régions «historiques», «culturelles», en tout cas «authentiques», rhétorique qui relève d'une approche statique du territoire. On parle ainsi de *la Catalogne*, de *la Bretagne*, de *la Bavière*, de *la Transylvanie*, du *Pays Sicule* ... Cependant, comme nous l'avons observé, il n'existe pas une seule *Transylvanie*, mais plusieurs, et autant de manières de concevoir ce territoire et les rattachements à lui. Le processus de construction territoriale est une négociation permanente entre individus ou groupes différents, qui entrent en compétition pour définir le territoire.

Si l'analyse des constructions territoriales doit s'inscrire dans une approche dynamique, cela n'exclut pas l'existence d'un discours d'essentialisation des territoires de la part des acteurs impliqués dans ces projets et à des fins de légitimation culturelle, politique, etc. Cette dimension est présente aussi dans le discours de *Provincia*. Le moteur principal de ses actions est la croyance dans une «différence culturelle transylvaine». Il s'agit plus largement d'une conception unitaire de la *Transylvanie*, territoire conçu comme un espace homogène, historiquement et culturellement distinct du reste de la Roumanie. Même si quelques personnes dans le groupe ont critiqué cette vision unitaire du territoire, ces voix furent plutôt marginales. Le ton général fut donné par une certaine volonté de diffuser une parole politique (dans le sens élargie du terme) autour de la question transylvaine, une parole performative qui produise une réalité sociale. Affirmer publiquement une «spécificité transylvaine», sous-entendait de partir du postulat d'une Transylvanie considérée comme entité discrète, substantielle, historiquement et culturellement distincte de la Roumanie. Une tension permanente entre deux régimes d'énonciation différents, scientifique (lié au profil de certains membres du groupe) et politique, a accompagné les actions du groupe. Cette parole performative et politique fut encore plus manifeste quand certains membres de *Provincia* ont souhaité légitimer par leurs actions la construction d'un territoire administratif ou politique transylvain et la création même d'un parti politique régional transylvain. Ces deux projets n'ont jamais abouti.

Deux idées sont centrales dans la conception de *Provincia* concernant la Transylvanie: la spécificité culturelle transylvaine par rapport au «Sud» de la Roumanie et en tant qu'espace des diversités et des interférences culturelles. La spécificité transylvaine est justifiée par l'appartenance à la *Mitteleuropa*, considérée comme plus proche culturellement de l'Occident, et à laquelle l'autre partie de la Roumanie n'aurait pas eu historiquement accès. De cette appartenance découlerait une supériorité culturelle pas toujours formulée, mais sous-entendue. Ces rapports entre la Transylvanie et le «Sud» de la Roumanie sont pensés selon un principe proche de l'«orientalisme» (Saïd 1980). Ce principe, appliqué au sud-est européen, comporte un discours à la fois de proximité vis-à-vis de l'*Occident* et d'éloignement des *Balkans*. Ce discours se rencontre dans cet espace sud-est européen soit dans des processus de différentiations entre des pays voisins, soit au sein d'un même pays (Bakić-Hayden, Hayden 1992, Antohi 2002, Turda 2001). Un *orientalisme interne* est perceptible également en Transylvanie. Comme le remarquait Marius Turda, en rejetant les *Balkans* de l'autre côté des Carpates on se réserve à soi une appartenance à la *Mitteleuropa*. Le rôle des Carpates est ici très important, marquant la frontière avec l'espace *balkanique*.

La parole performative sur la Transylvanie véhicule une autre idée plus ou moins constante dans le discours de *Provincia*: cette région apparaît comme le berceau *in illo tempore* de la diversité culturelle et de la cohabitation harmonieuse entre Roumains, Hongrois et Allemands. Cependant, les références aux Roms (numériquement plus nombreux aujourd'hui en Transylvanie que les Allemands) sont inexistantes ou, parfois, ils sont évoqués comme des «étrangers» à ce territoire, arrivés plus tard et altérant dans une certaine mesure la tradition de vie en Transylvanie. Ni la dimension des flux migratoires interrégionaux ou de type urbain-rural n'est prise en compte, face à un discours qui insiste sur le «noyau dur» transylvain, resté presque inchangé jusqu'à nos jours, et cela malgré les mutations survenues.

Sans nier l'existence d'un sentiment d'identification régionale ressenti par les habitants de cet espace, la parole performative de *Provincia* laisse souvent entendre que cette distinction culturelle transylvaine repose sur l'existence d'un ensemble statique d'éléments culturels substantiels et atemporels. Alors qu'en réalité cette distinction est un élément construit, mouvant et stratégique de la part des individus.

Par conséquent, si l'*Europe* est un moteur de la production du lien au-delà des différenciations ethniques dans des régions caractérisées par une tradition ancienne de «tolérance sans interférence», elle est en même temps un moteur pour des mobilisations qui tendent parfois vers de nouvelles formes de repli sur soi. Les constructions régionales témoignent quelques fois des approches essentialistes; ces régions ne reposent plus sur des *communautés de sang* (comme dans le cas des nationalismes classiques), mais sur des *communautés de sol* qui sont souvent tout aussi exclusives. La terre et le territoire apparaissent comme une source d'identité culturelle et historique authentiques de laquelle ne peuvent pas se revendiquer ceux qui viennent de l'extérieur (et cet extérieur ne se situe parfois qu'à un pas au-delà d'une frontière physique). Des exclusions ethniques sont transgressées, mais des nouvelles frontières peuvent surgir dans ces nouvelles mobilisations régionales.

Bibliographie

Antohi, Sorin 2002: Romania and the Balkans. From Geocultural Bovarism to Ethnic Ontology. In: Transit - Europäische Revue 21 (http://www.iwm.at/index.php?option=com_content&task=view&id=235&Itemid=411).

Bakić-Hayden, M., R. Hayden 1992: Orientalist Variations on the theme «Balkans»: Symbolic geographies in Yugoslav cultural politics. In: Slavic Review 51, 1: 1-15.

Ballinger, Pamela 2004: «Authentic Hybrids» in the Balkan Borderlands. In: Current Anthropology 45, 1: 31-60.

Bensa, Alban, Fassin Eric 2002: Les sciences sociales face à l'événement. In: Terrain 38: 5-20.

Dupoirier, Elisabeth (ed.) 1998: Régions. La croisée des chemins: perspectives françaises et enjeux européens. Paris: Presses de Sciences Po.

Esposito, Roberto 2000: Communitas. Origine et destin de la communauté. Les essais du collègue international de philosophie. Paris: PUF.

Feischmidt, Margit 2003: Ethnizität als Konstruktion und Erfahrung. Symbolstreit und Alltagskultur im siebenbürgischen Cluj. Münster: LIT.

Groza, Octavian, Muntele Ionel 2003: Le maillage sans territoire - la région de développement en Roumanie. Communication au Colloque «Refonder les territoires». Lyon: Ecole Normale Supérieure.

Hayden, Robert 2002: Antagonistic Tolerance. Competitive Sharing of Religious Sites in South Asia and the Balkans. In: Current Anthropology 43, 2: 205-232.

Kabakchieva, Petya 2001: From Local to Regional Identity? The Possible Construction of «Cross-Border» Regional Identity. Case study of the Border Region: Smolyan. Sofia: Academic Nexus Project.

Karnoouh, Claude 1998: Un logos sans ethos. Considérations sur les notions d'interculturalisme et de multiculturalisme appliquées à la Transylvanie. In: Discussion Papers 44 (Collegium Budapest). Budapest.

Kötek, Jöel (ed.) 1996: L'Europe et ses villes-frontières. Bruxelles: Editions Complexe.

Lazăr, Marius 2003a: Cluj - 2003. Metastaza ostentatiei. Ilustrate in alb şi negru din orasul tricolor [La métastase de l'ostentation. Des illustrations en noir et blanc de la ville tricolore]. In: Ideea 15: 125-134.

Lazăr, Marius 2003b: Identités urbaines et styles de vie à Cluj-Napoca. In: Cerclet Denis (ed.), Patrimoine et dialogue entre les cultures. L'exemple de Cluj en Transylvanie Roumanie. Rapport de recherche réalisé par EPACTE en partenariat avec le CREA. Tome 1.

Losonczy, Anne Marie 1999: Le refus de l'exil. Migrations, autochtonie et patriotisme entre la Hongrie et la Transylvanie. In: C. Giordano, J. Rolshoven (ed.),

Ethnologie européenne. Ethnologie de l'Europe. Fribourg: Ed. universitaires, 111–122.

Lie, Rico 2002: Spaces of Intercultural Communication. Conference Paper, 23rd Conference IAMCR, Barcelona, 21–26 July.

Nancy, Jean-Luc 1990: La communauté désoeuvrée. Paris: Christian Bourgeois.

Palard, Jacques 1998: Vers l'Europe des régions? La Documentation Française. Paris.

Rey, Violette (ed.) 1998: Les territoires centre-européens. Dilemmes et défis. Paris: La Découverte.

Roth, Klaus 2006: Living Together or Living Side by Side? Interethnic Coexistence in Multiethnic Societies. In: Reginald Byron, U. Kockel (ed.), Negotiating Culture. Moving, Mixing and Memory in Contemporary Europe. Berlin: LIT, 18–32.

Turda, Marius 2001: Transylvania Revisited: Public Discourse and Historical Representation in Contemporary Romania. In: B. Trencsenyi et al. (ed.), Nation-Buiding and Contested Identities. Romanian and Hungarian Case Studies. Budapest: Regio Books. Iasi: Editura Polirom, 197–209.

Zempléni, András 1996: Les manques de la nation. Sur quelques propriétés de la «patrie» et de la nation en Hongrie contemporaine. In: D. Fabre (ed.), L'Europe entre cultures et nations. Paris: Maison des sciences de l'homme, 121–157.

Abstract

With its dispute about territory between the local Romanian and Hungarian elites, which is also a sensitive issue between the neighbour states, Transylvania has been studied most often from the perspective of ethnic identity construction and nationalism. Before the background of the production of two competing symbolic nationalisms, Transylvania today is going through a process of territorial "renewal" where the transnational and European factors play a central role. Globalization translates into the rebirth of regional identity politics, a process that is also visible in other countries in Central and South-East Europe. The emergence of regional phenomena which are here analysed on the example of Cluj-Napoca, must be placed first of all in the context of the historical cohabitation or "coexistence", i.e., the tendency (of both Romanians and Hungarians) to "ethicise" the social, cultural, economic, and political networks. By taking the "Provincia" (Province) initiative as an example, the paper analyses this revival of regionalism from the point of view of the territorial concepts on which it is based. While in some regards it helps overcome the existing nationalisms, this new regionalism also introduces new forms of exclusion based not on "blood communities" but on "soil communities".

The Cross With Four Pillars as the Centre of Religious Gathering: Discussing Micro Regional Identity

Aleksandra Đurić, Belgrade

Banat, both a geographical and a historical region, is currently divided up between three countries: the eastern part lies in Romania (the counties of Timiş, Caraş-Severin, Arad, and Mehedinţi), the western part in Serbia (the autonomous province of Vojvodina and Belgrade City District), and a small northern part in Hungary (Csongrad County). In 1779, the Banat was incorporated into the Habsburg Kingdom of Hungary. In 1848, the western Banat became part of the Serbian Vojvodina, a Serbian autonomous region within the Habsburg Empire. In the eighteenth and nineteenth centuries, under Habsburg rule, a planned colonization took place which brought German, Hungarian, Slovak, Romanian and Ruthenian settlers to the region. Romanians have lived in the Banat since the Middle Ages, with the oldest Romanian settlements dating back to the fourteenth and fifteenth centuries. Among them are Sočica, first mentioned in 1421; Kuštilj, in 1361; and Jablanka (Jabuka at that time) in 1385.[1] More settlements with a majority Romanian population were founded during the great migrations of the eighteenth and nineteenth centuries. Mirjana Maluckov states that the Romanians in the Serbian Banat are of three different origins, coming from the Banat, from Transylvania, and from Oltenia. They did not settle separately but mixed in the settlements of southern and central Banat (Maluckov 1985: 31).

There are differences between the Romanians living in the hills in the Vršac hinterland and those in the plain. This paper focusses on the hill settlements of Kuštilj, Sočica and Jablanka, whose material cultures and dialects resemble those of the inhabitants of the Carpat region in Romania. Maluckov holds that there are no exact data concerning the time or manner in which their settlements were founded, although there is some evidence that they are among the oldest Romanian settlements in thc Serbian Banat. The names of the Romanians in Serbian Banat are not related to their origins:[2] Romanians from the hills around Vršac are called *Codreni* (highlanders) and those from the plain *de la Pustă* (lowlanders).

The Romanians from Transylvania and Banat accepted the jurisdiction of the Orthodox metropoly of Karlovac (Karlowitz). By the decree of Emperor Franz

[1] Cf. Măran, Mircea 2003: 35.

[2] Maluckov states (1985: 31) that the Romanian hill settlements in Serbian Banat are Malo Središte, Markovac, Kuštilj, Sočica, Jablanka, Mesić, and Vojvodinci.

Joseph I of December 1864, the Romanians obtained their own national church. Ecclesiastical independence was a very important factor in the development of national consciousness. Following autocephaly, a great number of Romanian churches were built in Banat, most of them shortly after in order to confirm or develop national independence (Maluckov 1985: 13). The Romanians of the Serbian Banat also belonged to other religions. The Romanian Greek-Catholic (Uniate) church[3] was established in 1864, and in the early twentieth century, various Protestant denominations such as Nazarenes[4], Adventists and Pentecostals appeared.

The villages of Sočica, Jablanka, Kuštilj and Vrani, inhabited by Romanian settlers from Banat, form the hill settlements called *de la Codru*. Endogamy was strong in Romanian villages, so marriage between inhabitants of Banat, Oltenia and Transylvania were rare. Kinship ties were very important for the four villages, and people intermarried within very small circles of neighbouring villages.

The religious monument called *Crucea cu patru stâlpi* (The cross with four pillars) or *Ruga albă* (The white prayer) is the most important religious symbol for the Romanians living in the border area. The monument was erected in the mid-nineteenth century at the crossroads of the four villages of Sočica, Kuštilj, Jablanka and Vrani. The joint settling in the hills of Banat, the relationship between natives and settlers, the autocephaly of the Romanian Orthodox Church, as well as other dramatic changes of that time, all led to the formation of a community of the four villages around this religious monument.

This paper is based on field research in March 2007[5] in the villages of Sočica (Sălciţa), Kuštilj (Coştei), and Jablanka (Iablanca) near the town of Vršac in the Serbian Banat. The villages, only a few kilometers away from the Romanian border, are inhabited by Romanians (except for Jablanka which also has a Serbian population). Our interviews focussed on the *Ruga albă*. They were conducted in the mother tongue of our informants and were open-ended, in the interests of eliciting the best possible information. There are no written records of this place (except for some data found in a monograph on Sočica village). This paper is therefore based on the testimony of our interviewees, mostly elderly people, born in the villages where the research was done. The information we gathered gives the impression of a unique perception shared by the inhabitants of these places and

---

[3] There is a Greek Catholic Church in Markovac which, until 1963, was in Jankov Most in the Serbian Banat.

[4] The largest Nazarene community is in the village of Lokve. It consists of some 500 believers.

[5] The field research was carried out by a team from the Institute for Balkan Studies in Belgrade; the team consisted of the socio-linguists Biljana Sikimić, Annemarie Sorescu-Marinković, Svetlana Ćirković and Aleksandra Đurić.

Picture 1: Map indicating the territory of the four villages and the monument – The Cross with four pillars

of a general idea of the role that the *Ruga albă* plays to this day. In the development of local identity, *Ruga albă* is certainly more than only a religious monument. The oral testimonies present a picture that I will present in more detail.

The cross was the centre of religious gatherings for the inhabitants of the four villages. As one of the informants said, the cross was raised precisely at the point where the borders of the four villages meet. People would go there on a dirt road by horse-drawn cart or on foot. Every year on the day of the Christian Orthodox holiday of Pentecost[6] (Romanian *Rusalii*), fifty days after Easter, a procession of priests and peasants travelled from the villages to the monument site. The celebration would begin in the morning in the church and after lunch they would arrive at the Cross. A liturgy with the priests from all four villages was held, in the

6 The holiday of Pentecost marks the descent of the Holy Ghost upon the apostles which happened (1) on the Jewish holiday of Pentecost celebrated according to the Old Testament, or (2) on the fiftieth day after the resurrection of Christ.

Picture 2: The Cross with four pillars-Ruga albă

presence of the followers and the church choir. Each village set up a stone pillar which had been brought from the region of Fizegi near Sočica village (Vulcu-Pleşu 2005: 155).

Customs related to the holiday of Pentecost usually have to do with the protection of the living space and with stimulating the fertility of the land. As a specific kind of pilgrimage, the main purpose of the custom of going out to the fields was to protect the land and the crops from drought, bad weather and hailstorms. However, the one thing that makes the celebration of this holy day so unique in these four villages is the *Ruga albă* as a sacred place, a place for prayer, a symbol of unity for all Romanians living in these villages. People would go to the cross several times a year, mostly on the days of the patron saint of their village. The patron saint of Sočica is St. George (April 23), of Jablanka the Holy Trinity (the date changes every year depending on the date of Easter), Kuštilj celebrates Spasovdan (July 13), and Vrani celebrates the day of St. Teodor Tiron (February 17).[7]

[7] According to both Romanian and Serbian tradition, the patron saint's day of the church corresponds to the patron saint's day of the village. This is when visitors arrive from all the neighbouring villages.

Picture 3: The reconstruction of the monument, professor Bălteanu and pupils 1937

The monograph on the village of Sočica says that Ion Bălteanu, a contract teacher in Sočica, and his students, restored the Cross in 1937. After the borders had been established in 1918, the cross was now in the Serbian part of Banat and belonged to the Kingdom of the Serbs, Croats and Slovenes. One of the informants who had participated in the restoration gave a description of that event:

> *We fixed it, we painted the roof and we did everything in that year. I was seven back then. But I remember that our teacher was organizing balls. We said balls (...) and with collected money, the children from the school and professor Bălteanu fixed the Cross with four pillars. We fixed it and we bought a metal roof. I think it had a shingle roof before* (U. I., born 1930, Sočica).

Pupils of the local primary school would perform their ritual walk "with the star" (Romanian *cu steaua*) around the village[8] and sing religious songs on Christmas Eve and Christmas Day. The teachers would give them the words of the songs and

[8] The walk with the star was quite common in all parts of Banat in the inter-war period.

rehearsals were held in the church. Boys would knock on the doors of all the houses, sing Christmas carols and receive presents in return. That was how they collected money for the restoration of the cross. The first contract teachers arrived in 1935, after the signing of the Yugoslav-Romanian agreement on schools for ethnic minorities in Vojvodina in 1933. The teachers came from Romania and brought with them new folk dances and songs, thus influencing the cultural life of the villages.

Only few people in the villages remember what the gatherings around the cross looked like in the early decades of the twentieth century. The informants we spoke to were born after the establishment of the national border and have only vague memories of the 1930s.

A look at the historical conditions under which the cross was erected reveals that the period from 1718 to 1867 was a time of Austrian political domination and a policy of Germanization. However, this period is also marked by an even stronger and ever-present influence of the Transylvanian Latin School on the Romanian intelligentsia, the result of which was a certain kind of elite nationalism. The period between 1867 and 1918, after the Austro-Hungarian agreement and the establishment of the Banat borders in 1873, was characterized by an energetic policy of Magyarization. The institutions responsible for the rise in national awareness (libraries, choirs, orchestras and art societies) grew in strength, but the most significant fact was that the church gained independence in 1864. It was in this period of rising national feelings that the *Ruga albă* was erected.

After the First World War and the disintegration of the Austro-Hungarian Empire, new sovereign states and national borders were created. The decision that the Banat should be divided between Romania and the Kingdom of Serbs, Croats and Slovenes was reached at the international peace conferences in Paris. The territory of the Serbian part of Banat included some forty settlements with a Romanian majority.[9]

The establishment of borders in 1919 did not prevent people from crossing them, and according to the agreement between the two governments the land could be used freely. The borders remained flexible until 1949, when relations became strained and the borders were closed. Contacts between Serbia and Romania were considerably hindered by the Iron Curtain and the political conditions between 1945 and 1990. People had no religious freedom, and gathering around the cross was strictly forbidden. There were several attempts to destroy the cross. The priest of the Romanian Orthodox church in Jablanka told us that the communists had tried to knock down the pillars of the cross. On one occasion they tied horses to

[9] More about the history of Romanian settlements in the Serbian Banat in Măran 2003.

Picture 4: The Cross with four pillars today

them, on another they even fired at them, but despite all their attempts the cross has remained almost intact to this day. After the end of communism, the visits to the cross continued, but there were only visitors from the villages in the Serbian Banat. People from the Romanian village of Vrani found it difficult to join again, even though there is a strong cultural connection between the two countries.

The interviews that make up the oral corpus were taken from seven adults in the three Serbian villages of Kuštilj, Jablanka and Sočica. The following points reflect the interviewces perception of the cross and its past and present significance:

1. All interviews have in common that they point out the unsuccessful attempts of the communists to knock down the cross. Only one of them said "they were not communists but drunkards". A second thing they have in common is the awareness of the border which has destroyed the former union of the four Romanian villages: *There is a road, a road to Vrani. You can go directly on this road. Before, those from Romania came, they came here together.*
   But the interviews do not show explicit nostalgia for the times when they lived in community. The reason for this is probably the lack of personal memories of those earlier times, since those who witnessed them are dead. The only memo-

ries are those of the futile attempts of knocking down the cross "at the orders of communists", a deed which even today is unanimously criticized.

2. The reduction of the function and meaning of the cross during the twentieth century: People now gather only once a year, for Pentecost, although they used to celebrate four different saint's days, one for each village: *Before, these villages gathered here four times a year. We celebrate in February St. Teodor Tiron, in Iabuca their saint's day is Pentecost, in Sălciţa St. Gheorghie, Arhanghelu* [Vrani] *Yes, theirs is St. Peter.*
3. The reasons for erecting the cross have always been of great significance for the entire community of four villages. The reasons for both the individuals and the communities are: *to come out at a particular moment to pray for the rain to begin to fall or to stop ... // they prayed for fertility of the fields ... There is something special about that. // People from four villages would come there and pray with many priests, against cholera, against plague, wars and storm or if there was a drought they prayed for the rain to fall.* Entirely different reasons are given for the erection of a new cross (very similar to the old one, at the entrance of the village) in Kuštilj: *prayer to feel reverence on leaving or returning to the village.*
4. The reasons for the existence of two names for the cross, based on its appearance and its colour: *We call it the cross with four pillars, but those from Kuštilj call it white prayer*[10]. *// And because of that we call it white prayer, with four pillars. It is white from white marble.*
5. Views of religious beliefs now and before: *People used to believe in God ... // They all used to believe in Him but they do not anymore.*

Today, this symbol helps to recognize other elements which took their place in the preservation of tradition and in shaping the group identity of the community of the villages. As a sacred place of pilgrimage of some sort, the cross today serves both social and religious functions, namely in the creation of a microcosm and definition of borders separating "our" world from "other" worlds.

> *And it was a sacred place of pilgrimage. People from four villages would come there and pray with many priests, against cholera, against plague, wars and storm or if there was a drought they prayed for the rain to fall. And because of that we call it the white prayer with the four pillars. It was white, because it was made of white marble (...) and we gathered there four times a year* (I. R. C., born 1946, Kuštilj).

As historical conditions changed, the role of this place changed accordingly. At the time when the cross was erected, Banat was part of the Habsburg Empire with

---

[10] In Christianity, white symbolizes virtue and purity.

a different ethnic structure. Kravanja (2005: 143) explains that in anthropological literature the placement of religious signs in the landscape is generally discussed under the heading of "sacred places" which are seen not only as places of worship and ritual, but also in the context of the specific historical settings in which they arose and changed.

Deep social changes create a need to protect one's identity. Religion connects people and is thus an instrument for creating and maintaining group identity. Golubović (1999: 50) writes that group identity links origin and history, past and future, tradition and rituals practised in collective ceremonies and celebrations, and with their help feelings of affiliation and solidarity are strengthened. Both individual and group identity have always been established in relation to differences which are commonly known, but while personal identities are based on differences, group identities are based on similarities. They express the identification of people with each other, their equality and sameness. Awareness of equality within a group includes the awareness of differences with other groups (cf. Kuljić 2006: 151). Groups of people, no matter what their size or constitution, creatively utilize past practices as manipulative markers of a common identity. Every creation of public symbols is at the same time an attempt to found permanent places which mark the identity of the new owners of the territory or simply strengthen the unstable identity of its old owners (Kravanja 2005: 151). Thus, gatherings on Christian holidays represent the strengthening of group identities.

If we consider the creation of this place of worship as a result of the need of four villages to protect their religious and national identity under the given historical and social conditions, then we must assume that this need no longer exists today.

Questions of identity and those related to the preservation of borders are usually seen as relating to minorities, as problems of "endangered" or "weaker" groups, or as issues which tend to be raised at moments of rapid social change. The creation of national borders played an important role in the maintenance of contacts between the members of the cross-border community. Borders are a historical phenomenon and as such liable to change, but they give shape to identity and represent a space closely connected to a society and its history (Beker, Komlozi 2005: 73). Since identities are not static but continuously being (de- and re-) constructed, the process of identity construction requires permanent processes of bordering and "othering" (Houtum, Naerssen 2002: 63). In the same way as borders were rearranged after the First World War, today we are confronted with similar developments in the European Union, of which Romania became a member in 2007. While most borders within the EU have lost their relevance, the outward borders have become new barriers, making cross-border contacts more difficult. Vrani now belongs to the EU, and Serbs need a visa to cross the border.

Picture 5: Ruga albă with new cross in the middle

People from Sočica, Jablanka and Kuštilj continue to gather around the cross, with a clear picture in their minds of the period when the gatherings ceased, but only a vague memory of what the celebration used to look like. The connections with Vrani were broken in the period of socialism – and they have not been reestablished since:

> *But did they dance after the liturgy?*
> *No.*
> *With the fanfare and ... ?*
> *Only church choir. Maybe they danced before, I don't remember. I don't know, the borders were already closed.*
> *Where is Vrani now?*
> *In Romania. But then, they could come. Now only three villages. They hold the religious service with priests. There were also the choir and the priests from Coştei. Now ... But before, those from Romania would come all together. Before the borders* (A. G., born 1937, Kuštilj).

After the smaller wooden cross between the four pillars was destroyed, local residents erected a new one in 1991. The inscription reads: "This Cross was

Picture 6: Celebration ceremony – The descent of the Holy Spirit (see also picture 7)

erected in the spring of 1991 in the place of the one erected in 1843, so that the religion of our ancestors and the love of our fellow men can be preserved at the crossroads of the villages of Kuštilj, Jablanka, Sočica and Vrani." During the past few years, local residents of Jablanka, Kuštilj and Sočica gathered here only once a year, at Pentecost. Apart from the church choir from Kuštilj, women from Oastea Domnului also sang church songs. As one of the informants explained:

> *Oastea Domnului belongs to the church and it is not a sect. During the ceremony, songs dedicated to that holiday were sung. However, perhaps some other customs existed before. Nowadays we go regularly. Even people from Romania were ready to come but they couldn't because of the visas. They were invited but they didn't come. People are eager to come and revive the tradition. Since children today have classes of religious instruction, priest take them to visit the Cross, too* (M. S., born 1975, Kuštilj).

People from Vrani do not come here anymore and it is assumed that 1949 was the they came here. Instead, more and more Romanians and people from other places, especially from the town of Vršac, come here. Recollections of the gatherings around the cross show a need to establish continuity with the period before the

Picture 7: Celebration ceremony – The descent of the Holy Spirit

borders were closed and when people from all four villages would come together. One of the informants explained that the people from the three villages now gather in order to revive this tradition. Traditions can be changed to suit the needs of the day, and the changes can become accepted as a part of the old tradition. This creation of continuity with the past after several decades, and with the participation of town-dwellers, can be seen an invention of tradition, a deliberately created symbolic or ritual behaviour which sets certain values and norms in order to establish continuity with a past period of time. The need for such inventions is felt particularly strongly in societies which undergo deep changes (Hobsbawm, Ranger 2002: 6). Groups of people of whatever size or constitution thus make creative and manipulative use of past practices as markers of their shared identity.

Conclusion

The paper investigates the changing roles of a cult place in the creation of group identity for Romanians living in a micro region in southeast Banat, but in different social worlds due to new national borders and historical changes. Modernity produces contradictory processes which change people's understanding of identity and their sense of affiliation. The tradition of gathering around the cross has been revived, but for many reasons the cross no longer has the importance it used to have from the time of its erection until the closing of the border. Today it is only a testimony of past times and of the events that took place in this area. Regarding the question of the future of this and other micro communities in Banat, the story of the cross with four pillars allows a better understanding of such phenomena. Micro communities and their cultural inheritance play an important role in the preservation of cultural pluralism in multiethnic regions such as Banat, but at the same time the divisive power of political borders cutting through a region must not be underestimated.

Literature

Anderson, J., L. O'Dowd 1999: Borders, Border Regions and Territoriality: Contradictory Meanings, Changing Significance. In: Journal of Regional Studies 33, 7: 593–604.

Armbruster, H., C. Rollo, U. H. Meinhof 2003: Imagining Europe: Everyday Narratives in European Border Communities. In: Journal of Ethnic and Migration Studies 29, 5: 885–889.

Beker, Joahim, Andrea Komlozi 2005: Granice u savremenom svetu [Borders in the present world]. Belgrade: Filip Višnjić.

Cerović, Ljubivoje 2000: Srbi u Rumuniji [Serbs in Romania]. Temišvar: Savez Srba u Rumuniji.

Ćorković, Mirjana 2006: Nostalgia în literatură şi viaţă: povestea despre învăţătorii dintre cele două războaie mondiale [Nostalgia in literature and life. A story about teachers between the two World Wars]. In: Tradiţia 29, 30: 12–13.

Fabijeti, Ugo, Maligeti Roberto, Matera Vinčenco 2002: Uvod u antropologiju – Od lokalnog do globalnog [Introduction into anthropology: from the local to the global]. Belgrade: Clio.

Golubović, Zagorka 1999: Ja i drugi [I and the others]. Belgrade: Republika.

Kravanja, Boštjan 2005: Macedonian Crosses. In: Zmago Šmitek, Aneta Svetieva (eds.), Post-Yugoslav Lifeworlds Between Tradition and Modernity. Ljubljana, Županičeva knjižnica, 143–162.

Kuljić, Todor 2006: Kultura sećanja [The culture of remembering]. Belgrade: Čigoja štampa.

Hobsbom [Hobsbawm], Erik, Terens Rejndžer 2002: Izmišljanje tradicije [The invention of tradition]. Belgrade: Biblioteka XX vek.

Măran, Mircea 2003: Localităţi bănăţene: trecut istoric şi cultural, Panciova, Libertatea [Banat localities: historical and cultural past]. Timişoara: Augusta.

Madsenn, K. D., T. V. Naerssen 2003: Migration, Identity, Belonging. In: Journal of Borderlands Studies 18, 1: 61–73.

Maluckov, Mirjana 1985: Rumuni u Banatu [The Romanians in the Banat]. Novi Sad: Vojvodjanski muzej.

Sikimić, Biljana 2006: De la Torac la Clec: Informaţia minimală de teren [From Torac to Clec: minimal field information]. In: Annemarie Sorescu-Marinković (ed.), Torac - metodologia cercetării de teren. Novi Sad: Editura Fundaţiei, 173–201.

Sorescu-Marinković, Annemarie 2006: Identitatea - o ecuaţie cu mai multe constante. Cazul românilor din Voivodina [Identity - an equation with too many constants. The case of the Romanians in the Voivodina]. In: Tradiţia 29, 30: 6–8.

Vulcu-Pleşu, Gheorghe 2005: Monografia satului Sălciţa [Monograph on the village of Sălciţa]. Vârşeţ: Tuli.

Zanini, Pjero 2002: Značenja granice [The meaning of borders]. Belgrade: Clio.

Abstract

The paper presents field research in three villages in the Serbian Banat inhabited by Romanians (Sočica, Jablanka and Kuštilj), and a Romanian village (Vrani) on the other side of the Serbian-Romanian border, which have had contacts for many decades. Romanians have settled in the Banat since the Middle Ages, but massive Romanian immigration took place as part of the Habsburg colonization in the eighteenth and nineteenth centuries. The religious monument called *Crucea cu patru stâlpi* (the cross with four pillars) was erected in 1843 in the central area between the four villages. This place became the centre of religious gatherings for the villages. Every year at the holiday of Pentecost the peasants would go there, accompanied by their priests. In 1918, with the establishment of the Kingdom of Yugoslavia, the area was divided by a new national border, and the village of Vrani became part of Romania. The research focusses on the question of how strong the influence of this border and historical developments was on keeping the tradition and contacts alive in this region, how the people living in the three Serbian villages perceive the border, and what role this sacred place plays in these processes.

Narratives About Dissenter Neighbours and Their Place in the Cultural Strategy of Coexistence in the Western Rhodope Region of Bulgaria

Magdalena Lubańska, Warsaw

The aim of my analysis is to indicate cultural functions of narratives told by Bulgarian speaking Muslims[1] (Sunni) and Orthodox Christians living in the Western Rhodopes. I distinguish several types of narratives concerning dissenter neighbours: Muslim-Christian narratives about neighbourliness and about resentments (resulting from slaughters in the nineteenth and twentieth centuries), Muslim narratives about Christianity as a "false" religion, Christian narratives about Muslims as Crypto-Christians, and Christian narratives about Muslims as "people of the Orient". I consider all of them crucial for understanding the grassroots cultural strategy[2] of coexistence developed by Muslims and Christians as members of the local community. This strategy is not introduced by any superior authority, but built on a shared social experience of Muslims and Christians, leading to the affirmation of neighbourliness (cf. Roth 2006). I do not regard it as a permanent cultural pattern, but as a dynamic process influenced by many factors.

In their narratives, my interlocutors have revealed some of these strategies. When compared, their accounts show hidden tensions lying behind declared brotherhood and solidarity. It seems that neighbourliness is something rather worked out by both religious groups than given for granted. It must constantly be reasserted in everyday life through relations of reciprocity. The latter can sometimes turn into hostility as is described briefly in Evgenia Ivanova's book

---

[1] I use the term "Bulgarian speaking Muslims". In the literature, their endoethnonym "Pomaks" is employed. However, my interlocutors asked me not to use that name, as it has derogatory overtones, stemming from the words "tortured", "tormented" and expressing the popular conviction (derived from Bulgarian national historiography till the late 1980s), that they were forced to convert to Islam during Ottoman rule. According to recent research, the conversions, mostly voluntary, had economic and social reasons (Željazkova 1997: 52). They themselves usually reject a view of their conversion that turns them into martyrs, as it categorizes them as traumatized and "second class" Bulgarians who were not strong enough to protect their faith and nationhood. At the same time, there are opposite theories in Bulgarian historiography which regard them as the "purest" Bulgarians who safeguarded their blood and language from mixing with the Turks (see Neuburger 2004: 41).

[2] Cvetana Georgieva uses the term "code of coexistence" (Georgieva 1994: 153). I prefer to use "strategy", as "code" suggests something rather unchangeable, exacting conformity, and inhibiting the initiative of individuals who are not entirely determined by social patterns, but are social actors. As such, they may not only adopt, but also create social reality.

(Ivanova 2002). She quotes examples of harms which Rhodope Muslims and Christians inflicted on each other in the past despite apparent peaceful coexistence, and presents Muslim and Christian testimonies from the Central Rhodopes concerning the "National Revival" process connected with assimilative measures taken towards Bulgarian speaking Muslims in the period 1912–1989. These actions threatened the traditional neighbourliness system and led to incidents directed against Muslims based on nineteenth century resentments.[3]

Other more traumatic cases of deterioration of long-term peaceful Muslim-Christian relations of neighbourliness concern former Yugoslavia. Before the war of 1993–95 they resembled those in the Western Rhodopes. I found many similarities between my data and those of the Norwegian anthropologist Tone Bringa (1995) who describes peaceful and friendly relations between Catholic Christian and Sunni Muslim neighbours in a Bosnian village near Sarajevo. Her fieldwork was carried out only a few years before the war, when there were no signs of future disaster. However, during the war their relations became extremely strained and hostile:

> After I had revisited the village in May 1993 and had seen almost every Muslim house destroyed and all the Muslims gone, it was very difficult to sit down in peaceful Cambridge and continue writing this book. Nothing of what I had earlier said seemed real or to matter. At the same time however, it became even more important to write about the community and the lives that had once, not long ago, existed. It had been a community where people treated each other with dignity and respect, and understood how to accommodate each other's cultural differences (Bringa 1995: xvii).

The Bosnian example provokes the question, what external and grassroots factors must occur to jeopardise the status quo of long neighbourly Muslim-Christian relations and trigger off mutual hostility. The conflicts in former Yugoslavia in the 1990s as well as Islamophobic moods spread by global media after September 11 certainly have a negative impact on Muslim-Christian relations worldwide, including the Muslim-Christian local community I describe in this article. Therefore I consider it important to look carefully at the feelings and symbolic messages

---

[3] Some Pomaks took part in the April Uprising of 1876 on the Turkish side. At that time the massacre on Christians in Batak took place, when Bulgarian speaking Muslims from Barutin murdered Christians, including women and children, who found shelter in the church. Their remains in the church became Bulgarian national relics (for more on this see Lubanska 2006). After Bulgaria's liberation, Muslims were persecuted and Bulgarian speaking Muslims were forcibly converted to Christianity at the initiative of the Bulgarian Orthodox Church, King Ferdinand, and the government. They were obliged to abandon their faith, traditional costumes, and Muslim names. Although they returned to them a year later, similar assimilative actions occurred several times in the 20th century on behalf of different governments.

revealed in my interviewees' narratives. What do they say about present and past Muslim-Christian relations and prejudices? As Frankie Wilmer (2002: 31) noticed, "stories contain the emotions of past experiences, including trauma, and collective memories that can be conjured up by warmongering political wizards in the present", and therefore, in order "to understand how communities[4] are created and destroyed, we must understand the construction and deconstruction of the narratives that underlie them".

The present paper is based on research conducted in 2005 and 2006 in Southwest Bulgaria in the Goce Delčev region, in the villages of Ribnovo, Satovča, Gărmen, and Ognjanovo. I lived in Muslim houses and observed their everyday life. The research was done with a sample that took into account the impact of "important" people, the functional élite, on the local community.[5] It resulted in fifty-two ethnographic interviews, twenty-five of them with Muslims, twenty-two with Christians, three with atheists, and two in mixed Muslim-Christian groups. My fieldwork methodology is based on Hans Georg Gadamer's hermeneutics, adopted for ethnographic purposes by the Polish anthropologist Joanna Tokarska-Bakir (1992, 1995). I analyse my interviews in accordance with Clifford Geertz's (2005: 19) interpretative anthropology, based on Max Weber's definition of culture as "a web of significance that man himself has spun". Accordingly, anthropological analysis is not a faithful and objective culture description, but rather its subjective interpretation aimed at finding elements most meaningful for the participants of a culture. Interpretations are not considered equally valid and unlimited in number: if the hermeneutic recommendation to consider the text as a whole by the reference to its parts, and the parts by the reference to the whole is met, the scope of possible interpretations is strongly narrowed.

I regard my interviewees' narratives to be accounts of their attitude toward dissenter neighbours. Simultaneously, I enquire into the narrative's symbolic messages and the situational context in which it was told. During my fieldwork, I noticed that the narratives told by my interviewees often constituted a reply to other stories on a given topic in the form of their extension or denial.

Each narrative told by my interlocutors deserves a deeper anthropological analysis. However, the purpose of this article is not a detailed investigation into the narrative components, but rather the depiction of relations between them.

[4] Wilmer here refers to national communities.

[5] Among my interlocutors were: the mayor of Gărmen and his wife, eight *hodjas* (teachers of Islam), among them the *mjufti* of the Muslim Municipality for the region of Goce Delčev, two Christian Orthodox priests, three officials working in the Gărmen municipality, the headmistress of the school in Satovča, two workers from the House of Culture (in Gărmen and Dăbnica), five teachers, three atheists (previously communists), and two faith healers (one Muslim and one Christian).

I will specify narratives shared by both religious groups as well as those particular for each group and concealed from dissenter neighbours.

Narratives shared by both religious groups: narratives about neighbourliness and narratives about resentments

Narratives about neighbourliness (turk. *komšuluk*) and about resentments are popular in both religious groups. The most favoured one is the narrative about neighbourliness which seems to showcase the local community to the newly arrived. It describes the neighbourliness principle as reciprocity relations and is accompanied by fixed phrases saying that dissenter neighbours are "like brothers", "closer than family", "the same as we are":

> *They* [Muslims] *are as ours. We are constantly together. We are not divided or something. We are neighbours* (Orthodox Christians, women, pensioners, Satovča, 2005).[6]

This narrative, if told by a Muslim, is often supported by an illustration of Prophet Muhammad's life[7] recommending practice based on neighbourliness. According to it, neighbourliness is not only a social duty, but also a religious one. Some of my interlocutors believe that the salvation of the soul depends on it:

> *Islam is constraining us to maintain neighbourly relations. Prophet Muhammad himself, in one of the hadiths, says that those who are on good relations with their neighbours will obtain a high position in paradise. Later, in some other statement, he emphasizes that one condition to be fulfilled by a pious person is to respect one's neighbours. Muslims have the same obligations toward close and distant neighbours. Close neighbours are those living in the same part of the village. Distant ones are those in general. Where did it come from? Prophet Muhammad was putting it into practice himself. He had a Jewish neighbour who had the habit of throwing his rubbish on Muhammad's courtyard during his absence. One day, the Prophet, surprised not to see the rubbish on his courtyard, understood that his neighbour was ill and decided to pay him a visit. The man asked him: "How did you know that I am ill?" He answered: "You were throwing the rubbish on my courtyard every day, but today I haven't found any. I came to the conclusion that you were ill and I came to see you." This is the very*

---

[6] All interviews, originally in Bulgarian, were translated into English by the author.

[7] According to Islam tradition, the Prophet's religious teachings are *sjunnet* (tradition), while obligations imposed by Allah are *farz*.

> *reason why he* [Muhammad's neighbour] *converted to Islam* (hodja, 36 years, Ribnovo, 2005).

> *Neighbours are even more important than relatives. Neighbours are the most intimate people. At the worst moment, a neighbour will show up. If something happens, a neighbour will show up (...). They say that when you go to the other world, the first thing they will ask you will be: "What kind of relations did you have with your neighbours?"* (Muslim women, 58 years, unemployed, Ribnovo, 2005).

> *Now listen, when you die, on the way from here to the graveyard, they will stop you in a few places and ask what kind of relations you had with your neighbours. Even if your neighbours are not nice to you, don't be angry at them. Pray Allah to be in favour of them and to take care of them. In the other world you will go to the prettier place and they* [will go] *to the bad one. He* [the neighbour] *dislikes you, but you don't. If you don't help one man and you disapprove of him,* [actually] *you disapprove of Allah, of God* (Muslim woman, seventy-two years, pensioner, Ribnovo, 2005).

This narrative also mentions reciprocity relations such as the exchange of gifts and festive food, mutual help, paying visits to neighbours at life cycle turning points (childbirth, wedding, funeral). These practices[8] constitute a way of expressing willingness to maintain peaceful relations in the region. Sensitivity toward the religious feelings of dissenter neighbours is often associated with them:

> *Generally speaking, when I paint eggs, I bring them to them* [friendly Muslim family]. *However, I've even asked them recently ..., because I've noticed that they've become more religious ... they are doing bows and all these things, required by religion ... Not so long ago, they were not doing that, but now I feel it to be inconvenient to bring them those eggs. I didn't know whether it was a sin or not for them to accept it. So I asked them: "If it is a sin, I won't give them to you. I won't feel bad because of this, but please tell me if you can't accept them." "It is not a problem. We haven't done those eggs. They give as pleasure. Children may clink with them. They will compete whose egg is the strongest and they will eat them. It is not a problem. We haven't pained anyone"* (Christian woman, about forty years, teacher, Satovča).

---

[8] Marcel Mauss says that although reciprocity relations seem voluntary, they are in fact obligatory. Refraining from them may lead to "private and public war" (Mauss 2001: 170). When one stops to respect one's neighbours, e. g. to give them festive food or to greet them in the street, then suspicions about one's attitude towards dissenter neighbours will arise. When both religious groups want to keep peaceful relations, they have to find a way to communicate this.

Narrating about neighbourliness is part of the grassroots strategy of coexistence. It presents it as something natural, but in fact it reveals that it is not taken for granted. This narrative expresses the desire to keep peaceful relations between dissenters. Thus, it is a confirmation of the importance of reciprocity relations in everyday social life in the region:

> *When, for example, one Muslim cooks "banica" and carries it to his neighbour, a Christian, a Jew, or whoever else, if he doesn't take it, then something like hatred will come out (...). But if he takes it, then there is something like intimacy between good neighbours. And there is mutual understanding as Islam requires, not hatred and hostility* (hodja, about thirty-five years, Satovča 2005).

However, this type of narrative, common for both religious groups, is not the only one dealing with dissenter neighbours. The other two narratives are structurally the same for Muslims and Christians. Both of them refer to the history of slaughters experienced by the religious groups in the nineteenth and twentieth centuries. They are not told in the presence of local dissenters. The narratives display the existence of collective memories of former conflicts and can be recalled in case of lack of trust among the religious groups. During my fieldwork in Satovča, I found that such resentments are still alive. I listened to two narratives about resentments: one told by a group of Christian elderly women and the other one told by a Muslim group of two women and a man. The two groups were religiously homogeneous. The Christians revealed their fears when talking about the Batak massacre which, as they told me, "has nearly happened" in Satovča as well.

> C1 *Listen now to what I will tell you. One day they were sharpening knives to kill us ... We had here* [at home] *an old woman in the family ... She told me about all this. They were sharpening them there, we are telling this to you. There were such stones and willows and the Turks were sharpening their knives, because they wanted to come here and kill all the village. But ... They went to Batak to kill. If only you could go there and see it, how it did look there. There are heads and everything. How they killed small children! And they had closed the church and massacred everybody with knives!*
>
> C2 *Church. The Turks had closed the church and small children, men, women, everyone. Blood remained in the courtyard* (Christian women, about ninety years, pensioners, Satovča 2005).
>
> C1 *Listen now to what I will tell you. We get on very well together. God, don't let something happen, because they will slaughter us like mice. What can happen?*

C2 *If there is war, they will kill us all.*
Are you afraid?
C1 *Of course we are* (Christian women, about ninety years, pensioners, Satovča, 2005).

As long as the Muslim woman was among the Christian women, they tried to convince me of the neighbourly relations with Muslims, but as soon as she had left, they began to talk about the Batak massacre and their fear of Muslims. A local Muslims' story about the extermination of the Muslim elite performed by Christian neighbours in Satovča in 1912 sounds similar:

Did the local Muslims take part in the 1876 April Uprising?
M1: No, no ... only Bulgarians took part in it. At that time, one "baši buzuk" came. That is what we call it.
What does "baši buzuk" mean?
M1: Independent army. Because all the richest and most intelligent Muslims were living in Satovča. They, our local Bulgarians, all gathered them as they said, seemingly for the meeting. And they went for the meeting, but they tied them up by means of a rope. There is a hill over there. There, they killed them. Fifty men standing in one line were slaughtered.
M2: That was in 1912.
M1: My grandfather was murdered and my grandfather's brother.
M2: They tied up and killed seventy people.
M1: Over there. On the hill. My grandfather and his brothers were slaughtered by local Bulgarians.
Bulgarians living here?
M1: Yes, living here. Our neighbours. It happened in 1912.
M2: When Bulgaria was liberated (Muslim woman, about eighty years, pensioner, and a Muslim man, about seventy years, pensioner, Satovča 2005).

It is impossible to say whether the mentioned slaughter in Satovča refers to real historical events. Bulgarian osmanists whom I consulted with (Antonina Željazkova and Mihail Gruev) could not answer that question for lack of historical sources. As far as the structural level is concerned, the specificity of this narrative is similar to Bulgarian folk songs about Turkish slavery, only that the roles of victims and perpetrators are exchanged, depending on the religious group of the victim.

M2: And then the sky opened. A horrible light started to shine during the night. That is the reason why they [people] *tell that the sky opened. I believe in this, because I asked Christians. I thought that we* [Muslims] *may be exaggerating a little. My grandfather and my grand-*

mother remember this. They told me this. I asked elderly Christians: "Do you believe that the sky opened?" "I do believe." "Did you see it?" "I saw it." It is interesting that all of them, being hodjas, were praying while going there. These were all people knowing the Qur'an and praying. They had told them that there was a meeting, a lecture in the House of Culture. They gathered them in one house.
Where is that place? Where did they take them?
M2: Here. At the outskirts of the village, on a hill.
Is this place somehow distinguished and demarcated presently?
M2: No.
M1: We are afraid. What shall we do? They will come again, they will come again in the evening. We live together, we celebrate together, we drink together, [but] *we are afraid! We feel like in captivity (...). My grandfather was stabbed eighteen times with a knife* (the same two Muslim interlocutors).

These accounts express hidden fears of the same dissenter neighbours who, in earlier neighbourliness narratives, were called "brothers":

M1: Bulgaria has always been persecuting Muslims. Always. It wants to make us one ...
M2: Nation.
M1: But we don't want them. The wolf won't become a cow and a cow won't become a wolf (the same two Muslim interlocutors).
We live on very good terms. We don't have any problems. Politics, government are the source of problems (Christian woman, retired teacher, Gărmen 2006).

Although narratives about resentments were present only in two interviews quoted above, I think they tell something crucial for understanding interreligious relations among members of Rhodope local communities. Their components are similar to those of Ivanova's sources, supporting Cvetana Georgieva's thesis that the Balkan "code of coexistence" is twofold: on the one side it is responsible for neighbourliness,[9] on the other it is connected with collective memories and conflicts[10] (Georgieva 1994: 154, 2003: 28). Narratives about resentments express feelings of fear and mistrust toward dissenter neighbours hidden behind good neighbourly

---

9 On the basis of data collected in 1993–94 together with students from Sofia University in the Asenovgrad, Razgrad, Zlatograd, and Ruse regions, she presented *komšuluk* to be a manner of managing peaceful coexistence between different ethnic and confessional groups, typical for the Balkans in general.

10 Georgieva mentions the second "code", but she does not give examples of it (Georgieva 2003: 28).

relations. To overcome them, Muslims and Christians in the region have begun to work up a strategy for peaceful coexistence. Their relations are in fact ambivalent, as they are at the same time friends and potential enemies.

Narratives specific for Muslims and Christians

Narratives that are specific for each religious group express the attitude to the religious practices and beliefs of dissenter neighbours. They usually confirm the rightness of one's own religion compared to the other, and help to cope with the cognitive dissonance produced by the fact that there is more than one way of worshipping God and obtaining salvation. These narratives constitute the hidden background for the overtly peaceful coexistence. They express the will to maintain a separate religious identity. The function of such narratives is antisyncretic. Muslims who want to confirm the rightness of their religion tell stories depreciating Christian faith. Christians neglect the separateness of local Islam and consider it as Crypto-Christianity or attribute the religious practices of Muslims to a stereotypical "Orient".

Muslim narratives about Christianity as a "false religion"

Some Muslim narratives, invoking various "sacred stories", portray Christianity as a false religion. They are usually told by old hodjas practising a traditional *(adat)* Islam rather than the official one. They present figures such as Adam and Eve, Saint Paul, or the four Evangelists as performing fallacious religious gestures based on incorrect interpretations of God's revelation. The latter is said to be spoiled by the Evangelists and distorted in the Gospel *(Indžil):*

> *Christians, Christians, but please do not feel offended, they are deluding themselves. They are deceiving themselves when they believe in the cross and in the hazeti Isa* [Jesus Christ]. *Hazeti Isa was created and his mother was Miriam (...).*
> *What else did the Christians understand wrongly?*
> *They wrongly understood, they rejected the Qur'an, the Christians. They do not believe in the Qur'an. And this is an offence that they do not believe in it. They will be punished for it. Those who believed in Qur'an became Muslims and those who did not – Christians, Jews and infidels.*
> *Kjafirs*[11]?

[11] The Unfaithful.

> *Kjafirs, ha!* [laughing]. *Lady, you know everything!* (hodja, eighty-one years, pensioner, Ribnovo, 2005).

The other erroneous element in Christian religion was the recognition of Christ as God's Son:

> *I haven't read those Gospels ... but it is written that there is a discrepancy.*
> *Is it written in the Qur'an that there is a discrepancy?*
> *Yes, yes. But in the Qur'an there isn't (...). Christianity was spoiled by people who thought that they knew Christianity, but wrote something different* (hodja, 82 years, pensioner, Ribnovo 2005).

> *They make the sign of the cross, because Jesus was crucified. Now, they are showing this in the cinema. However, it was not him who was crucified, but his friend Judas. Jesus was taken to heaven together with his book Indžil. That is how your Bible is called. Indžil is a Christian book. And his book was taken together with him* (Muslim woman, introduces herself as hodja, seventy-four years, pensioner, Ribnovo, 2005).

The Christian religion is considered by my Muslim interlocutors as being "polluted" with the sin of idolatry *(širk)*, understood as a false recognition of the sacred. One of its symptoms are icons and cults of the cross. One of my interlocutors said that the apostles wrongly interpreted Christ's gesture, and that the sign of the cross originated from this. According to him, the Apostles saw Christ making this sign while talking to God, just a moment before his ascension:

> *Icons – it is strictly forbidden to believe in them. Because the cross and Jesus Christ, whom they circulate in churches, it is absolutely proscribed in the Qur'an. The cross can not help you in anything, when you pray to the cross. If you pray to Allah, he might help you. But if you stare at the cross, you pray to the cross. You pray to Jesus Christ. But Jesus Christ is a man as we are. And they, when they crucified him in order to kill him, to destroy him, God had already taken him to heaven. And as God commands, we call him Isa and you Jesus. "What does God command him?" "Now, Isa", he says, "ascend to heaven, you". He looked up and saw in the heights one little hollow, then he said "But Arabi, my head will make its way, but this arm and that arm, how will they make their way?" And those who saw that, who were there, began to make the sign of the cross as he did. He saw this* [he shows me how Jesus made the sign of the cross, saying the words of Jesus], *that the head will make its way, but this arm and that arm, how will they make their way? Allah commanded this and gave him strength and he rose to heaven. And now he is alive* (hodja,eighty-one years, pensioner, Ribnovo, 2005).

> M2: *Isa is recognized in the Qur'an. Isa is a prophet. He is recognized in the Qur'an, but not in the way Muhammad is. He is a little bit lower. The Qur'an recognized also Jesus. Christians call him Jesus and the Arabs Isa. They acknowledge him. Do you know anything about Isa? Is he resurrected or is he going to resurrect?*
> *According to Christians, he is resurrected.*
> M2: *He isn't resurrected. He will resurrect now. The Qur'an says that he is not yet resurrected.*
> *So why do Christians believe that he has resurrected?*
> *Here is the Christian mistake. A man like you or me cannot be God. Isa and Muhammad are people like you and me. Do you know what the Qur'an says? That he* [God] *was not born, but Muhammad and Jesus were. You cannot be God and I cannot be God* (Muslim woman, about eighty years, pensioner, and Muslim man, about seventy years old, pensioner, Satovča, 2005)

As one old hodja told me, Christians believe in the Holy Trinity as a result of apostle Paul's manipulation. According to him, Apostle Paul intentionally preached heresies about Jesus, as he wanted to continue his struggle against Christianity:

> *He gathered one group and started to explain them that Isa was Allah. He told the other group that he* [Jesus] *was Allah's son, that was how it was. He told the third group that Isa was a messenger. And he* [Paul] *disappeared. And they, for example, gathered and began talking. Some said that he was Allah, others that he was Allah's son, the third ones that he was a prophet. And it made all Christians confused. But in fact he* [Jesus] *was created, "azeti" Isa. Allah was someone else. And that was how they began to murder each other* (hodja, eighty-two years, pensioner, Ribnovo, 2005).

When I asked him to tell me how he learned that Apostle Paul introduced the Holy Trinity worship, he showed me a handwritten book entitled *The Garden of Believers*, whose cover was missing, so that the author's name and the date of publication are unknown. The photograph shows the pages about Apostle Paul's false teachings.

When I asked a couple of teachers from Satovča about Apostle Paul, they recommended that I read the second edition of Maurice Bucaille's book *Bibljata, Koranăt i naukata*[12] which was for sale in their bookshop. A separate chapter is devoted to Apostle Paul, who is introduced as the creator of a new stream in Christianity in conflict with Orthodox (Jacob) Christianity, and finally superseding

---

[12] The book was published by Glavno Mjuftijstvo in Bulgaria in 2004 (2nd edition).

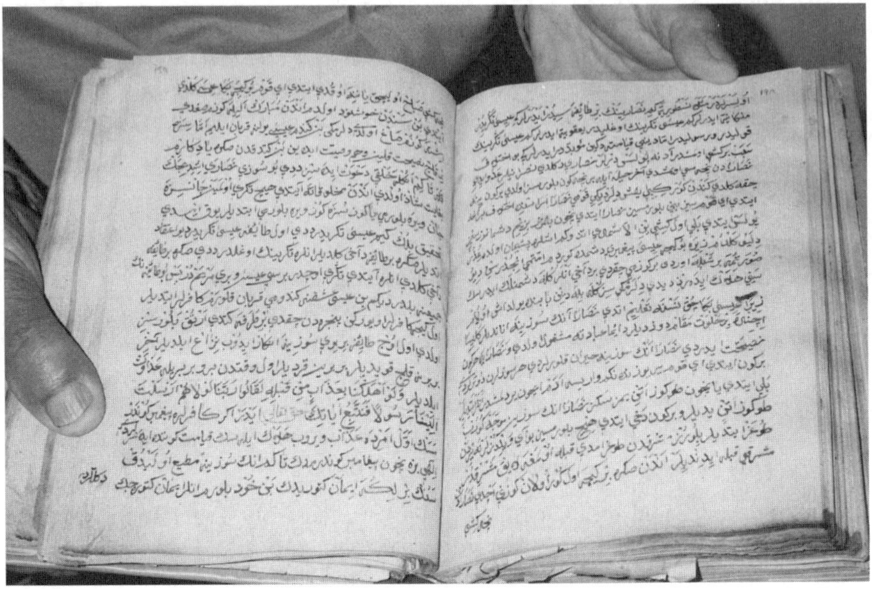

Pages from the book "The Garden of Believers"

it. The council in Jerusalem in the year forty-nine, relieving Christians from circumcision and other Jewish religious practices, gives evidence to this (Bucaille 2004: 76). According to Islam, the abolition of these rituals discredits Christianity, because it lacks some religious practices compulsory for Muslim believers, e. g. circumcision. As one of my interlocutors told me, human souls obliged themselves to obeying Islamic religious practices, as they were created in paradise. The Qur'an confirms their validity and the submission to them.

> *They didn't accept the prayer ("namaz"). They didn't accept important things which have to be followed in Muslim religion. And that is why they are now separated, Muslims and Christians.*
> *Can you tell me what things they did not accept?*
> *They didn't know, you have to forgive me, but when men and woman gather, they immediately take a bath after that,* [because] *this is a sin. But they* [Christians] *didn't accept this. They go on Sunday to take a bath. You don't take a bath when women and men gather, do you? That is what they didn't accept. "Abdest"*[13]*, washing oneself up to here, face, hands and legs up to here* [shows me how Muslims make "abdest"]. *You are doing all*

[13] Ritual ablution.

> *this, you are doing "abdest" for the sin to fall off. One should pray five times a day, pray. That is what they didn't accept. They rejected those things. That is why they will be severely punished. Every man should do those prayers* (Muslim woman, about eighty years, pensioner, and Muslim man, about 70 years, pensioner, Satovča, 2005).

The religious negligence of dissenter neighbours as presented in the above-mentioned narratives, which excludes them from the community of the saved, is deliberately concealed and remains untold in the relations between both religious groups. I did not encounter analogous narratives about the religion of Muslim neighbours among Christians. This may arguably be connected with their often inclusive attitude to Muslim neighbours. If differences between Muslims and Christians are mentioned, they concern only the religious form, not its content, and relate to customs:

> *What are the similarities between Islam and Christianity?*
> *Between Muslims and Christians? So, the difference is that they have separate names, separate customs. Our customs are disparate. The wedding is the same everywhere, but funerals differ. We bury our deceased in coffins, while they bury the members of their communities naked, wrapped up in linen. There are differences between Muslims and us. But in general we are the same. Even when a Muslim meets you and you have a problem where to sleep, he will immediately invite you to come to his house. Our people are not that warm. Also among us you will find such people, but Muslims are much more hospitable* (Christian woman, about eighty years, pensioner, Osikovo, 2005).

The absence of Christian narratives about the beliefs and religious practices of Muslims can partly be explained by the poor theological knowledge of my Orthodox interlocutors. They define their own religion not in terms of theology, but of traditions and customs with which their religion was contaminated. Not only does the Christianity they observe have weak ties to the "official" faith, but it is also insufficient as concerns their familiarity with biblical figures and events.

Christian narratives about Bulgarian speaking Muslims: Crypto-Christians and "People of the Orient"

The phenomenon of Crypto-Christianity, i.e., the secret fostering of Christian practice while officially confessing Islam, was described by historians of the Ottoman Empire. It occurred in the period from the sixteenth to the nineteenth centuries, and there are no grounds to claim it continues until today. Stavro Skendi (1967) states that this phenomenon was most conspicuous among Cypriots who, although they adopted Islam in the sixteenth century, continued to baptize their children for four centuries and gave them both Muslim and Christian names, observed Christian feast days, venerated the Holy Communion, and married women who upheld Christian traditions (Skendi 1967: 230). Skendi points out the existence of Crypto-Christian communities in Crete, Albania, Serbia, and Bosnia. As far as Bulgaria is concerned, he suggests that although there is no reliable information about Crypto-Christianity in this area, this does not mean that there was no Crypto-Christianity (Skendi 1967: 234). Nevertheless, the thesis of the Crypto-Christianity of Bulgarian speaking Muslims was spread by some Bulgarian scholars, among them Krasimir Stoilov, even with regard to present times. It is used as an argument that Bulgarian speaking Muslims are true Bulgarians, and is meant to level out differences undermining their national identity. The authors of this thesis seem to confuse some secondary cultural practices (such as making the sign of the cross over cakes before putting them into the oven) with factual religious commitment.

It is impossible to indicate the exact source of my interlocutors' knowledge about the Crypto-Christianity of Bulgarian speaking Muslims. According to them, it is displayed in such practices as Muslim church attendance in hope to recover from physical or spiritual illness, drinking alcohol, and eating pork. My interlocutors gave the example of the Muslim habit of inviting themselves to Christian houses in order to eat pork in "conspiracy":

> *Baj Dančo* [informant's husband], *will you invite me for pork? – Come if you wish. – Tell your wife not to tell anybody that we were at your place. And they came, five to six people.*
> *Were there women as well?*
> *Only men. And they wanted us to cover the windows, so that nobody can see that they were there* (Orthodox woman, pensioner, Gărmen, 2006).[14]

> *Do Muslims drink?*
> *They do, they do. They eat pork, they do everything. You can find among them fanatics as well. But, for instance, they used to bring me pork fat and salami for New Year, when I was a teacher there, years ago. They brought pork fat. They wanted me to fry it and to eat it together, as we are people who would understand this, friends. I told them that if they are hungry next time they shouldn't bring anything, because I have both: pork fat and meat. There is no need for them to buy it.*
> *Couldn't they prepare it themselves?*

---

[14] The same interlocutor claimed that, sometimes, Muslims bred pigs at their dissenter neighbour's place, because they liked to add pork to their home-made salami (bulg. *lukanka*) which was too dry without it.

> *I asked him: Imir, why don't you buy it in the shop, so that your mother could fry it for you at home? "It won't happen even in a dream. Even if I am going to put it in the frying pan myself, she will throw away the pan and the pot into the garden." So as not to tease them* (Christian woman, retired teacher, Gărmen, 2006).

> *They eat everything except pork. The elders do not eat, but the younger ones do. One of them told me: Be it shame or not, I will breed a pig, in Debren. When one takes some, all will take* (Orthodox woman, seventy-two years, pensioner, Gărmen, 2006).

Christians associate the ban on eating pork with another tale told half-seriously:

> *Why can't they eat pork according to them?*
> *The tale is, as they say: at the Turkisk-Bulgarian border, there was once a boiled pig. They say that they had to split it according to how it was. Very well, but the Turks happened to have the back and they felt disgusted. That is why they don't eat pork* (Christian women, seventy-two and seventy years, pensioners, Gărmen, 2006).

Those who talk about the specific Crypto-Christianity of the Bulgarian speaking Muslims are concurrently "orientalizing" them. This constitutes another way of depreciating dissenter neighbours based on the "ontological and epistemological differentiation of others" (Said 1991: 25), i.e., of "people of the Orient" from themselves. The orientalizing image of Muslims is characterized by women subordination, higher birthrates in Muslim families or women covering their body. Although not said openly, these characteristics are taken as evidence of Muslim inferiority. One interlocutor made an interesting distinction between "modern" and "backward" Islam. According to her, the uncovered woman stands for the first orientation, while the obligation of covering the female body stands for the second. She gives the example of a hodja who blamed women exposing their body for causing natural disasters:

> *By and large, the Muslim religion keeps women under cover. The Qur'an says that men may have as many wives as they wish. For them, the woman belongs in the second category. This means that in some way she is not a human being. There [in the neighbour village] they are, how to say, very modern ... I am talking about the outward appearance. While here, it is an oriental way of thinking. Here, older women gossip about short skirts, while over there they say: my granddaughter is dressed prettier than yours* (Christian woman, factory worker, about thirty-five years, Satovča, 2005).

> C1 *They are even more exposed than Christian girls.*
> C2 *If they like to dress like that, let them do so. (...).*

C1 *The hodja even goes to cafés. One woman came to the café and what happened? "Those short skirts cause hail, floods"* [he said]. *They think that those floods are Allah's punishment.*

C2 *Because we do not believe, we do not cover ourselves. I don't consider this to be good, either* (Orthodox woman, about seventy years, pensioner, and her daughter-in-law, about thirty years, Satovča, 2005).

The narrative is based on resentment.[15] The dissenter neighbour is depicted as a person who is disparate, backward, and driven by prejudices rather than by rational thinking.

Summary

Both Muslims and Christians consider the narratives about neighbourliness to be an official version of relationships between dissenter neighbours. By telling them, both religious groups confirm and cherish their peaceful coexistence. Concurrently, among themselves, they tell other narratives, often inconsistent with the official ones, expressing prejudices and fears about their dissenter neighbours. Muslims develop narratives depreciating Christianity as a religion, inconsistent with God's revelation. They demonstrate this by pointing out the "genuine" origin of elements of Christianity which, in their eyes, appear to be idolatry *(širk)*. Christians make use of two narratives contrary to each other. The first one uses symbolic violence to reduce differences between themselves and their Muslim neighbours by calling them "Crypto-Christians". The second one depreciates Muslim customs as pertaining to the backward "Oriental culture". Narratives told only in their own religious groups fulfil the cultural functions of maintaining separate religious identities and express the need to set oneself apart from the dissenters.

The coexistence of all these different narratives is typical of "common knowledge", which is "unmethodical" and inconsistent (Geertz 2000: 97). In this "everyday knowledge", one can say with Nižnik (1991: 164), different narratives "coexist side by side, not only without conflict, but supporting each other mutually". They do not constitute a coherent image of the dissenter neighbours but express and rationalize ambivalent prejudices and emotions towards them. Narratives about neighbourliness show the grassroots cultural strategy of religious coexistence in the region. Other narratives reveal the secondary feelings both religious groups have towards each other, which are suppressed by them, however, in order to make neighbourliness work. But they are also testimony of the fact that Muslims and Christians are aware that any unstable political situation in

---

[15] The same Christian group, gathered at Saint Ilija's feast, complained that they felt dominated by Muslims in the local power structures.

Bulgaria can disturb their neighbourliness, arouse resentments, and make their relations more strained.

The findings of this paper may be useful for social initiatives or regional policy makers wishing to use grassroots cultural strategies of coexistence developed by Muslims and Christians in the region as tools for strengthening religious tolerance. The findings are also an illustration of the double "code of coexistence" described by Cwetana Georgiewa (1994) and are thus applicable to all Balkan countries.

Literature

Bucaille, Maurice 2004: Istoričeski pregled. Judeo-hristjanstvoto i sveti Pavel [Historical survey. Judeo-Christianity and St. Paul]. In: Bibljata, Koranăt i naukata. Sofia: Glavno Mjuftijstvo na Mjusulmanite v Republika Bălgarija, 75–79.

Bringa, Tone 1995: Being Muslim the Bosnian Way. Identity and Community in a Central Bosnian Village. Princeton: Princeton UP.

Geertz, Clifford 2005: Opis gęsty. W poszukiwaniu interpretatywnej teorii kultury [Thick description]. In: Interpretacja kultur. Wybrane eseje. Kraków: Wydawnictwo Uniwersytetu Jagiellońskiego, 17–47.

Geertz, Clifford 2000: Myśl potoczna jako system kulturowy. In: Wiedza lokalna. Dalsze eseje z zakresu antropologii interpretatywnej. Kraków: Uniwersytet Jagielloński, 81–100.

Georgieva, Cvetana 2003: Hristjani i mjusulmani v bălgarskoto prostranstvo [Christians and Muslims in the Bulgarian space]. In: Balkański identičnosti IV. Sofia: Fondacija otvoreno obštestvo, 7–29.

Georgieva, Cvetana 1994: Săžitelstvo kato sistema văv vsekidneven život na hristjani i mjusulmani v Bălgarija [Coexistence as a system in the everyday life of Christians and Muslims in Bulgaria]. In: Vrăzki na săvmestimost i nesăvmestimost meždu hristjani i mjusulmani v Bălgarija. Sofia: IMIR, 140–158.

Ivanova, Evgenija 2002: Othvărlenite, priobšteni, ili procesa narečen văzroditelen (1912–1989) [The rejected, included, or the so called Renaissance Process (1912–1989). Sofia: Institut za iztočnoevropejska humanitaristika.

Lubańska, Magdalena 2006: Uraz historyczny jako polityczne narzędzie kreowania tożsamości narodowej Pomaków w Bułgarii [Historical trauma as a political tool of creating Pomaks' national identity in Bulgaria]. In: Joanna Tokarska-Bakir (ed.), Cóż po antropologii. Prace Katedry Antropologii Kulturowej Collegium Civitas. Warsaw: Collegium Civitas Press.

Mauss, Marcel 2001: Szkic o darze. Forma i podstawa wymiany w społecznościach archaicznych. In: Socjologia i antropologia. Warsaw: KR, 211–415

Neuburger, Mary 2004: The Orient Within. Muslim Minorities and the Negotiation of Nationhood in Modern Bulgaria. Ithaca, London: Cornell UP.

Nižnik, Józef 1991: "Potoczność" jako kategoria teoretyczna. In: Kategoria potoczności. Źródła filozoficzne i zastosowanie teoretyczne. Warsaw: Instytut Kultury, Instytut Filozofii i Socjologii PAN, 159–165.

Roth, Klaus 2006: Living Together or Living Side by Side? Interethnic Coexistence in Multiethnic Societies. In: Reginald Byron, U. Kockel (eds.), Negotiating Culture. Moving, Mixing and Memory in Contemporary Europe. Berlin: LIT, 18–32.

Said, Edward W. 1991: Orientalizm. Warsaw: PIW.

Skendi, Stavro 1967: Crypto-Christianity in the Balkan Area under the Ottomans. In: Slavic Review 26, 2: 227–246.

Tokarska, Bakir Joanna 1992: Hermeneutyka gadamerowska w etnograficznym badaniu obcości. In: Polska Sztuka Ludowa. Konteksty, XLVI, 1: 3–16.

Tokarska, Bakir Joanna 1995: Dalsze losy syna marnotrawnego. Projekt etnografii nieprzezroczystej. In: Polska Sztuka Ludowa. Konteksty, XLIX, 1: 13–22.

Wilmer, Frankie 2002: The Social Construction of Man, the State, and War. Identity, Conflict and Violence in the Former Yugoslavia. New York: Routledge.

Željazkova, Antonina 1997: Formirane na mjusjulmanskite obštnosti i kompleksi na balkanskite historiografii [The formation of Muslim communities and the complexes of Balkan historiography]. In: Mjusjulmanskite obštnosti na Balkanite i v Bălgarija. Istoričeski eskizi. Sofia: IMIR, 11–56.

Abstract

The Western Rhodopes are mainly inhabited by a Slavic population of Orthodox Christian or Sunni Islam confessions. The paper describes the relationship between different types of narratives about dissenter neighbours which I heard in Muslim-Christian communities in 2005 and 2006. They are crucial for understanding the grassroots strategy of coexistence between Bulgarian speaking Muslims and Christians. Two narratives are prevalent among Muslims and Christians, the first one being fundamental for supporting the region's neighbourliness, as it depicts the others as "brothers", "the same". The second one derives from mutual resentments and hidden fears, evoking collective memories of massacres. Other narratives unveil prejudices and negative attitudes to the other religion, but they are told only within each group. In Muslim narratives, Christianity is considered a fallacy based on misinterpretations and on heresies spread by the Apostle Paul. Christian narratives do not perceive Muslims as distinct from Christians, ascribing to them a Crypto-Christian identity, but on the other hand orientalising local Islam as backward and patriarchal. The first narrative, told by both religious groups, makes the existence of the separate narratives possible without upsetting the neighbourliness in the region.

Translated from the Polish by the author and Agnieszka Krześniak

Magazines as a Way of Maintaining Regional Intra-Ethnic Communication. The Case of Balkan Jewish Periodicals

Dimitrije Pešić, Belgrade

Introduction

In 1492 the Catholic monarchs Isabel and Ferdinand issued a decree, by which the Spanish Jews, the Sephardim, were obliged to leave Spain. Searching for a new homeland, they populated North Africa, the Middle East and other parts of Europe, mainly in the Ottoman Empire, where Sultan Bayazit II offered them significant privileges, should they settled permanently. He was aware that the Jews, being versatile merchants, would contribute to the economic development of the Empire. Hence, in the sixteenth century, Sephardic communities were formed on the Balkan Peninsula, with two main centres, Salonica and Istanbul.

In certain aspects the Jewish community differed from other minority groups in the region. Firstly, the Jewish population did not occupy a compact area as other groups did but was dispersed throughout the region (Popović 1997: 203). Secondly, the Jews were late in coming to Eastern Europe and the Balkans, and arrived everywhere as foreigners entering existing societies (Sowards 1996: 2).

The life in the Jewish community originally revolved in a set circle – patriarchal family, cultivation of tradition and religious commitments, raising children and their employment as soon as possible. At the end of the nineteenth century this way of life was opposed by a group of young intellectuals, who stressed the importance of emancipation and the further education of children, which would procure the spiritual development of the community (Popović 1997: 51, Alkalaj 1962: 86 f.). In this regard, it was not very distinctive from the other communities of the area, but the Jews experienced very diverse treatment from their neighbours in different parts of the region (Sowards 1996: 3).

It is important to point out that never in the history of Balkan Jews did their urban quarters represent a ghetto. They were allowed to settle outside of their quarters, but the majority of the Jews chose to live with other Jews. Trade was the main, but not the only contact with the surrounding population, while the Sephardic communities were tightly linked with each other, both on a cultural and an economic level. This fact facilitated the maintenance of the Judeo-Spanish language, literature and culture. On the other hand, as a consequence of this way of life, modernization and especially the emancipation of women, came very late.

It is important to mention that there are two varieties of the language of the Spanish Jews, Judeo-Spanish and Ladino. Judeo-Spanish is the name of the linguistic variety used for everyday communication and oral literature. The Sephardim used Ladino, together with Hebrew, as the language of written literature and religion. Ladino can be defined as a language of translation of holy scripts, the Talmud and the Bible. It differed from Judeo-Spanish because it was heavily influenced by Hebrew in lexicology as well as in syntax. Almost until the second half of the nineteenth century literacy was the privilege of men, but even among them the level of education was not the same, because the quality and the length of schooling was unequal.

Serbia

Taking into consideration that the journals, on which this article focusses, were published in Belgrade, I will briefly outline the historical and social background of the Serbian Jewish community. Belgrade became one of the most important centres of Sephardic culture in the Balkans in the seventeenth century (Popović 1997: 56, Vidaković-Petrov 1986: 20). The early foundation of educational institutions led to further improvement of the community.

As early as in the second half of nineteenth century, first among their community in the central Balkan region, the Belgrade Sephardim began to modernize their way of life, to open themselves up to the outside world and to incorporate themselves into Serbian culture. They took part in public activities, founded numerous societies and accepted the Serbian language, while still maintaining Judeo-Spanish and Hebrew (Vidaković-Petrov 1986: 35 f.). Of course, the conservative part of the community strongly resisted these processes. The shift from Judeo-Spanish to Serbian can be followed with statistics. In 1895, 3.88% of the Jews in Belgrade stated Serbian and 77.2% Judeo-Spanish as their mother tongue. Almost forty years later, in 1931, the census indicated a significant change in ratio: 54.2% stated Serbian and only 29.72% Judeo-Spanish as their mother tongue (Popović 1997: 151). In the period between the two Wars, the Sephardim were mostly bilingual, but not all equally. In addition, a lot of young Sephardim spoke German, as many of them studied in Vienna (Vidaković-Petrov 1986: 79 f.). Official documents and the correspondence of the Sephardim's organizations in Belgrade were kept exclusively in Serbian (Popović 1997: 153).

The Jews also began to add, at their own will, the Serbian suffix *-ić* to their family names, such as Davidović, Avramović, Aronović, Isaković, etc. (Popović 1997: 21). In political struggles, the Jews defended their interests, but without clashing with any party. They supported the Serbian state and its national interests, and the state had a very benevolent attitude towards them. King Petar I Karadjordjević, for example, laid the corner-stone for the new synagogue in 1907 and attended its inauguration in the following year (Popović 1997: 22).

The Sephardim in Serbia considered themselves "Serbs of the Moses faith". The Zionist idea never picked up, because during that time anti-Semitism, the basic moving force of Zionist ideas, was almost non-existent in Serbia. It is recorded that the Public Prosecutor's Office banned the publishing of the *Protocol of the Elders of Zion*. The only political party which openly promoted anti-Semitism, *Zbor*, and their leader Dimitrije Ljotić, won only 1% of the votes in the 1935 and 1938 elections (Popović 1997: 160 f.). The main promoters of Zionism were young and educated Sephardim, while the older generation stood for the integration into Serbian society (Popović 1997: 73).

Women emancipation among Serbia's Jews also began in Belgrade. By the second half of the nineteenth century they no longer dressed traditionally, and they started living more freely, establishing contact with outside circles. In spite of everything, until the First World War, marriages between Jews and non-Jews were rare. Any girl who married a Serb was considered a betrayer and conversion was met with public contempt (Alkalaj 1962: 89).

Romania and Bulgaria

The situation of the Jews in Serbia compares favourably to the one in Romania, which had the largest Jewish population in Southeast Europe. Jews were seen by the Romanian population as an alien element that would not be assimilated. This prejudice was exploited by ethno-nationalist leaders. In addition, Jews suffered from prejudices based on both political and economic myths, although they had little political or economic power. As non-citizens, Jews were barred from holding public offices, from voting and from owning land. As a consequence, they were forced to pursue social and economic lives that further distinguished them from the mass of Romanians. This fact added socio-economic tensions to the obvious religious and linguistic differences (Sowards 1996: 3 f.). This situation did not change until after the First World War, when foreign pressure eventually forced Romania to grant its Jewish residents full citizenship and civil rights in 1923, when the Constitution was rewritten (Sowards 1996: 9).

Compared to Romania, Bulgaria had a relatively small Jewish population. They had been living there since medieval times and were not treated badly. When Bulgaria gained autonomy in 1878 (and full independence in 1908), the Jewish community retained a special status with substantial self-administration under the chief rabbi (Sowards 1996: 6). Bulgaria's Jews lived separate lives but without being faced with prejudice. Although they were not fully integrated into national life, neither the state nor the local population created impediments for their businesses, and there was little resentment of Jews. Local Zionist groups were active and created a good alternative educational system, which was paid for mostly by the Jewish community itself (Sowards 1996: 11).

Magazines and their role

In the broadest sense, the term "Jewish periodicals" includes all journals and newspapers which appealed particularly to Jewish readers, either because of the language in which they were published or because of the special nature of their contents. The first Jewish periodical, *Gazeta de Amsterdam* (Amsterdam's news) was published in 1678 in Amsterdam, in Judeo-Spanish. Nine years later, in the same city, the first magazine in Yiddish, *Kurant*, was printed. In contrast to the Ashkenazim (Yiddish-speaking Jews) who published periodicals in many countries (Netherlands, Germany, England, USA, Austria, France, etc.), almost two centuries passed before the appearance of a new Sephardim magazine, the *Chronica Israelita*, which was printed in 1842 in Gibraltar (Gottheil, Popper 1906: 602–604); thereafter Sephardic periodicals began to spread to other regions as well.

The first magazines in Judeo-Spanish on the Balkan Peninsula appeared in the second half of the nineteenth century, first in Turkey, then in Romania, Greece, Bulgaria and Vienna (Gottheil, Popper 1906: 606). Towards the end of the century the first Sephardic magazines were published in Serbia and Bosnia. At first they were published in Hebrew and Judeo-Spanish. Later magazines used the Latin script, with articles in Serbian and Judeo-Spanish.

Two themes figured particularly prominently in these journals: the description of Jewish history and famous persons, and the attitude of other peoples towards the Jews. In the beginning, the magazines aimed to be mainly informative. Factious and independent publications only appeared after the First World War and many societies and organizations published their own periodicals.

The first Sephardic periodicals in Belgrade appeared at the end of the nineteenth century. They were published in *Rashi* letters[1] because their purpose was not to confer Sephardic culture to external circles but to gather the Sephardim from Serbia, Romania and Bulgaria, and to maintain their unity. The Belgrade Jewish community started the magazine *El amigo del puevlo* in 1887 ("People's Friend", on the cover page it also read, in Serbian and with Cyrillic letters, *Narodni prijatel*). It contained 24 pages in 14 × 14 cm format. The founder and editor was Jacob M. Alkalai, the president of the Belgrade Jewish community of that time.[2] "People's Friend" was published as a monthly publication "for Jewish

---

[1] *Rashi* is a semi-cursive typeface for Hebrew letters, used by Sephardic Jews.

[2] Alkalai was born in 1843 in Belgrade, where he finished the *yeshiva* (Jewish male educational institution). He was fluent in Hebrew. Although he was educated to become a rabbi, he

news, literature and science *(por novedades israelitas literatura i sensya)*". Although published in Belgrade, it was the voice of "Jews in Bulgaria, Romania and Serbia". All articles were written in Judeo-Spanish, in *Rashi* letters. The texts were anonymous, and the best known contributors were Simon Bernfeld[3] and Abraham Bezerano[4]. In 1890 Samuel Bohor Elias became the editor of the journal, and from 1893 it was published in Sofia (Vučina, forthcoming). The magazine was solely aimed at the Sephardim audience, and published information on everyday life and general Jewish issues. The aim of the magazine was expressed in the introductory article by the editor: Our intention is to gather all conscientious people of our nation (...) to engage seriously in favour of Jewish communities in the Balkans (...) (Amigo I, 1: 2).[5]

The journal was greeted with enthusiasm. Letters of support came from Jews all over the region. Already in the second issue, published one month later, the editorial board thanked "all our friends from Vienna, Constantinople, Sofia, Plevna [Pleven in Bulgaria], Iaşi, Šabac and other places who honoured us with words of support" (Amigo I, 2: 16). The letters of support expressed the feedback, which the magazine received from the Jewish communities, as the following two examples illustrate; the first letter came from the rabbi of Belgrade, the second from the rabbi of Istanbul:

> The foundation of a journal in the Spanish language in our capital is a very important action and through the course of time will bring fruitful benefits to all our brothers in the Balkans (Amigo I, 1: 5).[6]

---

worked as a tradesman in export. In 1883 he was elected president of the Jewish community in Belgrade. He died in 1903 (Lebl 2001: 199 f.).

3 Simon Bernfeld was born in 1860 in Stanislav, Galicia. He acquired a basic education from his rabbi father, and from the age of thirteen he was already translating German into Hebrew. He worked in the editorial board of several magazines in Germany. He obtained a doctoral degree in philosophy at Berlin University in 1885. He arrived in Belgrade in March 1886, where he was appointed rabbi and the principal of the Jewish school. He immediately started to learn Ladino, the language of believers, and frequently wrote introductory articles in *El Amigo del puevlo*. In 1893 he left Belgrade and died in 1940 in Berlin (Wiernik 1906: 93, Lebl 2001: 160).

4 Abraham Bezerano was born in Stara Zagora, Bulgaria. Before his arrival in Belgrade he worked as a teacher in Jewish schools in Istanbul and Rusčuk (today Ruse). He was a rabbi in Belgrade and often wrote articles for *El Amigo del puevlo* (Lebl 2001: 158–162).

5 *"Muestra intesyon es de sontraer a todos los ombres aklarados de muestra nasyon (...) a ke se okupen seryozamente en favor de las komunes čudias del Balkan (...)."*

6 *"La fundasyon de un čornal en lengua espanyola en muestra kapitala es una ovra muy importante ke kon el tyempo trayera frutos delisyozos para todos muestros ermanos del Balkàn."*

> It substantially strengthens our relations with our Sephardic brothers from Turkey, Bulgaria and Serbia (Amigo I, 3: 10 f.).[7]

> An approach of hearts, harmony and agreement between our brothers from Turkey, Serbia, Bulgaria, Romania and Germany, to strengthen our relations, to generally act much better for the honour of our sacred nation (Amigo I, 5: 8).[8]

The second Sephardic journal in Belgrade was *Hashalom* ("Peace") and it was published from 1903 until 1906. The number of pages differed from 8 to 24 and the format was 15 × 23 cm. The editor was Isaac Mitrani, articles were written in Judeo-Spanish in *Rashi* letters, and it basically published "national news, Jewish history, religious education, very interesting stories" *(novedades nasyonales, istorya de los đudeos, sensya reližyoza, kuentos muy kuryozos),* as stated on the cover page. The magazine was decidedly Zionist-oriented, and called for Jewish unity and the creation of a Jewish state. News usually concerned the persecution of Jews in Europe and appeals for help. Literary texts described themes from history or prominent persons from that time. The magazine did not have a precise publishing schedule, but depended on subscription payments. For example, the second issue of the third year was published at the beginning of spring 1906, on Purim, and the third one not before the beginning of summer of that year. At the end of that issue, the editorial board wrote an apology *(Eskuza)* in which they asked for understanding for the delay and informed their audience that timely subscription payments would enable bi-monthly publishing.

Although the magazine was printed in Belgrade, the editorial board moved from one city to the next. It shows that the state boundaries did not represent any obstacles and that the circulation of Jews among their communities throughout the Balkans went undisturbed. The editor of the second issue in the third year was Isaac Mitrani from Belgrade, while the editor of the third issue of the same year was his relative Barouh Mitrani from Sofia. In one of the articles, the editorial board acknowledged the receipt of donations and appealed to readers to donate. It proves that the destiny of the magazine depended solely on its readers. This text also evinces that the magazine was read throughout the Balkan Peninsula:

> To our friends in Belgrade! We thank you for your promises: the anonymous reader who helped us with the costs of this issue! We praise him from the depth of our heart, hoping that others will do the same! Friends in Sofia

---

7 *"(...) aze atar bastante las relasyones kon nuestros ermanos los sefardim de la Turkia, la Bulgaria i la Serbia (...)."*

8 *"(...) un aserkamyento de korasones i armonia i akordo entre nuestros ermanos dela Turkia, Serbia, Bulgaria, Vlahia i Nemcia, por atar byen rezyas nuestras relasyones, por ovrar munčo bueno por la onor de nuestra santa nasyon en čeneral."*

> and Filipolje, we await your good will; to our subscribers in Pazardžik, Niš, Vidin, Yambol, Varna, Kragujevac, Dupnica, thank you for your ongoing support which has enabled us to continue; subscribers in Sarajevo and Šabac, we thank you as well (Hashalom III, 2: 16).[9]

The third journal, *Jevrejski glasnik* ("Jewish voice") was published for three times, each for a short period: from 1909 to 1910, from 1920 to 1921, and from 1923 to 1925. It contained 8 pages, in 23 × 32 cm format. The founder of the magazine was David Alkalai (1862–1933). He belonged to the first generation of Belgrade Jews who acquired higher education outside of Serbia. He obtained a doctoral degree in law in Vienna and Tübingen and worked for the administration of the Belgrade Jewish community for eighteen years. Later, David Alkalai dedicated himself to Zionist work (Popović 1997: 192 f.). In this journal, texts were mainly written in Serbian, and just a few of them appeared in Judeo-Spanish with *rashi* letters:

> *Jewish voice* will in every issue publish a supplement in Ladino, Hebrew and in one European language (...). This supplement will contain the important news from the main edition and the articles that might be interesting to the Jews from the Orient (Jevrejski glasnik I, 1: 1).[10]

The magazine was Zionist-oriented. Similar to *Hashalom*, the texts were mostly about political issues, calls for Jewish unity and the creation of a Jewish state, as well as about anti-Semitic incidents throughout Europe.

All magazines published essays by scholars on the situation in which the Jews lived, which, sometimes, turned into severe polemics. In the news section, the texts mainly informed readers about activities of Jewish communities in Serbia, Bulgaria and Romania, but also from all over the world: Russia, Austria-Hungary, Turkey, USA, England, Italy, Germany, Palestine, France, Tunisia, Argentina, Abyssinia, Greece and Egypt. Especially interesting are the parts with news from the Belgrade Jewish community, as they reflected the everyday life of Jews in Belgrade. This news concerned, for example, scholarships for students, the work of Jewish schools, permits for selling kosher foodstuff, etc. Furthermore, the

---

9 *"A nuestros amigos en Belogrado! Agredesemos sus prometas: anonimo ke nos ayudo kon gaste de este numero! Lo bendezimos delas entranyas de nuestro korason makare uviera otros aziendo semežante! Amigos en Sofia i Filipole esperamos sus buenas prometas: a nuestros abonados en Bazarđik, Niš, Vidin, Yambol, Varna, Haskovo, Kragujevca, Dupnica, grasyas en rogando kontinuasion de sus favoros para poder nozotros kontinuar: abonados en Sarayvo i Šabca grasyas lo mizmo."*

10 *"La boz žudya va imprimir en kada uno de sus numeros un suplemento en ladino, ebreo y en una lengua evropea (...). Este suplemento va kontener las novedades importantes de la edisyon prinsipala y artikulos ke pueda intresar los žudiyos del oryente."*

magazines published articles from Jewish periodicals from other countries, announcements, as well as literary texts. The large number of news articles indicates that the main aim of these Belgrade periodicals was to spread information among the Balkan Jewish communities.

Due to their low circulation and their systematic destruction during the Holocaust, only a small number of copies of these and other Sephardic periodicals were preserved. The largest number of magazines are kept in the National and University Library in Zagreb, the Jewish Municipality in Sarajevo, the Jewish Historical Museum in Belgrade and the Ben-Zvi Institute in Jerusalem.

The influence of Balkan languages

Bilingualism is a consequence of direct language contacts and it is defined as the use of two or more languages in one community. These contacts between speakers of two languages provoke a number of changes in one or both languages. The Balkan Peninsula represents a unique contact area among languages of different language groups. The centuries of language mixing have led to linguistic commonalties called *Balkanism*. It is very hard to determine whether one common language phenomenon came, for instance, directly from Turkish or through other Balkan languages that had already adopted that linguistic borrowing from Turkish. After the expulsion of its speakers from the Iberian Peninsula, Judeo-Spanish had its own development, very different from the one of the peninsular Spanish (Castilian), archaism being its main characteristic. Some features of medieval Spanish, especially in the field of phonetics, are maintained until the present day. The speakers of Judeo-Spanish in the Balkans represent an interesting sociolinguistic phenomenon. They were bilinguals in a mostly monolingual environment and maintained their language with great effort, but, nevertheless, were not left immune to the influences of other languages spoken in the region, especially Serbian and Turkish. Serbian was the language of the surrounding population, and Turkish, due to the long Ottoman rule, is woven into all the languages of the Balkan Peninsula. Almost all linguistic fields of Judeo-Spanish spoken in Belgrade, therefore, experienced a number of changes. In phonology, for example, the phonemes /dž/ and /đ/ were adopted under the influence of Turkish loan-words:

Džami. Tur. *cami* – mosque.
"Salimus dil maldar, taman vinimus fin la džami."
"We went out of the school and just had arrived near the mosque."
Điger. Turk. *ciğer* – liver.
"Ke vos se kemi el điger ke no stuvitiš oj al kal."
"Your liver is going to burn because you haven't been to the synagogue today."

Jorganđi. Turk. *yorgancı* – quilt maker.
"(...) otra noće onde tiju Mušon il Jorganđi."
"(...) the other night at Muson's, the quilt maker."

The adoption of new phonemes and pronunciation rules was facilitated by the fact that the phonemic systems of Judeo-Spanish and the Balkan languages are generally very similar. The place of pronunciation of voiced [k] was moved toward the palatal region and, as a result, the affricate [č] appeared. It can be seen in loan-words from Turkish where the initial *k-* was changed into *č-* or *ć-:*

Čupri. Tur. *köprü* – bridge.
"In ansina una timpesta sta Mušon il kazaminteru dilantri di čupri (...)."
"In one such storm Muson the matchmaker is standing in front of the bridge (...)."

In morphology, the increase of affixes is evident, i.e.,the borrowing of morphemes used for the derivation of alterable types of words. The typological relatedness between Judeo-Spanish and Balkan languages also served in this process. All of them, with the exception of Turkish, belong to the flective type, so the word derivation is performed in a similar way. On the other hand, the structure of words from Turkish, a language that belongs to the agglutinating type, segments the root from other morphemes, so the affixes from Turkish are borrowed unchanged *(-li-, -ci-/-çi-):*

Monastirli. toponym Monastir [the Greek and Turkish name for the Macedonian city of Bitola] + Tur. suffix *-li.*
"In dialekto monastirli."
"In Monastir dialect."
Ojanđija. JudSp. *oja,* Sp. *hoya* – jewelry + Tur. suffix *-ci-* + Ser. suffix *-ja.*
"No ja jamavan dibaldis 'la ojanđija'."
"They do not call her 'jeweller' in vain."

It is interesting that in some cases, the Spanish suffix *-s,* used for the creation of plural of nouns, is added to the loan-word already in plural form:

Štifletes. Ser. Štiflete < Germ. *Stiefeletten* – type of ladies boots.
"(...) i un par de štifletes (...)"
"(...) and a pair of ladies boots (...)"
Pravilas. Serb. *pravila* – rules.
"(...) i restante de todos los ovligos ke tienen los vendedores de karne segun las pravilas de la opština serbeska."

"(...) and the rest of all the obligations which meat sellers have by the rules of the Serbian municipality."

Verbs were constructed by adding the Spanish suffix *-iar* to the Serbian root. Verbs of Turkish origin were constructed in a similar way (the infinitive suffix in Turkish is *-mek* or *-mak*):

Kazniar. Serb. *kazniti* – to punish.
"(...) el skup tiene la derečedad de kazniarlo por kada yero a 100 dinares."
"(...) the group has a right to punish him with 100 dinars for every mistake."

Since the contact with Balkan languages was long and intensive, the syntax of Judeo-Spanish suffered many significant changes, which could be explained by the influence of Serbian. Briefly speaking, those syntactic rules that do not exist in Serbian were lost in Judeo-Spanish. The most obvious consequences were the loss of subjunctive forms and changes in word order. However, the most notable influences were lexical in nature. Many Turkish words became naturalized among the Sephardim throughout the Balkan Peninsula, and can be found both in Serbian and Judeo-Spanish:

Kira. Turk. *kira* – rent.
"(...) kale ke (...) tomen a kira kaza para azer la orasyon."
"(...) they should (...) rent a house to pray."
Tefter. Turk. *defter* – notebook.
"(...) a todos tenia eskritos en su tefter."
"(...) they were all written in her note book."
Kavane. Turk. *kahvehane* – inn.
"Si estava el tiempo luviozo o si era invierno, si asentava en la kavane (...)."
"If it was raining or if it was winter, he was sitting in the inn (...)."

Loan-words from Serbian are relatively young. There are many Serbian words that completely overrode Spanish words. One characteristic of the Belgrade variety is the abundance of Serbian words of German origin, which do not occur in other varieties. Due to the application of Serbian phonetic rules, they acquired totally distinctive forms.

Farba. Serb. Farba < Germ. *Farbe* – paint.
"(...) farba muy vieža (...)"
"(...) a very old paint (...)"

Šances. Serb. šančevi < Germ. *Schanze* – trenches.
"(...) pelyaron oy komo unos leones de los muevos šances ke fraguaron la noče."
"(...) fought today as lions from new trenches, they dug the night before."
Štof. Serb. štof < Germ. *Stoff* – cloth.
"Kada anyo eyos mandan para la fiesta de Hanuka 12 pares de vestidos de buen štof."
"Every year they order 12 pairs of suits of good material for the Hanukkah party."

This can be explained by the influence of German language speakers from neighbouring Austro-Hungary, which was, until 1918, divided from Serbia only by the rivers Sava and Danube and had a strong economic and cultural presence in Serbia.

The largest number of loan-words belongs to semantic fields related to professions, human attributes, emotions, home and food. This is not a surprise, given the frequency of the use of those words in everyday communication. As usual, the majority of the new lexical elements belong to nouns and verbs, especially nouns that represent new items and products or parts of Balkan culture:

Clothes
Čakširis. Tur. *çakşır* – trousers.
"(...) la varda jerva es in bašu, ma kun todu si puedin inatakar lus čakširis."
"(...) it's true, below is the grass, their trousers could become dirty."
Feredžes. Tur. *ferace* – veil of Muslim women.
"(...) konosjeron (...) feredžes"
"(...) they were aware of veils"
Mintine. Tur. *mintan* – type of coat with long, narrow sleeves.
"(...) la tapo kon el mintine, i tumo a fazer las kamas."
"(...) he covered her with the coat and started to make beds."
Šalvaris. Tur. *şalvar* – pantaloons worn by Muslim woman.
"Ti akordas ki ivavamus šalvaris, mi paresi in shuenju ki hue."
"You remember we walked in pantaloons, it seems I was in a dream."

Food
Baklaba. Tur. *baklava* – type of pastry.
"(...) ki venga di la manjana para tumaldi la masa di baklaba."
"(...) to come in the morning to take dough for baklava."
Burikita. Tur. *börek* – type of pastry filled with meet or cheese.
"(...) jevando debašo de la mano dereča el tifsiniko kon las burikitas (...)"
"(...) carrying under the right arm the copper pan with burikitas (...)"

Halva. Tur. *helva* – sweets.
"Inluego en esti tifsin azijamos halva."
"And then we made halvah in this copper pan."

Loan-words from this group include both typically Balkan food and food the Jews already had known, but which they gave names from the Balkan languages:

Kumpir. Serb. krompir < Germ. *Grundbirne* – potato.
"Lus šabatis a medjudija la kumida muestra era burek di kumpir (...)"
"On Shabbats at noon our meal was potato pie (...)"
But. Turk. *but*, *bud* – leg of an animal.
"Por lo esteso se ovliga a vender (...) karne de but (...)"
"Herewith he is obliged to sell (...) meat from leg (...)"
Piva. Serb. *pivo* – beer.
"(...) jo mi jami un đaru di piva."
"(...) I have ordered a glass of beer."
Raki. Tur. *rakı* – brandy.
"No vazjo el raki."
"He did not spill the brandy."

This practice should not be surprising as the groceries were bought at the market and in non-Jewish stores, so the local terms had to be used. Similar loan-words can, therefore, be found for household items:

Fulđan. Tur. *fincan*, *filcan* – coffee and tea cup.
"Na ti il fulđan."
"Here is your cup."
Ibrik. Tur. *ibrik* – narrow-necked vessel made from copper with a cover used as a water pot.
"Las mosas ja estavan prontas kon el ibrik i el legen en sus manos."
"The girls were ready with the water pot and the washbowl in their hands."
Kalup. Tur. *kalıp* – mold.
"Un dija, mi mandi mi madri ki vajga ondi tija Lunača para ki li enpresti lus kalupis di lukumis."
"One day my mother sent me to aunt Lunača to borrow molds for lokum from her."

Frequent use of household items and the purchasing or repairing thereof in non-Jewish shops provoked the use of lexemes from the language of the local population. Of course, a large number of dishes, vessels and other items were unknown to them, so they took the lexemes directly from Balkan languages. It was facilitated by the fact that the Jews did not live in a ghetto, but mingled with the local population, and it can be assumed that the conversation among neighbours was mostly related to home and domestic care. The same can be said for professions:

Burekon. Turk. *börek* - burek + Span. suffix - *ón* - one who makes and sells burek.
"Ja abasta ki lu jaman a el Avramači il burekon (...)"
"It is enough that Avramači is called the burekon (...)"
Kasap. Turk. *kasab* - butcher.
"(...) partjo onde Jusufači el kasap a merkar karni para šabat."
"(...) she went to Jusufači the butcher to buy meat for Shabbat."
Pekar. Serb. pekar < Germ. *Bäcker* - baker.
"(...) tu ja savis ki il pekar alado del Bujrum si jama Simo."
"(...) you know that Simo is the name of the baker near Bujrum's."

From a sociological point of view, these phenomena confirm that the influence of one language increases with more intensive contact with the members of another linguistic community. When Jewish children began to attend public schools and emancipated women began leaving their homes, the language of the local population entered Sephardic homes, which was a milestone in the language shift process. However, although Judeo-Spanish had an "inferior" status, the language shift to Serbian was relatively slow due to the efforts of the Sephardic community to maintain their language.

Conclusion

The Sephardim from Serbia, Romania and Bulgaria formed an entity, as they lived in the same geographic area and under similar conditions. It is apparent that there were no insurmountable boundaries for the Sephardim and it is, therefore, difficult to talk about the Sephardim in Serbia independently from those in Romania or Bulgaria. Living relatively isolated from the rest of society, the Sephardic communities maintained their unity in spite of state boundaries.

The Sephardic periodicals *El Amigo del puevlo*, *Hashalom* and *Jevrejski glasnik* contain valuable information about the everyday life, culture, customs and beliefs of the Sephardic Jews and their relationships with other ethnic groups. They informed their readers both about the position of the Sephardim in the Balkans and in the world, worked on the gathering of Jews and promoted the Jewish cultural heritage.

For the relatively small Balkan Sephardic communities, the publication of journals such as these was a kind of luxury. Nevertheless, the need to have newspapers emerged with the modernization of life and the turbulent political changes at the dawn of the twentieth century. Besides the ties with the domestic population, the Sephardim in Serbia, Romania and Bulgaria apparently also felt the need to create a bond among themselves in the Balkan region and to maintain a certain level of communal spirit, especially during the intensive development of Zionism in Europe. Therefore, the main role of the magazines was not to bring the Sephardim closer to other people, but to establish and maintain the unity of Sephardic communities dispersed throughout the Balkan Peninsula.

Bibliography

Sources

El Amigo del puevlo, anni I, VI and VII 1888–1889 i 1893–1895. Belgrade, Sofia: Jewish Community.

Hashalom, annum III 1905–1906. Belgrade, Sofia: Isaac and Barouh Mitrani.

Jevrejski glasnik, annum I 1924. Belgrade: David Alkalai.

References

Alkalaj, Aron 1962: Život i običaji u nekadašnjoj jevrejskoj mahali [Life and customs in the former Jewish quarter]. In: Jevrejski almanah 1961–1962. Belgrade: Savez Jevrejskih Opština Jugoslavije, 82–97.

Gottheil, Richard, William Popper 1906: Periodicals. In: The Jewish Encyclopedia, vol. 8, 602–633 (http://www.jewishencyclopedia.com).

Lebl, Ženi 2001: Do "konačnog rešenja". Jevreji u Beogradu 1521–1942 [Until the "Final Solution". Jews in Belgrade 1521–1942]. Belgrade: Čigoja.

Mihailović, Milica 1982: Jevrejska štampa na tlu Jugoslavije do 1941. godine [The Jewish press on the territory of Yugoslavia until 1941]. Belgrade: Savez Jevrejskih Opština Jugoslavije.

Popović, Nebojša 1997: Jevreji u Srbiji, 1918–1941 [Jews in Serbia, 1918–1941]. Belgrade: Institut za savremenu istoriju.

Sowards, Steven 1996: Nation without a state: The Balkan Jews. (http://www.lib.msu.edu/sowards/balkan/lect17.htm).

Vidaković-Petrov, Krinka 1986: Kultura španskih Jevreja na jugoslovenskom tlu [The culture of the Spanish Jews on Yugoslav territory]. Sarajevo: Svjetlost.

Vučina, Ivana 2008: Uslovi i brzina zamene jezika u sefardskoj zajednici u Beogradu [Conditions and speed of language change among the Sephardic community in Belgrade]. Forthcoming.

Wiernik, Peter 1906: Bernfeld, Simon. In: The Jewish Encyclopedia, vol. 1, 93 (http://www.jewishencyclopedia.com).

Abstract

This study concentrates on the *El Amigo del puevlo, Hashalom* and *Jevrejski glasnik* magazines, which were published in Belgrade and Sofia in the period from 1888 to 1925, analysing their role in the social, cultural and political life of the Balkan Jews. These periodicals aimed at providing Jews with news and information from the whole region and enabled communication among them, as well as expression of their cultural and political views. They contain a valuable source of information but are difficult to access because they were written in Judeo-Spanish with Hebrew characters.

The study also draws special attention to the historical and social analysis of the texts and the influence of other Balkan cultures in them, especially in the areas of language, folklore and tradition. The beginning of the 20th century was a time of modernization and cultural transition for the whole region. In this context, the Balkan Jews represent an interesting sociolinguistic phenomenon. They were bilinguals in a monolingual environment and maintained their language with great effort, although they were not immune to the influences of other languages spoken in the region. This work examines the extent and the type of these influences.

BalkanBeats Berlin: Producing Cosmopolitanism, Consuming Primitivism

Rozita Dimova, Berlin

Introduction

This analysis is a biography of commercial success.[1] I trace the ways in which the spontaneous efforts of a group of refugees from the Former Yugoslavia during the mid 1990s gradually (and unexpectedly) initiated a successful commercial enterprise. This stream of events, I insist, should be analysed in the context of larger ideological processes, inextricably linked to the rise of the World Music phenomenon in the late 1980s, when a group of musicians agreed on coining the label "World Music" and thus, on creating a legitimate way for third and second world artists to participate in the Western music industry. Although the initial efforts of the "World Music" creators were not driven by major economic interests, or by explicit intentions to exoticize the artists coming from more "exotic" parts of the world, the subsequent rise of the World Music genre in general, and the Balkan ethno music in particular, would affect the way this music has been viewed, consumed and disseminated in the West.

The emergence of BalkanBeats Berlin, the musical trend that is the focus of this analysis, is deeply embedded in the World Music setting. Indeed, it is part of the late capitalist, urban-class quest for the ethnic and exotic. The Balkan musical space in Berlin, however, has a very distinct trajectory which testifies that Berlin's urban context has informed multiple social processes: it fostered social bonding among refugees from Former Yugoslavia, induced political action by questioning predominant nationalistic tendencies prevalent in the Balkans, and resisted the dominant expansion of turbo-folk music. Berlin's urban space has also produced the contemporary BalkanBeats musical network as a neo-liberal commodity *par excellence*, in which the politics of branding, copyright and profits become crucial for its contemporary outlook.

---

[1] I am greatly indebted to Marko Valić for his invaluable research assistance in conducting interviews, recalling past events, explaining music and contextualizing networks and individuals for me. I would also like to thank Robert Šoko for his patient tolerance with my, often excessive, intrusions into his DJ space and for the generous time he devoted to answering my questions. Tatjana Šoko provided crucial analytical insights into subtle matters surrounding the rise of the BalkanBeats scene in Berlin. The research for this article was generously supported by the Max Planck Institute for Social Anthropology in Halle/Saale, Germany.

The Origins

In 1992, at the dawn of the war in Bosnia and Herzegovina, an underground club in Berlin established itself as an important landmark for a group of young refugees who had fled their war-torn country. Nestled in the heart of Berlin's Kreuzberg, between Bergmann Strasse and Tempelhof Airport, the Arcanoa club was visited by people from different ethnic backgrounds who were primarily "misunderstood" rebels, unsuccessful artists, junkies or other kinds of marginal(ized) individuals – "people who did not fit into the mainstream society". Several newly-arrived refugees from Former Yugoslavia were introduced to this club by people from Former Yugoslavia who already lived in Berlin and frequently visited clubs such as Arcanoa and Monaco.[2] Several of those who discovered Arcanoa, soon realized that their "lifestyles before their flight as refugees fit in with the overall mood in Arcanoa: alternative, underground and punk/rock". They found solace in the burden-free atmosphere of Arcanoa, "where everyone was left alone", and where smoking joints and taking drugs in the club's gallery was allowed and even encouraged. Soon this place became a regular meeting point *(Treffpunkt)* for a dozen refugees from Former Yugoslavia.

Caught up between the ongoing disbelief regarding the full-scale war in Bosnia, the different experiences related to their displacement, and their newly-found freedom in Berlin which was still wrapped in its post-unification euphoria, the refugees started gathering in Arcanoa almost every day. The owner of the club, Petra, "an interesting character with frequent mood swings", allowed people to DJ and play music in the evenings and before long Yugoslav Rock music was part of the weekly repertoire at Arcanoa. As word spread in Berlin that there was a club playing rock music from Yugoslavia, Arcanoa started attracting a new crowd of regulars. The Yugoslav rock scene (both formal and informal) was strong, well-developed, and similarly as in the Czech Republic, for instance, rock music was a powerful and subversive space and tool where the dominant Yugoslav, and later nationalistic ideologies could be challenged.[3]

The music, the shared Yugoslav experience, and the bonds with Germans, many of whom also felt dislocated from and misunderstood or mistreated by the mainstream German society, encouraged more people from Former Yugoslavia to gather in Arcanoa. Soon the club became a central gathering place for a group of people who, in the next four to five years, would become its regular visitors. The weekly Yugoslav parties played music from Ekaterina Velika (EKV), Edo Maajka, Azra, KUD Idioti, and other rock bands from the Former Yugoslavia. On the one

---

2 This group of people was primarily first or second generation *Gastarbeiter*, and since many of them were from the Croatian coastal town of Split, they were introduced to me as *Spličani*.

3 For more see Gordy 1999, Gourgouris 2000.

Photo 1: Bernd Potschka, club Arcanoa

hand, this was the music that had been popular during their youth and which now encouraged the young refugees to reconstruct and embrace this place as a shelter that offered "something familiar that we all knew and liked". Arcanoa's unconventional interior on the other hand, comprised of recycled old furniture, represented a piece of a cosmopolitan world which many of the young people in Yugoslavia, looking for alternative lifestyles outside of the borders of Yugoslavia, longed for.[4] The art work on the walls and the ceiling, the dentist chair, the pieces of gravestones assembled together and used for the bar, along with the strong colours, created a surreal atmosphere, where "you lose sense of time and space". Many of the refugees arrived in Berlin alone, without their parents, and the relationships they formed with the people in Arcanoa became the most meaningful social network for most of them. An important feeling that Arcanoa evoked in

[4] Due to the Yugoslav politics of open travel, with noneeding visas required for most of the Western and Eastern European countries, London, Paris, and Amsterdam were the main destinations for young people eager to go to rock concerts. Travelling abroad to buy new records and attend the rock concerts of world stars was one of the main features of symbolic capital prevalent among many people, making an explicit class statement of being urban, cosmopolitan and rich enough to afford these travels.

many of these people, indeed, was *Urlaub osječaj*, "a feeling that you are on vacation by yourself and are allowed to do whatever you like".

The world's attention was captured by the war in Bosnia and Herzegovina, instigating unprecedented humanitarian relief operations from many EU countries. Germany in general, but Berlin in particular, accepted large numbers of refugees.[5] The formal arrangements, however, required that the refugees would be accepted on a temporary basis only, with a *Duldung* status, which prevented most of them from being allowed to work legally, or obtain further education. The state provided them with financial support and most of them (officially) lived and were registered in collective reception centres. Many, however, arranged for alternative dwelling possibilities in squat houses or friends' places and did not remain in the reception centres. By receiving regular financial support from the state, many of the refugees had a lot of free time on their hands. Even those who had jobs, or were working illegally (*na crno*, primarily on construction sites), regularly visited Arcanoa after the end of their working hours to seek comfort with people who "enjoyed the same music and laughed at the same jokes".

Coming from different class and ethnic backgrounds, common features shared by most of the people gathering in Arcanoa were anti-nationalistic and anti-turbo folk sentiments. Although this was a time of pronounced intensity of ethnic differences which had initially led to the outbreak of the war, many of the people who visited Arcanoa were from mixed marriages with an open longing for Yugoslavia and the lives that they had left behind. The core group that gathered in Arcanoa initially consisted of six to seven people only. Samir[6], for instance, arrived in Berlin with his parents after a long ordeal – first waiting for his father to be released from a concentration camp, and then having to flee via Serbia because they were only able to arrange Serbian passports that would allow them to leave Bosnia. Upon their arrival in Berlin, he was separated from his parents, because he was already eighteen, and was placed in a collective reception centre where he made friends with an Arab and a Turk. It was through them that Samir was introduced to the Arcanoa club.

There he met and befriended several other people from Yugoslavia who shared similar experiences and had been through similar struggles in Berlin. One of them was Amela, whose displacement to Germany was marked by many ordeals. However, the fact that her brother was living in Berlin, where he had already formed a family, helped her immensely in finding her way around. But given that she could not attend school or work, she was clinging desperately to the places where refugees from Former Yugoslavia gathered to "kill time". Arcanoa was a

---

[5] On the effects of refugee experience and the legal status of *Duldung* in Berlin see Dimova 2006a, 2006b, 2007.

[6] The real names of the informants have been changed.

revelation for her – her brother, who had become a regular visitor there, introduced her to the people. Without her mother around, she felt as if she was on a holiday and could do whatever she liked. She soon started taking drugs. After several years of intense "hanging out" in Arcanoa on a daily basis, she realized she had to leave Berlin for a while to go back to Zagreb and finish school. Upon her return from the six-month stay in Zagreb, in 1997, Amela realized that the refugees had already started going back, either to Bosnia or to a third country, and it was obvious that the Arcanoa Yugoslav network would soon fade out.

Similarly to Amela, Ivana was also fortunate that her brother was already living in Berlin prior to her arrival. He was a regular at Arcanoa and introduced her to the Yugoslav circle hanging out there. As a Serb coming from the Serbian part of Sarajevo, she never felt excluded or singled out by the people who visited Arcanoa. According to her, "ethnicity did not make any difference at all".

The idea to play Yugoslav rock/punk music in Arcanoa came from a young man in his early twenties. Robert arrived in Berlin in 1990, prior to the outbreak of the war in his native Bosnia and Herzegovina. Born to parents from mixed ethnic backgrounds, a Croat father and a Serb mother, he was brought up in a genuine spirit of Yugoslav "brotherhood and unity", never differentiating between people according to their ethnic backgrounds. Although he himself was not a war refugee, Robert soon became involved with refugees when they started arriving in Berlin on a massive scale. A large section of the ethnographic data in this article is based on information provided by Robert. I followed his BalkanBeats project for two years, from 2005 to 2007. I attended the contemporary parties he organized in a club in Berlin's Mitte district, and we also had numerous lengthy conversations about the initial Arcanoa moments as part of the contemporary development. This analysis describes Robert's efforts to elevate BalkanBeats to a professionally-managed DJ and music enterprise. As he points out, his story is not of a "glamorous DJ career, but of the vital survival training of émigrés. In the Arcanoa, a Kreuzberg underground punk bar, they tried to regain their lost past and identity" (quoted from balkanbeats.de), since those who were gathering in Arcanoa never paid attention to ethnic differences. Nevertheless, their clique was marked by pronouncing class distinctions, expressed primarily through their music taste and standing strong against turbo-folk.

The turbo-folk music in former Yugoslavia began its continuous rise in the mid 1980s, but the early 1990s brought along an unprecedented proliferation of this kind of music. Gordy (1999) analysed this process in his book, *The Culture of Power in Serbia,* where he identified that Milošević and his regime had strategically worked to destroy any alternatives, especially in music, by promoting the ascent of the turbo-folk genre that had been carefully stripped of the subversive elements present in rock music. While rock music was a marker of urban lifestyle and pro-western elements, turbo-folk was identified with nationalists, *seljaci* and *narodnjaci*.[7] The struggle between rock and turbo-folk music soon mirrored the larger class struggles during the late Yugoslav period, and also after its dismemberment.

This class differentiation prevailed, and even became exacerbated during the extraordinary circumstances of the displacement and the flight among the refugees in Berlin, where different social strata socialized in, and created their own distinct places. The turbo-folk fans frequented several places in Berlin, such as the Hollywood discotheque, while for the rock/punk fans it was primarily Arcanoa that provided them with the space to enjoy their music.

In December 1995, the signing of the Dayton agreement introduced a new phase in the life of the refugees: the war in Bosnia officially ended and the German authorities proceeded with a firm policy of repatriation. Those who had arrived in Berlin as individual refugees belonged to the so-called "group 1", the category of people who were to be repatriated first. Many of them returned to Bosnia, others left for the US or Australia; those who remained, managed to do so by marrying German citizens. In the period from 1996 to 1999, numerous *Abschiebungsparties* (deportation parties) took place, organized by those who were required to leave Germany. The massive departures coincided with the closing-down of the Arcanoa club in 1998, marking the end of the Yugoslav rock/punk presence in Berlin.

New spaces and the music shift: from punk/rock to Gypsy grooves

In 2000, several people from the former Arcanoa clique who managed to avoid repatriation and remain in Berlin, organized a party on November 29, the *Day of the Republic* that marked the formation of the Yugoslav Federation in 1943. In Yugoslavia this was the most important national holiday, and the idea of having a party celebrating this day had a nostalgic but also an ironic feel to it. Unexpectedly, 300 people showed up at this event. Another party was organized for March 8, International Women's Day, and yet another for May 25, Tito's Birthday. Tito became a mascot for these parties.[8]

Although the Arcanoa core was involved in the organization of these parties marking former Yugoslav holidays, there were several important changes in the music style: the predominant music played at these parties was Goran Bregović's

---

[7] The literal translation of *seljaci* would be village people, but there is a strong pejorative connotation to this word, a very negative value judgment representing non-urban and non-cosmopolitan preferences.

[8] The BalkanBeats website points out that "thus, the fascinating, bizarre, somehow tragicomical celebration of the exiled became a regular event that soon had to take place in larger venues" (http://www.balkanbeats.de).

Photo 2: Flyer for the BalkanBeats party on May 25, Tito's birthday, Youth Day (photo: by Rober Soko)

Roma(gypsy)music inspired soundtracks from the famous Yugoslav, Emir Kusturica's movies.[9] The success of his *Underground* and *White Cat, Black Tom-Cat* soundtracks enabled a commercial and popular introduction of Balkan Music into the World Music genre.[10] The people who attended these parties came from

---

[9] Emir Kusturica, Bosnian-born movie director, achieved major success in Yugoslav times with his films *Do You Remember Dolly Bell?* (1981, Sječas li se Dolly Bell?), *When Father was Away on Business* (1985, Otac na službenom putu), and *Time of the Gyspies* (1988, Dom za Vešanje). After the break-up of Yugoslavia he was heavily criticized in his native Bosnia for his outspoken pro-Serbian support during the Yugoslav wars in the 1990s. His conversion to Orthodox Christianity, followed by his adoption of a new orthodox name, Njemana, marked him as a Serbian nationalist. He has lived and worked mainly in France. The two movies that brought him major international success were *Underground* (1995, Podzemlje) and *Black Cat, White Tom-Cat* (1998, Crna macka, beli macor). The music for these two films was composed by Goran Bregović, who paved the way for the wide-spread popularization of Balkan Roma music.

[10] Balkan music in Berlin was inaugurated as World Music through the summer festival organized by Piranha Music in 1988. The group was founded in 1987 in Berlin and its mission was to bring "world music – the international soundtrack of Anti / Globalization in all its variety – to Berlin, Germany" (quoted from piranhamusic.de). The concerts organized in the

different ethnic, but especially different social backgrounds. More so than for the rock fans, these parties became compelling for people who did not mind listening to turbo-folk, because Bregović's music, along with other popular ethno-Balkan music styles, such as the Serbian singer Luis, borrowed styles and sounds from different genres. One reason for this switch may be found in the topographical resizing of the spaces in Berlin which are inhabited by people from Former Yugoslavia. Given that many of those with preferences for rock/punk had to leave, the ones who remained were increasingly trespassing the previously more rigid class boundaries in the various clubs that they frequented.

In any case, the anti-nationalistic mood remained and it was now coupled with a more theatrically displayed nostalgia for Yugoslavia: the person at the door, for instance, was dressed in communist pioneer style with a red scarf and a blue pioneer's cap with a red star attached to it. The entrance stamp to the club was a former Yugoslav border-crossing passport stamp. In addition to the party, Yugoslav movies were shown on a few occasions and there was a performance by a female group singing *a capella* polyphonic tunes from the Balkans, promoting the rich folk tradition in music – vastly different from the turbo-folk style. The audience, however, was not too interested in this and primarily responded to the popular tunes, which had a specific Balkan ethno-sound with a dynamic rhythm. Not only refugees, but also second generation *Gastarbeiter* frequented the club. For many, the YU rock music no longer had the same meaning as it did for those who arrived in Berlin in the 1990s; it was certainly not as meaningful for the young refugees who had socialised in Arcanoa.[11]

The most important turning point that shifted the way in which these parties unfolded, was the professionalization of the role of the DJ. After the first party where almost 300 people showed up, Robert realized that the main profit from these parties was going to the German bar owner who, at the end of the party, when most of the people had already left, had the audacity to unplug the music system. This act of disregarding the smaller group of people who remained at the end of the party was, in Robert's own words, the moment when he realized that all profits were going into the wrong pockets, despite the fact that the majority of the people there bought drinks because they wanted to listen to the music at these

---

Tempodrom in the early 90s featured musicians such as Boban Marković and Fanfare Ciocârlia, although I was told that the interest at that time was not wide-spread.

[11] Several of the second generation *gastarbajteri* whom I interviewed observed that their memories and feelings concerning Yugoslav rock music were closely linked to their summer visits to relatives and vacation places in Yugoslavia. It was obvious to me that this music did not have the same political and subversive meaning as it had for those who were born and raised in Yugoslavia and who considered music to be the most effective way of voicing rebelliousness or individualism.

Photo 3: DJ Soko and DJ Marko, the current tandem playing BalkanBeats music in the Mudd Club (photo by Alen Hebilović)

parties. Robert recognized the DJ's market factor and for the upcoming parties he insisted on receiving a percentage of the sales from the entrance tickets.

BalkanBeats™

This led to the official introduction of the BalkanBeats brand, represented with a professionally-designed logo, which would evolve over the years to become a recognizable brand in the realm of DJ and music producers in Germany and in Europe. The BalkanBeats project has been running full steam ever since. The incorporation, however, caused factions within the group that had originally initiated the parties. Tension and bickering mounted when it came to deciding how the workload and profit should be divided between the members of the group involved in organizing BalkanBeats.

Robert explained that he was the most engaged person and that he had invested the majority of his efforts into promoting BalkanBeats to different guide-magazines promoting weekly events in Berlin, such as Zitty and Tipp, as well as giving interviews, posting flyers, etc. Consequently, he believed that he deserved most of the earnings. This triggered conflict among the group of people involved in the organization of the parties, which were now continuing as a trademark enterprise. Although Robert included other DJs and tried to maintain a small circle of friends from the previous Arcanoa scene, this clique soon dissolved and BalkanBeats became solely Robert's enterprise.

Since 2001, BalkanBeats has followed an upward trajectory in terms of financial success. Its permanent house is the Mudd Club, which is situated in a dim cellar, and owned by an American who opened a similar place in New York. After visiting Berlin, the owner was confident that a similar club in Berlin's central district of *Mitte* would attract large numbers of people. Contrary to previous versions, when refugees and people from Former Yugoslavia were the main visitors, the audience now consists primarily of German or international students, or second generation *Gastarbeiter* who enjoy surrendering to the "wild sounds" of Balkan music. According to Robert and some other people from Former Yugoslavia who were involved in organizing the BalkanBeats parties in their early stages, rather than delving into any nostalgic memories or fostering deeper sentimental connections with the music's historical background, the new audience enjoys the momentary feeling. Several concerts, for instance, that Robert organized in the club, when musicians from Former Yugoslavia performed, did not attract the same attention from the new consumers of the music as they did before. The "crowd" usually arrives after the end of the concert when the "real" party begins.

Robert explains the shift from Yugoslav rock music to primarily Balkan Gypsy music, designated also as Ska, Ethno-Beats and Tribal, with the proliferation of Kusturica's films. The music put together for the soundtracks by Bregović, with its danceable and lively rhythms is liked by many – not only by people from Former Yugoslavia. It has attracted many Germans, who now attend these parties more frequently than the previous visitors from Former Yugoslavia. As the main goal of a DJ is to "light fire" on the dance floor for everyone, the most popular tunes became *Mešecina* and *Kalašnjikov,* the two major hits from the film *Underground,* arranged by Goran Bregović. Despite criticism from the original Arcanoa group that Robert and his DJs betrayed the initial rock and punk bond and turned to folk or *narodnjaci*, his firm belief is that popularizing this music is the right and good thing to do, and that "when you play opa, opa, everyone is jumping. It is the audience, after all, who determines the repertoire".

Nowadays BalkanBeats participates in an extended network of Djs – all over Europe and a few in the US – who exchange music among themselves and promote this style of music. The network of DJs and the bands focussed on, or inspired by Balkan rhythms, share music, compete, and also collaborate with each other digitally (through My Space), or by forming coalitions such as BalkanBeats

Berlin-Paris and London, for instance, in which DJ Soko and DJ Tagada play music at common parties and invite each other to different gigs.[12]

The release of two BalkanBeats CDs marked the formal incorporation of the brand into a musical/economic enterprise. Charlie Gillet, one of the founders of the World Music project reviewed vol. 1 of the CD on the BBC air show:

> "Balkan gypsy music basically has two speeds – breathlessly fast and heart-stoppingly slow. BalkanBeats virtually dispenses with the slow ones, so the whole thing is a bit like Madness on speed. One strand of the music is called Turbo, a sort of post modern disco music, with a four-to-the-floor drum on quite a few tracks, and an Abba-style chorus on others. But the wild horn arrangements and manic singing dispel any thought of slick formulas, and you flail around the room, glad that somebody somewhere is unashamedly offering you a good time, no strings of self respect attached (...) Where reggae and funk once trod the dance floors, Turbomania stomps with mighty steps" (from http://www.balkanbeats.de).

Several of the most regular visitors to the BalkanBeats parties, German students, explained to me that this was exactly what drew them to the parties: the raw primitive energy that was "freed" by the essential beats of the music. In a similarly essentializing manner the BalkanBeats website "reveals" why this music is so special:

> The secret lies in the rough energy, the colourful, fresh timbre, the savageness, passion and danceability. The inexhaustible diversity stems from Slavic, Oriental, Jewish traditions, and from the culture of the Roma people. Many of the bands are inspired by completely different traditions. The mixture of old and new, of urban and rural influences is the essence of the south eastern European soul – diverse, explosive, and just over the top. BalkanBeats is a rich culture's musical underground ambassador (from http://www.balkanbeats.de).

In lieu of a conclusion: explicating the shift

In an article published in the New York Times in October 2006 (quoted from FRoot Magazine 2007), rock star David Byrne explained why he hated World Music: In my experience, the use of the term world music is a way of dismissing artists or their music as irrelevant to one's own life (...) It's a way of relegating

[12] Other DJs involved in this network are Gaetano Fabri, working in Brussels and Paris; Dunkelbunt in Vienna; Penny Metal in London; and DJ Delay from Melbourne.

this "thing" into the realm of something exotic and therefore cute, weird but safe, because exotica is beautiful but irrelevant; they are, by definition, not like us ... It groups everything and anything that isn't "us" into "them". This grouping is a convenient way of not seeing a band or artist as a creative individual, albeit from a culture somewhat different from that seen on American television. It's a label for anything at all that is not sung in English or anything that doesn't fit into the Anglo-Western pop universe (fRoots Magazine 2006).

Responding to this and similar accusations directed at World Music, Ian Anderson, one of its founders, claims that conspiracy theories have been dismissing "World Music" as irrelevant, as a "Bullshit Detector" (where) "anybody from the Third World is allowed to join through the paternalistic assumption of rudimentary, exotic and inaccessible qualities" (fRoots Magazine, 2007, World Music History). In a similar vein, others have accused World Music "as ghettoising third world artists". Despite these accusations, however, Anderson foregrounds that the group of people who came together in a pub in 1987 and reached a decision to form this "label" did not have any thoughts of "ghettoising third world artists as irrelevant exotica or dressing them in Aran sweaters" (ibid.).

The main idea to coin the name World Music, which wasn't a new name, just one of many that had floated around in the preceding decades ... was that an established, unified generic name would give retailers a place where they could confidently rack otherwise unstockable releases, and where customers might both search out items they'd heard on the radio ... and browse through wider catalogue. Various titles were discussed including "Worldbeat" (left out anything without drums), "Tropical" (bye bye Bulgarians), "Ethnic" (boring and academic), "International Pop" (the death-by-Johnny-and-Nana syndrome) and "Roots" (left out Johnny and Nana). "World Music" seemed to include the most and omit the least, and got it on a show of hands. Nobody thought of defining it or pretending there was such a beat: it was just to be a box, like jazz, classical or rock ... (fRoots Magazine 2006, World Music History).

It can be successfully argued that the World Music genre introduced a new tendency, a trend which in social theory has been theorized as "culture as commodity". Appadurai (1986) and Kopitoff (1986), for instance, have shown how "culture" becomes packaged in a marketing brand, and thereafter represents a region, an ethnic group, by circulating and creating different meanings. This commodification of third or second world music has amply illustrated that contemporary markets and consumer choices determine the production and circulation of ethno-music. Indeed, contemporary BalkanBeats belongs to the World Music genre, especially because Ian Anderson's first label was recorded by a Bulgarian singer. The grand commercial entry of Balkan music into the World Music genre, however, occurred with Kusturica's films and Goran Bregović's soundtracks for the films. Stefan Hantal of Frankfurt, DJ Shantel, was responsible for the promotion of Balkan music in Germany on a massive and commercial level; the release of his first CD, Bukovina Club, made a major breakthrough in the popularization of this music. The second CD released in 2004, with the music used for several films such as *Alles auf Zucker* and *Borat*, enabled circulation of the music by reinforcing regional stereotypes, but also blurring boundaries: it becomes irrelevant whether the music comes from the Balkans, Eastern Europe, or Central Asia.

The contemporary BalkanBeats parties in Berlin have evolved (or mutated) from rock/punk parties with Yugoslav bands into ethno-beat, gypsy-groove, Ska and "tribal parties", gypsy brass music, and freshly produced traditional music. This process of transformation is deeply embedded in the larger dynamics of postmodern (late capitalist) lifestyles where the quest for authenticity, exoticism and "freedom" becomes a driving force of a specific urban social class. The Balkan Beats music thus becomes an exemplary case of what Rastko Močnik calls "generic ethnicity", ethnicity without specific roots, but with enough exotic flavour to it, and easily distinguishable from Western sounds.

Robert insists that although there is something "exotic and primitive" attached to the Balkans on the dance floor, BalkanBeats makes a real difference in redefining the negative connotation of this region. Could there be a process of subversion, similar to the one described by Hall in his article "Signification, Representation, Ideology: Althusser and Post-Structuralist Debates" (Hall 1985), in which he argues that music proved to be a powerful tool and a site for contesting the dominant colonial ideology in Jamaica? Reggae music initiated and carried their successful cultural revolution. Similarly, Gilroy has argued for the political and subversive role of music in his book, *The Black Atlantic* (1993).

The question is whether BalkanBeats can launch something similar for the Roma or for the Balkans and redefine the stigmatized place that this region occupies in the Western imagination. One has to consider, though, that in our case the process is rooted in an entirely different world context. Reggae music and its revolutionary character were not part of the World Music genre, in which, as Byrnes rightly pointed out, "World Music groups everything and anything that isn't 'us' into 'them', which is a 'convenient way of not seeing a band or artist as a creative individual". This feature is deeply embedded in a late capitalist trend that relies on multiple presences, multiple voices, multitudes with constant shifts and metonymic sliding. These discourses successfully prevent effective ways of broader alliances between individuals where music could merge with vocal political claims, which in turn can foster ruptures and subversions of dominant Western hegemony through late capitalist consumer culture in which profit becomes the ultimate goal.[13]

---

[13] For more on this see Hardt and Negri 2000, Butler, Laclau and Žižek 2000.

And yet, Robert is right when he claims that BalkanBeats parties and music do not merely reproduce stereotypes about the region, but also build a bridge between Germans, the predominant visitors at the BalkanBeats parties nowadays, and the Balkan region, by exposing them to, and entrancing them with, the fast rhythms. While highly sceptical about the lasting effect of this bridge after the end of the parties, from the outset I have been fully aware that different perspectives clash at the parties: the ethno-music and gypsy grooves which are packed in a World Music wrap, are sold as a cosmopolitan product and polished through transnational channels of music exchange. The audience, however, is hungry to consume "primitive" sounds that unlash primordial energy. This paradox between the transnational cosmopolitan connections involved in the act of production and circulation disappears in the process of consumption, a paradox that is, arguably, the driving force of contemporary globalization: a universalizing phenomenon that nonetheless rests on unequal distribution of wealth, marginalizing regions and people through subtle mechanisms of the dissemination of popular forms.

References

Appadurai, Arjun (ed.) 1986: The Social Life of Things: Commodities in Cultural Perspective. Cambridge: Cambridge UP.

Butler, Judith, Ernesto Laclau, Slavoj Žižek 2000: Contingency, Hegemony, Universality: Contemporary Dialogues on the Left. London: Verso.

Dimova, Rozita 2006a: From Protection to Ordeal: Status of Bosnian Refugees in Berlin. Max Planck Institute Working Paper Series, Paper No. 83.

Dimova, Rozita 2006b: Duldung Trauma: Bosnian Refugees in Berlin. Conference Proceedings from the Workshop on Developments and Patterns of Migration Processes in CEE. Prague, 25–27 August 2005.

Dimova, Rozita 2007: Strategische Erinnerungen als "Kampf um die Lebenden". Das Gedenken an das Massaker von Srebrenica bei in Berlin lebenden Bosniern. In: Berliner Debatte 4/5 (October 2007) 96–104.

Gilroy, Paul 1993: The Black Atlantic: Modernity and Double-Consciousness. Cambridge Mass.: Harvard UP.

Gourgouris, Stathis 2002: Hypnosis and Critique (Film music for the Balkans). In: D. Bjelic, O. Savic (eds.), Balkan as Metaphor: Between Globalization and Fragmentation. Cambridge, Mass.: MIT Press, 323–350.

Gordy, Eric 1999: The Power of Culture in Serbia: Nationalism and the Destruction of Alternatives. University Park, PA: Pennsylvania State UP.

Hall, Stuart 1985: Signification, Representation, Ideology: Althusser and Post-Structuralist Debates. In: Critical Studies in Mass Communication 2, 2: 91–114.

Hardt, Michael, Antonio Negri 2000: Empire. Cambridge, Mass.: Harvard UP.
Kopitoff, Igor 1986: The Cultural Biography of Things: Commoditization as Process. In: Arjun Appadurai (ed.), The Social Life of Things: Commodities in Cultural Perspective. Cambridge: Cambridge UP, 64–94.
Ramet, Sabrina 1994: Rocking the State: Rock Music and Politics in Eastern Europe and Russia. Short Disc. Boulder: Westview Press.

Web sources
http://www.balkanbeats.de
http://www.piranhamusic.de
World Music History. fRoots Magazine 2007 (initially published in fRoots 201, March 2000) (http://www.frootsmag.com/content/features/world_music_history/).

Mask Customs and Identity in the Region of Southeastern Europe. The Case of Macedonia

Eli Miloševska, Prilep

Introduction

The aim of this paper is the study of traditional cultural values that stimulate the building and promotion of various types of identity in Macedonia, as manifested through mask customs. The examination of the present-day manifestation and modification of traditional mask customs in the Republic of Macedonia can elucidate patterns of local, national and supranational identification. Thus, the basic aim of the research is to contribute towards a better understanding of the construction of identity in its broadest sense and to examine the possible consequences of the current processes of globalization, Balkan regionalisation and European integration, on different levels of identity in Macedonia.

These processes can be framed within the concept of "healthy glocalization", as developed by Thomas Friedman in his analysis of globalization and responses to it. According to Friedman, "healthy glocalization" requires that the capacity of any given culture be able to embrace, in its encounter with other dominant cultures, influences which it can integrate for its own benefit and enrichment, to reject the elements it finds truly foreign, and to appropriately regulate the elements which, although different, it can still enjoy (Friedman 2003: 242). In a similar vein, the discussed case study can also be framed within the concept of regionalism, which in part has emerged as a manifestation of the process of globalization and in part as a defence against this very process – as being "a project of unfair relations and new inequalities in the world" (Mitrović 2002). I believe that the analysis of mask customs in contemporary Macedonia can serve as a link between these theoretical processes and the understanding of identity patterns in the contemporary Balkans. For the purpose of my case study, I start from the following two premises:

1. The contemporary processes of post-socialist transformation, integration and globalization have affected both the structure of the existing, historically emerged society and the individual and collective identity of persons and ethnic communities.
2. In the construction of identity within these processes, traditional cultural values play an important role on account of their extraordinary capacity for active acculturation and participation (cf. Roth 1992: 44).

The exploration of mask customs, thus, can reveal the role of "traditional" culture in modern society for the formation of various types of identity - local, regional, national and supranational - and how society, in a specific situation, falls back on "tradition" for articulating new forms of identity; an issue, to which little attention has been paid in recent empirical research, despite the surge of interest for identity issues in the former Yugoslavia in the 1990s. However, the work of ethnologists such as Dunja Rihtman-Auguštin (1988), Slobodan Naumović (1996), and Ivan Čolović (2000) already suggested the significance of "tradition" for the realities of late Yugoslav and post-Yugoslav everyday life and identity. In this article, the focus is laid on traditional seasonal mask rituals in Macedonia which serve as vehicles for promoting various and multiple identities against the background of major political, social and economic changes experienced in Macedonia in the last decade. I start from Harrop's assertion (2003) that mask-wearing is not an auxiliary prop and that the person beneath the disguise does not become someone else. The masked person is "the very thing" the mask expresses, because daring to behave inversely is ingrained in the person and the disguise merely enables them to show their other face. Masks allow the articulation of (new) identities and in this manifestation, the traditional corpus of masks, used in certain rituals, is modified by new forms.

Traditional seasonal mask customs in the Balkans and Macedonia

Balkan ethnological and folklore studies have carried out extensive research into mask customs, based on written, material and visual sources (Kulišić 1970, Prosić-Dvornić 1978, Gavazzi 1988, Čajkanović 1994, Arnaudov 1996, Antonijević 1997, Svetieva 1998b). The material evidence indicates that, unlike the mask customs of Western and Central Europe (Roth 1992: 44), mask customs in the Balkans originated in distant, pre-Christian times. According to Dragoslav Antonijević this is a result of the fact that this part of Europe retained older cultural patterns for a longer period of time as a consequence of the centuries-long era of Ottoman rule and the belated emergence of modernization (Antonijević 1997: 20). Indeed, mask customs and the practice of masking are characteristic of all ethnic communities in South Eastern Europe. Notwithstanding the widespread insistence on their originality, authenticity and uniqueness, these mask customs are part of the shared Balkan and European matrix of religious systems and beliefs (Čolović 2000: 96). Over time, these customs have developed mechanisms to sustain and gradually transform themselves following the development of society as a whole. In the last few decades they have become a constituent part of the identity of ethnic communities, of states, and regions. In certain areas in the region, this has resulted directly from the need to secure ties with the tradition because "that is what the ancestors did" (in some areas of Bulgaria, Macedonia, Greece - especially in Thrace - and in Romanian Banat, etc.), while elsewhere they have been elevated to national symbols (such as in Patras in Greece, Pernik in Bulgaria, Strumica in Macedonia, Herceg Novi in Montenegro, Mohacs in Hungary, Ptuj in Slovenia, Istria in Croatia, etc.; Marjanović 2004: 158). However, at the same time they are considered a part of the shared European cultural heritage and these towns have become members of the Foundation of European Carnival Cities.

Starting from these general assumptions, and on the basis of content, the semiotic and contextual analysis of my ethnographic material centred on mask customs in Macedonia over recent years (2002–2007), I will try to establish the basic principles and mechanisms of the creation of local, national, and supranational identities through mask customs. I want to specifically stress the importance of contextual analysis (cf. Roth 1992, Sztompka 1994) which argues that, without the knowledge of the social, political and cultural situations in which rituals are performed, we cannot properly understand either the content or the meaning that a certain mask represents and communicates. It should also be noted that the ritual dances with masks in Macedonia have not been sufficiently researched, especially with regard to the emergence of new forms of integration and identification of this ritual practice.

Both older and more recent works on masks in Macedonia discuss the annual calendar of the performances of mask rituals: the earliest date in the year is *Kolede* (*Badnik*, Christmas Eve), followed by the "not-christened" or pagan days before *Vasilica* (St Basil's Day); then, the days before the start of Lent; at the very beginning of Lent *(Pročka, Trimeri);* then on the holidays of Lazarus Day, Easter, St George's Day, and Ascension Day; there are mask rituals at weddings and, amongst Muslim Macedonians, circumcision (Makedonski Folklor 1975, Običai so maski 1998). Most of the mask customs represent an integral part of the New Year's festive-ritual cycle; to be exact, they are connected with the critical interval of the so-called "not-christened days" from 7 to 19 January (Svetieva 1998b: 58, 63 f.). According to folk beliefs, the souls of the dead, together with various demons and evil forces - vampires, fairies, witches, diseases, wolves and bears - roam the earth in this period, and to encounter such souls is considered very dangerous. As a measure of protection from these evil forces, particularly before *Vasilica*, masked processions at night visit people's homes and circle the inhabited areas (Miloševska 2003: 157–163). Most probably, after the substitution of the Julian calendar, some of these ritual masked processions were moved to the period before the forty-day Lent before Easter, as well as on the first three days of Lent, called *Trimeri*.

Depending on the time and the place of their performance, the masked customs are called by different names: *Džamalari* (in the villages in the Skopje region and

Photograph 1: The “Mečkari” from Prilep

in the village of Sopot in the Kavadarci region), *Maškari* (villages in the Mavrovo, Ohrid and Debar regions), *Surati* (Ohrid), *Babari* (villages in the Kičevo, Mariovo, Bitola and Prilep regions), *Karnavali* (Mijak region), *Surovari* (villages in the Strumica region), *Surovaskari* (villages in the Osogovija, Pijanec, and Maleševo regions), *Mečkari* (Prilep), *Džolomari* (village of Begnešte in the Kavadarci district), *Vasiličari* (village of Vevčani in the Struga region), *Survari* (village of Dzvegor in the Delčevo region), *Trimeri* (Strumica), etc. (Svetieva 1998b: 63, Bocev 1993: 115). All these masked processions have specific local characteristics and differ from one another in various particularities as regards their appearance and the performance of the ritual.

In this paper, I examine the mask customs in Prilep, Strumica and Vevčani, mainly because the customs in these areas have undergone gradual transformations over time; and because presently, these customs, together with traditional masks, demonstrate certain elements of mass culture – entertainment, attractions, presence of mass media, commercialism, etc. (cf. Bocev 2004: 96). I shall begin with a description of the particularities of traditional masked customs in these three areas.

One of the most idiosyncratic masks, which diverges from the characteristics typical of other masked processions in Macedonia, is the masked company of

Photograph 2: The "Groom" and the "Bride" on St. Basil's Day

butchers from Prilep, called *Mečkari* (photograph 1). This company celebrates the religious holiday of *Pročka* (beginning of Lent) as the day of their trade. The fascinating and sensational appearance of this male masked company is achieved through the zoomorphic characters they assume; more precisely, their disguises in an unusual attire of raw sheep and lamb hides, in masks *(surati)* made of black cloth and decorated with beads, pendants, animal teeth, goat horns, beards, and strings of many bells and rattles hanging from their waists. The overall effect is reinforced by their particular ritual movements: they shake and roll over like bears; they pound their sticks against the ground and thrust them at the gathered crowd like phalluses, making clear and grotesque allusions to erotic arousal and sexual acts. They dance their ritual dance to the rhythm of drums and the music of wooden pipes *(zurla)* from morning till night, both on the streets and in people's homes. The onlookers and hosts are expected to reward the performers with money and beans. Refusing to reward them or allow them to enter your house results in a symbolic punishment; you will either be assailed on the street or you can expect some disturbances in your yard. If anyone should refuse to reward them or let them enter their home, they punish such people symbolically, either by assailing them on the street or by making a disturbance in the house-owner's yard.

The masked customs in the village of Vevčani (Struga district) take place on the eve of *Vasilica* (St. Basil's Day) and on the same day as the religious holiday. Their procession is characterized by two groups of *Vasiličari* from the upper and the lower part of the village. Each group consists of younger and older men, but the leading roles in the performance are played by the three masks of the "Groom", the "Bride" (photograph 2), and the "Clown". The other *Vasiličari* are masked in zoomorphic and anthropomorphic masks bearing a variety of names: the "Grandfather", the "Grandmother", the "Hangman", the "Devil", the "Policeman", etc. The *Vasiličari* of both groups, after having danced the *Vasiličari oro* in the centre of the village to the music of drums and *zurla* pipes, journey through the village visiting every house without exception, dancing and blessing their hosts. Then they gather again in the village centre, where the ritual ends with a great festivity involving everyone.

The traditional ritual dance with masks in the town of Strumica is dedicated to betrothed girls. Many women gather in their homes on the eve of *Trimeri* (the third day of Lent) and generate a specific atmosphere by singing songs with erotic connotations. Later, the masked male groups arrive and the girls have to recognize their fiancé among the masked men. This is not a very difficult task because the fiancé can be easily recognized by the accentuated phallus made from a bottle or similar objects. The most common masks in these male groups are the "Groom and the Bride", the "Gypsy Man and Woman with a Baby", the "Priest", the "Devil", etc. They are accompanied in their procession by musicians playing the accordion, the guitar and the tambourine, all of which help create a general joyful and festive mood.

According to folk beliefs, these masked customs represent a ritual blessing for health, fertility and prosperity – an embodiment of Good and a means of expelling Evil and sickness. This is expressed in the theatrical improvisation of a caricatured wedding in which the leading roles are given to the "Grandfather" and the "Grandmother" or the "Groom" and the "Bride" as the basic fertile couple and representatives of the unity of the male and female principles. Through simulations of sexual acts and the singing of a certain type of erotic songs, they generate an orgiastic and erotic charge which is typically explained as a vital aspect of the rituals of fertility. The other masked participants in the ritual – with their frightening appearance, the tumult they create, and the slogans they chant – are believed to expel demonic and impure forces, and they appear in the role of mythical protective ancestors who secure fertility and prosperity (Svetieva 1998a: 7–13, Ristovski 1975: 219–228, Bocev 1993: 114–124).

Mask customs as vehicles for promoting different and multiple identities

Today, however, in the performance of the mask rituals of any given community, both in Macedonia and other countries of Southeastern Europe, we can recognize that religious beliefs have disappeared from the rituals themselves, which are carried out automatically, out of tradition. Vesna Marjanović (1996: 103) observes that even though some archaic reminiscences of the cults of the ancestors, of fertility and new vegetation, have survived in certain rituals, the masking itself has lost its magic significance and has been turned into a powerful tool for entertainment and relaxation, and an opportunity for transformation of the self (see also Marjanović 2004: 156, 160 f.). This interpretation is further corroborated by the emergence of new forms and contents which diverge from the original ritual masked processions. In the last fifteen years, in the three aforementioned areas, an ever-increasing number of masks has been recorded which, through their non-verbal symbols (appearance, movements, dances) and verbal symbols (text, dialogue), reflect domestic and international issues of social, political, economic, cultural and public life. As a result of their increasing popularity, but also under the influence of the new processes of Macedonia's "opening" towards Europe and the world, these masked customs have acquired the institutional form of organized carnivals under the initiative of local, socially integrative agents. In addition, masking has been transformed into a symbolic object which facilitates communication within the community and beyond. The mask in this context obtains the new function of a socially acceptable new identity.

By maintaining such formal ties with rituals and cults from the past, a variety of communities in Macedonia have upheld their mask customs and rituals as a component of local culture, so that today they represent a symbol of the identity of their cultural heritage. In support of this claim, we can refer to the ongoing revitalization of mask customs and many other folkloric traditions in various areas – customs and traditions which were forcibly abandoned in the socialist period. A logical question arises: Why, now, in the process of the democratization of society and European integration, do the trends of turning back to traditions gain such momentum? This trend is typical not only of Macedonia but also of other countries throughout the region (cf. Balandier 1981). According to Slobodan Naumović, this represents a type of reaction characteristic of the incompletely or unsuccessfully modernized societies faced with comprehensive and long-lasting crises as a result of endogenous or exogenous forces, or both of them (Naumović 1996: 111).

This crisis in Macedonia was instigated by the long period of transformation which, unfortunately, has still not been brought to its end. This process has affected stagnation in every sphere of life as well as great uncertainty among people with regards to their future. This has resulted in a crisis on all levels of identification, both individually and collectively. In the pursuit of confirmation of their own identity, the individual, as well as the community, have returned to the presumed values of folk culture, which are traditionally observed as most sacred (cf. Durkheim 1972: 292). By falling back to their traditional values, the individual and the community feel safer. They strengthen their shared consciousness and their internal mutual relationships, and as a consequence they bring about affirmation of their community at all levels: social, economic and ritual (cf. Bocev 2004: 98).[1]

Mask customs in Macedonia serve as an excellent example of how tradition can be established as a fundamental value on which to base one's identity, that is to say, the sense of belonging to a specific human community. From this point of view, mask customs as a constituent of tradition secure some essential contents as values, symbols and techniques of passing traditions. Collective memory is founded upon these essential contents and the development and survival of the identity of any given community is unimaginable without it (Connerton 1989: 96–104). These contents unite several different identities: local, national and supranational.

Local identity

Local identity is demonstrated through the strengthening of the unity of the individual and the community on a local or micro-regional level (belonging to a certain town or village). This is displayed in the traditional and contemporary components of present day masks and masking. The most important traditional elements are:

1. Equal devotion of all members of the community, those with masks and those without, participating in the organization of the mask customs and rituals.
2. The presence of the traditionally established characters and processions, including their appearance, accessories and conduct.
3. Observation of the traditional dates of mask customs.
4. The calls on people's houses by the masked people and donations from the hosts.

The following are some of the contemporary components:

5. The presence of a larger number of people masked in the masks traditional for the community, mostly from the younger population, including children as young as one year (as confirmed by the photograph of a "Little *Mečkar*" from Prilep, photograph 3).

[1] The website of the Strumica carnival reads: "The Strumica Carnival is a centuries-old tradition of the town under the Tsar's Tower" (http://www.strumickikarneval.com); in the same vein, the website of the Vevčani carnival says: "The Carnival of Vevcani, older than 1400 years, is an interesting mix of paganism and modernism" (http://www.vevcani.org.mk/karnevala.html).

Photograph 3: The "Little Mečkar" from Prilep

6. The presence of masks derived from certain verbal symbols specific to a particular place. The people of Prilep are pejoratively called "monkeys" based on the anecdote "No monkeys dance in Prilep". In time this name was so widely accepted by the local inhabitants that it has come to represent a certain kind of identity. This claim can be confirmed by the existence of many individual and group masks representing monkeys.
7. The increasing presence of masked people performing certain folk customs typical of other local environments and cultures: for example, the *Gjurgjovden* (St. George's Day) custom from the village of Krivogaštani or the *Sv. Trifun* custom (Saint Trifon) performed by the masked procession *Džamalari* from the village of Sopot near Kavadarci.
8. The presence of masked people performing present-day local folk material culture: The "Vegetarian" (photograph 4), a mask made from various vegetables and industrial crops common in the Prilep area, and the mask called *Trajan Čatalot* from the village of Bučin, made from the same vegetables and industrial crops as the Vegetarian mask, but styled as a folk costume from the Prilep and Bitola region.

The words of one of the participants in the *Vevčani* festival illustrate this local identity quite clearly: "I participate in the carnival to show that I come from Vevčani!" (Bocev 1998: 148). I would like to add that the villagers of Vevčani,

Photograph 4: The "Vegetarian", region of Prilep

who work and live abroad, feel a moral obligation to be in the village at the time of the performance of the ritual. If they cannot attend, they enact the ritual in the place of their residence. This demonstrates how strongly the integrative and identification power of the mask customs is felt.

This is revealing of another contemporary dimension of the local identity of the villagers of Vevčani demonstrated through their mask customs. After 1990, the processes of globalization and transformation only worsened the dichotomy between the highly developed (metropolitan) and the underdeveloped (peripheral) regions, in this case rural regions. Looking for a way out of the unfavourable situation, the village community began to rely increasingly on these symbolic activities which were to lead, on the one hand, to "nostalgic regionalism", through popularization of the local masking custom in the regions abroad, where persons from the village resided temporarily or permanently; and on the other, to an expansion of tourism and "festivalization" of their rural environment as a counterbalance to intensifying urbanization and globalization (cf. Roth 2008).

National and ethnic identity

During the observance of the mask customs in the three investigated places, national (or ethnic and ethno-national) identity is demonstrated alongside the local identity. My interest in this paper is not in the complex classification of national

Photograph 5: "Philip II the Macedonian"

identity, nor in its final definition, but in its influence on the individual and collective sense of belonging to the same ethnic group.

In the mask rituals in Macedonia, national or ethnic identity is demonstrated with historical romanticism and ethnocentrism. A plausible explanation of this phenomenon is offered by recent history. The emergence of ethnic and national movements in the former Yugoslavia in the late 1980s/early 1990s and the subsequent break-up of the country into several smaller ethnically and nationally differentiated states instigated new crises of identity and produced dilemmas as regards national, state and ethnic identifications. One of the mechanisms applied in the construction of national and ethnic identity in the Republic of Macedonia and in its neighbouring countries was to refer to history and tradition, i. e., to mythologize selected "sacred" historical figures and events. Today, political anthropology makes it quite clear that identification mechanisms are based, above all, on elements of a political nature, followed by elements coming from other social and cultural contexts. These mechanisms are introduced and supported mostly by the ruling structures of the state. By this means, a certain body of historical and folkloric symbols are selected to be installed in the new social and political ideology which then instigates the creation of a new political and ethnic mythology (Rihtman-Auguštin 2001, Risteski 2001: 295).

In this context, on the basis of a short semiotic analysis of masks over the past few years, we can establish the mechanisms on which the methodology of cre-

Photograph 6: "The Macedonian Phalanx of Alexander III the Macedonian"

ation of national identity is founded and, specifically, of the elements that encourage and determine the ethnic consciousness of communities. An important characteristic of Macedonian ethno-national identity, particularly evident in the period after the declaration of independence in 1991, has been the establishment of two ethnic myths regarding the origins of the Macedonian people. Both of these myths were promoted by certain political centres of power. The first ethnic myth declares that Macedonians are direct descendants of the ancient Macedonians, while in the second the genesis of Macedonians is linked to the history of the Slavs (Trpeski 2003: 94).

In mask rituals, the most evident is the first ethnic myth, as is corroborated by the large number of masks representing significant historical figures: the mask of "Philip II the Macedonian" (photograph 5), where the most distinctive feature is the symbol on the shield, the golden-yellow two-tailed lion; the mask of Philip's son, "Alexander III the Macedonian and His Soldiers"; and perhaps the most impressive of all, is the mask "The Macedonian Phalanx of Alexander III the Macedonian" (photograph 6). The soldiers-lancers' costumes are representative of the ancient Macedonians: the clothes, the shields, the spears and the flag with the golden-yellow sun with sixteen rays. This attire of the mask is accompanied by a text emphasizing the continuity of the Macedonian people through the centuries.

Photograph 7: Komiti – Freedom Fighters

As far as this emphasis on ethnic continuity and longevity is concerned, i.e., continuity in the ethnic, cultural and social-political development of the Macedonian people, the best example is the group mask called "Macedonia throughout History to Present Day Democracy". In this case, the mask bearers are disguised as Alexander the Great (in Macedonian, *Aleksandar Makedonski*) with his mother Olympia; as Tsar Samuil with his wife Agrippa; as King Marko; as the leaders of the national revival in the nineteenth century; and as present-day government officials. The preference for national elements is also evident in the masks representing national heroes, such as the mask "King Marko" and the masks inspired by the *Ilinden* period in the history of the Macedonian people, e.g. the "The Little Voivodi for Macedonia" where boys are disguised as a *komiti*, i.e., freedom fighters against Ottoman domination (photograph 7). At the opening of the Strumica carnival, flag bearers wear this *komiti* attire as a national folk costume.

When we discuss national and ethnic identity and the strengthening of the sense of belonging to a particular ethnic group, we must not overlook the mask "The Three-headed Dragon" (personifying Macedonia's three neighbouring states, Greece, Serbia and Bulgaria) with enormous gaping jaws in which it tries to swallow a girl in white – the personification of Macedonia – who tries to avoid this at any cost (Mitrova 2001: 333). This mask symbolizes the partition of Macedonia after the Balkan Wars were sanctioned by the Treaty of Bucharest in 1913. Macedonia is represented by the young girl in white not allowing herself to be swallowed or dismembered, which unmistakably suggests its indivisibility, that is, its virtue and incorruptibility. The idea of the virtuous, incorruptible girl allegorically refers to the organic entirety of the ethnic body of Macedonia. When borders change, the issue of upholding ethnic integrity, according to Ivan Čolović, "becomes a highly problematic and traumatizing experience of the same consequence as guarding one's mother's honour" (Čolović 2000: 43) – or female honour in general, as is the case with the mask we have discussed. This strong allegorical and personifying motif, present in the mask, involves visual images of the mythical and folkloric perception of Macedonia's ethnic and cultural space and actualizes the political myth about the ethnic unity of partitioned Macedonia (Risteski 2001: 300).

European and supranational identities

In recent years, topics concerning Balkan regionalization and European integration have come increasingly to the fore in the politics and economy of the country – and consequently in its cultural and social life in general. A characteristic of mask customs is their swift reaction to such processes, mainly owing to their amazing capacity for the non-conflicting adoption of anything foreign, that is, their "capacity for acculturation and participation" (Roth 1992: 44, cf. Ivanova 2004: 93). By transforming themselves, they have an effect on the identity structure of both individuals and communities. The emergence of a supranational identity was inevitable and has manifested itself in the masked customs of these three areas in several components:

1. As a result of inter-regional cooperation between towns and villages which cherish this tradition, masks characteristic of the local traditions of neighbouring countries have started appearing in Macedonian carnivals, such as the mask "Playful Combination" where the basic elements of its manufacture and its symbolism were borrowed from the *Kukerska* mask from Bulgaria (photograph 8).
2. The participation of masks and mask companies from neighbouring countries in the parades in Strumica and Prilep, and vice versa; the participation of masks from Macedonia in international carnivals in the region.
3. The joining of Vevčani (1993), Strumica (1995), and Prilep (2006) in the Foundation of European Carnival Cities (FECC).
4. Membership in the FECC gave the mask customs a new form, resembling that of the festivals and carnivals in western European cities. In addition to the performance of the ritual activities by the masked processions on the traditional day, the duration of the Vevčani, Prilep and Strumica carnivals has been extended, either by a few days before or after the original day.

Photograph 8: "Playful Combination", based on Bulgarian masks

5. As a result, novelties are introduced in the traditional appearance of the masks which are not derived from the local culture. This is most evident in the Strumica carnival, where we can observe influences in the stage performances originating from other European cultures, adopted by the population mostly through the prototypes of *commedia dell'arte* and Italian Renaissance carnivals (photograph 9).
6. The supranational identity can be observed in the younger population participating in various carnival activities and clearly expressing their support for the European community. As the most characteristic example we can cite a drawing by a student (photograph 10). He used the drawing assignment entitled "Masks – Tradition and the Present" to express his supranational identity. With the intention of emphasizing his supranational affiliation, the student added the following words to his depiction of the symbols and the representatives of the European Union: "For homework you need to write a hundred times: we all love each other and we want to join the European Union and NATO."

In support of this supranational identity, the president of FECC, Henry F. M. van de Kroon, said the following at the opening of the Prilep carnival in 2006: "Don't

Photograph 9: Masks from the Strumica region, adopted from the *commedia dell'arte*

forget Macedonia belongs to Europe. We are one people. If I seem a big man with this cap[2], I am one of you."

Conclusion

The analysis of the empirical material related to the mask customs of Macedonians over recent years indicates that traditional cultural values have greatly contributed to the establishment of identity at the local, national and supranational level. This means that traditional cultural values and identity are coexistent factors or, in other words, that mask customs as an element of the folklore tradition of a certain community

> "cannot explain the change in quality of their own content without taking into consideration the identity of the corresponding group; and vice-versa – if one wants to explain the identity of a group, the community will have to look at the content, changes and the applications produced by this group" (Lafazanovski 1999: 304 f.).

We should note that the influence of culture on the development of the identity of individuals and communities differs at different stages in the development of the society. The demise of socialism caused an identity crisis in the formerly socialist societies in the Balkans, which subsequently replaced their communist ideology with ethno-nationalism. This involved reverting to a primordial religious matrix in

[2] He referred to the special FECC presidential cap. For the FECC, see their homepage at http://www.carnivalcities.com/.

Photograph 10: Drawing by student "Masks – Tradition and Present"

which ethnic communities sought a foundation for the renewal of their identity. This is corroborated by the emergence of masks equipped with a rich repertory derived from national mythology, whose sole purpose was to prove ethnic and historical continuity. As these societies grew more open due to ensuing modernization and urbanization, traditional cultural values reacted promptly to the current social and political changes. The choice to turn towards Western culture has had an effect on the dynamics of individual and collective identities. Individuals and the communities increasingly considered themselves a part of the globalizing world and this might be an indication of the acceleration of current processes of Balkan regionalisation and European integration. The dynamic changes in the mask customs, thus, reflect the ongoing processes of political and socio-cultural transformations, with all their ambivalences between Europeanization, centralization and decentralization.

This analysis of the relation between mask customs in Macedonia and local, national, and supranational identity offers insights into the concepts and mechanisms of identification. In fact, this represents a relevant problem for ethnological research because similar processes, taking into account specifics and similarities in contemporary social, political, cultural, and economic processes, can be observed in other countries throughout the region of Southeastern Europe as well.

References

Antonijević, Dragoslav 1997: Dromena. Belgrade: SANU, Balkanološki Institut.

Arnaudov, Mihail 1996: Očerci po bălgarskija folklor [Essays on Bulgarian folklore], vol. 2. Sofia: Marin Drinov.

Balandier, Georges 1981: Sens et puissance. 2. éd. Paris: Quadrige/PUF.

Bocev, Vladimir 1993: Maskiranjeto i običaite pod maski vo Makedonija [Disguising and mask rituals in Macedonia]. In: Etnolog 3: 114–124.

Bocev, Vladimir 1998: Tradicionalnoto i sovremenoto vo vasiličarskiot običaj vo seloto Vevčani - Struško [The Traditional and Modern of the Vasilica custom in the village of Vevčani near Struga]. In: Običai so maski. Trudovi od Meğunarodniot simpozium održan vo Vevčani - Struga 1996 [Mask rituals. Proceedings of the International Symposium held in Vevčani, Struga 1996]. Skopje: Muzej na Makedonija, 145–149.

Bocev, Vladimir 2004: Karnevalite kako sovremeno gradsko praznuvanje na primerot na strumičkiot karneval [Carnivals as contemporary urban festivites. The Strumica carnival as example]. In: Etnolog 10: 92–99.

Čajkanovič, Veselin 1994: Studije iz srpske religije i folklora [Studies from Serbian religion and folklore], 1925–1942. Ed. Vojislav Đuric. Belgrade: Prosveta, Partenon.

Čolovć, Ivan 2000: Politika simbola. Ogledi o politickoj antropologiji [The politics of symbols: Essays on Political anthropology]. Belgrade: XX vek.

Connerton, Paul 1989: How Societies Remember. Cambridge: Cambridge UP.

Durkheim, Emil 1972: O podeli društvenog rada [Division of Societal Labor]. Belgrade: Prosveta.

Friedman, L. Thomas 2003: Lexus i maslina [Lexus and olive]. Zagreb: Izvori.

Gavazzi, Milovan 1988: Godina dana hrvatskih narodnih običaja [One year of Croatian folk customs]. Zagreb: Kulturno-prosvjetni sabor Hrvatske.

Harrop, Peter 2003: The Ma(s)king and Unma(s)king of Strangers: Verfremdungseffekt and Its Antithesis. London: Folklore Society Centenary, University of London.

Ivanova, Radost 2004: Bugarske praznično-obredne tradicije u eri globalizacije [Bulgarian festive-ritual traditions in the era of globalization]. In: Etnokultorološki zbornik (Svrljig) IX: 89–96.

Kulišič, Spiro 1970: Iz stare srpske religije: novogodišnji obicai [From the old Serbian religion: New Year's customs]. Belgrade: Srpska književna zadruga.

Lafazanovski, Ermis 1999: Folklor i identitet [Folklore and identity]. In: Makedonski folklor 53: 304–311.

Makedonski folklor 1975, vol. 15–16. Skopje: Institut za folklor.

Marjanović, Vesna 1998: Masks and Ritual Processions in Traditional Culture of Vojvodina. In: Običai so maski, Trudovi od Megjunarodniot simpozium odrzan vo Vevčani - Struga 1996 [Mask rituals. Proceedings of the International Symposium held in Vevčani, Struga 1996]. Skopje: Muzej na Makedonija, 103–110.

Marjanović, Vesna 2004: Maskiranje i balkanski kulturni prostor u svetlu novih istraživanja [Masks and Balkan cultural area in the light of new research]. In: Etno-kulturološki zbornik (Svrljig) IX: 155–162.

Miloševska, Eli 2003: Tradicionalnata kultura vo opština Krivogaštani [The traditional culture in the municipality of Krivogaštani]. Krivogaštani: WNGO Horizont.

Mitrova, Dragica 2001: Tradicionalnoto i sovremenoto vo Trimerite, običaj pod maski vo Strumičko [The traditional and modern aspect of the Trimeri, custom with masks in the Strumica region]. In: Makedonski folklor 58–59: 325–336.

Mitrović, Ljubiša 2002: Sudbina kulturnih i etničkih identiteta u procesima globalizacije i regionalizacije na Balkanu [Destiny of the cultural and ethnic identities on the processes of globalization and regionalization in the Balkans]. Internet: http://www.komunikacija.org.yu/komunikacija/casopisi/junir/IX/index_html?stdlang=ser_lat.

Naumović, Slobodan 1996: Od ideje obnove do prakse upotrebe. Ogled o odnosu politike i tradicije na primeru savremene Srbije [From the idea of renewal to the practice of instrumentalisation. An Essay on the relation of politics and tradition in contemporary Serbia]. In: Od mita do folka [From myth to folk]. Belgrade, Kragujevac, 109–145.

Običai so maski 1998: Običai so maski. Trudovi od Megjunarodniot simpozium održan vo Vevcani - Struga 1996 g. [Mask rituals. Proceedings of the International Symposium held in Vevčani, Struga 1996]. Skopje: Muzej na Makedonija.

Prošić-Dvornić, Mirjana 1978: Teorijsko-hipotetički okvir za proučavanje poklada kao obreda prelaza [Theoretical-hypothetical frame of studying of the "Pokladi" as customs of passing]. In: Etnološke sveske 1: 33–50.

Rihtman-Auguštin, Dunja 1988: Etnologija naše svakodnevice [Ethnology of our everyday life]. Zagreb: Školska knjiga.

Rihtman-Auguštin, Dunja 2001: Etnologija i etnomit [Ethnology and ethno myth]. Zagreb: Publica.

Risteski, Ljupčo 2001: Novosozdadenite narodni pesni i socio-kulturniot kontekst vo Makedonija [Recently created popular songs and the socio-culture context in Macedonia]. In: Makedonski folklor 58–59: 293–304.

Ristovski, Blaže 1975: Maškite erotski narodni pesni okolu koledniot ogin vo nekoi mesta vo Makedonija [Male erotic songs during the *Koleda* fire in some places in Macedonia]. In: Makedonski folklor 15–16: 219–228.

Roth, Klaus 1992: Narodnata kultura na Jugoistočna Evropa v modernoto vreme [Folk culture of South-East Europe in the Modern Times]. In: Bălgarski folklore 1: 38–48.

Roth, Klaus 2008: What's in a region? Southeast European Regions between Marginalization, Globalization and EU-Integration. In this volume.

Svetieva, Aneta 1998a: Erotski elementi vo obredite so maski kaj Makedoncite [Erotic elements in the mask rituals of Macedonians]. In: Običai so maski, Trudovi od Megjunarodniot simpozium održan vo Vevčani - Struga 1996 [Mask rituals. Proceedings of the International Symposium held in Vevčani, Struga 1996]. Skopje: Muzej na Makedonija, 7–14.

Svetieva, Aneta 1998b: Obredi so maskiranje kaj Makedoncite i drugite balkanski narodi za vreme na sezonskite promeni [Rites with masking among the Macedonians and other Balkan peoples during the time of seasons change]. In: Balkanoslavica 25: 55–70.

Sztompka, Piotr: 1994: The Sociology of Social Change. Oxford, Cambridge: Blackwell.

Trpeski, Davorin 2003: Etnomitovite na makedonskata politička scena [Ethno-Myths on the Macedonian political scene]. In: EtnoAntropoZum 3: 90–100.

Abstract

Since the 1990s, the Republic of Macedonia has been going through a period of democratization and transition. This process triggered a crisis and introduced great uncertainties into every sphere of life, which resulted in identity crises of both the individual and the collective. In pursuit of the confirmation of their own identity, individuals, as well as the community, returned to the values of folk culture, which have traditionally been held as most sacred. By referring to these traditional values, the individual and the communities feel safer, strengthening their consciousness and their internal relationships, resulting in the affirmation of their community at all levels: social, economic and ritual. In this regard, mask customs in Macedonia and in the wider region of Southeastern Europe represent a typical example of one of the forms of articulating identity for both the individual and the ethnic community. For this paper, mask rituals and carnivals in three towns in Macedonia (Prilep, Strumica and Vevčani) are analysed in order to explain changes in the symbolism of the masks by relating them to the social and political contexts. Masks are a dynamic form of representing identity on the local, national and supranational levels. The paper, thus, argues for the significance of "tradition" which is being appropriated to manifest new forms of identification.

Translated from the Macedonian by Matthew and Marija Jones

Sulina – the Dying City in a Vital Region
Social Memory and the Nostalgia for the European Future

Petruţa Teampău, Cluj Napoca, Kristof van Assche, Minnesota

> And suddenly it came to his mind – as a verdict of fate ... the death of Sulina. Yes! This city is doomed ... cities have their lives and deaths ... The gate of Sulina is closing for ever. Abandoned, Sulina disappears as a city. Sulina will represent just a small village of fishermen on the map, forgotten on the shore (Bart 2004: 195).

A romantic novel, "Europolis", written between the World Wars by the former Marine officer Jean Bart about the city of Sulina, begins with a phrase that has, ever since, been adopted to predict the future of the city (or used as an argument for its current fate):

> Day and night they worked to load the ships. Only in the middle of the day the harbor was dead. Earth and water, people and animals were suddenly falling into a deep lethargy. [...] When the sun reached the horizon, the muted harbor, gilded in a dazzling light, it seemed, in the heat of the day, a dead city, put to sleep by a spell, turned to stone for centuries – a phantom city (Bart 2004: 5).

To this day, the metaphor of death seems to have been the most appealing in describing the fate of the city.[1]

Sulina, the only town in the Danube Delta, is a small place at the mouth of the Danube, the easternmost locality of Romania, and since 1 January 2007, of the European Union. The "city" is actually built on a narrow tongue of land between the Danube and the Black Sea; surrounded by water, it has no land connection to neighbouring localities. In order to visit Sulina during the summer time it is necessary to depart from Tulcea and travel by boat for a minimum of one and a half hours. In winter, when the Danube is frozen over, the travel time needed to reach the nearest city, with a special ice-breaking ship, is extended to about eight hours. In the early mornings, upon arrival from Tulcea, one is confronted with the desolate image of the remains of the former fish factory and the naval shipyard cloaked in a timid coat of sunlight, as soon as the boat approaches the waterfront,

---

[1] Jean Bart was probably influenced by the Belgian symbolist Georges Rodenbach, with his "Bruges-la-Morte", late 19th century, who was widely read throughout Europe.

the place unfolds its strange, unique beauty. Street I, running parallel to the silent flow of the Danube, is an eclectic succession of crumbling old buildings, terraces, blocks of flats, stores, closed off towards the northern end with the Orthodox cathedral and the Palace of the former European Danube Commission.

The city in itself consists of six main parallel streets, crisscrossed by smaller ones, following the stream of the Danube.[2] When passing through Street I to II and III, all within the space of just a few hundred metres, one can note the gentle transition from an urban to a rural landscape. If Street I (once King Carol I) represents the "urban" space, a space of socializing and maximum interaction with tourists, Street II is already the interface for a different style of living. Losing the quality of façade, it still maintains a rather urban "air", although one of past epochs, with old and grimy edifices. From Street III and IV onwards we are already in a rather rural space, with dusty roads and countryside architecture, small houses in front of which people sit and chat on wooden benches. On Street IV and V we can sense the nearness of the sea, from the air and the sand that covers the roads. The houses have iron fences, with the gates painted in blue or green, adorned with metal figures representing dolphins, fish, or hearts. The borders of the sidewalks are decorated with small shrubs of colourful flowers. Street VI is already nature's territory, with only a few houses stretching towards the channel, full of reeds and other vegetation, along the margins of the city. Cows and horses walk freely on the "street"; here and there we can see a rusty boat "parked" in front of a house near an old *Trabant*. All over the place there are small, friendly dogs wandering through the city or sleeping in the shade on the terraces, mingling freely with the tourists.

During the summer, the place is usually crowded with tourists, hosted in one of the many pensions; unofficially, almost everyone would offer you a room for a much smaller price. The winters, although not as cold as in the rest of the country, are terribly windy: "the Russians turn on the fans", as a local saying goes. People spend their time indoors, meeting each other, playing cards, or just watching TV.

A small, insignificant place on the margins of Romania, lost in between waters, a town looking rather like a village, with a dwindling population and a decaying urban landscape, Sulina has a bewildering, savage beauty, a lure of its own. Whether it is the vicinity of water and its peaceful flow, or just its unusual

---

2 Unlike most towns, Sulina has no centre, even though, across the water, there is another small neighbourhood, Prospect, even more gloomy and poor than the rest. People from Prospect rarely come to the main city, and when they do, they have to pay a small tax for a boat to cross the Danube. In fact, the grid pattern might be related to the street pattern of other 19th century merchant cities, such as Odessa and Batumi, also influenced by Western European architects.

isolation, the place offers its visitors a rare sense of serenity, combined with a bizarre feeling of ephemeral, of the transient flow of time – and life.

The aim of this paper is to explore the making of social memory in Sulina, in connection with strategies and plans for a European future. Bearing in mind that social memory entails a particular management of the past in light of the requirements and necessities of the present, a collective project of a group or community in order to enhance its identity and ensure a desirable future, we are interested in how "collective" memory is "made" and instrumentalized for (not only) political purposes; and in how people articulate their own memories and respond to the dominant production of memory in this specific environment. In order to investigate these research questions,[3] we have corroborated in depth interviews with local people (both native and newcomers), conducted as part of our anthropological fieldwork in the summers of 2006 and 2007, with an analysis of discourses, emanating from several sources (official local speeches, local political and social events, local and national media portraying the city and its fate, and several documentaries and films about Sulina).

Mapping the terrain of memory studies

The field of memory studies owes much, unquestionably, to Maurice Halbwachs. His most significant contribution to this field was his insistence on the social character of memory. The process of "remembrance" is always socially "framed"; every memory we have as individuals, we have as members of a community, of a social group, and must be consequently validated within it. The social – par excellence – character of memory explains its functions as a cohesive element of a community: we are a group because we have common memories or, rather, because we belong to a group we have to remember what that group validates as "legitimate" memory.

We should also mention the formative contribution of Frederic C. Bartlett, who claimed, in the early 1930s, that "our memories are *social* to the extent that they codify perceptions on the basis of their meanings, i.e., on the basis of a structure of knowledge of the world which in turn is the expression of the individual's membership of a culture"; and, also, "normally the recollections that individuals have of a certain event are influenced by the others' recollections of those

[3] This research is part of the larger ongoing international research project, "Nature, Culture, Planning in the Danube Delta". Our gratefulness goes to our colleagues Patrick Devlieger (Catholic University of Leuven) and Cristi Suciu (University of Cluj). Also, our host in Sulina, Mrs. Nela Mitache, as well as the local authorities and informants in Sulina were very supportive and helpful.

same events. Hence recall is constituted and stabilized within a network of social relationships" (Jedlowski 2001: 31). Thus, memory has everything to do with the common identity of a group:

> Collective memory unifies the group through time and over space by providing a narrative frame, a collective story, which locates the individual and his and her biography within it, and which, because it can be represented as narrative and as text, attains mobility. The narrative can travel, as individuals travel, and it can be embodied, written down, painted, represented, communicated and received in distant places by isolated individuals, who can then, through them, be remembered and reunited with the collective (Eyerman 2004: 161).

In other words, memory must be conceptualized as a dynamic process, moving beyond a cognitive understanding of it: "collective memory [should be understood] not as a collection of individual memories or some magically constructed reservoir of ideas and images, but rather as a socially articulated and socially maintained 'reality of the past'" (Irwin-Zarecka 1994: 54), a "set of *social representations concerning the past* which each group produces, institutionalizes, guards and transmits through the interaction of its members" (Jedlowski 2001: 33).

Memory has an active life; it is never static or finite. On one hand, it "is defined as recollections of a shared past which are passed on through ongoing processes of commemoration", which are "as much physical and emotional as they are cognitive in that the past is both embodied and recalled through such cultural practices" (Eyerman 2004: 161). Memories travel across generations in order to perform their meaning. But, on the other hand, it entails more and more a "plurality of interrelated functions. What we call 'memory' is a complex network of activities, the study of which indicates that the past never remains 'one and the same', but is constantly selected, filtered and restructured in terms set by the questions and necessities of the present, at both the individual and the social levels" (Jedlowski 2001: 30). Thus, memory is a Janus-faced idea. On the one hand, it is concerned with managing the past and its present representations; on the other hand, this very administration of the past is always performed looking towards future.

Philosophically speaking, what we call "memory" can be described as the field of a complex temporal dialectic: while on the one hand the flow of life over time entails effects that condition the future, on the other it is the present that shapes the past, ordering, reconstructing and interpreting its legacy, with expectations and hopes also helping to select what best serves the future (Jedlowski 2001: 30). The paradox of memory is the same as that referred to by the "hermeneutic circle": the past structures the present through its legacy, but it is the present that selects this legacy, preserving some aspects and forgetting others, and which constantly reformulates our image of this past by repeatedly recounting the story (Jedlowski 2001: 41).

Building on Susan Sontag's insights regarding the role of photography in the representation of pain, Eyerman observed the preeminence of "collective instruction" over "collective memory":

> All memory is individual, irreproducible – it dies with each person. What is called collective memory is not a remembering but a stipulating: that *this* is important, and this is the story about how it happened, with the pictures that lock the story in our minds. Ideologies create substantiating archives of images, representative images, which encapsulate common ideas of significance and trigger predictable thoughts, feelings (Eyerman 2004: 162).

Since memory entails process, negotiations, and changes, all around a double dialectics (between past and present, individual and community), its understanding also brings about issues of power. "The past, as it is formally coded in texts, embodied in rituals, landscapes and commemorative built spaces, and buried deep in the unconscious body of individual memory, becomes fundamental in power struggles", insofar as "conflicting memories are not only about what 'really' happened. They are also about identity claims, identity formation and identity politics. In the most basic sense, legitimation of and through memory is an ideological tool" (Pine, Kaneff, Haukanes 2004: 3 f.). The battle for memory is borne not only for legitimizing present power through a monopoly over the "truth" of the past, but also between individuals (or subgroups) and community. "By keeping alive and reiterating counter memories, by producing and reproducing interpretations which challenge the hegemonic account, individuals and groups outside the official corridors of power offer alternative routes to legitimacy, and alternative, if often muted or hidden, criteria for shared identity. [...] Implicitly or explicitly, fragments of the past carried in and reproduced by the rememberings of marginal or subordinated groups often challenge hegemonic discourses. In so doing, they introduce and perpetuate the possibility of alternate presents and futures" (Pine, Kaneff, Haukanes 2004: 3 f.).

Not all individuals voluntarily accept the "official memory" of an event, especially when their own biographical details feed a different remembrance of it. "The 'realities of the past' as they pertain to individuals are not carbon copies of publicly available accounts. They are often worked out within smaller and larger communities of memory, their shape and texture reflecting a complex mixture of history and biography" (Irwin-Zarecka 1994: 56). This is not to say that the official framing of what is being remembered collectively has no relevance. On the contrary, "beyond providing resources to work with, public discourse may validate (or discourage) particular ways of seeing the past. It may also create an altogether new community of memory, where bonding extends well beyond individuals' own experience" (ibid.). Memory can bring people together, or can work to ensure that they stay that way.

Urban places as spaces of nostalgia. "Remembering" the city

In the modern world, memory could not find a better home than the complex and intricate space of the city. Suffused with meaning, laden with memories, the urban landscape can provide a suitable apparatus for anchoring processes of remembering.

> Privileged places of social interaction, and yet too vast to be imagined in their entirety, cities are probably the most dense and complex reservoirs of memorative signs, and thus key nodes in the geography of nostalgia. [...] They have never ceased to accumulate strata of meaning, expressed in their landscape through memorative signs, or even (– no less significant –) absences. [...] Whether consciously or unconsciously, physicality and memory, urban geography and history, memorative sign and nostalgia intertwine in complex urban "topologies of memory". Buildings, sites, and landscapes, in their shape and material substance ... are more complex than a written source, although less easy to read. And the genius loci ... makes people feel that they share past experiences, as if there were a direct access to history (Della Dora 2006: 212).

Urban places, as dynamic contexts of social interaction and memory, are not only ideology-informed, but have the power to coalesce and sustain a community. Fluid and unsettled, places are never innocent settings, but political stakes of symbolic (and physical) appropriation. In discussing memory in connection to place, we owe it again to Halbwachs for having maintained that "group memory was so deeply entrenched in genuine places and social experiences that 'place and group each received the imprint of the other'" (Jacobs 2003: 255). In other words, "while collective memory is shaping the urban spaces, a city's social memory is at the same time being shaped by symbolic places" (Jacobs 2003: 255).

On one hand, we have to keep in mind that memory often works retrospectively to alter the past, to render it unambiguous and coherent, not as much to itself, but to the present. In this respect, when it comes to urban landscapes, they not only trigger certain memories, but "are also simultaneously sites of forgetfulness/forgetting; spatial tactics of erasure are thus manifested through urban demolition, clearance of squatter communities and the rebuilding of new symbolic landscapes. Memory formation thus has both a creative and destructive dimension, with implications for place identity and meaning" (Chang 2005: 248).

Moreover, even though memory evokes itself in urban settings through space, those particular places that memory "revives", "remembers", do not have to necessarily exist (or have existed). Memory can work with absences, too. Absence can sometimes manufacture a more powerful evocative effect. As Veronica Della Dora observes,

> In "landscapes of memory" [...] imagination works better with decay and absences rather than with reconstructions, for certain remains from the past carry a potential evocative power – potential because their evocative power is not an inherent property of themselves; the most perfectly preserved building or document becomes evocative, indeed, "historical", only through imagination (Della Dora 2006: 230).

Open spaces very easily allow for various kinds of projections and encourage imagination, triggering different memories. Needless to say, cities are sometimes too complex and heteroclite for one singular, articulate thread of memory to occur from certain places. Some groups choose to invest particular urban spaces "in ways that escape, at least partially, the orchestration, values, and control of the dominant discourses. [...] In addition, the same places and spaces around the city can be invested with different experiences and narratives simultaneously or at different times" (Bélanger 2002: 82). Memory, as always, entails a process of selection, followed by the validation and endorsement of a certain narrative.

The workings of memory on the public remembrance of urban places (or the public framing of the memories produced by individuals) is even more perceptible when "space and time are produced as cultural commodities in the form of nostalgic discourses, images, or renovated heritage areas". In such cases, the past "is often reclaimed and represented in one-dimensional and unrealistic ways. Past struggles and differences in perspective [...] are typically ignored or re-articulated in comforting sepia tones that locate them as part of the 'good old days'. Most significantly, there is often an implicit discourse of continuity between past and present, between older uses and meanings of space and newer ones" – although this imaginary continuity is only possible with a degree of rupture (Bélanger 2002: 74).

Longing for the future: nostalgia and urban life

"The past as a cozy home, however imaginary or sentimentalized, *is* nice to return to" (Irwin-Zarecka 1994: 88). A vague feeling of being apart from a *topos* invested with personal affection, longing for or having lost such a *topos*, nostalgia is, more than anything, related to space and place:

> Nostalgia as a feeling arises from place in two ways: from its idealized image in the geographical imagination of the individual (or of a commu-

> nity), but also from "material" topographical features (like landmarks or buildings), objects and even names. In order to chart "space on time and time on space" and hinder "the distinction between object and subject", nostalgia draws by handfuls from the vast repertoire of symbols and signs which constitutes territory (Della Dora 2006: 211).

Svetlana Boym distinguishes between at least two threads of nostalgia: a "restorative" nostalgia, focussing "on *nostos* which aims to reconstruct the lost home, often in association with religious or nationalist revivals" and "reflective nostalgia" which "dwells on *algia*, and has no place of habitation. It is embodied in the essence of movement, not destination. If restorative nostalgia ends up reconstructing emblems and rituals of home and homeland in an attempt to conquer and spatialize time, reflective nostalgia cherishes shattered fragments of memory and temporalizes space" (Legg 2004: 100); it "lingers on ruins, on the patina of time and history, on uncanny silences and absences and on dreams" (Della Dora 2006: 210).

Nostalgia is not only a benign feeling, set off by autobiographical details, but tends to be employed for political (in the large sense of the word) purposes. "The emotive capacity of nostalgia gives it the future (rather than just the past) relevance that explains its recurrent manipulation as a political tool" (Legg 2004: 100). In a similar vein, Veronica Della Dora, writing about Alexandria, argues that "nostalgia can be both a powerful political weapon and an active force subverting the political as it moulds literary and material cityscapes" (Della Dora 2006: 209). Most importantly, nostalgia is connected to the present in that, as David Lowenthal has reminded us, in some cases "both nostalgia and heritage rely on interpretations of history to compensate for a present malaise, for a lack of community and a need for identity in place" (Mills 2006: 371). When the present is not satisfying enough, when the strength of a community is fading or the group decides to invest in a novel project for the future, revolving to the past and producing a favourable narrative of it turns nostalgia into a programmatic community assignment. And, as Irwin-Zarecka pertinently observes, "often, it is the telling itself, the ongoing articulation of the 'reality of the past' that forms and informs a community. For that matter, the past so told need not be real at all to offer the basis for communal solidarity. All that is needed is active remembrance, communally shared and deemed important for the community's self-definition" (Irwin-Zarecka 1994: 57).

A glimpse at history

What is being "remembered" in Sulina about its past covers, actually, a particular slice of the past, coinciding with the functioning here of the European Danube Commission, i.e., roughly the second half of the nineteenth and the first half of the twentieth century. It is the "golden age" of Sulina, which tends to wipe out the period before it, and especially the one that followed.

Among the first references to Sulina, we discover a small locality with a very unpleasant reputation, especially for the period before the middle of the nineteenth century. As described by a French marine officer, who travelled here in 1784:

> Sulina is a small village situated at the mouth of this Danube arm. The ships anchor at five to six *stânjeni* (ten to twelve metres) away from the houses, where the water is fifteen feet (almost five metres) deep. There are about twenty houses, one mosque and some *feredele* (public baths) built on the ruins of an old edifice. The mosque is wooden (quoted in Tatu 2005: 114).

Sulina's bad reputation was related to it being a pirates' nest and home to all kinds of evil-doers. A Romanian traveller described it, in 1856, as "a collection of adventurers that came from the entire Orient to settle here in a very humid environment, full of mosquitoes, waiting to find an opportunity to make money, even with the risk of their own life, which they do not cherish too much" (quoted in Tatu 2005: 229). Home of pirates, not a very welcoming place either, with an extremely unpleasant fiscal regime and high taxes for transit, Sulina was also the end of the line for many ships (up to twenty-five shipwrecks a year) that sank in its perilous waters. By the end of 1856, Sulina reportedly had between 2000 and 5000 inhabitants, dealing with navigation most time of the year and engaging in heavy drinking for the rest (according to a report written by an employee of the newly established Danube Commission; Tatu 2005: 287).

During the nineteenth century, the political-administrative authority in Sulina belonged, in turn, to the Ottoman and the Russian Empire, which encouraged, or at least tolerated, this state of affairs. But the economic interests of the other European powers transformed, by the middle of nineteenth century, the problem of the Danube into an issue of international politics. Thus, following the Crimean War, through the Peace Treaty in Paris (March 1856) the European Danube Commission was established (with representatives of France, England, Austria, Prussia, Russia, Sardinia, and the Ottoman Empire), setting its headquarters in Sulina, for an initial mandate of two years.

Actually, the European Danube Commission would stay in Sulina for almost a century, marking what came to be remembered later as the "golden age" of the city. Besides its duty regarding the amelioration of navigation on the Danube, rendering the Sulina channel safe and navigable, the Commission was actively involved in the life of the community. In a kind of beneficial colonization, the commission built a hospital (1867–1869), the commission palace (1868), the water castle (1903), a telegraphic line linking Sulina to Tulcea and Galaţi (1857), and a telephone line (1903); it organized the cemetery (1864 for the Christian population, 1871 for the Muslims), introduced public illumination with petroleum (electricity since 1910). Also, the Danube Commission had a very active role in sponsoring all religious confessions, contributing to a milieu of multicultural tolerance (it paid for the Catholic Church in 1865, the Russian Orthodox in 1866, the Protestant and Greek Orthodox in 1869, and the mosque in 1870). At the beginning of the nineteenth century, there were two Romanian schools, two Greek, one German, one Jewish, and one French pension. On the beach there was a casino; the city had many restaurants, a theatre, a publishing house and newspapers. By 1930, the commission had 359 employees (208 of them Romanians) and 746 temporary workers (567 Romanians), all generously paid in golden francs.

All this incredible progress was cut short by the First World War, during which Sulina was literally reduced to ruins. But after 1920, the city was reconstructed, with more schooling institutions (teaching languages: Romanian, French, Italian), and in 1932 Sulina became a fashionable resort for thousands of tourists. This period also brought strategies of Romanian "colonization" of this cosmopolite city to the fore. Part of the newly born Romanian Kingdom since 1878, Dobrudja was the subject of what Constantin Iordachi called "internal colonization":

> Its organization was characterized by administrative distinctiveness and excessive centralization supported by claims of cultural superiority of the core region, by intense ethnic colonization, and by uneven regional economic development tailored to the needs of the metropolis (Iordachi 2001: 121 f.).

For this end, the Romanian political authorities employed a "threefold mechanism composed of ethnic colonization, cultural homogenization, and economic modernization. The most important stimulus behind the annexation of Dobrudja was economic: due to its strategic geographical location, the province was regarded as a vital commercial outlet of Romania, granting it access to the sea and facilitating thus its elevation into the world economy, from periphery to semi-periphery. Demographically, Northern Dobrudja served as an 'Internal America' for Romania, a dynamic frontier zone of new settlements for expanding the national economy and ethnic boundaries" (Iordachi 2001: 122).

Between 1878 and 1913, Northern Dobrudja was subject to a separate, extra-constitutional administrative organization, meaning that the inhabitants were denied political participation and the right to acquire properties outside the province. Dobrudja became "a melting pot of regional differences and a laboratory for fostering Romanian national identity"[4] (Iordachi 2001: 135). Due to its multicultural character, Dobrudja, an important economical asset, was indeed a tough challenge for the young Romanian state, interested in homogenization and in building a coherent, strong national identity. According to Iordachi, "Dobrudja was the first major test of Romania's national institutions and power of assimilation, which explains the importance assigned by Romanian political elites to administrative centralization and cultural homogenization in the province. [...] Dobrudja's integration was celebrated by Romanian political elites as a success, a self-congratulatory evidence of Romania's civilizing power" (Iordachi 2001: 145).

The prosperous life of Sulina started to decline after Constanţa, another harbour city on the coast of the Black Sea, became the new focus of development, and was definitely brought to an end with the Second World War, when the place was heavily bombed by both Allied and the Axis powers. After the war, power in Romania was seized by the communists, who inaugurated a totally different path of development for Sulina, thus ending an epoch. Moreover, the construction of the Danube-Black Sea Channel cut Sulina off the map of navigation and gave priority to Constanţa as harbour. During communism, Sulina developed a local industry (mainly fishing and tinning fish, carpet production, and naval ships repair). The demographic structure changed radically; most Greeks, Armenians, Jews – urban populations par excellence – left the country; due to the communist policies of intense urbanization; the population was heavily "Romanianized", and many Lipoveni (Russian Old Believers) from the neighbouring villages in the delta came "to the city" in the 1970s to find work.

After 1989, after the revolution that brought down the communist regime, most of the local industry was dismantled; people lost their jobs, the unemployment rate became one of the highest in the country, and the town continued to destroy itself. Sulina lost its centripetal forces of attraction as "the city" of the region – most visible in the 1970s – and became the place everyone wanted to leave behind. This is, roughly, the context in which people in Sulina began to "remember" and celebrate the past, or specific slices of it.

Commemorating the past

> Pasts are being both renegotiated and reclaimed, through texts, through control of space and place, and through performance of ritual. [...] In all of

---

[4] We could also argue that, due to the fact that many people, especially Turks, Greeks, Armenians, have emigrated from Dobrudja after WW I, the melting pot metaphor does not hold completely. See for further reference "Dobrogea", published in 1940 by The Romanian Academy, Bucharest.

> these different types of ritual, repetition and symbol are directed towards the evocation of past events and former epochs; in calling up memory they claim the right to bear the mantle of the past (Pine, Kaneff, Haukanes 2004: 5 f.).

In August 2006, the local authorities of Sulina celebrated, for the first time, the establishment of the Danube Commission, more precisely, 150 years since its establishment. This event deserves our analytical attention for at least several reasons: first of all, the commemoration was framed as a celebration of the city of Sulina (*"Zilele oraşului",* "The Days of the City"), which included all kinds of happenings, concerts, sport events, etc. Second, it was not a mere coincidence that the events were held in the middle of August and culminated on August 15, when most Romanians celebrate Virgin Mary's Day. St. Mary is considered the benefactor of seamen, and August 15 is the official Navy's Day. Third, the month of August ensured the desired audience (lots of tourists, students on their holidays, etc.).[5]

On the second day, a "symposium" took place in the building of the local disco, "Coral", which included the mayor and all kinds of guests (it was easy to observe that there were no "ordinary" local people[6]). All the people who talked at this meeting, besides the organizers, were in fact people that no longer lived in Sulina, and had come back with lots of memories about it. All these discourses were past-oriented ("to restore", "to revive", "to bring back", etc.), and when other people (from NGOs or government bodies) proposed different approaches, more future-oriented, arguing that "Sulina cannot live from memories", they tended to get angry and impatient reactions. Although the symposium was entitled "Sulina – Past, Present and Future", we heard only about the past. On the one hand, the dominant discourse was an elitist one, focussing on revitalizing navigation and the specificity of Sulina as a harbour, with clear undertones of contempt towards fishing, tourism, and any alternative development projects. As one of the participants claimed, "this is a city not only of tourism and fishing, but a city of sailors, a border on the road of Europe; not out of marsh or fish will the life of other times be revived; we have to give back to Sulina its greatness as a Danube harbour". On the other hand, there were plans for reviving Sulina by focussing on

---

[5] Actually, according to an informant, August 15 is the peak of the season: "After St. Mary's Day, everything dies, everybody is leaving, it's over."

[6] In front of the place, there is a small park, seemingly with a long tradition, where older people, mostly men, preserve the habit of meeting on Sundays and discussing different matters, preferably politics. Since it was Sunday, there were some men outside. But when asked why they didn't go in, they answered "We are not as white as those" (obviously, referring to their social status).

tourism[7] and on marketing the "local colour". Hence, we have a macro-perspective (to restore navigation on the Danube for the benefit of Sulina, but this is not something for the local community to decide) on the one hand, and a rather micro-perspective, focussing on local resources and people, on the other.

On the same occasion, the local authorities produced a brochure (Micu, Bucur 2006), suggestively entitled "Sulina – European Destiny", and a CD with a presentation of the city with data and pictures "from the life of the community". Using an interwar tune for the soundtrack (underlying the nostalgic tone), the presentation employs an enthusiastic voice in describing the city: "God has blessed this city. The sea, the Danube, and the Delta support us in feeling this way." The presentation ends with images from traditional celebrations (Christmas, New Years' Eve, and Easter), with the idea of "light" as a red thread: "The people of Sulina, the first Romanians to see the sun every morning, truly love light, with all their heart." Actually, the presentation tries to assert a local identity (a city of fishermen and sailors, with the sea and the river as constant features) and to project a positive picture of the future, using images of children ("Children are the most precious gift; they learn and respect the traditions") and repeating the word "hope".

The festivities ended on August 15, with a special religious ceremony, performed in front of the town hall, on the very shoreline of the Danube, in the presence of all local authorities, including several police officers. The service was followed by an allegoric staging, the god Neptune arriving on a boat, together with a few young and beautiful, tanned girls. Finally, this mixture of symbols and discourses was followed by a series of sport contests for the youth. All in all, the whole event seemed a little too overloaded with significance and symbols, and somewhat confusing. What clearly came out of the festivities was a strongly perceived need for local identity, for definition of community, for commonality of projects and visions for the future.

Guardians of Sulina's memory and "remembering" the past

Sulina also has a few "professional" guardians of memory. Some were "recommended" as such (elderly people who "knew" stories about old Sulina, but who were so used to telling those stories, perhaps even to journalists, that it altered the whole narrative), some were discovered during the research process . One of them

---

[7] It is not clear if there is a real interest in developing tourism, if this means legal measures, taxes, and legal standards of comfort (Sulina is very cheap for tourists now, but with little comfort, usually no bathrooms etc.); the general problem is the canalization of the city, which is of course a political issue, but nobody seems to care too much. Tourism in Sulina is a bit informal, everybody seems to take in tourists, at different prices, but very few have actually made it a permanent business.

was the local photographer, a passionate collector of old pictures of Sulina and the depository of all current photographs of Sulina's places and faces, acting as a semi-official guardian of memory. In his own words, "as a photographer, I know half of the houses, inside out. And I know their events, their parties, the most important moments of their lives. Sometimes I was shocked to find a wedding, a funeral, and a baptizing, all on the same negative". He has developed a visible passion for "remembering" the old face of the city, searching for special places, for places imbued with history, or just for expressive absences in the urban landscape.

> When I first got a camera, I went to shoot the houses that were gone, destroyed as if after a bombardment or war. [...] By 1975, they started to build the blocks, and they had big trucks driving all over the city, and Sulina, where you could walk around without a bit of dust on your shoes suddenly became full of mud and holes ... for a few blocks of flats (quote from the documentary *Porto Franco*).

In Sulina, people tend to recollect the past (a particular past, i.e., that of the Danube Commission period) in the frame of two main intertwining narratives: of the prosperity of that time and of multicultural tolerance. Sulina was a *porto franco* and a harbour; people came and went. There was indeed a unique blend of ethnicities, religious confessions, and languages. But, retrospectively, nostalgia tends to even out the rough edges, to "forget" the conflicts and to present the past in a blissful colour. Writing about a certain melancholy when remembering the *mahalle* (the old neighbourhood) in Istanbul, Amy Mills uncovers a rarely mentioned truth about the workings of nostalgia:

> The nostalgia for tolerance and close community relations of the mahalle of collective memory betrays a deep and polarizing difference in identity. Greek and Jewish minorities are beloved, and their homes restored, only after they themselves have abandoned the city and no longer pose a challenge to the space of the nation. They are present in contemporary urban culture today, then, only through their very absence (Mills 2006: 388).

Actually, those very ethnic groups which made Sulina the "most cosmopolite city in the country" are no longer there. Jews, Armenians, Turks, and Greeks were traditionally urban populations, involved in commerce and trade; they made the city a multicultural space built around these occupations and embedded into a particular fashion of urban inhabitancy. Today, most of the inhabitants are either Romanians or Lipoveni, who came to Sulina, "to the city", from neighbouring villages. Very few are old enough to actually remember Sulina before the war; some of them learn anew about Sulina's glorious past, and are less likely to long for a past they have no connection to (biographical and/or affective).[8] However, if memory does work as a cohesive element of a group, and can even create a new community whose recollections go beyond people's own direct experiences, as Irwin-Zarecka has shown, then it is only natural that all current inhabitants of the city seem to agree on Sulina's wonderful history. Generally speaking, they "remember" pre-war Sulina as a place that was flourishing, attracting resources from the region, especially from the Vâlcov area (now on the territory of Ukraine). Stories about huge amounts of vegetables, piles of butter, meat, and other foods being sold on the streets by peasants and merchants constantly pop up in interviews, together with details of places and locations of urban cosmopolitan life.[9]

In opposition to this quasi-mythical prosperity "remembered" by older informants as part and background of a happy childhood, come the years of the Second World War, which brought for Sulina – and the region – a series of tragic events: an earthquake followed by flooding in 1941, then a period of drought, hunger, and poverty immediately after the War – the end of an epoch. The 1950s witnessed a constantly modifying demography, with old bourgeois habits and places dying out, all to the background of general transformations induced by the communist regime. The communist period, at least in the beginning, seems to have kept Sulina, unlike other places in Romania, still in a marginal position, in a kind of grey zone, with no clear rules (or not so harshly enforced). Long Mitza, the owner of a brothel, was still there in the 1950s as a respectable tobacco shop owner, with her stylish blue dress as a reminder of another time. People may or may not have had jobs (many of them came to Sulina from the rural area, trying to escape the collectivization of land) and life carried on.

Moreover, some of the informants "remember" the good times of the communist period when the *porto franco* functioned in one part of the city and allowed people, using different semi-legal strategies, to sneak in and buy cheaper merchandise, later sold at a higher price in the "other" part. Others remember, with visible satisfaction, how they used to steal from the huge amounts of sugar, for example, that was being loaded on ships in that area. The methods and occurrences are strikingly similar to those of the pirating and thieving inhabitants of nineteenth century Sulina. This is in fact part of a recurrent narrative that seems to inform the present local identity, as a kind of pride taken in avoiding taxes and gently working around the law. The prosperous – for some people – period of the

---

8 In fact, many newcomers are being assimilated into this narrative and they appropriate space and time according to it, and simultaneously they can reinvent themselves as cosmopolitan *"Sulineni"*.

9 One of our informants is currently putting on paper his memories of Sulina, with precise details of the locations and owners of cafes, butcher shops, restaurants, brothels, cinemas etc. Their number is quite telling for the development and prosperity of the interwar city.

communist regime seems to act, in certain narratives, as a compensation for the affluence of the interwar period and in contrast with the current uncertainty of the transition period.

This is where the waters of "memory" come apart. Even if there is an official, somehow "programmatic" nostalgia for the period of the Danube Commission, most people also yearn for the (presumed) security – both social and economic – of the communist period. And, strange enough, memories about this recent past are being wiped out by an alternative nostalgia. Nonetheless, as Pine, Kaneff, and Haukanes have made clear, conflicts over memory are not only about the historical truth, but also about identity claims and power (Pine, Kaneff, Haukanes 2004: 3 f.). In this case, divergence over memory can hide an underlying, tacit divergence between groups, who develop loyalties and memories of different times. After all, many of the Lipoveni and Romanians used to work for the Greeks and Armenians, the main characters in the nostalgic narratives, sometimes as domestic servants. Even when they participate in a common mnemonic account of Sulina's "good times", details of their own biography locates them in different social strata and places.

Furthermore, Sulina still has to cope with its marginality (both geographical and socio-cultural) and with its ready-made destiny, trying to develop a new sense of identity of place, of local pride, and a feasible project for its (European) future, in an ongoing context of ambiguous dialectics of European identification. At this moment, Sulina sees its future, once again, in connection to the European project; and tries to symbolically regain access to a prosperous past in order to ensure a similar future. The almost mythical prosperity of the Danube Commission period is being projected into the near future – when Sulina will be a "European" city – in a kind of cyclically replicating fate. If the Europeans came once and made Sulina the beautiful, rich city it was, they can do it again. Appropriating a particular segment of the past, celebrating it, building anew a social memory of it, seems critical for projecting the future and eluding the tedious present.

Sulina – the dying city at the end of the world

When moving to Sulina with her husband in 1962, after being born and raised in Bucharest, one of our respondents reportedly was asked in horror by colleagues: "How can you go there, to the end of the world"? Most probably, they have read newspapers articles with headlines such as: "Sulina, the town frozen in-between waters". A painter and art teacher in Sulina seems to have framed her own biographical narrative in the same way:

> When I got off the train and the lines were actually over, I truly felt like I was being deported, like I'd come to the end of the world. […] But after-

> wards, I started to perceive it as a space of freedom and independence, which only such an open landscape can give you. This openness of the horizon allows you to find yourself (quote from the documentary *Porto Franco*).

In 2006, after three decades, Sulina seems to have undergone a process of programmatic oblivion, orchestrated by mass media, in the very year before European accession. Most of the articles (and there were several in 2006, including TV reports) about Sulina circumscribe its destiny between a glorious history and a disappointing present: "The history is a dream, the present is a nightmare" (*Jurnalul Naţional*, 10 October 2006). Sulina is either "dead", or "asleep", "frozen in-between ages, intoxicated with its own memories" (*Jurnalul Naţional*, 28 June 2004). The newspapers do not hesitate to write that "the European Union was born in Sulina, 150 years ago, since through here Europe has entered Romania. In Sulina, there are tombstones to prove that we have been in Europe for a long time". Retrospectively, the Sulina of those happy times, "when Europe was floating on the Danube", is "remembered" as a place of abundance, an El Dorado, "a city where a simple worker earned enough money every day to feed thirty people at the restaurant. A locality integrated with Europe, with no unemployment" (*Adevărul*, 23 August 2005). All of these events were projected by newspapers in a mythical time, with undertones that made things seem somewhat unreal: As soon as the first Europeans landed in the middle of the marsh [...] and the European money started to flow in the city faster than the waters of the Danube into the sea, the life of the place took off as nowhere else in the country. A simple porter in the harbour would earn 500 lei per day. In the morning, before going to work, he would eat a steak at the restaurant and drink a bottle of red wine for only 15 lei (*Jurnalul naţional*, 26 June 2006).

Moreover, there were theatres, cafes, and, of course, brothels. It is easy to observe that most references of a good life revolve around urban entertainment: eating at restaurants and participating in an urban public life. Also, speaking about the "life of the place" is no coincidence; it is meant to emphasize again, by way of comparison, the death of this city in our days:

> At Sulina, the sun gets up earlier than in the rest of the country, but its urgency is useless, because it only reveals the poverty of a city which lives from beautiful memories. Blocked in-between waters, the inhabitants of Sulina are prisoners in their own city [...] Buildings once appealing, a deserted church, roads as dusty as countryside ones, abandoned plants. [...] The time of Sulina is dead (*Jurnalul naţional*, 28 June 2004).

Documentaries and TV reports about this topic employ the same language of nostalgia in describing a city which fails to revive its past life: "Sulina, a unique, in its way, city, today bearing the mark of degradation, has the life of the moment but also that of the centuries, fed with the vitality which the wild nature continuously renews." The idea of memory, of time passing by, is effortlessly connected to the familiar image of water flow: "The memory of the Danube is constantly renewed in present tense." The water is the perfect witness to the life of the city: "Watersheds come and go. What image would they bear over the years, when we will be long gone?" (quotes from the documentary *"Sulina – oraşul soarelui-răsare"*). All of these media products have an unfortunate effect on Sulina's image and self-identity; what they do is nothing more than to imprison Sulina into an implacable destiny, closed between a fascinating history and an inevitable death.

Conclusion

Sulina is a small town at the mouth of the Danube, a region that has always been the focus of political and economic interest; once a pirates' nest, then a humble rural settlement, Sulina set off for its urban golden age with the establishment here of the European Danube Commission in 1856. Up until 1939, this would turn Sulina into "the most cosmopolite city in the country", a fashionable resort and a flourishing *porto franco* of over 10000 inhabitants, with about twenty different ethnic groups and several confessions. Beside its unique multicultural history, Sulina is also a post-socialist town, with a former prosperous local industry during communism, now sharing the decaying fate of many of the small towns of Romania. Opening both to the Danube and to the Black Sea, Sulina is still only accessible by water. The town, thus, bears witness to different historical epochs and subsequent functionalities through its architectural blend of nineteenth century buildings, interwar houses, modern terraces, and distasteful blocks of flats. Passing from Street I to the other five parallel streets of the town entails a unique gradual translation from urban to rural, each with specific architecture and routine.

Described by newspapers as "a dying city, lost between two ages", the town of Sulina struggles to have an implausible future by reviving a past it has long lost. Once part and nexus of one of the first European organizations, today doomed to isolation, Sulina is trying to recuperate a regional identity and position. The official discourse increasingly pinpoints to European integration, portraying Sulina as "the gate of Europe", thus reversing symbolically its – both geographical and socio-political – marginality, as summarized in the favourite catch phrase of the locals: "We are the first to see the light and the last to see justice." At this moment, the future of the town is seen, once again, in connection to the European project. The almost mythical prosperity of the Danube Commission period is being projected into the near future, when Sulina will be a "European" city, in a kind of cyclical fate.

In this regard, local and regional authorities struggle to recover the historic cosmopolitanism and the European atmosphere of the city, by privileging a certain collective memory. The memory of a particular period becomes instrumental for the current projection of Sulina's future, even though there are at least two levels of nostalgia: while official discourse enforces the nostalgia for the European past of the city, most people actually yearn for the (presumed) economic and social security of the communist period. Moreover, even if not uttered as such, there is also nostalgia for the marginal position, with all the advantages deriving from it (avoiding the firm grip of control emanating from the centre).

As of January 2007, the easternmost town of Romania is now the easternmost town of the European Union. Whether the former headquarters of the Danube Commission will be able to once again be a point of reference on the map of Europe, one century later, when obviously the new political and economic realities have significantly modified the geo-strategic relevance of the region, remains a question. Being a relatively small city, with a fascinating and unique history of multicultural urban life, situated as ever at the crossroads of empires and histories, Sulina can be a great location for mapping the sinuous fate and prospect of European integration on the margins of Europe.

Nevertheless, as Boym has cautioned us, "while yearning for Europe in the past was a defiant stance against authoritarianism, following the fall of the Iron Curtain the European Union's Golden Curtain has arisen in its place. Cities such as Prague are shown to be nostalgic for an image of an inclusive Europe that they once desired but with which they are now disillusioned: nostalgia for nostalgia itself. Contesting nostalgias have emerged, whether for Europe, for the Prague of 1968, for the post-Velvet Revolution enthusiasm for the city or for Kafka's cosmopolitan presence" (quoted in Legg 2004: 102). The cosmopolite, prosperous life of Sulina can hardly be re-enacted; and neither can the nineteenth century Europe.

Postscript: Sulina and the construction of regional identities. Sulina and/in the Delta

Sulina was and was not a part of the Danube Delta, the Delta was and was not a part of Dobrudja/Dobrogea, Dobrogea was and was not a part of Romania and Romania was and was not a part of Europe. The history of Sulina and the wider regions reveals a pervasive ambiguity and volatility in the construction of identities on all these scales. Reconfigurations on one scale can trigger re-definitions and changing identifications on the other scales. Sulina's layered re-writing of its European connection is an integral part of the re-writings on the other scales, and these latter processes will determine the chances of a revised local narrative to succeed. A strong accent in Sulina on a European past is less likely to occur, if

Romania was adamantly anti-European, and if it would occur nevertheless, it would have a slim chance to be picked up elsewhere, and to be reinforced. On the other hand, portrayals in the national and regional media, e. g. the image of the dying city, can spark local counter-discourses.

But what region will include Sulina? Despite the historical unity of Dobrogea, especially in antiquity, we argue that nowadays, it is the Danube Delta. Few people other than administrators and scientists assume a regional identity for Dobrogea. Few tourists know the region as a unity, and it is rarely presented as a single touristic product. Tourists rather visit the Danube Delta, and Sulina would be one of the highlights. The Danube Delta, with its clear natural boundaries, is recognized much more easily as a unity, even when the regional identity has strong overtones of marginality.

As Iordachi (2001) pointed out, the Dobrogea after its incorporation into Romania was seen by many in Bucharest as a non-Romanian area (initially, ethnic Romanians were actually a minority), a potentially unstable area. It needed to be modernized, and modernization was simultaneously Romanization. At the same time, the Danube Commission was perceived as an asset as well as a nuisance for the new state working on the consolidation of the territory. Constanţa developed as a competitor for the harbours controlled by the Danube Commission. After the arrival of communism, the political leadership continued the Romanization of Dobrogea, including the Delta.

Nowadays, very few people in Sulina feel they are part of Dobrogea and its regional identity does not seem strong anywhere else we spoke to people. The Delta, however, is another case. Most people in Tulcea, on the western edge of the Delta, would consider Sulina a part of the Delta, but for many locals in Sulina, this amounts to an insult. Sulina is a free port; it belongs to the Sea and to the Danube, not to the swamp that surrounds it on three sides. It belongs to the fostered and revitalized image of the European Sulina, not to the land of impoverished, barely literate and rather aggressive fishermen – as the Delta is often depicted in opposition to the cosmopolitan and highly educated city environment.

The fishermen in question are mostly Lipoveni, and despite the negative imagery of the Delta region in Sulina, many more present-day inhabitants of Sulina have their roots in these Delta communities than in the old cosmopolitan town. As described earlier, newcomers have become assimilated into the pre-existing social memories, and the topography of memory rejuvenates the European narrative. Interestingly enough, the image of the Delta region as one vast marginal area, far from the centres of power, their regulative controls and value systems, is closely related to another narrative of self produced in Sulina: the pirates' nest. Region and city are opposed on one level, and merge into one big narrative of proud marginality and defiance of authority on another.

Sulina nowadays lacks the schools, the social, cultural, economic networks, the resources, infrastructure, and the strategic importance, which made it cosmopolitan for a while. During the Danube Commission era, Sulina was detached from its Delta context, and a new identity was rapidly constructed which turned the margin into a centre. Keen observers like Jean Bart knew that these favourable circumstances were not likely to last forever. Bart's premonitions turned out to be true; the state of Sulina declined, transformed and was gradually given back to the Delta and the economies it could sustain. Against all these odds, amidst competing layers of social memory, and despite the drastic demographic transformation of the place, the European identity survived. The intricate mechanics of local and social memory analysed in this paper have sustained this site of identification, while simultaneously creating a counter-discourse on regional identity.

References

Ashworth, G. J., J. E. Tunbridge 1999: Old Cities, New Pasts: Heritage Planning in Selected Cities in Central Europe. In: GeoJournal 49, 1: 105–116.

Bart, Jean 2004: Europolis. Bucureşti (first ed. 1933).

Bélanger, Anouk 2000: Urban Space and Collective Memory: Analysing the Various Dimensions of the Production of Memory. In: Canadian Journal of Urban Research 11, 1: 69–92.

Chang, T. C. 2005: Place, Memory and Identity: Imagining "New Asia". In: Asia Pacific Viewpoint 46, 3: 247–253.

Comisiunea Europeană a Dunării şi opera sa de la 1856 la 1931. Ed. Primăria Oraşului Sulina. Bucharest 2006 (translation Constantin Bondar). [1st edition, Paris: Imprimérie Nationale, 1931].

Della Dora, Veronica 2000: The Rhetoric of Nostalgia: Postcolonial Alexandria Between Uncanny Memories and Global Geographies. In: Cultural Geographies 13: 207–238.

Eyerman, Ron 2004: The Past in the Present. Culture and the Transmission of Memory. In: Acta Sociologica 47, 2: 159–169.

Fentress, James, Chris Wickham 1992: Social Memory. Oxford: Blackwell.

Iordachi, Constantin 2001: "The California of the Romanians": The Integration of the Northern Dobrogea into Romania 1878–1913. In: Balàsz Trencsényi et al. (eds.), Nation-Building and Contested Identities. Romanian and Hungarian Case Studies. Budapest: Regio Books, Iaşi: Polirom, 121–152.

Irwin-Zarecka, Iwona 1994: Frames of Remembrance. The Dynamics of Collective Memory. New Brunswick, New Jersey: Transactions Publishers.

Jacobs, A. J. 2003: Symbolic Urban Spaces and the Political Economy of Local Collective Memory: a Comparison of Hiroshima and Nagoya, Japan. In: Journal of Political and Military Sociology 31, 2: 253–278.

Jedlowski, Paolo 2001: Memory and Sociology. Themes and Issues. In: Time & Society 10, 1: 29–44.

Lee, Y. S., B. S. A. Yeoh (eds.) 2004: Special Issue on Globalization and the Politics of Forgetting. In: Urban Studies 41,12.

Legg, S. 2004: Memory and Nostalgia. In: Cultural Geographies 11: 99–107.

Low, M. Setha 1999: Spatializing Culture: The Social Production and Social Construction of Public Space in Costa Rica. In: Setha M. Low (ed.), Theorizing the City: the New Urban Anthropology Reader. New Brunswick: Rutgers UP.

Markusen, Ann 2004: The Work of Forgetting and Remembering Places. In: Urban Studies 41, 12: 2303–2313.

Micu, Cristian, Sorin Bucur (eds.) 2006: Sulina - European Destiny. The 150th Anniversary of the European Commission of the Danube. Tulcea, Sulina: Tulcea County Council and Sulina City Hall.

Mills, Amy 2006: Boundaries of the Nation in the Space of the Urban: Landscape and Social Memory in Istanbul. In: Cultural Geographies 13: 367–394.

Pine, Frances, Deema Kaneff, Haldis Haukanes 2004: Introduction: Memory, Politics and Religion: A Perspective on Europe. In: Pine Frances, Deema Kaneff, Haldis Haukanes (eds.), Memory, Politics and Religion. The Past Meets the Present in Europe. New Brunswick, London: Transactions Publ.

Tatu, Tudose 2005: Cărţi vechi, corăbii, reisi, neguţători şi diplomaţi, Dunărea de Jos, 1745–1856 [Old books, ships, Turkish captains, merchants and diplomats, Lower Danube, 1745–1856]. Galaţi: Editura Istru.

Zerubavel, Eviatar 1996: Social Memories: Steps to a Sociology of the Past. In: Qualitative Sociology 19, 3: 283–299.

Visual materials

Sulina - oraşul soarelui-răsare ("Sulina, the city of sunrise"), Societatea de televiziune Electron M-bit, a film by Paul Prisada (2001).

Porto Franco, a film by Anca Damian, Editura Video (2000).

The Problems and Potentials for the Regionalization of Serbia

Dragutin Tošić, Marija Maksin-Mićić, Belgrade

Introduction

In 1929, the Kingdom of Yugoslavia was divided into administrative-control macroregions *(banovine),* which were spatially differentiated into economic and transport entities according to the drainage areas of the largest rivers.[1] They replaced the hitherto existing division of the country into historical-regional entities. The basic political aim of this change was to overcome the historical divisions, thus consolidating and integrating the parts of different entities (Stanković 1981, Petranović 1988). Today, this idea could be associated with European meso trans-border regions. At the same time, governance at the local level was decentralized, thus forming 6645 municipalities, which would today correspond demographically, spatially and functionally with local communities in the EU countries.

After the Second World War, the only attempt to divide the Serbian territory into macro-regions, i.e., into thirteen inter-municipal regional communities, was made in the 1980s, parallel to the liberalization of economic development and governance decentralization. However, these macro regions never had all necessary administrative and control functions and did not enjoy the desired degree of autonomy. Although they disposed of specified investment funds and had the authority to direct regional development, they never took root completely and did not persist. During the last decade of the twentieth century, the republican administration was re-organized into thirty districts, with the detached services of the republican ministries, so that one cannot speak about a new model of regionalisation, except with respect to the spatial coverage of these districts, which have a meso-regional dimension.[2]

---

[1] The names of the *banovine* formed in 1929 were: Danube Banovina with the seat in Novi Sad, Sava Banovina (Zagreb), Vrbas Banovina (Banja Luka), Drina Banovina (Sarajevo), Zeta Banovina (Cetinje), Vardar Banovina (Skopje), Drava Banovina (Ljubljana) and the Littoral Banovina (Split). The separate Administration of the City of Belgrade was established under the imposed so-called September Constitution of 1931, and covered Belgrade, Zemun and Pančevo (Petranović 1988).

[2] In 2004, the Human Development Index (HDI) for the Republic of Serbia, calculated according to the UNDP methodology, was 0.811. According to this index value, the Republic of Serbia was ranked as the 56th most developed country in the world and the fifth among the countries of South Eastern Europe. During the period 2000–2004, the HDI value in Serbia was continuously increasing. In the same period, such a markedly continuous increase in the HDI

The third and last attempt to regionalise Serbia at the conceptual and planning level at the end of the twentieth century was made under the Spatial Plan of the Republic of Serbia (1996), which anticipated functional macro regions and meso regions, that is, the functional regions of the major urban centres in Serbia. Until now, the attempts to regionalise Serbia have not produced any significant effect on the integration and balanced development of the entire territory of Serbia and its parts, so they are unable to provide a basis for Serbia's future regionalisation in accordance with EU principles and policies.

On the other hand, Serbian geographers still have no common stand on the theoretical and methodological framework in developing regional geography. Some authors, especially M. Vasović, argue that the foundation of scientific regional geography in Serbia was laid by the complex studies of the Balkan Peninsula and its parts, that is, regional entities, conducted by J. Cvijić (Vasović 1985, 1997). Although at that time there was neither the clearly established criteria for regionalisation nor the theoretical and methodological basis for its development (after all, Cvijić did not use the terms "region" and "regionalisation"), it can be stated that his work and research methodology laid the foundation of Serbian regional geography. Cvijić's work underscores the idea of the unity of nature and man - organized into societies, which was advanced by K. Ritter and A. Hetner, and about the reciprocal influence of nature and man/society in shaping the geographic landscape, which was advocated by Vidal de la Blache. On the basis of Cvijić's work and the concept of possibilism, which he had adopted through French geography, B. Milojević conducted a number of exhaustive studies about some spatial entities in Serbia and Yugoslavia (Milojević 1956). In the 1990s, in the spirit of classical regional geography, M. Vasović proposed the division of the

---

value in South-eastern Europe was also recorded only by Romania and Greece. An analysis of the HDI during the observed period points to a more significant improvement in the quality of life in the Republic of Serbia due primarily to an increase in the education index and the GDP per capita (Vlada Republike Srbije 2005).

At the same time, an analysis of the HDI points to great regional differences at the district and municipality levels in Serbia. The highest index value was recorded in the City of Belgrade (0.927). The highly developed districts include the South Banat (HDI value of 0.882), South Bačka (0.858) and West Bačka (0.849) districts. In the same period, the lowest HDI values were recorded in the Toplica (0.610), Raška (0.609), Bor (0.570) and Jablanica (0.563) districts. On the basis of an analysis of the HDI it is concluded that the quality of life is the highest in the municipalities of Apatin, Pančevo, City of Belgrade, Novi Sad and Bečej, and the lowest in the municipalities of Medveđa, Trgovište, Preševo, Bosilegrad and Tutin. This shows that the long-lasting trend of the regions in southern Serbia lagging behind in their development continued, coupled with the emergence of newly underdeveloped regions during the transition period - so-called "transition poverty" municipalities in the functional regions of one-time large industrial centres (Vlada Republike Srbije 2005). Huge differences in the HDI values are the result of uneven urbanization and the unbalanced agglomeration of functions in few urban centres.

Balkan part of Serbia into five macro-regions and 27 meso-regions. Apart from their physiognomy, he also determined their anthropo-geographic and cultural-geographic characteristics (Vasović 1985, 1997). The question remains as to whether and to what extent the regional structure of the Serbian geospace has changed in the new political and socio-economic circumstances?

In Serbian regional geography the functional paradigm took root in the 1970s. Its development has three, conditionally parallel, directions: economic regionalisation, nodal regionalisation[3] and planned regionalisation. Certain attention to functionalism, as the principle and paradigm in the economic-geographic and socio-geographic exploration and organization of space in Serbia, and the regionalisation of the country based on that principle is devoted by O. Savić and J. Ilić in an analysis of the relations of cities and the surroundings gravitating towards them (Savić 1965, Ilić 1977); by V. Djurić in an analysis of the functional classification of cities (Djurić 1970); by D. Perišić in studying the development patterns of agglomerations and agglomeration systems (Perišić 1985); by A. Veljković et al. in interpreting and analysing the city as an autonomous system and the role of growth and development centres (Veljković 1991); by B. Derić in defining the concept of regional development (Derić, Perišić 1996); by M. Stepić in determining the significance of regionalisation in the administrative-territorial organization (Stepić 2002); by B. Stojkov and others in determining the social and economic significance of Serbia's regional differentiation (Stojkov 2007). This form of regionalisation is also faced with problems, dilemmas and open scientific questions. In Serbia there is no scientific consensus on the concepts of economic-geographic, socio-economic, nodal and planned regionalisation. In other words, we have not developed the concept for an integrated approach to regionalisation.

---

[3] In regional geography there are two directions. The proponent of structural functionalism is Hartshone (Hartshone 1959), who is influenced by German social geography. The other approach is process functionalism, which is concerned with the functional organization of space. The nodal region in geography is a synonym for the functional region. The concept of nodal region is in the core of process functionalism in regional geography. It is based on the fact that, through their functioning, urban settlements exert influence on regional integration and differentiation of the space being heterogeneous from a natural-ecological, socio-economic, settlement-demographic, physiognomic and functional aspect. The specific spatial systems so created are called nodal or functional regions. The concept has gained its significance under conditions of accelerated urbanization, which is characterized by a pronounced concentration of population and functions in cities and their surroundings, i.e., under conditions of creating new regional structures such as urban regions. The nodal region is the space of functional integration and complementarity of the city in its zone of influence and represents an open and dynamic system. As early as 1959, in his article "The Concept of a Planning Region", J. R. P. Friedmann placed the nodal region in the centre of regional planning, stating that it provides the basis for planning in "industrial economics" (Friedmann 1959). Today, it could be said that the nodal region is the basis of post-industrial (global) economics and spatial development.

During the last decade, a number of papers and research projects appeared, devoted to European regional initiatives and regionalisation schemes, which were conceived in the EU countries and adjusted to the specifics of our territory. It is increasingly held in the scientific circles that the functional paradigm is an imperative in conceiving the model of Serbia's sustainable spatial development. It is expected that the conditions for the rational decentralization of functions and the new spatio-functional organization and regionalization of Serbia will be created by implementing that model. Proceeding from the concept of polycentric development, which is favoured in the European Union, it seems that functional urban areas can provide an adequate basis for the formation of socio-geographic regions that would also be entrusted with the administrative-control function. This paper analyses these problems and points to the possibilities for the establishment of functional links and the integration of space at the level of national macro and meso regions and meso transborder regions.

The integration and regionalisation process of the EU – Can Serbia cope?

The integration of national urban systems into a coherent European urban system is taking place parallel to the integration of European countries and the globalization process. An integrated European urban system is intended for the realization of the concept of polycentric development as the instrument for achieving the economic competitiveness, cohesion and balanced territorial development of the European Union (European Commission 1999). At the beginning of the twenty-first century, this resulted in the adoption of the paradigm that functionally linked (networked) large cities are assuming the role of support to the economic and political integration of Europe (European Commission 1999, Faludi 2000, 2005). Therefore, the use of the concept of polycentric development in the European Union is based on the functional networking of metropolitan regions and their infrastructural linkages by trans-European transport corridors.

With the enlargement of the European Union from fifteen to twenty-seven member countries, the spatial and economic relations within it also changed. Under the Interreg IIIB programme, the model of Metropolitan European Growth Areas (MEGAs) has been proposed as the most coherent model of the EU's decentralization and balanced development. In determining the model, the indicators of population concentration, transport location and accessibility level, concentration of capital, intellectual potentials, private sector participation in investments, development level of the public sector and the like were used. According to this model, two global cities (Paris and London) and seventy-four MEGAs were defined and classified according to a four-level hierarchy. In the future polycentric urban integration, the classical socio-geographic regions, i.e., Functional Urban

Areas (FUAs), would be proposed as subsystems. The European MEGAs should exert influence on urban control and balanced growth, integrated development of agglomeration systems, lessening of regional development disparities, etc. (PlaNetCenSe 2006).

In the European Union there are also sceptical views on decentralization and balanced development based on the mentioned model, because the question that imposes itself is whether and how the strongest centres will transfer some of their competences and functions to lower ranking centres and the like. On the other hand, South-eastern Europe has no unique urban system or joint association of cities. This is understandable if one considers its socio-historical development and historical discontinuity, as well as the complexity of its natural basis, its geographic location, unequal level of economic development, political fragmentation and the like. Its urban network is comprised of functionally maladjusted and hierarchically incompatible national urban systems.

In view of the fact that Hungary, Greece, Romania and Bulgaria are EU members, Serbia's urban network will have to adjust to its immediate surroundings and find the appropriate role in the regional-integration processes of South Eastern Europe. This should be favoured by Serbia's central location in the Balkans, which enables its capital, Belgrade, to assume the position of the northern gate of the Balkans and the southern gate of Central Europe. This view is also supported by the typology of the spatial structures of the region of Central and South-eastern Europe (Fig. 1), which is based on the population density and existence/accessibility of Metropolitan European Growth Areas (MEGAs) and transnational/national Functional Urban Areas (FUAs). The designated spatial structures should ensure the transnational identity of urban regions as a basis and a chance for the integration of urban systems and national territories into the European space (PlaNetCenSe 2006).

The question is whether functional urban areas can be acceptable as the model for the decentralization and regionalisation of Serbia and its integration into the European surroundings. Second, what should be undertaken as to fulfil those tasks and implement the proposed model?

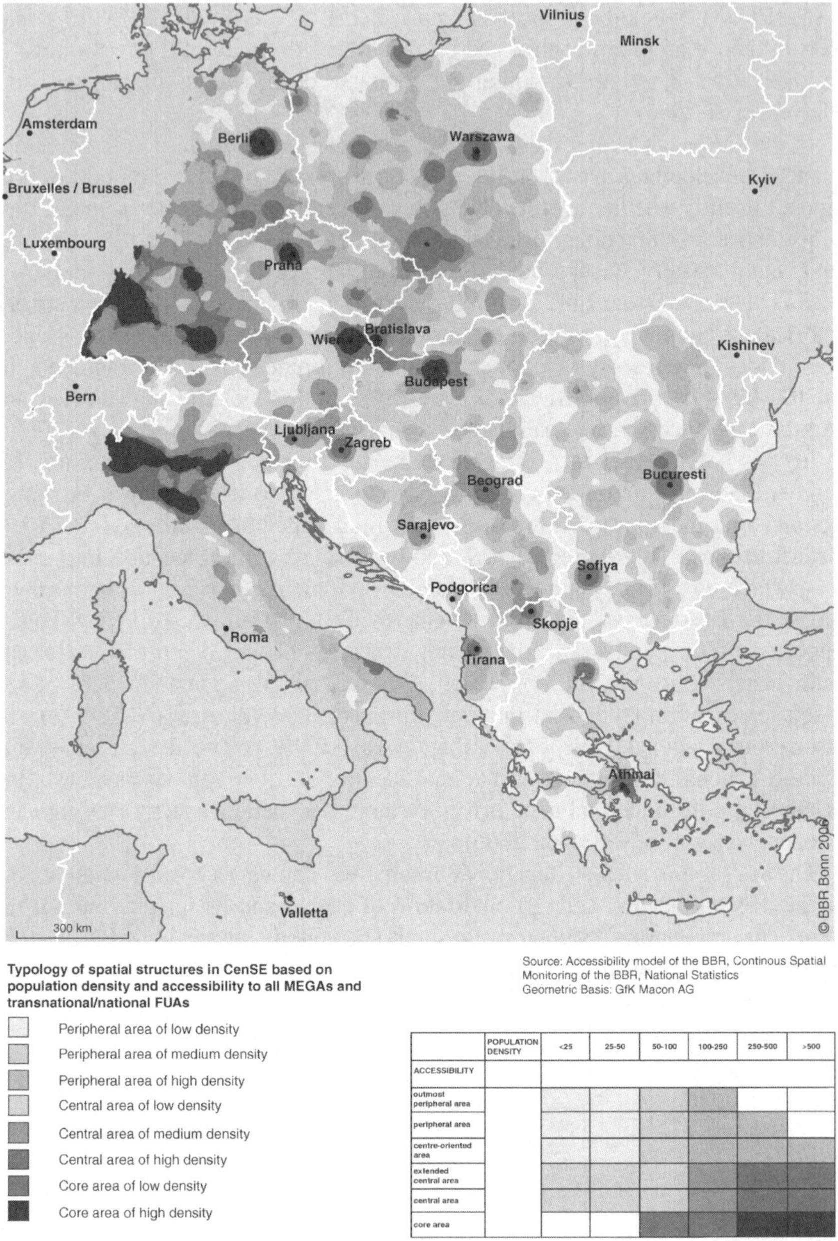

Figure 1. Spatial structures in the region of Central Adriatic, Danubian and South East European Space (CADSES) (Source: PlaNetCenSe 2006, http://www.planet-cense.net)

Urbanization in the function of Serbia's regionalisation

1. The urbanization process in Serbia

Like a large part of Southeastern Europe, Serbia is not sufficiently urbanized. The phenomenon of urbanization and urban development in Serbia is not older than 300 years. One can speak of intensive urbanization only since the second half of the twentieth century. According to the 1953 census, about one-fifth of the total population (22.5%) lived in urban settlements, while about two-thirds of the active population (67%) were engaged in agriculture. Vojvodina was the most urbanized region with 29.5% of urban population; it was followed by central Serbia with 21.2%, and Kosovo and Metohija with only 14.6%. The growth of urban population was not uniform in certain inter-census periods. The highest growth rate was recorded in the period 1961–1971 (41.7 ‰ per annum), while in the last inter-census period (1991–2002) it stagnated (about 2 ‰ per annum). In central Serbia, the share of urban population rose from 21.2% in 1953 to 47.8% in 1981, 54.1% in 1991 and 56.2% in 2002. Compared to the neighbouring countries, Serbia is less urbanized than Bulgaria, Hungary and Romania, more urbanized than Albania and Bosnia and Herzegovina, and at similar levels as Croatia and Macedonia (Tošić, Krunić 2005).

Over the past two decades, the number of inhabitants has been increasing only in urban centres. In other words, there has been a distinct polarization between the regions with increasing population and regions with a decrease in population. The first group includes urban regions in which the highest population increase is recorded in peripheral and peri-urban zones, while rural and hilly and mountain regions are characterized by depopulation (Fig. 2.).

There is a distinct geographical differentiation of the Serbian territory, primarily into lowlands, which include larger river valleys and plains, and mountain regions. This differentiation has been enhanced by differences in the development level and the degree of utilization of available natural and man-made resources. In our circumstances, the concentration of the economy, especially industry, in the river valleys and along the major transportation routes, brought about the accelerated concentration of population, that is, the movement of population from the underdeveloped and peripheral regions in Serbia to the zones and centres of economic concentration. During this process, the network of cities and economic centres was established, on which the territorial integration of the economy and economic polarization of Serbian space are based.

Research has pointed to the interdependence of road infrastructure and the concentration process in the Serbian territory or, in other words, the emergence of the zones featured by a more distinct agglomeration of the economy and population along the European transport corridors – in the Danube-Sava, Velika Morava, Zapadna Morava and Južna Morava development belts (Fig. 3). It is difficult to determine precisely to what extent the centres of these zones have become attractive for development thanks to their location on the major transportation routes. The same applies to the influence of the existing concentration on changes in the road network, that is, in the functions and significance of specified routes. It can only be said with certainty that there are pronounced interaction and high level of correlation (Perišić 1985).

2. The Serbian Urban System

According to the methodology of the Republican Statistical Office, the current network of urban settlements consists of 194 settlements: 114 in central Serbia, 52 in Vojvodina, and 26 in Kosovo and Metohija. Since the 2002 census did not include the inhabitants of Kosovo and Metohija (Fig. 2), we will point to some basic demographic characteristics of 168 urban settlements in central Serbia and Vojvodina.

The significance of these settlements in the urban system and regional organization of the Republic and its parts varies. The spatio-structural and functional organization of the settlement network is dominated by small urban settlements (Table 1). Out of 168 urban settlements, 51 have less than 5000 inhabitants, 41 from 5000 to 10000 inhabitants, 58 from 10000 to 50000 inhabitants, 14 from 50000 to 100000 inhabitants, and only 4 have more than 100000 inhabitants (there are 3 settlements with less than 200000 inhabitants and Belgrade with more than one million inhabitants). In 25 municipalities in central Serbia and Vojvodina there are no urban settlements at all.

Table 1: Distribution of urban settlements in Serbia according to population size, based on the 2002 Census.

Population size (inhabitants)	Number of urban settlements	Population	Urban population in percent	Cumulative sums
< 5000	51	135500	3.21	135500
5001–10000	41	306860	7.27	442360
10001–50000	58	1207430	29.10	1649790
50001–100000	14	900980	21.36	2550770
100001–200000	3	519880	12.08	3070650
200001 and more	1	1118980	26.53	4189630
Total	168	4189630	100.00	—

Source: 2002 Census.

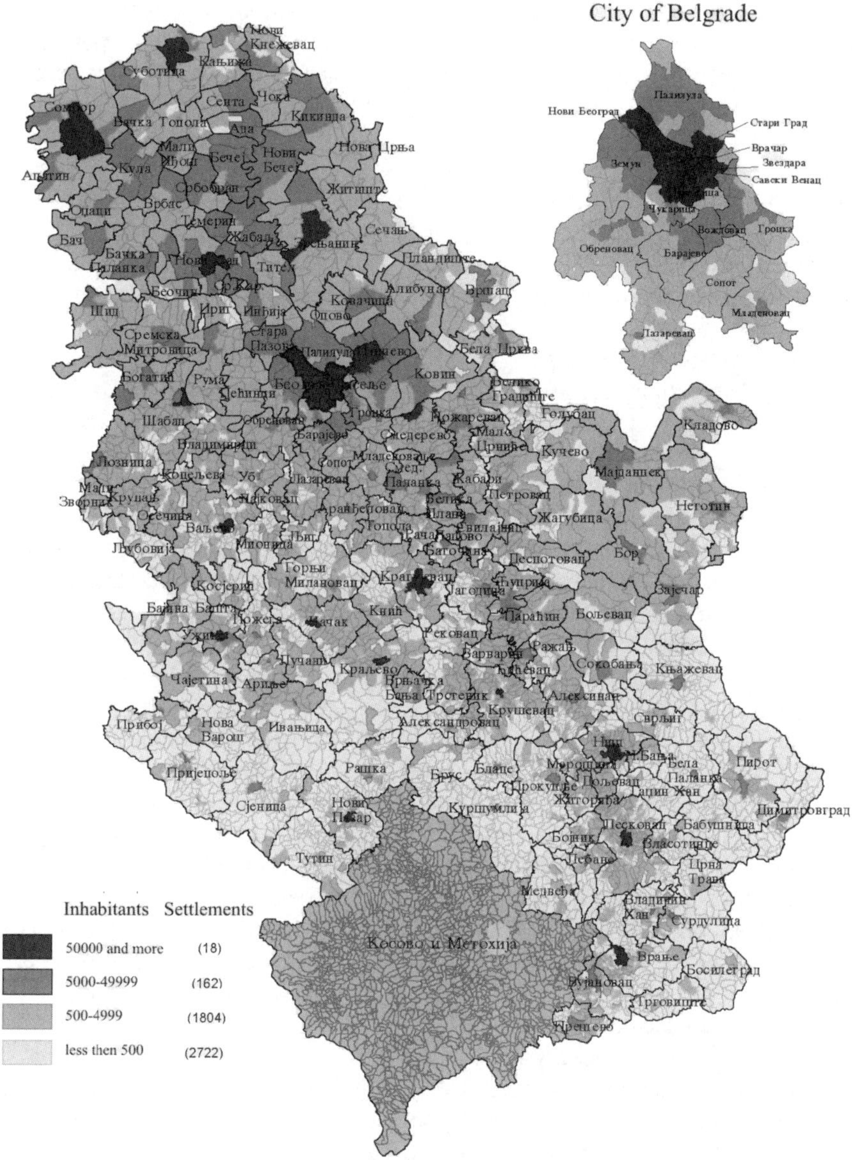

Figure 2. Settlements according to population size in Serbia, 2002 (Source: 2002 Census).

At first glance one might conclude that the distribution of settlements in the Serbian urban network is favourable. However, the zones and belts of population and activity concentration point to the contrary. In addition, about 26% of Serbia's urban population (without Kosovo and Metohija) live just in Belgrade. This discrepancy in the number of inhabitants between the major and other urban settlements shows that Serbia has no uniformly developed and interconnected urban system, that is, its urbanization flows were not directed at the proper time. If we analysed the statistical and administrative criteria for identifying cities and urban settlements, and applied scientifically more accurate methods, the degree of Serbia's urbanization would even be lower, while regional polarization and disparities more pronounced.

The dominance of Belgrade (1 118 980 inhabitants in 2002), or the Belgrade urban agglomeration (1 574 000 inhabitants with the suburban municipalities in 2002) as well as a strong demographic polarization are confirmed by the size of the ten largest urban centres. The dominance of the state centre is also pointed out by the index of urban primacy, whose value is 5.87 (the population ratio of Belgrade to Novi Sad, as the second largest city). The population size of Valjevo, the tenth largest urban centre, is only about one-twentieth of that of Belgrade (index of 0.054). The indices shown in Table 2 lead to the conclusion that the scientifically presented and socially justified concept of de-metropolization, decentralization of urbanization, regionally balanced and dynamic polycentric urban systems as anticipated by the Spatial Plan of the Republic of Serbia (1996) have not been implemented.

This disproportion in the population size of Belgrade and other larger urban centres is the result of Serbia's incoherent and asymmetric urban system. It is evident that there are no urban settlements, except of Belgrade, with 200 000 to 500 000 inhabitants and the macro-regional functions, which would be the agents of Serbia's balanced development and the hubs for integrating the urban system into the European urban system and development trends.

In Serbia, many types of more or less urbanized regions and of regional urban systems can be identified, as well as the hierarchy of their spatial and functional systems. As for continuity in the duration of urbanization and its spatial types there are pronounced differences among:

- polycentrically urbanized Vojvodina;
- somewhat less urbanized central Serbia with an irregular hierarchical structure of the urban settlement system and a large span between the functional capacity of Belgrade and other cities in central Serbia, and
- low-urbanized Kosovo and Metohija (Tošić, Krunić 2005).

With such a structure, the Serbian urban system is neither compatible nor complementary with the aims of establishing the European urban system. Since the European strategy (ESDP) is aimed at the future integration of polycentric urban

Table 2. Population size relations of the top ten urban centres in Serbia, according to the 2002 Census.

Urban centre	Population	Index in relation to Belgrade	Index in relation to the previous urban centre
Belgrade	1 118 980	1.000	—
Novi Sad	190 162	0.169	0.169
Niš	173 390	0.154	0.911
Kragujevac	145 890	0.130	0.844
Subotica	99 471	0.088	0.676
Zrenjanin	79 545	0.071	0.957
Pančevo	76 110	0.068	0.955
Čačak	73 152	0.065	0.832
Smederevo	62 668	0.056	0.861
Valjevo	61 406	0.054	0.964

Source: 2002 Census.

structures, it is important that the Serbian urban and regional development models are adjusted to that concept. The question here is whether the model of a polycentric urban system and functional regions of urban centres adopted by the Spatial Plan of the Republic of Serbia, coupled with the necessary adjustments to the changes occurring in the last decade, provides a sound basis for integration into the European urban system and development trends. Does the problem lie in the planned model, or the failure to implement it, that is, in the un-readiness to implement this or some other model of Serbia's development decentralization and regionalisation displayed at the national and other levels of government?

Which solutions are possible?

1. "Belts of More Intensive Development" and "Functional Urban Areas" in the Spatial Plan of the Republic of Serbia

The Spatial Plan of the Republic of Serbia points to the potentials and basic solutions: the initial strategic commitment of the Plan is to reach a higher level of Serbia's overall functional integrity and much better transport and economic linkages to the neighbouring and other European countries. This aim implies the reduction of regional disproportions or, in other words, qualitative changes in the spatial, economic and social structures, including specifically the regions with pronounced dysfunctions in social and economic development. Proceeding from the current concentration of population and activities in the basic development belts, the commitment to reduce excessive concentrations in these belts was affirmed. The principle of polycentric development and greater attractiveness as well as of activating other development belts and zones - with substantial natural and man-made potentials and a relatively good transport location and accessibility - was established.

The belts of more intensive development (Fig. 3) were defined by proceeding from the existing and planned routes of trans-European and national transport corridors in which the potentials for developing economic activities, increased concentration of population and urban settlements, and improving technical, public social infrastructure were activated, or is planned to do so.

For example, the urban centres and peripheral regions in eastern Serbia will get access to the trans-European transport corridor X, primarily through the connections of class I and II state roads to the highway, so that travel to the corridor takes between 1.5 and 2.5 hours; those in western and, in particular, central Serbia will lie within 2.2 and 4.5 hours from the corridor. Only after the construction of the planned highways in the Zapadna Morava valley and towards the southern Adriatic, the peripheral western parts of central Serbia will be equalized with eastern Serbia with respect to transport accessibility. The reconstruction and modernization of the state and local road networks can also shorten the travel time, that is, facilitate access and ensure better conditions for the integration of the eastern and western parts of central Serbia with each other and with the neighbouring countries. In ten to fifteen years, assuming the construction of the highway network and the improvement of the quality of the state road network, the shortening of the travel time between the neighbouring, larger urban centres within the primary development belts and trans-European transport corridors (twenty-six urban centres in Vojvodina and thirty urban centres in central Serbia) to about forty minutes and up to two hours between the peripheral regions and the belts of primary development and the trans-European transport corridors can be regarded as ensuring adequate accessibility of specified regions (Maksin-Mičić 2003, 2004). In addition, the planned and potential routes of state highways will also enable better connections of the Serbian urban system to the urban systems in its surroundings (Figure 3).

In the development of the Serbian urban system, the emphasis in the Spatial Plan of the Republic of Serbia is put on reducing the concentration of population and activities in the state and provincial centres, that is, on qualitative changes in their economic and socio-economic structures, in addition to the more intensive use of available building funds, land and other advantages, intellectual, scientific, and development potentials. Priority is given to the de-metropolization of Serbia and the implementation of the principle of polycentric development by spurring development and improving the quality of life in macro-regional (Niš, Užice and

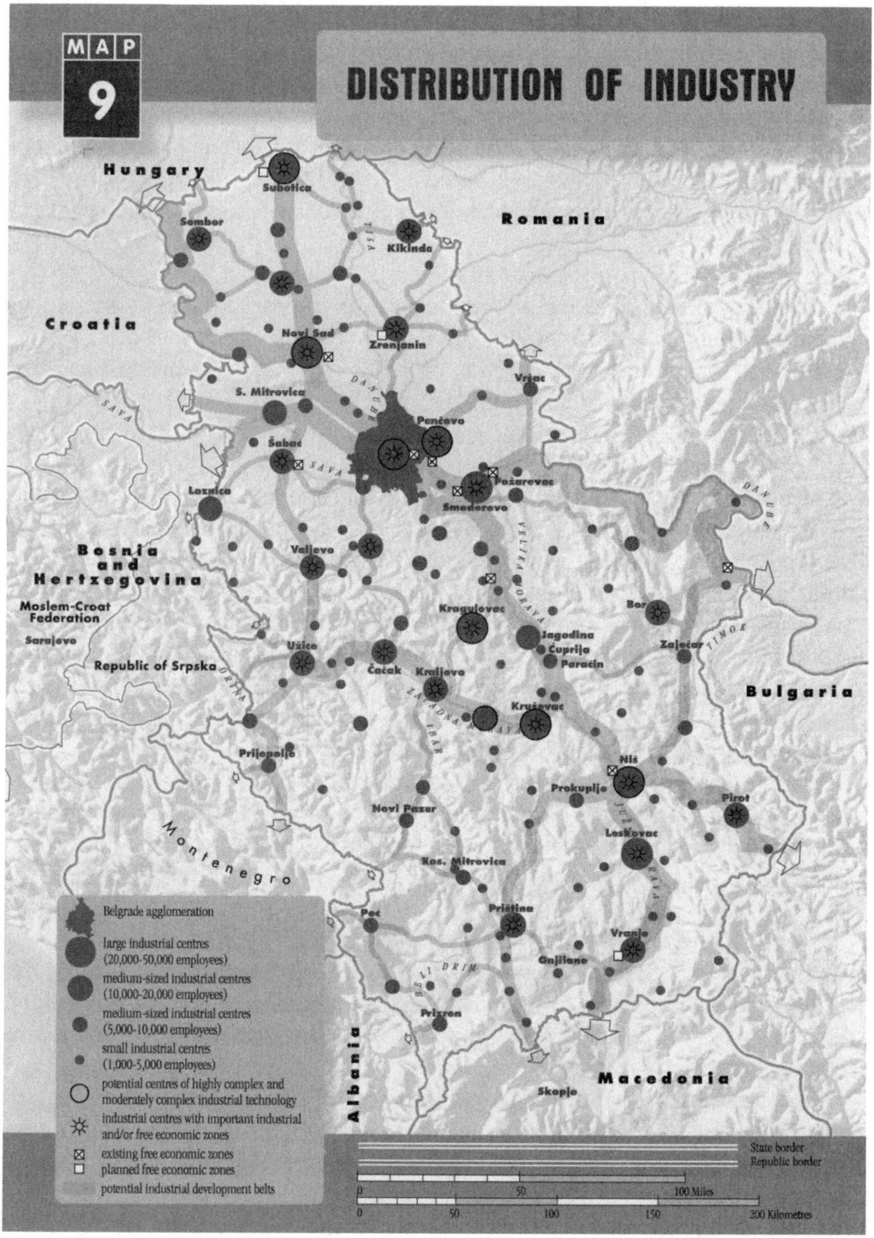

Figure 3. Belts of more intensive development in Serbia (Source: Spatial Plan of the Republic of Serbia, 1996, Map 9)

Kragujevac) and regional centres and smaller cities in the territory of the Republic and especially in the peripheral zone of Belgrade.

The Spatial Plan of the Republic of Serbia anticipates thirty-four functional regions, which are formed by state, macro-regional and regional centres (Fig. 4). This spatio-functional re-organization of the Republic, as one model of its regionalisation at NUTS 3 level, should ensure:

- sustainable development at the level of meso-regional entities – functional urban areas;
- better networking and efficiency of the urban system;
- government decentralization and rationalization in order to achieve more efficient satisfaction of the citizens' daily needs;
- better adjustment of the organization of public services to the needs, possibilities and interests of local communities;
- more efficient coordination of the activities and programmes of local communities.

It is interesting to note that during the public debate about this plan (1994–1996), it was relatively easy to reach the consensus on the number and spatial limits of the proposed thirty-four functional regions which are, with respect to territory, similar or identical to some districts. At the same time, the greatest number of remarks and opposing views were expressed with respect to the proposed territory of six macro regions at the NUTS 2 level, that is, functional regions of the state, two provincial and three macro regional centres in the Serbian urban system. Since a consensus could not be reached for the macro-regional level, macro regions were not included in the procedure of the national spatial plan.

Apart from the anticipated role of integrating republican space, some centres in the Serbian urban system have a predisposition to become the centres of future trans-border regions – transnational, functional urban areas.

2. Potential metropolitan and transborder regions

In the process of Serbia's functional integration with Southeastern Europe, the dominant place will be held by the Belgrade agglomeration (Fig. 1), which will be followed by the Niš agglomeration and then by the agglomerations of the future centres of trans-border regions.

Within the administrative borders of the City of Belgrade, there are 157 settlements, of which 18 are urban. In a functional sense, the Belgrade agglomeration connects the Vojvodina-Pannonian-Danubian and Central-Balkan parts of Serbia (Tošić 2000). It has developed by spatial integration of urban settlements along the Novi Sad-Zemun-Belgrade-Pančevo-Smederevo routes. According to the 2002 Census, the City of Belgrade had 1 574 000 inhabitants, of whom 1 280 639, or

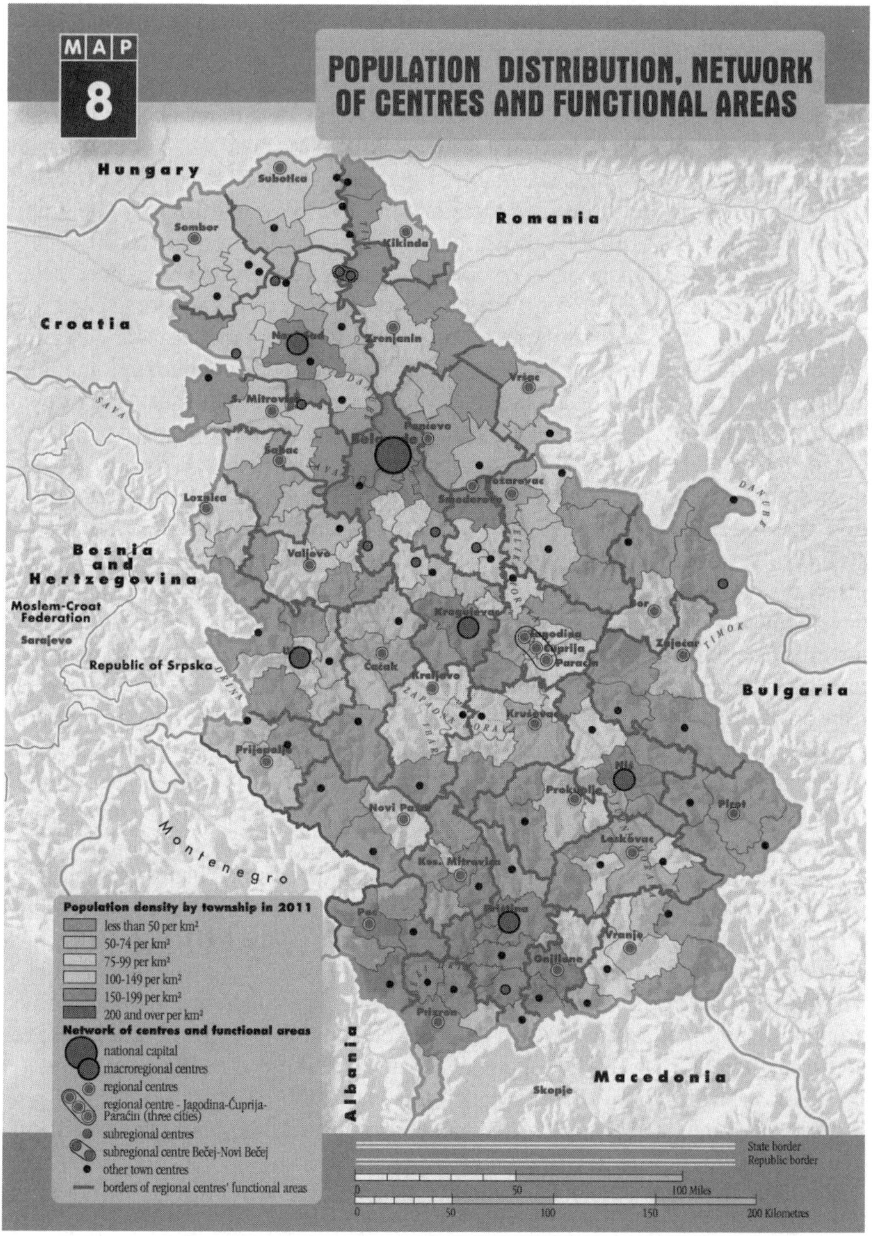

Figure 4. Functional regions of Serbian urban centres. – Potential Trans-border Region Area (Source: Spatial Plan of the Republic of Serbia, 1996, Map 8)

82.3%, lived in 18 urban settlements, while 1118980 inhabitants or 87.4% of the urban population lived in the urban area of Belgrade proper.

In relation to its European surroundings, the Belgrade agglomeration has developed as the nodal point of the Pannonian-Sava development axis (Vienna, Budapest, Belgrade, Bucharest), the primary Balkan Morava-Vardar development axis (Belgrade, Niš, Skopje, Thessaloniki, Athens), the north-Sava axis (Maribor, Ljubljana, Zagreb, Belgrade) and the Šumadija-Ibar development axis (Belgrade, Kraljevo, Kosovska Mitrovica, Prishtina, Skopje). The position and importance of Belgrade in the functional organization of Southeastern Europe have been determined by its role as the hub for the trans-European transport corridors X and VII. The Belgrade agglomeration can develop into the bipolar Belgrade-Novi Sad agglomeration, thus forming a two-and-half-million metropolitan agglomeration and having the potential to assume the role of a Metropolitan European Growth Area in the future, akin to Prague, Warsaw, Bratislava, and Budapest.

In the second group of urban agglomerations Niš distinguishes itself as the main complement to the Belgrade metropolitan region in joining European integration processes (Tošić, Nevenić 2006). So far, this macro-regional centre has not sufficiently valorized its regional location along significant transport corridors, insufficiently equipped with high-quality infrastructural facilities - the eastern development axis towards Sofia and further southwards, along the Maritsa valley, towards Istanbul, and the continuation of the Morava-Vardar development axis towards Athens, via Skopje and Thessalonika (the section of trans-European transport corridor X). In 2002, the city of Niš had 250180 inhabitants, of whom 177823 lived in urban settlements (Niš and Niška Banja). According to socio-geographic methods the Niš agglomeration can be said to have over 350000 inhabitants and a large area of influence, acting as a gravitational zone in southern and south-eastern Serbia.

Apart from Niš, the second group of urban agglomerations includes the macro-regional centres of Kragujevac and Užice and the regional centre of Subotica, as the potential centres of macro urban functional areas (at the NUTS 2 level), which can contribute more significantly to Serbia's more balanced development (ibid.). The third group of urban agglomerations includes the functional regions formed around the regional centres, which have the potential role as transborder linkages and trans-border regions. The potential centres of these transborder regions (at NUTS 3 or NUTS 2 level) are, among other:

- Užice, Loznica and Šabac, which can cooperate with the Federation of Bosnia and Herzegovina and the Republika Srpska;
- Sombor and Bačka Palanka, which can cooperate with Eastern Slavonia in Croatia;
- Kikinda, Zrenjanin and Vršac for the cooperation with Romania;
- Zaježar and Pirot for the cooperation with Bulgaria; and

– Vranje as centre of a trans-border region with Macedonia.

Other functional urban areas, designated in the Spatial Plan of the Republic of Serbia, can fall into the fourth group of urban agglomerations with the integrative role at the intra-regional level, that is, functional urban areas being significant for integration of the territory of Serbia.

Final Considerations

The attempts to regionalise Serbia in the twentieth century had no significant effects on the integration and balanced development of Serbia's entire territory and its parts, so that they cannot provide a basis for its future regionalisation in accordance with the EU principles and policies.

The situation at the beginning of the twenty-first century is similar. In the latest official document for medium-term plans, designed to provide answers to the future regionalization of Serbia, there is no vision of regional development (Regional Development Strategy of the Republic of Serbia for the Period 2007–2012, passed in 2005; see Vlada Republike Srbije 2005). Instead, it offers variations of formal-statistical regions, which are designed in order to approach EU funds (at NUTS 3 or NUTS 2 level). At the same time, the basic conclusion of this document is that the regional disproportions are increasing,[4] and there is still no regional policy, coordination or appropriate support to the balancing of Serbia's regional development. On the other hand, it is anticipated that uneven urbanization is both the cause and effect of Serbia's unbalanced socio-economic development. However, a more balanced regional development can be achieved only by relying not on formal-statistical regions, but on functional or nodal ones.

Disproportions in population size between Belgrade and other major urban centres in Serbia are the result of its incoherent and asymmetric urban system. There is an evident lack of urban centres with 200000–500000 inhabitants and macro-regional functions, which would be the agents of Serbia's balanced endogenous development and linkage to the European urban system. Due to such a structure, the Serbian urban system is neither compatible nor complementary with the aims of establishing the European urban system. Since the European strategy is geared to the future integration of polycentric urban structures, it is important that the Serbian urban and regional development models are adjusted to that concept.

Proceeding from the concept of polycentric development and the models which are favoured in the European Union, the functional regions of urban centres can

---

[4] According to the Regional Development Strategy of the Republic of Serbia for the Period 2007–2012, regional disproportions in the development level in the Republic of Serbia are the highest in Europe (Vlada Republike Srbije 2005: 82).

provide an adequate basis for the formation of socio-geographic regions, which would also be entrusted with the administrative-control function. The model of polycentric urban system and functional regions of urban centres adopted under the Spatial Plan of the Republic of Serbia, coupled with the necessary adjustments to the changes occurring in the last decade, provides a sound basis for inclusion in the European urban system and development trends.

The first precondition of the successful implementation of this plan is to reach a consensus on the concept of polycentric development and the appropriate model of national and transnational functional urban areas. The second precondition is to ensure that all key actors are ready to take part in the implementation of the adopted model, which was the major problem in enforcing planning decisions in the past period.

Therefore, it is necessary to perform a number of activities aimed at improving the efficiency of managing and directing Serbia's more balanced development and its integration into the European development trends and policies, including specifically:

- the provision of the appropriate legal and planning basis;
- the formation of functional and nodal regions with the appropriate administrative-control competences and institutions, while at the same time carrying out decentralization and strengthening the local level of governance;
- the development of the hitherto non-existent instruments and measures of various policies (general economic, regional, sustainable development, land and other general and sectoral policies) and the improvement of the existing ones;
- improvement of horizontal and vertical coordination;
- the further promotion and development of cooperation between the public and private sectors;
- the improvement of information dissemination and the development of modalities for including the public and key actors in the making and implementation of planning decisions at all level of governance and in all sectors, etc.

Only in this case, the adopted model of government decentralization and regionalisation of Serbia will stand a realistic chance of success.

References

Derić, Branislav, Dimitrije Perišić 1996: Kriterijumi regionalizacije teritorije Srbije [Criteria for the regionalisation of the territory of Serbia]. In: Prostorno planiranje, regionalni razvoj i zaštita životne sredine [Spatial planning, regional development and environmental protection). Posebna izdanja 28. Belgrade: IAUS.

Đurić, Vladimir 1970: General Approach to Functional Classification of Urban Communities in Serbia. In: Geographical Papers (Department of Geography, University of Zagreb), 83–95.

European Commission 1999: European Spatial Development Perspective (ESDP). Potsdam.

Faludi, Andreas 2000: The European Spatial Development Perspective: What Next? In: European Planning Studies 8, 2: 237–250.

Faludi, Andreas 2005: Polycentric Territorial Cohesion Policy. In: Town Planning Review 76, 1: 107–117.

Friedmann, J. R. P. 1959: The Concept of a Planning Region. In: Economic Geography 35: 147–195.

Government of the Republic of Serbia 1996: Spatial Plan of the Republic of Serbia. Belgrade.

Hartshorne, R. 1959: Perspective on the Nature of Geography. Survey of Current Thought in the Light of the Past. Chicago et al.: McNally (= Association of American Geographers, Monograph series, 1).

Ilić, Jovan 1970: Karakteristike funkcionalnih odnosa između gradova i okoline sa posebnim osvrtom na Srbiju [The characteristics of functional relations between cities and their environment with special emphasis on Serbia]. In: Stanovništvo 8, 3–4: 163–178.

Maksin-Mićić, Marija 2003: Uticaj transevropskih saobraćajnih koridora na regionalni razvoj i aglomeracione sisteme – iskustva evropskih zemalja [The influence of trans-European transport corridors on regional development and agglomeration systems in European countries]. In: Ekonomski anali 157: 123–134.

Maksin-Mićić, Marija 2004: Uticaj transevropskih saobracajnih koridora na regionalni razvoj i aglomeracione sisteme – iskustva u Srbiji [The influence of trans-European transport corridors on regional development and agglomeration systems in Serbia]. In: Ekonomski anali 163: 165–182.

Milojević, Ž. Borivoje 1956: Opšta regionalna geografija [General regional geography]. Belgrade: Narodna knjiga.

National Assembly of the Republic of Serbia 1996: Prostorni plan Republike Srbije [Spatial plan of the Republic of Serbia]. In: Službeni glasnik Republike Srbije 13: 331–429.

Perišić, Dimitrije 1985: O prostornom planiranju [On spatial planning]. Belgrade: IAUS.

Petranović, Branko 1988: Istorija Jugoslavije 1918–1988 [History of Yugoslavia 1918–1988], vol. I. Belgrade: Nolit.

PlaNetCenSe 2006: Mobilising the Potentials of Central and South East Europe – Chances, Challenges and Choices for Future Development. Internet: http://www.planet-cense.net.

Republički zavod za statistiku 2003–2004: Popis stanovništva, domaćinstava i stanova 2002 [Population, household and housing census 2002], vols. 1–8. Belgrade: Republički zavod za statistiku.

Savić, Olga 1955: Uticajne sfere gradova u dolini Velike Morave [Spheres of influence of the cities in the Velika Morava valleys]. Belgrade: Geografski institut SANU. Posebna izdanja, 7.

Stankovic, Đorđe 1981: Administrativna podela Kraljevine Jugoslavije/SHS [Administrative division of the Kingdom of Yugoslavia/Serbs, Croats and Slovenes]. In: Istorijski glasnik 1–2: 33–46

Stepić, Milomir 2002: Regionalizacija u funkciji unutrašnje političko-teritorijalne organizacije Srbije [Regionalisation in the function of Serbia's internal political-territorial organization]. In: Zbornik Matice srpske za društvene nauke 112–113: 127–147.

Stojkov, Borislav 2007: Status grada, policentrizam, decentralizacija i novi status grada u Srbiji [City status, polycentrism, decentralization and new city status in Serbia]. Belgrade: PALGO Centre.

Tošić, Dragutin 2000: Gradski centri – faktori regionalne integracije Srbije [Urban centres – factors of the regional integration of Serbia]. In: Glasnik Geografskog društva Republike Srpske (Banja Luka) 5: 83–96.

Tošić, Dragutin, Marija Nevenić 2006: Metropolitan Regions in Serbia and Their Potentials for Integration of South East Europe. In: Borislav Stojkov (ed.), Metropolitan Networking in CADSES. Belgrade: Faculty of Geography University of Belgrade, 139–147.

Tošić, Dragutin, Nikola Krunić 2005: Urbane aglomeracije u funkciji regionalne integracije Srbije i Jugoistočne Evrope [Urban agglomerations in the function of the regional integration of Serbia and South-eastern Europe]. In: Glasnik Geografskog društva Republike Srpske (Banja Luka) 9: 83–96.

Vasović, Milorad 1985: Regionalna geografija s posebnim osvrtom na njen razvitak u Srbiji [Regional geography with special emphasis on its development in Serbia]. In: Razvitak i primena geografske nauke u Srbiji za proteklih devet decenija [Advancement and application of geographic science in Serbia during the past nine decades]. Belgrade: Odsek za geografiju i prostorno planiranje PMF-a Univerziteta u Beogradu, 155–171.

Vasović, Milorad 1997: Regija i regionalizacija u geografiji; geografska struktura i regionalizacija Srbije [Region and regionalisation in geography; Serbia's geographic structure and regionalisation]. Belgrade: Geografski institut SANU. Posebna izdanja, 51.

Veljković, Aleksandar 1991: Gradovi – centri razvoja u mreži naselja Srbije [Cities – development centres in the Serbian settlement network]. In: Geografski institut SANU. Zbornik radova 43: 161–195.

Vlada Republike Srbije [Government of the Republic of Serbia] 2007: Strategija regionalnog razvoja Republike Srbije za period 2007–2012 [Regional development strategy of the Republic of Serbia for the period 2007–2012]. In: Službeni glasnik Republike Srbije 71: 33–99.

Abstract

The attempts to regionalise Serbia did not have much success in the twentieth century. The last attempt, at the conceptual and planning level, was made under the Spatial Plan of the Republic of Serbia. This paper proceeds from the concept and the model of decentralization and balanced development, applied in the European Union. It analyses the characteristics and problems of Serbia's urbanization and urban system. Serbia is not sufficiently and uniformly urbanized. There is a distinct polarization between the zones of concentrated population and activity in urban regions and of depopulation in rural, hilly and mountain regions. Disproportions in population size among the ten major urban centres and relative to other urban settlements are the results of Serbia's incoherent and asymmetric urban system. The paper also analyses whether the model of polycentric urban system and functional urban areas, established by the Spatial Plan of the Republic of Serbia, provides a sound basis for the integration of the Serbian urban system into the European one. In this connection, the Belgrade agglomeration distinguishes itself as the potential metropolitan growth area, in addition to Niš and other agglomerations, which can play a significant role in the formation of national and transborder functional urban areas. In the final considerations, the papers argues that a vital prerequisite for the implementation of any model of decentralization and regionalization is a consensus, whereby the key players should display the readiness to reach it and carry out the activities aimed at improving efficiency in managing and directing the development of Serbia's territorial development and its integration into European development trends and policies.

Addresses of authors and editors

Editorial Board

Prof. Milena Benovska-Sabkova, e-mail: mbenovska@yahoo.com
Prof. Keith Brown, e-mail: Keith_Brown@brown.edu
PD Dr. Ulf Brunnbauer, e-mail: ulf@zedat.fu-berlin.de
Dr. Jasna Čapo-Žmegač, e-mail: capo@ief.hr
Prof. Nicolae Constantinescu, e-mail: nicolacon@from.ro
Prof. Christian Giordano, e-mail: christian.giordano@unifr.ch
Prof. Robert Hayden, e-mail: rhayden@ucis.pitt.edu
Dr. Deema Kaneff, e-mail: kaneff@eth.mpg.de
Prof. Karl Kaser, e-mail: karl.kaser@uni-graz.at
Dr. Jutta Lauth Bacas, e-mail: bacas@academyofathens.gr
Damiana Otoiu MA, e-mail: damiana.otoiu@icp.ro
Prof. Klaus Roth, e-mail: K.Roth@lrz.uni-muenchen.de
Dr. François Ruegg, e-mail: francois.ruegg@unifr.ch
Stephanie Schwandner-Sievers MA, e-mail: Sschwand@aol.com
Dr. Vesna Vučinić-Nesković, e-mail: vvucinic@f.bg.ac.yu

Authors of volume 11

Prof. Wolfgang Aschauer
Kultur- und Länderstudien Ostmitteleuropas, Studiengang European Studies, TU Chemnitz
Thüringer Weg 9, Zi. 319, D - 09107 Chemnitz
e-mail: wolfgang.aschauer@phil.tu-chemnitz.de

Prof. Kristof van Assche
Community Development Program, Minnesota State Universities - St Cloud State
Steward Hall, 720, 4th Avenue South, St Cloud, MN 56301–4498, USA
e-mail: kvanassche@stcloudstate.edu

Prof. Pamela Ballinger
Bowdoin College, Department of Sociology and Anthropology
7000 College Station, Brunswick, ME 04011, USA
e-mail: pballing@bowdoin.edu

Bianca Botea PhD
4 rue Bechevelin, F - 69007 Lyon
e-mail: ebbotea@yahoo.fr

Dr. Rozita Dimova
Osteuropa-Institut, FU Berlin
Garystr. 55, D - 14195 Berlin
e-mail: rozita@zedat.fu-berlin.de

Aleksandra Djurić
Grčića Milenka 4b/53, 11000 Belgrade, Serbia
e-mail: saskadjuric@yahoo.com

Prof. Christian Giordano
Department of Social Anthropology, Université de Fribourg
Route des Bonnesfontaines 11, CH - 1700 Fribourg
e-mail: christian.giordano@unifr.ch

Magdalena Lubańska, MA
ul. Indiry Gandhi 35 m.290, PL - 02–776 Warszawa, Poland
e-mail: magdalena.lubanska@gmail.com

Marija Maksin-Mičić, PhD
Faculty of Tourism and Hospitality Management, Singidunum University
Danijelova 32, 11000 Belgrade, Serbia
e-mail: micic70a@yahoo.com

Prof. Alexander Maxwell
School of History, Victoria University of Wellington
PO Box 600, Wellington, New Zealand
e-mail: alexander.m.maxwell@gmail.com

Eli Miloševska, MA
Institut za staroslovenska kultura - Prilep
ul. Kicevsko dzade bb., MAK - 7500 Prilep, Republic of Macedonia
e-mail: eli_miloseska@yahoo.com

Dr. Claire Norton
St Mary's University College
Waldegrave Road, Twickenham TW1 4SX, UK
e-mail: nortonc@smuc.ac.uk

Dimitrije Pešić, MA
16. oktobra 19, 11160 Belgrade, Serbia
e-mail: pesic@unhcr.org

Prof. Klaus Roth
Institut für Volkskunde/European Ethnology, Munich University
Ludwigstr. 25, D – 80539 München
e-mail: k.roth@lrz.uni-muenchen.de

Petruţa Teampău, MA
Str. Rasinari 1, ap. 8, RO – 400457 Cluj Napoca, Romania
e-mail: mindrut_petruta@yahoo.com

Dragutin Tošić, Ph. D.
Faculty of Geography, University of Belgrade
Studentski trg 3, 1100 Belgrade, Serbia

Instructions to Authors

Ethnologia Balkanica is a refereed journal. We welcome submissions by ethnologists, folklorists, ethnographers, cultural and social anthropologists as well as scholars from related disciplines working on the ethnology of Southeast Europe. Submissions should meet the criteria below. The decision about acceptance or rejection rests with the editorial board. When a manuscript has been accepted the full text incl. notes, references, and summaries must be forwarded as a printout and as a data file on diskette or by e-mail. Data files should contain no styles and a minimum of formatting. Authors should send their full postal and e-mail addresses as well as their affiliation together with their paper to the editors.
Length: Articles should have a minimum of 4500 and a maximum of 9000 words.
Languages: Manuscripts can be submitted in English, French or German. Authors who are not writing in their mother-tongue must have their text checked by a native speaker of the language of the text. Titles of publications in southeast European languages must be followed by a translation in the language of the text in brackets [ ].
Abstracts: All manuscripts must be supplied with an English summary of 150 words that summarises the main arguments and findings of the article.
Spelling: Though we prefer British spelling for texts in English, American spelling is also acceptable. In any case the spelling must be consistent.
Transcription from Cyrillic alphabets should follow the scientific style (ISO standard). Do not use ch, zh, sh, iya but č, ž, š, and ija (see transcription list on next page). If your programme does not know these letters, use the popular form of transcription but mark all letters that require diacritical marks with a "*". Romanian names must be written in the original, i. e., with all diacritical characters.
Citations and References: Citations should be in Harvard style, author, date and page as follows (Verdery 1983: 27); if there are two or more authors, separate authors with commas. This applies also to footnotes. No comma after the author's name. Don't use p. or pp. Always cite page numbers where you are quoting or paraphrasing from a specific part of a text, and avoid too much citation where a work in its entirety is referred to. Avoid the use of ibid. and op.cit, but if you do so, make sure you use them correctly. Note that "cf." means "compare to", not "see also"; if you mean the latter, say so. If a cited scholarly work is not (yet) published, use for example (Smith forthcoming) if the work will be published with certainty. References to archival sources should be given in footnotes, particularly when they are lengthy. Make sure that you use dashes between numbers and dates, for example April – May, 22–30, and not hyphens (-). All references cited, and only these, should be listed under the heading "References" or "Literature",

according to the style indicated below. Always give page numbers for papers in edited volumes or journals. Do not forget to mention the publisher.
For all questions of style, format, headings, quotation, notes, and references please take earlier volumes of this journal as a model. Other styles are not accepted.
Pictures and diagrams: Please always send photographs, graphics, and diagrams separately, never imported into the text. Photographs should be saved in the TIF format; please avoid all compressed formats such as JPEG. Resolution should be from 300 dpi (photographs) up to 600–800 dpi (drawings, caricatures). If you send pictures taken with a digital camera please adjust to maximum resolution and minimal compression.
The author will get one free copy of the journal and a free supply of 10 offprints.

Table: Transliteration of south slavic cyrillic characters (ISO standard):

а	a	к	k	ф	f	ю	ju
б	b	л	l	х	h	я	ja
в	v	м	m	ц	c	ђ	đ, (dj)
г	g	н	n	ч	č	ѕ	dz
д	d	о	o	ш	š	љ	lj
е	e	п	p	щ	št	њ	nj
ж	ž	р	r	ъ	ă	ћ	ć
з	z	с	s	ы	y	џ	dž
и	i	т	t	ь	j	ѣ	ě
й	j	у	u				